MCGRAW BROTHERS

MCGRAW BROTHERS

Of One Blood are All People

1   Darrell V. McGraw, Jr.   Warren R. McGraw

To whose benefit are the actions of government and big corporations?

Do we ask? Do we know?

Jorea Marple

This book is dedicated to those who stay in the arena and work for the

good of all people.

"Of One Blood Are All People."

A special thanks to Elliott Catherine Zekany McGraw, daughter of Darrell V. McGraw, Jr. and Rebecca McGraw Thaxton, daughter of Warren. R. McGraw who contributed time to research and editing. And a deep appreciation to Patrick C. McGinley, Judge Charles H. Haden, II, Professor of Law, WVU College of Law, for his continued encouragement, advice and support in both development and editing.

Table of Contents

Preface

Darrell Vivian McGraw, Jr. and Warren Randolph McGraw were born to a destiny of service shaped by their provenance in Appalachia's simultaneously exploited and neglected mountains. The plight of their beloved state had a profound impact on these two brothers, stoking a fire to right the injustices perceived in their community. Their public service occurred in a political arena rift with corporate and private greed through thirty-eight elections and service in 8 elected offices—county school board member, delegate, senator, senate president, prosecuting attorney, justice, chief justice, attorney general and judge.

Their dramatic and controversial history was the subject of two documentary films: *If Elected* (1972), broadcast by Bill Moyer's Journal, and the award winning *The Last Campaign (2005)*. Wayne Ewing's *If Elected* was labeled a documentary for the ages by critics. "It could be placed tomorrow in the civics visual library of any educational system in the land and still be of immense value a decade from now, probably a century from now."[1] The *Last Campaign* is the backstory for the seminal U.S. Supreme Court case, *Caperton v. Massey* that provided real life inspiration for John Grisham's novel *The Appeal* . Their struggles against injustice, special interests and "dark money" are cited in Laurence Leamer's *The Price of Justice: A True Story of Greed and Corruption.*

Big coal and unscrupulous elected officials, more interested in wealth and power, exploited the vulnerability of West Virginians for decades with Big Pharma ravishing already devastated families and communities. In recent years, in the McGraws' rural county of birth, population 23,766, drug wholesalers shipped 10 million doses of opioid drugs.

The McGraw brothers' stories are important because they challenge us to look beyond what seems apparent and what appears right and ask "to whose benefit" is the obstruction of and resistance to mine safety enforcement; environmental requirements; strip mine regulations; black lung benefits; coal severance taxes; state Supreme Court decisions that protect workers' rights, health and safety, equality of educational opportunity for all students, juvenile rights, mental health care, employee pensions, and a host of consumer litigation cases against big tobacco, drug and insurance companies? The McGraw brothers' actions were based on what was legally and culturally just. They remembered the essence of the Berea College motto on a pennant that hung beside their childhood orange bunk beds—"Of One Blood Are All People," taken from Acts 17:26: "God has made of one blood all peoples of the earth." During their professional careers criticisms for their progressive actions were unrelenting from a multitude of wrongdoers, angling to maintain their own power and influence over public policy.

Often the electorate, lacking time and expertise to sort out conflicting claims of politicians and deceits propagated in the media and on the internet by unidentified interests who seek to confuse and distract, finds it exceedingly difficult to sort fact from fiction. In an age of 24/7 proliferations of social media, news and fantasies, it is increasingly important for citizens to become better informed through a higher level of understanding of civics and engagement in election processes. It matters who is elected. Everywhere and in every community voters hear disparate assertions from those seeking office and those who are already elected. Unraveling these economic, social and political assertions requires much diligence to determine "to whose benefit" are these assertions? Without such analysis voters often unwittingly vote against their own interests. The McGraw brothers routinely faced special interest groups determined to sway the electorate for their own financial or political benefit. The *McGraw Brothers* is a civics lesson of the best kind; it is entertaining, informative and motivating.

Prologue

I met the McGraw brothers in 1972 and my life was ᵢᵤ changed. I was a 23 year-old daughter of a small-town businessman, Republican politician and Barry Goldwater supporter. Warren was married with three children and Darrell divorced with two. My mother wanted to know what I was thinking, "God forbid, they are Democrats." But I found them handsome and compelling. They had an edge, a maturity that left me intrigued. Everyone in my world was conforming and accepting of the status quo, and these men challenged it. The influence of their convictions finds expression in the fact that when approaching seventy, my Dad became a Democrat.

Where I lived, coal mines were present but not part of my everyday life. I was a county seat girl, from a family of farmers, merchants and businessmen. My only exposure to the dangers of underground coal mining occurred when Bill Brown was killed in the mine at Widen, WV. Miners, including Bill, struggled to unionize the mine. Bill worked part-time for my dad as an ambulance driver and was a common presence around my home. I still remember the night dad returned from the Widen where he recovered Mr. Brown's body. Mr. Brown was killed in a coal mine. His death was "an accident" to the company but a disaster for his family.

When I was about eight years old, Mr. Brown gave me a rhinestone gold colored little mirror and fingernail file for my birthday. Somehow, I knew it was a treasure. Its value lay not in monetary value, but because it was a gift from a man who sacrificed every day in the most grueling job to make a life for his family, and who perished from this earth by the time I was ten. I've wondered why he gave me such a gift. Perhaps I represented something Mr. Brown hoped for his own children—my family never worked in the mines; they were educated; they traveled, and they never doubted life would be better for the next generation. I kept my Bill Brown treasure, despite my general inclination to shed tchotchkes and tokens. The McGraw brothers knew far better the travails that Bill Brown faced as he descended into the darkness and dangers of the mine. Bill, like countless other miners, knew there were two realities—death in the mines or death outside the mines from what was then called miner's asthma caused by exposure to silica and coal dust, later called "black lung" by miners and or pneumoconiosis by medical professionals.

When I met the McGraw brothers they were already actively engaged in doing "right" for all the Bill Browns. But doing what is culturally just, as they were taught within the dimension of the culture of the region, was and is still often met with resistance. This conflict between justice versus power and moneyed interests lies at the core of much of the McGraw brothers' life journey.

For more than a century, big coal and elected officials, more interested in wealth and power, cynically exploited the vulnerability of Appalachians. Many others followed suit. West Virginia, once called *Almost Heaven,* has seen the exploitation of its vast resources for the benefit of a chosen few. The resulting mono-economy focused on advancing the interests of the coal industry to the exclusion of the broader public interest. West Virginia is where the McGraw brothers were born and raised, where they were called and committed to make life better for others. They grew to adulthood in a land of abundant mineral resources, a land rich with forests, water, game, minerals and hard-working people whose lives revolved around love of family, friends and the mountains. But their family was grounded in the reality of the Appalachian coalfields and helped them see what was happening right in front of their eyes. Their mother, Julia, often lamented, "The coal trains are hauling my West Virginia away. What is left behind for the people who live here?"

Their southern West Virginia is a land of majestic mountains resting atop thick beds of the rich bituminous coal that stoked the furnaces of the industrial revolution, fueled two world wars and the economic development for a nation. West Virginia is a picturesque place. The forests remain, but markedly depleted of maple, walnut, and hickory trees from clear-cutting its primeval forest. The streams and rivers run clear for fishing and whitewater rafting, except where mine waste and slurry from strip and deep mines have taken their toll.[1] Near the time the McGraw brothers were born it was estimated that more than two-thirds of West Virginia held minable seams of bituminous coal. Even with the net national coal production decline, WV remains a significant component of the estimated $41 billion dollar a year U.S. coal mining industry.[2]

West Virginia, blessed with abundant resources including huge reserves of coal, gas, and timber, suffers from what economists refer to as the natural resource curse or the curse of plenty. Economists use this term to explain the paradox that occurs in countries with an abundance of natural resources but have less economic growth and poorer development outcomes than countries with fewer natural resources. The natural resource curse exists in states where there is an overinvestment in a natural resource instead of sectors that are conducive to long run growth. This overinvestment in a natural resource results in a decrease in Total Factor Productivity which is vital for any state's continued economic growth.[3] Total Factor Productivity defines the amount of growth in real output that exceeds the growth in capitol and labor inputs.

The natural resource curse paradox is evident in West Virginia—a state rich with natural resources that evolved into a one-industry coal-driven economy that rewarded out-of-state investors rather than fostering economic, cultural, social and educational development and prosperous communities. "Economists sometimes write about the natural resource curse…In this sense, few places have been as cursed as West Virginia. Even when the mines were at their most productive, West Virginia ranked among the poorest and most poorly educated states. Coal wasn't taxed heavily and the coal companies weren't asked to contribute much in the way of corporate citizenship."[4]

West Virginia, a resource rich state, ranks last in overall well-being and happiness, emotional and physical well-being as well as last in economic activity, health and potential.[5] West Virginia's senior population is one of the highest in the nation. Its unemployment rate is 7.3 %. Twenty-one percent of the population lives below the national poverty level.[6] Equally alarming are West Virginians rates of smoking, obesity, diabetes, heart disease, cancer, suicide and opioid overdose deaths.[7] West Virginia's workforce is the lowest paid and is the least educated of any state.[8]

As the nation's electric generation industry moved away from coal as its fuel of choice, West Virginia's coal-dependent economy suffers from drastically reduced revenues from waning coal production and an attendant decline in severance taxes. Politicians' decisions to cut tens of millions from already insufficient business and corporate taxes burden the state with increasing fiscal debt and limited alternatives for replacing lost revenue. Already inadequate government services continue to decline as the state faces revenue shortfalls and deficits.[9]

Most recently the state is experiencing a boom in natural gas with production spiking more than five fold in the past decade and gas related jobs increasing to over 13,000. With the state's continued low severance tax, the mistakes made with coal resources are repeating. In 2018 when teachers, frustrated by low pay and inadequate services for students, went on strike the Legislature refused to increase severance taxes on gas to fund a salary increase. Instead the Legislature chose to finance a meager raise through cuts to state programs already inadequately funded: "Hampering a growing industry in a poor state is something that most West Virginia politicians had no interest in doing. The No. 1 tax that everyone said we should raise was natural gas severance. But they just have overwhelming power."—*Ted Boettner, Executive Director West Virginia Center for Budget and Policy*

How can a state so rich in natural resources continually rank last or next to last in so many indicators reflecting quality of life including wellness, education, economic security and living conditions? Within the McGraw brothers' stories are answers. In West Virginia, generation after generation, political decisions support the maintaining of a defined wealth that negatively impacts schools, social and health resources, roads, housing, jobs, the judicial system and government services.[10] At the end of the nineteenth century West Virginia's agrarian social and economic structure was transformed by an ascendant coal industry that created rural industrial conclaves with landless workers and a managerial class overseen by politically influential coal barons and the wealthy elites. Mining, drilling, timbering and manufacturing created jobs without investment in a sustainable community infrastructure. For well over a century the resulting wealth from the extracted resources elude most communities and the wealth produced by West Virginia labor enrich investors who often live in distant places.[11]

The McGraw brothers recognize and resist this disproportionate allocation of wealth from the exploitation of the state's workers and natural bounty. There exists much evidence of the failure of elected

representatives to insist on the enactment and enforcement of health and
safety regulations to protect workers, and the adverse impact of special
interest groups more focused on profits than community needs. The
McGraw brothers' stories provide insight into why so many people are
disillusioned with existing political systems and underscore the
importance of asking "who benefits" from any proposed action, assertion,
legislation, legal opinion or political platform.

Many West Virginians feel left behind, abandoned by their
government and invisible, except during election years, to political
leaders. They crave a better quality of life and the stability of an
economy that provides a safe workplace and a living wage. They want to
actually experience and live the American promise; i.e. the opportunity
for prosperity and success. A drive through West Virginia's former
industrial communities finds boarded up businesses and bankrupt
companies that once offered jobs to thousands of proud, hardworking
individuals who made a contribution in their community. The view
includes dilapidated houses that haven't seen a coat of paint in decades if
ever. Homes once occupied by coal miners, steelworkers and others
supporting an industrial economy now show disintegrating steps and
sidewalks, disconnected gutters and crumbling porches, stacked with the
remnants of broken toys, appliances and furniture. Inside the houses are
people who spend their days trying to figure out how to stretch the
unemployment, public assistance, social security, disability or tenuous
retirement benefits to meet the basic needs of their families. Alarming
drug and suicide rates are reflective of the residents haunting belief they
are powerless to change their circumstances. They crave leaders who can
make life better.

All too often leaders of coal, drug, tobacco, insurance and other
powerful companies frame their message to appear to embrace the hopes
and dreams of West Virginians who produce, but seldom enjoy, an
equitable share of the wealth they create. For more than a century those
same corporate interests lend financial and material support to elect
officials whom, once in office, do their bidding. As with any other
endeavor which aspires to an ideal to advance human progress, this book
reveals the McGraw brothers' pursuit of a cultural standard of "justice"
for all participants in the community. The pursuit of "justice," often

fraught with controversy and set backs, must inhibit those who set a higher value on power and money, that fortifies institutional wrong. In the McGraw brothers' individual and collective struggles making law, interpreting and enforcing the law, they encountered wrongdoers, snake oil salesmen types, more interested in power and money and self-advancement than the good of the community. The McGraw brothers' unraveled legal, social and political considerations while seeking the answer "to whose benefit" are the actions of government officials, business and corporate leaders, legislators, media, and many others. By relentlessly seeking to answer this fundamental question, the McGraw brothers discerned ways forward and these are the stories of their journey.

As the author I clearly admit up front that I make no effort to concentrate on the negative aspects of the complex personalities of the McGraw brothers. I know, particularly Darrell's, all too well. As young men they were hot-headed, intensely passionate, impatient, out-spoken and often abrasive. But it was those characteristics that made them courageous enough to take tough stances against the establishment interests. Critics will be quick to say there is another side to the McGraw brothers that I ignored. Perhaps that is so. But for the fifty years I've been part of the McGraw family, all the brothers' foibles have already been well exposed and many times well exaggerated in the media. This is a book about the well-intentioned work of two individuals, with all the prerequisite human flaws, who tried mightily to make a difference in their West Virginia.

9

Chapter I   The McGraws and West Virginia

Learning Duty to Others

1866, Wheeling

West Virginia was born out of in-fighting in Virginia. In 1866, West Virginia's Capital was Wheeling, then a booming Ohio River valley industrial town underlain by the fabulously rich "eight-foot" or "Pittsburgh" coal seam in the state's northern panhandle. The industrial behemoth that soon blossomed as Pittsburgh, the Steel City, was fueled by this nearby and plentiful West Virginia coal and coke.

Governor Arthur I. Boreman, a Republican, was in his third year of a four year term. Forty year old John McGraw was elected to represent the 6th District in the state House of Delegates, one of only eight Democrats elected to that body.[1] McGraw traveled nearly 300 miles from his home in the southern West Virginia to Wheeling to take his seat in the Legislature. To travel from the settlement at McGraws, in Wyoming County where he lived among a few handfuls of relatives, John rode his horse through miles of narrow hollows along circuitous trails dimmed by the surrounding mountains. But the mountains lent protection and fostered allegiance among settler families like the McGraws. The McGraw family and other early inhabitants of the region knew of the coal beneath these mountains, having harvested the outcroppings of coal for their own use in cooking and heating their homes. John McGraw believed that coal mining development in other parts of the state would eventually reach southern West Virginia, and so it did in the 1870's.[2]

By horse and steamboat John made the difficult journey to Wheeling's Linsley Institute, where the Legislature met. John no doubt stood in wonder when he first saw the engineering and architectural marvel of the Wheeling suspension bridge, which was until 1851 the largest suspension bridge in the world.

John met his first challenge as a legislator on opening day. John was a religious man. Among other pieties, he did not swear. During the Civil War, West Virginia's Republican Legislature, fearing disloyalty from Democrats, passed a law requiring all elected officials swear to a "test oath" affirming that since June 20th, 1863 they had not "borne arms against the United States or West Virginia."[3] McGraw had not taken to arms to support the Confederate insurrection, but his religious conviction prevented him from swearing to anything that was not totally accurate. During the War John McGraw was authorized payment to haul dead soldiers to the Virginia militia cemetery. According to family legend, when John McGraw arrived in Wheeling, David Pinnell, the Republican House Speaker requested the entire class of new delegates to stand and take the oath of office, as remains the tradition. Then the Speaker began to administer the "test oath." John stood with everyone but did not utter a word as the test oath was read. A few weeks later Pinnell received a letter from a political opponent of John McGraw, a man named Roach, claiming that John was a Rebel. Pinnell convened a committee to determine John's allegiance. Brought before the committee, John was asked to name his sons. John McGraw had eight sons and one was named Bobby.

"What's Bobby's full God given name?" asked Pinnell. "Bobby," said John.

"Robert Lee," offered another, unknown Delegate, and, "Confederate."

With that, Speaker Pinnell clacked his gavel and sent John home, leaving only seven Democrats in the House. John's answer gave the committee a pretext for thinning the Democratic ranks. Virginian McGraw had no allegiance to the South. Indeed, on one foraging raid Confederate Virginia Militia confiscated one hundred head of cattle and two horses for which he was not compensated.[4]

John returned to southern West Virginia from Wheeling the same way he came and continued to work his land, developing three stores, a sawmill and a gristmill where he ground both meal and flour. John bought his wife, Mahala (Cozart), the first sewing machine in the county—deemed a progressive action by some.[5]

Gristmills were popular meeting and loafing places. It was there that John built a base of supporters and was elected twice more to the Legislature to represent Raleigh, Wyoming and McDowell Counties. By the time he returned to Wheeling in 1870 the Test Oath had been abandoned. A few months after he arrived, state officials boarded a steamboat christened *The Mountain Boy* at the Wheeling levee to begin a

11

journey transporting all state records down the Ohio River and up the Great Kanawha to the new Capital City in Charleston.[6]

1884 Tax Commission

In 1884 a Tax Commission was formed to provide recommendations to the Legislature to promote and ensure the development of the state and its people. The Commission recognized the immense mineral wealth as tenuous if not properly managed for the benefit of all of the state's citizens. The Commission's report warned of dire outcomes if West Virginia failed to internalize and capture fair and appropriate revenue from the exploitation of its coal bounty and its other valuable natural resources:

The wealth of this state is immense; the development of this wealth will earn vast private fortunes far beyond the dreams even of a modern Croesus; the question is, whether this vast wealth shall belong to persons who live here and who are permanently identified with the future of West Virginia, or whether it shall pass into the hands of persons who do not live here and who care nothing for our state except to pocket the treasures which lie buried in our hills. If the people of West Virginia can be roused to an appreciation of the situation we ourselves will gather this harvest now ripe on the land inherited from our ancestors; on the other hand if the people are not roused to an understanding of the situation in less than ten years this vast wealth will have passed from our present population into the hands of non-residents and West Virginia will be almost like Ireland and her history will be like that of Poland.[7]

To whose profit was it to resist appropriate fair taxation of WV's abundant resources? Powerful big coal and railroad interests, and their minions, worked hard to maintain and accumulate wealth, and had no intention of sharing. Increased taxation reduced profits. The Tax Commission's report ran counter to the core purpose of securing the highest possible profits for the industrialists. These industrialists crafted a powerful pointed message for succeeding generations of industrial managers that has successfully reverberated for more than a century: Increased taxes, as well as mine safety and health regulations, drive away industry and cost people their jobs. To effectively propagate their message, these industrialists made it a top priority to back candidates for elective office who carry their water once in office. Politics was, and remains, important to implementing an anti-fair tax and increased coal production message over tax support for economic development and miner workplace safety and health.

John McGraw's family called him "Bige." John's son, William Henry Harrison McGraw, went by "Pole," and Pole's son, James Herford McGraw, went by "Fud." In 1911, Fud's son was born, Darrell V. McGraw. These sons and grandsons continued to dutifully work the farm where they raised hogs, cattle, sheep; milked cows and produced large truck gardens. The farm's bounty was used by the family and anything extra was sold to earn needed income. Every Sunday they attended the Methodist Episcopal Church.

In 1930, Darrell, Fud's son, had the good fortune to attend Berea College, where hard working young people from less advantaged Appalachian families attend school tuition-free in exchange for work in campus service. Darrell met his wife, Julia Zekany, at Berea. Julia was the first generation daughter of Hungarian immigrants who settled in Logan County, West Virginia where mining jobs were plentiful. After their graduation in 1934, Darrell and Julia returned to southern West Virginia to teach school. In the early days of World War II, when his teaching hours were over, Darrell was assigned to work as a "fire boss" in the coal mines. The job of the fire boss was to make sure the mine was safe for the miners.

Warren and Darrell V., Jr. 1940

13

Brothers Always

As Methodists and alumni of Berea College, Darrell and Julia McGraw instilled the values of learning, hard work, duty to others in their young sons, Warren and Darrell V., Jr. As a constant reminder of these values, Julia hung a Berea pennant on their bedroom wall which included the words "Of One Blood are All People." John G. Fee, an abolitionist preacher, founded Berea College before the Civil War to educate both black and white students. Today Lyle Roelofs, President of Berea College reminds us that "diversity is in our DNA...but in order to face the challenges of our day, and ultimately, to live up to the legacy of our founder, John G. Fee, we must work to create that world where we recognize that 'God has made of one blood all peoples of the earth,' as outlined in the book of Acts, Chapter 17."[8]

The parents always aimed to make everything a learning experience for the boys—the weather, the War, the coal trains rolling by or the flooding of creeks rushing down nearby hollows. As the family gathered for dinner, almost every night Darrell Sr. quizzed his boys asking: "What did you learn today in school? What causes thunderstorms? How many counties are in West Virginia? Who is the Vice President of the United States? Where should we locate plants in the garden to produce the best?" Their responses were discussed, challenged, rejected or accepted.

In the schools where they taught, the McGraws worked hard to provide assistance in any way they could to the children. They packed extra sandwiches for the hungry; found glasses for those squinting to read the chalkboard and routinely engaged in other simple acts of kindness to help families in need. These values were reinforced on the brothers' frequent visits to their Grandpa McGraw's farm, just down the mountain from their home. Their grandparents always placed an extra plate and chair at the dinner table for anyone who might be passing by the house at mealtime. The strangers who graced the table often became friends and were sometimes given work to do on the farm.

The senior McGraws frequently started life lesson conversations with their sons with "at Berea we were taught..." Berea's doctrine of equality of all humankind was apparent in how Darrell V. and Warren addressed each other. They called each other "brother" not by their given names.

On trips to Logan County to see their mother's parents, the brothers loved to watch their grandfather, Alexander Sandor Zekany work in his forge and machine shop making tools for his job at the coal mine and for his family and neighbors. The brothers grabbed their snacks from the grape arbor as they listened to their Grandfather tell of his life as a cadet and horse soldier (Hussar) in the Austro-Hungarian Army. The grandfather told the brothers of the time he was chosen by the cadre to repair and shoe the Emperor Franz Joseph's horse. He proudly recounted how the Emperor had proclaimed it "good work."

The brothers were always anxious to garner their grandfather's praise and sought out work that needed done in the machine shop, relishing the thought that on the ride home they could say their grandfather had offered an approving "Good work my son, good work."

Grandfather Alexander Zekany in the Austro Hungarian Army

After the Japanese attack on Pearl Harbor thrust America into a world war, the boys and their parents spent every morning and evening listening to the War news on their Montgomery Ward Airline console radio. Warren, perhaps too small to understand the significance of the attack when it occurred, nevertheless realized the family time around the radio was important. It was there, around the Airline that their parents listened, learned and took every opportunity to offer an expanded history lesson to their sons. Julia loved President Franklin and Eleanor

Roosevelt, but she frequently took the opportunity to tell the boys about FDR's cousin President Teddy Roosevelt. Their mother especially lit up relaying details of Teddy Roosevelt's glorious *Man in the Arena*. "If he fails, at least fails while daring greatly," she extolled. "Know victory and defeat," she urged them, "they go together." Julia's middle name was Rozelle, in honor of the first President Roosevelt, who was president during the time her father worked to become an American citizen.

Beyond the radio, the boys already understood the impact of the war as their uncles and cousins joined military service and scattered overseas in fighting the nation's enemies. In their small community of McGraws twenty men, mostly relatives, had gone off to war.

Low Gap House at McGraws, West Virginia

The War's influence crept closer to home when their dad was drafted by the Navy in May, 1945. Their father left for basic naval training camp in Great Lakes, Illinois, but not before sitting the young brothers down to remind them how thankful they should be for all their blessings. He further emphasized to the boys his expectation that they were to assume the roles of men of the family while he was gone and do their best to help their mother.

Warren and Darrell were apprehensive about their new "duty" and melancholy about their father's absence. Not long after their father's departure, Julia gathered the boys on the porch swing to help her write their first letter to the father they missed terribly. Julia asked the boys what they wanted to tell their father. Enthusiastically, the brothers began to shout ideas, but their response was muted as they heard in the distance a heavy machine laboring up mountain to Low Gap, as they called their home at McGraws. A bus, *The Blue Goose,* reached the top and stopped at the gate. As the door opened, Darrell, Sr. stepped off the bus. The boys ran ahead of their tearful mother to reach their father and hug him.

After their father brought his government-issued bag into the living room and sat down to enjoy his family, he explained the sudden change of events. The War was almost over and the need for fresh draftees was diminishing. Darrell was released from service not long after he'd arrived at Great Lakes, Illinois.

In the late 1940s the brothers helped their father build a duplicate of their great, great grandfather's settler cabin. The remnants of this cabin remained on the family's old homestead. The duplicate cabin, now behind their own house, had handmade riven shingles for the roof and deer hide leather hinges for the door. To build the cabin, they found and made timber from chestnut trees killed by the blight. They used a mule to pull the timber through the woods. The cabin project continued for almost two years, their father using the working hours to relay details of hundreds of years of family history in the Virginias. The brothers acquired their father's love of history and relished his stories, which were often parables of his strongest values: the importance of learning, duty to others and equality among men. They absorbed these lessons and would later use them to do what they believed was right and important. After completion, the model cabin was a barn and shelter for Bobtail, their milk cow. Their dad said to them, "You will be the last generation to live on the frontier."

Ira Brooks, a cousin, Darrell V. and Warren McGraw with "ole Bailey," circa, 1946

Warren and Darrell V. often spent hours in the woods surrounding their house, exploring and just looking to see what they could find. One day when they were on a mountain above the house Darrell felt a terrible headache coming on. As he felt the pulsing pains grow stronger, Darrell implored his brother to head home, but Warren wasn't ready. Darrell knew there would be hell to pay if he arrived home without his younger brother, who he was expected to watch. Warren refused to leave. In pain, Darrell didn't feel like cajoling Warren into moving. Darrell grabbed his brother's shoulders and gave him a shove forward. Gripping his forehead in pain, Darrell repeated his orders to move, but he knew his actions would not meet the approval of family.

As he made his way back through the woods, Darrell frequently glanced back to make sure Warren was following, but moved forward with greater speed. He knew all too well that the migraine would soon set in with full force. He needed to get home and lie down before it hit. Arriving home a few minutes before Warren, Darrell was greeted by his mother. Julia's Magyar eyes narrowed into slits whenever she smiled or- as now- scowled, a trait Warren famously inherited.

Julia's eyes were not the only thing she bequeathed to Warren and Darrell. She shared her deep sense of duty to others. But today Darrell knew his mother was not smiling as she realized Warren was not with him. Just as Darrell, Sr. entered the room, Warren burst through the front door in tears. Warren thought he was in trouble. As if in desperation, Warren proclaimed, "Brother said a cuss word!"

Their Daddy looked back at Darrell V. and scolded, "Don't ever leave your brother behind again." Just, right now, he had this headache, and he needed to lie down, so in a flash, before it could start, Darrell V. admitted his guilt and simply shouted out, "I won't." And he would not.

Darrell awakened that night to his mother stroking his forehead. His mother admonished him about cussing and then she kissed him on the forehead and whispered in his ear. When most mothers would whisper, "Good night," his mother, on that night, as she sometimes did, whispered the words he and his brother remembered and lived by, "Of one blood are all people."

For summers after the War, the family traveled to Morgantown to live while Darrell, Sr. completed work on his master's degree at West Virginia University. One summer the family rented a small house on Dunkard Creek in Mt. Morris, Pennsylvania. The commute to the University was longer, but the rent was more aligned to his teacher pay. When Darrell Sr. wasn't in class at WVU, he would join the boys fishing the creek that ran alongside their home.

Their daddy was interested in the political, social and economic history of West Virginia and how it impacted life in his local community, and he shared that interest with his sons. For most of the eight hour car ride from McGraws to Morgantown, he told stories of Wyoming County Virginia and West Virginia history and culture. He instilled an enormous amount of community pride in the boys, and educated them about their community industry's contribution to the world. Raleigh-Wyoming Coal Company operated one of the largest and most modern coal mines in the United States located just down the road from McGraws in Glen Rogers. The 720 foot mine shaft was driven downward to an 8 foot seam where coal was mined, hauled to the surface and loaded on railroad cars belonging to Virginian Railroad, a company built by Henry Huttleston Rogers, an associate of the industrial magnate John D. Rockefeller, Sr. It is said that Henry Huttleston Rogers, a visionary railroad builder and owner of Glen Rogers, perhaps had more to do with coal mining coming to Southern West Virginia than any other person.

Most days the family passed under and over railroad crossings where the trains hauled coal to destinations around the country, but mostly to Tidewater. The noise from the loaded railroad cars passing over the trestle to out of state destinations was not pleasant for Julia, as it harkened back to her childhood, growing up in a Logan County coal camp where she saw little evidence of coal's benefit to the community. When she heard the railroad cars, Julia often commented, "They are hauling West Virginia away." Julia's commentary confused the boys, who had been taught in school that West Virginia was lucky to have coal. Their father gently explained to them that it's not that simple: "We must use what God has given us wisely and for the community—and that's not what's done."

Perhaps Darrell, Sr. was ahead of his time. Decades later, John Prine wrote Paradise; vocalist John Denver Deutschendorf, Jr. popularized it:

Then the coal company came with the world's largest shovel
And they tortured the timber and stripped all the land
Well, they dug for their coal till the land was forsaken
Then they wrote it all down as the progress of man.
And daddy won't you take me back to Muhlenberg County
Down by the Green River where Paradise lay
Well, I'm sorry my son, but you're too late in asking
Mister Peabody's coal train has hauled it away[9]

For well over a century, only a few governors and legislators, at their individual political peril, heeded the 1884 Tax Commission's wise counsel and sought to establish additional taxes on mineral resources. In 1905 Governor A.B. White proposed a very modest one percent tax on gross receipts of extracted coal, oil & gas. It was firmly rejected by the Legislature.

In 1912 Henry D. Hatfield, a progressive old time Republican from the southern coalfields, was elected Governor and began efforts to place a tax on mineral production to support heath care, schools and a system of highways to serve as channels of commerce for the state. A medical doctor, Governor Hatfield contended the coal industry was "not liberal enough to admit that they should assume their equitable part of taxation"[10] even for taking care of the injured and sick miners admitted to the state funded miners' hospitals. Governor Hatfield said that without a fair tax on coal production that future generations, "when these vast resources shall have been exhausted and there is left only the empty shell, will rightfully blame us for such a course of action…"[11]

In speeches Governor Hatfield stated that millions of dollars in coal, oil and gas royalties were going to recipients who "pay no taxes to our state, but live in other states and other nations and care nothing for our future."[12] At a meeting of the State Labor Federation in 1914, Governor Hatfield offered that less than two hundred men controlled over two thirds of the mineral resources and pay practically nothing to the state: "Long years ago, most of it [was acquired] at public auction as delinquent and unappropriated land which should have reverted to the state and should have remained in the name of the state, but today these men own millions and millions of acres of this valuable land in West Virginia and they live in Boston, New York and Europe, surrounded by their millions."[13]

During a speaking engagement in 1915 Governor Hatfield posed a series of questions that remain pertinent: "Who is reaping the harvest from these riches? What are we laying away for inevitable rainy day? Why will not those who have large holdings in our common wealth assist in the up building of our state? Are we not entitled to a like treatment by corporations of our commonwealth as is exacted by other states contiguous to ours? When will relief come to us?"[14]

Hatfield's efforts to tax mineral production were not successful. Cognizant of the long arm of the industry Hatfield said, "You hear the statement that the combination of corporations will annihilate a man politically when he stands up for this kind of doctrine. I wish to say that I am not in politics for gain, not do I care to stay in the political arena if I must be subservient to selfish and unreasonable interests which are detrimental to the welfare of the state and its people."[15] After completion of his term as Governor, Hatfield entered the army medical corps serving as a chief surgeon during World War I. In 1928, Hatfield ran for the U. S. Senate, defeating the incumbent Democrat, Matthew Mansfield Neely, in the Hoover landslide that swept Republicans into office. Hatfield served only one term in the U.S. Senate where he achieved the successful establishment of the veteran's hospital in Huntington. Never entering the political arena again, Hatfield returned to private medical practice.[16]

And then there was William Casey Marland who was elected Governor of West Virginia and took office in 1953. The boys were in high school when Marland, who raised in Wyoming County, was Governor. The family knew Marland in his youth. The hardworking young Marland worked during his summers in the mine at Glen Rogers, where his father, called "Ole Man Marland," was superintendent. The elder Marland was neither big nor old, but a man in that position was one of the most important in all of Wyoming County. Marland Sr., the Governor's father, often visited the boys' Grandpa McGraw's farm in his big Chrysler to buy "roast'n ears" of corn. Marland filled the back seat and trunk with corn and drove to Glen Rogers where he gave the corn away to town's people.

When Warren was sixteen, he decided to use his connections to Governor Marland to secure the Number "2" license plate. The Governor is always issued the number "1" for his license plate, and is responsible for issuing the rest of the low numbers. Warren had recently acquired a Model A Ford for $35. He'd polished it to a spit shine, improvised a wire hanger antenna, and dug a radio out of another car and placed on the passenger side floor, but it was still in need of a license plate. Warren hitchhiked from Pineville to Charleston to ask the Governor for the number.

As the story goes, the governor's secretary stifled a laugh when the teenage Warren swaggered into her office and requested to meet with the governor to discuss "a matter." The secretary politely told the young man that an appointment was needed to speak with the Governor. Warren dutifully explained that he was from Wyoming County, and he was sure the Governor would see him if she would just tell him. Warren was right. The Governor Marland came out to greet Warren.

Warren made his request for the special plate, the "2." The Governor said he could not give out that number, explaining that the number is reserved for the Lieutenant Governor. With much patience, Governor Marland took the time to explain to his fellow young countian that the guy next in line for his job, in case anything happens to him, gets the number "2" plate. Continuing, the Governor told Warren that it required hard work to earn the right to have the number. First he has to be elected Senator, and he has to then be elected Senate President. Patting Warren on the back the Governor concluded that he couldn't give him the number. So, Warren hitchhiked all the way back home without the plate.[17]

The young Marland knew how to mine coal. As a student-turned-miner, Marland worked as a coal loader and set a one-day record for hand-loading coal. Marland became a member of the UMWA when he was only 15. Marland, fully appreciating the sacrifices of coal miners and the needs in a coal community, asked the legislature to impose a severance tax on coal.[18]

The young newly elected Governor William Casey Marland exerted his exuberance and conviction and proposed to tax companies that were depleting the state of its conspicuous natural resource, coal. Three days after taking office Marland dropped his tax bombshell which imposed 10 cents a ton on coal, 25 cents a barrel on oil and varying taxes on other natural resources. On February 22, 1953, five weeks after he became Governor, Marland made an appeal to the Legislature to support his severance tax in what was labeled as the most impassioned speech of his career:

"When our coal is gone, there will be nothing to which our people can turn for their livelihood. I say to you, let's use this suitable source of revenue, because whether we like it or not, West Virginia's hills will be stripped, the bowels of the Earth will be mined and the refuse strewn across our valleys and our mountains in the form of burning slate dumps. This refuse will continue to be dumped into our once clear mountain streams. We are paying a fearful price to allow the coal to be extracted from the hills of West Virginia. It is only right that we should be able to point with pride to improved roads and schools as a result of this awful toll that we are taking of this beautiful state of West Virginia."[19]

Marland's coal tax proposal, supported by the UMWA, WV-AFLCIO, and WVEA, was resisted by the Legislature. Big coal companies rejected any measure that reduced their profits, even marginally. Taxing coal was a slippery slope to diminished income for their investors and they wanted none of it. Marland's plea fell on deaf ears when the House of Delegates voted 56-41 to postpone any further consideration indefinitely.[20] Marland's attempt to retain for the state a small amount of the enormous wealth from extracted resources was termed by some as his "political suicide." Decades later Bob Mellace, a Statehouse reporter, lamented how West Virginia's economic future was negatively impacted by the failure to pass Governor Marland's severance bill, "If only others could have seen what Bill Marland saw, this state would have been in excellent financial health years ago."[21]

Historians concluded Marland's proposed tax on coal ended his political career.[22] Big coal ruined not only his career but his personal reputation. Marland's attempts to reform coal taxes were personally disastrous: "When he died in 1965, Marland was driving a cab in

23

Chicago. He is best remembered in West Virginia not for his daring actions as a reforming tax crusader, but as a drunk, an image affixed to him by the business leaders he had so incensed."[23] The truth was that Governor Bill Marland was a brilliant, highly effective governor who, after the defeat of his coal severance tax, devoted his efforts to securing new citizens—industrial and otherwise to share the tax burden. Marland secured 70 new industries, including Kaiser Aluminum's $216 million dollar plant in Ravenswood; nearly 15,000 new jobs and investments of over a billion dollars for West Virginia. And by the end of his term West Virginia was recognized nationally for its success in public school desegregation. Governor Marland, a self admitted alcoholic, successfully completed a treatment program in 1961 and never drank again.[24]

Despite knowing the dangers, the McGraw brothers, encouraged by their father and grandfather, grew up aiming to take a path toward advancing the public interest rather than special interests, similar to Marland's, though hoping for a better outcome. Their father encouraged them to study and then practice law, with the goal of making their community a better place.

Warren R. and Darrell V. McGraw, Jr. did go on to become lawyers, and to make West Virginia a better place for all. John McGraw's two great grandsons would both have offices in the West Virginia Capitol, now permanently housed in prominent architect Cass Gilbert's masterpiece. These two forces would be embedded in the collective psyche of West Virginia's working people—perhaps not because of a particularly winsome track record, but because of their remarkable fortitude in protecting the interests of regular citizens against powerful and moneyed special interests. They would go right at a coal tax and much more—enforcements against big drug and big tobacco; legislation protecting workers' health and safety insurance, including black lung compensation and strip mining regulations; legal opinions that recognized the rights of injured workers, mandated proper funding of public education and enforced human rights law, and a multitude of other culturally just actions. But like Marland, it would come with personal costs.

The Journeys

McGraw brothers' story is about two separate journeys that many times overlapped and were based upon an aligned sense of duty and commitment to the people they served.

Chapters I-IX unfold the life of Warren McGraw from a young man who held school districts' accountable for desegregation of public schools; to his struggles in the state Senate to enact coal severance tax, Black Lung and strip mining legislation; to his years on the state Supreme Court authoring opinions addressing medical malpractice and workers compensation; to his brutal attacks from Don Blankenship during his reelection bid and finally to his election as Wyoming County circuit judge. **Warren,** the husband and father, married to his high school sweetheart, Peggy Shufflebarger, was moved by his law school encounter with President Lyndon Johnson. After law school Warren worked in the U.S. Justice Department, Office of Civil Rights Division where doing his duty took on new meaning when he was tasked with enforcing the civil rights law in the south, Mississippi and then in his own state. Warren went on to take on the politically risky and often downright dangerous duty of resisting mountaintop removal of coal. He knew the facts—strip mining of coal devastated mountains, polluted streams, and the sludge dams created reservoirs of fluid waste, that if breeched were capable of burying people and their homes. Somehow, with ample conviction but without much money, he won a state senate election.

Warren went to Buffalo Creek when a collapsed mining impoundment produced a disastrous flood that killed 125 and injured 1,100 men, women and children. Big coal tried to convince everyone that the Buffalo Creek tragedy was an "Act of God." The state government provided only paltry assistance for the 4,000 victims who lost their homes. Government officials reneged on their promise to rebuild demolished homes and a community center, leaving devastated families to survive in temporary trailers provided by federal funds. Only days before he left office, then Governor Arch Moore, added insult to the flood victims' injury by secretly and inexplicably settling a $100 million dollar law suit against Pittston Mining, the company responsible for the waste impoundment's collapse. The "settlement"—a paltry million dollars, was $99 million less that the suit sought for damage.

Warren was in the state House of Delegates when miners began their fight to receive compensation for Black Lung, a terrible debilitating and often fatal respiratory disease caused by coal dust and silica. Coal companies, whose lawyers, lobbyists and captured politicians denied even the existence of the disease, opposed the movement to secure compensation for the miners. The Black Lung War saw thousands of miners marching on the state Capitol and 40,000 miners putting down their buckets and joining a state-wide strike. Warren led efforts in the House to secure passage of a Black Lung compensation bill. It was a real fight. In March, 1969 the Black Lung compensation bill passed, and West Virginia was recognized as a national leader in securing legislation to compensate victims of Black Lung.

In coal mining communities across the nation miners struggled to receive black lung compensation. Industry partisans, never at a loss for ways to deny responsibility, fought back, absurdly claiming that miners' diseased lungs were the result of tobacco smoking. Progress occurred at the national level with the passage of the 1977 Federal Mine Safety and Health Act. Warren stood next to President Carter when he signed Act that secured additional protection for miners.

As a legislator living in southern West Virginian, Warren was familiar with the outcomes of unsafe mining conditions—sick, injured and dead miners; of insufficient taxation of coal—poor basic infrastructures including roads, schools and community services and of inadequate regulation of strip and deep mining—polluted streams, slurry dam failures, soil erosion and flooding. Warren knew others had failed in their efforts to make the coal industry pay adequate taxes, and it had cost those advocates their political future, but it did not preclude Warren from leading the way to enact a coal severance tax in 1975. The coal severance tax provided needed money for schools and basic community services.

Dark money funneled into Warren's political campaigns. Don Blankenship, christened the Dark Lord of Coal by *Rolling Stone*, rose in prominence as the longtime CEO of the industry giant Massey Coal. As Massey's CEO Blankenship reduced mountaintops to heaps of rubble and harvested the valuable bituminous seams of coal to triple his company's revenue. A master at political manipulation, including channeling dark money contributions to so-called "friends of coal" who then defended the industry, Blankenship pumped millions into the political system to promote an anti-regulatory agenda.[25] Blankenship routed $3 million dollars to a pro-coal candidate in a successful effort to buy a seat on the WV Supreme Court and later bragged about his ploy. *Forbes* identified Warren, a justice on the WV Supreme Court, as one of the targets of big business in "waging a secret election-campaign war" on judges who favor plaintiffs in tort cases.[26] Ultimately Blankenship was convicted by a federal court jury of conspiring to violate mine safety laws. Blankenship served prison time for mining violations associated with the preventable deaths of 29 miners employed by his company.

Chapters X-XIX unfold the life of Darrell McGraw, Jr., from his rebellious youth to his Army service in the Chemical Corps; to his student days when he worked to bring the Mast from the sunken *U.S.S. West Virginia* home from Pearl harbor to West Virginia University as a tribute to the disproportionate number of West Virginians who gave their lives, and finally to his decades as WV Supreme Court Justice and Attorney General. Darrell was in the arena doing his duty as his parents had taught him.

Darrell learned how to organize grassroots campaigns through his work with Matt Reese, a national political consultant associated with the Kennedy supported campaigns. As a political consultant Darrell managed such grassroots efforts as Thomas Eagleton's successful campaign for the U.S. Senate in Missouri. These grassroots strategies were used in Warren's State Senate race as well as Darrell's run for Congress, where he first built his own name recognition, and in every subsequent campaign. The difference between grassroots campaigns and those campaigns financed by the "dark money" of special interest groups are presented in real life examples and illustrate the importance of campaign funding reform to the maintenance of a democracy.

In 1979 a youth hanged himself while incarcerated in an adult jail. Incarceration of minors with adult facilities was outlawed by the West Virginia Legislature in1936.[27] Then Justice Darrell McGraw investigated and ended up punched by deputies and thrust into a jail cell himself: "A large splotch of blood staining the left side of his white shirt, McGraw, 42, stood grim-faced as Magistrate Herb Pauley read the charges filed by the sheriff's department: two counts battery and three obstruction of justice. The magistrate once complained sheriff's deputies assaulted him at the same jail. He said he planned to step aside in the case." The incident made national news. Widespread disregard for the law was uncovered and reform occurred including the state Supreme Court's establishment of the first Juvenile Justice Committee to protect the rights of young offenders. The sheriff and prosecutor acknowledged that on occasion adults were housed in juvenile sections. They promised that Michael Jeffery's death would result in "sharp restructuring of the sheriff's department." and the practice of deadlocking juveniles would cease.[28] The promise was too late for Jeffery. But reform did occur: "It would appear that McGraw's swollen ear and bruised face may have been worth it. Out of crisis comes change."[29]—*Richard Grimes, Charleston Daily Mail*

As a state Supreme Court Justice, Darrell was one of a troika of justices whose opinions, based on allegiance to the language of the law, were resisted by power brokers and special interest groups. The rulings had "special significance not only in the lives of West Virginians but in the development of a national constitutional jurisprudence."[30] During Darrell's time as Justice, there were a number of landmark decisions that led to the evolution of the Court from one of the least to one of the most progressive appellate courts in the country. The Court's decisions held intentional violators of work place safety laws accountable; mandated equality of educational opportunity for all children and affirmed and advanced human rights law. The vignettes depict the Justices' level of commitment to legal and culturally right action and describe the resistance from those who objected to the Court's progressive opinions.

As the state's Attorney General, Darrell prosecuted law enforcement actions against big tobacco, big drug, insurance, telemarketers, pay day lenders, mortgage companies, and errant or corrupt government officials. Shortly before his last campaign for re-election as attorney general in 2012, Darrell prosecuted enforcement action lawsuits against many big drug companies. The suits alleged the drug companies shipped millions of addictive hydrocodone and oxycodone pills into West Virginia and that the companies knew the pills were diverted to street drug dealers. One of the companies prosecuted was Cardinal Health, the nation's second largest drug company that distributed excessive prescription opioids in West Virginias (over 241 million addictive pills between 2007-2012). Later Pulitzer prize-winning reporter, Eric Eyre revealed that a total of 780,000,000 opioid pills were funneled into West Virginia by a few drug companies that controlled 90% of the opioid distribution market.

The pharmaceutical companies fought back. The drug companies feared aggressive action by AG McGraw might expose what was essentially a "legal cartel" that earned billions in corporate profits while feeding a nationwide prescription opioid epidemic that has killed tens of thousands, including in West Virginia where the overdose death rate leads the nation. One way to avoid their responsibility for the epidemic was to defeat Darrell McGraw and elect a pharma-friendly attorney general. Drug companies were willing to spend large amounts of money for their own candidate, a New Jersey lawyer and Washington drug lobbyist who became a member of the West Virginia Bar just days before the deadline for filing to run for attorney general.

The McGraw Brothers know and appreciate the importance of coal, pharmaceuticals, doctors, large corporations, and business to the success of any community. One can value and appreciate corporate and business importance to the quality of life and remain committed to object whenever power and profit are placed above the people and the rule of law. As their stories depict, time and time again those who had much to profit created scapegoats—diversions to misguide and misinform the public. The McGraw brothers were only two targets of a now pervasive practice that divides the nation, as those who have much to gain create diversions to misguide and misinform the public.

Chapter II Warren McGraw Begins His Journey

During his first year of law school at Wake Forest, Warren met Lyndon Johnson. He regarded the meeting as having a substantial influence him. The future President energized Warren's desire to make a difference in his state.

Warren often found it difficult to concentrate on his studies, which he readily admitted were not a joy to him. Warren lived in student housing and any noise outside his door was a distraction, and as Warren said, was an excuse to leave his studies. In the fall of 1960, Warren was studying when the noise outside his apartment became too much for him to endure. Warren, known for jumping up and taking off at full speed, did just that when he yanked open his apartment door intent on admonishing the perpetrators.

Warren, wearing only his boxer shorts, ran straight into a tall, stately man in a suit and a Stetson cowboy hat (like Truman and Eisenhower before him) who thrust his hand out and said, "Hi, I'm Lyndon Johnson, and I'm running for Vice President of the United States." Warren flabbergasted and embarrassed, eyes narrowed, sheepishly flashed his pirate smile. Lyndon Johnson, future Vice President and President of the United States, laughed. He looked at Warren for a second, alternately at his smile and his boxers. Slapped him on the back and suggested, "Son why don't you get your britches on and join us."

Warren regained his composure, pulled on his pants and shirt and accompanied the entourage around campus. It was during this campus tour with Lyndon Johnson that Warren heard the future President talk about John F. Kennedy plans to abolish inequality, end poverty, improve housing for the low income and establish a Peace Corp program It was President Johnson who would later spearhead the "Great Society" policy initiatives, legislation and programs that advanced civil rights, public services, Medicare and Medicaid and Johnson's own "War on Poverty" designed to provide job skills, education and jobs for the underprivileged. These were all programs that were desperately needed in Warren's home county and West Virginia.

After law school Warren became a compliance officer for the Civil Rights Division at the Justice Department in Washington, D.C. Warren's job in the Civil Rights Division entailed reviewing the compliance form each school district submitted to affirm the district's desegregation status. Approval of the district's compliance form was necessary in order to receive federal funding. The protocol for review was a perfunctory approval unless the Office of Civil Rights received a previous segregation complaint against the school district. If a review of the record revealed a complaint then Warren authorized the FBI to investigate and evaluate the situation prior to any approval.

When Warren's home county's compliance form arrived at the Justice Department, he requested his supervisors assign the Wyoming County review to another evaluator. The supervisors were curt in their response to Warren's request: "McGraw, do your job." Their answer reminded Warren of something his mother would say. He knew what he had to do. Having grown up in Wyoming County, Warren understood the county's level of compliance with desegregation requirements. Warren denied approval of Wyoming County's compliance document. Within a few days Warren received a call from Wyoming County School Superintendent Robert Kuhn. Warren mowed Mr. Kuhn's lawn in his youth, as a neighbor in Pineville, but, Kuhn did not recognize Warren's voice. Mr. Kuhn demanded to know on what basis the compliance was denied.

Warren firsthand knowledge informed his reply: "Well, sir, I know the school board painted a 1960's hearse yellow and sends it out each morning to first go to Glen Rogers and pick up the Fuller children, and then it goes to Clearfork and picks up the McDonald children, and then it goes to Pineville and picks up the Warner children, and then it hauls them all to the Conley School for Black Children in Mullens." Mr. Kuhn was so shocked he hung up the phone. But Kuhn quickly called back and asked, "Who is this?" Warren, replied, "Mr. Kuhn, it is Warren McGraw." Mr. Kuhn said, "Warren, do you know that your denial of this compliance might cause your mom and dad (who were teachers) to lose their paycheck?" Warren said with all the conviction his parents had instilled, "Mr. Kuhn, my dad would want me to do the right thing. Your compliance form is denied."

The Wyoming County Board met that very evening to implement a desegregation plan for the school system.

In 1968, Darrell had finished his stint as legal counsel for Governor Hulett Smith and was working for Matt Reese Consulting, Inc. in Washington, D.C. (Matt Reese became known as the father of grassroots campaigning.) Warren was once again living in Wyoming County, the place where the brothers were born and raised.

Smoking as he paced the living room floor, Warren thoughts were on the coal miners who visited him in his office that day. One lost his job to a strip mine operation; the other suffered from black lung and received no benefits to support his family. The men were anguished and suffering from the hardships of trying to support their families.

Warren was now five years out of law school and practicing law in Pineville. Warren believed in his duty to the greater good of the community. It took precedence over everything except his family. He was married to his high school sweetheart, Peggy Shufflebarger. Peggy worked as a teacher to support them during his law school and was a State- Championship-winning high school girls' basketball coach on the side. She was now a music teacher in Pineville.

Peggy Shufflebarger and Warren McGraw, August 20, 1961

Warren and Peggy lived on the same street in their hometown of Pineville, and attended Pineville Grade, Middle and High School together. Warren and Peggy by now had a 5 year old boy, Warren Randolph II (Randolph), and a baby girl, Helen Suzanne, a third child,

Rebecca arrived in 1970. Warren's parents wanted the brothers to become lawyers to help their address community, but Warren now doubted his contribution. He needed to do something more meaningful.

Warren wanted to help the miners. He knew only members of the legislature could change the laws that allowed mountaintops to be stripped away and the miners to cough their lungs out without receiving compensation for their disease. Warren reached out to his brother Darrell to discuss the possibilities of running for House of Delegates. Darrell knew instinctively Warren already decided what he was going to do.

West Virginia House of Delegates

In 1968 Warren filed to run for the West Virginia House of Delegates. This was the first public election of the 38 elections spanning more than 45 years for the McGraw brothers. Darrell, through his work as counsel in Governor Hulett Smith's office, knew the established Democrat organization was not likely to be of assistance in Warren's election. Some West Virginia Democrats were much more reticent about social and economic reform issues than the McGraws. The West Virginia Democratic organization often curtsied in the attendance of big coal. Warren and Darrell McGraw were of a different mind.

Overcoming the existing Democratic organization list of preferred candidates required the McGraw brothers to think outside of the box. It required a strategy. For decades, political parties in West Virginia were driven to keep their candidate in office through orchestrating what were referred to as slates, the products of machine politics. Machine politics, where an authoritative boss or small empowered group commands the support of the electorate for their candidates, was alive and well in Wyoming County, and throughout West Virginia.

When Warren filed his candidacy papers for House of Delegates the brothers knew a major barrier to success was machine politics. They needed to determine how to overcome the impact of slate politics in Wyoming County. They determined a strategy that included Warren filing for a second office that of circuit judge of Wyoming County. They knew Democratic politicos would not want Warren elected judge, an office viewed to control the courthouse.

The next step was to convince the local Democrats that Warren was serious about securing the judgeship and willing to finance a competitive campaign. He was quite serious, because as a circuit judge he could be home every evening. He could eat Peggy's food, which he always preferred, read his magazines in in his favorite blue burlap chair and coach his son Randolph's little league. He wouldn't have to face the endless long drives to Charleston. The judge's pay was dependable, not like the law practice. The only problem with being a judge, as the brothers saw it, was that Warren wouldn't be able to enact laws that might help his community.

Of the two, Warren was the born legislator. Darrell knew through his work with the Legislature during Governor Hullet Smith's administration that serving in the Legislature wasn't for him. Warren's flair for public speech, acquired while on the debate team at Morris Harvey College, would serve him well if he became a legislator.

The element of surprise and timing were important in this and many of the McGraw brothers' future campaigns. Warren drove to Tesla, West Virginia in order to mail his filing papers for circuit judge. This ensured the candidacy papers were postmarked prior to the deadline but were opened in Wyoming County after the deadline. Filing for two offices was legal and easy to accomplish, but financing a campaign to run and win was more complicated for the money-strapped McGraws. For the McGraws it was always about strategy to out-wit the moneyed interests against them.

The brothers' needed to create an illusion that led opponents to the conclusion that Warren had sufficient campaign funds. Warren's friend, a merchant, arranged for a $10,000 loan from a Welch Bank in McDowell County for the campaign. Ten thousand dollars for a local campaign in the 1960s was a substantial amount. With check in hand, Warren drove his Plymouth Barracuda over the winding road across Indian Ridge Mountain from the Welch bank to deposit the $10,000 in the Pineville bank. Since the check was from another bank, Warren was able to immediately request withdrawal of $10,000 in $5 dollar bills. The curious request of a large amount of $5 dollar bills drew the attention of the teller and those with whom she shared the news of Warren's withdrawal request.

Word quickly spread that Warren withdrew a "large amount" of money for the election. People assumed the money was to pay people for votes, which was said to be a common practice in the 60s in West Virginia. No one made any attempt to correct the misconception. Warren redeposited the money in the Welch bank prior, of course, to the election. It was a great sense of relief to him to have the money back in the bank where it belonged.

Believing judges controlled courthouse politics, the local Democratic organization did not want the courthouse in Warren's purview. The politicos approached Warren with an offer not to fight his candidacy for House of Delegates if he withdrew from the judge's race. He was still a local boy, and well liked. Warren, not trusting the politicos long term level of commitment, kept his name on the ballot but agreed not to actively campaign for judge. Warren knew if he actually withdrew from the judge's race, nothing kept the anti-McGraw faction from changing their minds and campaigning against him in the House race. The tactic worked. Warren concentrated on winning the House seat and Democratic organization did not resist his candidacy. Warren won the primary and general elections. He was sworn in as a member of the House of Delegates member in 1969; the youngest member in the Legislature, and an ardent supporter of the needs of working people.

Warren made a name for himself as a vocal spokesperson for human rights, worker safety and the environment. For whatever reason, be it his youth and his handsomeness, his distinctive eyes and smile, or that he was a smart and poignant legislator, he was frequently featured in the state's most widely-circulated newspaper, the *Charleston Gazette*. As a freshman delegate, Warren introduced bills and struggled to receive good committee assignments while championing black lung compensation for coal miners and strip mining reform, controversial issues often not supported by members.

Farmington Mine Explosion—Consol No. 9
It was 1968 and the UMWA was under the iron fist rule of President W. A. Boyle. The union leadership was not always on the side of the miners. An old union story is illustrative of the vested interested Boyle had in his own power. On Saturday nights in Wyoming County

the Itmann union hall was usually filled with miners. One Saturday, a long black town car pulled up to the local hall. W.A. Boyle's right hand man, George Titler, emerged with a woman companion whom he escorted into the meeting. Titler held a baseball bat. Once inside the union hall, he thumped the end of the bat against his palm. He said, "Somebody in here's against our President Boyle." He walked between the aisles of seats, alternately slapping the bat into the palm of his hand and pointing its tip at the miners seated on the aisle. "What President Boyle wants to know, is which one of you is it?" It was this President Boyle who on the company's side when the disaster occurred at Consul No. 9.

On September 15th, 1968 the alarm on the safety fan at Consul No. 9 in Farmington, WV was disabled. [1] Ventilation safety fans are essential to push the highly combustible methane gas and coal dust buildup in mines from underground. Alarms on fans alert miners to impending danger.

Just a few days before November 20th, almost two months after the safety fan was disabled, one of the No. 9 miners told his wife that Consul stopped providing limestone "rock dust" commonly used to neutralize the combustibility of methane and coal dust.[2] On November 20, 1968, at 5:30 a.m., with the accumulated methane and coal dust at unreported levels, something ignited the hazardous mixture of gas and dust in Consol's No. 9. The disabled alarm did not sound. There was a monumental explosion felt as far away as 10 miles. Ninety-nine miners were underground at the time, and only 21 lived to come back to the surface. Seventy-eight miners died. Ten days after the explosion, Consol sealed the mine, shafts, slopes and all, in order to prevent the spread of fire. The concrete seal entombed bodies. The mine was unsealed about a year later, and bodies continued to be recovered for 10 years.[3]

Governor Hulett Smith said during the immediate aftermath of the Farmington disaster, "We must recognize that this is a hazardous business, and what has occurred here is one of the hazards of being a miner."[4] Assistant Interior Secretary Jay Cordell said, "The Company has done all in its power to make this a safe mine. Unfortunately, we don't know why these things happen, but they do happen."[5] UMWA President Boyle traveled to the disaster. His words supported the company, "As long as we mine coal, there is always this inherent danger of explosion... this happens to be one of the better companies as far as cooperation with our union and safety is concerned."[6]

But No. 9 had a history of safety violations. In 1954, a similar explosion killed 16 miners.[7] One Federal Bureau of Mines Inspector cited the company for violating Federal rock dusting procedures 24 times in the years leading up to the disaster. When asked why the Bureau didn't close the mine, he said, "Close a Consol mine? You must be kidding. Any inspector who closed a Consol mine would be looking for a job the next day."[8]

Flash Forward

Forty seven years after the disaster, in a sworn affidavit, Leroy Layne, MSHA inspector who was on the scene investigating Farmington on November 20, 1968, stated, "On September 15, 1970, Mr. Sacchetti told me that he and the chief electrician, Alex Kovarbasich, disconnected the FEMCO alarm on the fan before the November 20, 1968 explosion. Mr. Sacchetti further advised that 'they' told Alex Kovarbasich to disconnect the FEMCO alarm on the fan prior to the November 20, 1968 explosion..."[9] Mr. Layne further stated he sent a memo to his supervisors notifying that a Consolidation electrician told him that an alarm connected to the safety fan had been disconnected. Nothing was done. Widows and family members of the doomed miners only received $10,000 each from the coal company.

It wasn't until the publication of a book by Bonnie Stewart, a former West Virginia University professor, documenting the Consol Mine disaster, that Layne's memo was uncovered. Layne never spoke to anyone about his memo until after he visited Sacchetti in 2010 to talk about the explosion. Sacchetti didn't want to talk about the disaster and told Layne that better be careful; Layne considered it a threat.[10] Two Farmington widows ultimately corroborated the story.[11]

Almost 50 years later, the families of the miners killed at Farmington tried to find justice through the West Virginia court system. Professor Stewart's book uncovering key evidence of intent to harm, spurred the families to file a law suit. In November, 2014 the families sued the estate of Mr. Kovarbasich and Consolidation Coal for wrongful death seeking $110,000 for each victim's family and punitive damages. The suit alleged that defendants committed fraud and concealed vital information regarding why the explosion occurred. Consolidation, now Murray Energy, argued the lawsuit should be dismissed because it wasn't filed within two years of the explosion. The attorneys for the families countered that the two year statute of limitation should not commence until June, 2014 when Mr. Sacchetti's statement that Mr. Kovarbasich disabled the fan alarm was confirmed[12]

The statute of limitation issue eventually landed as a certified question to the newly constituted 2019 West Virginia Supreme Court. Justice Evan Jenkins, a former industry lawyer, delivered the Court's opinion negating the families' right to seek redress. Justice Jenkins' concluded "the law in effect at the time of this tragedy did not recognize a cause of action for fraudulent concealment with respect to at statutory wrongful death claim."[13]

Flash Back to 1968

The miners suspected foul play by the company contributed to the explosion at Consul No 9. And they knew Boyle was not to be trusted. Tony Boyle had long been in bad standing with West Virginia miners for his all too frequent alignment with coal operators and lack of support for black lung benefits for miners. Boyle's statements at Farmington aggravated one union trailblazer in particular, Jock Yablonski. He was a one time member of the UMWA's executive board. Yablonski said Boyle was taking the company's view. Yablonski believed Boyle was bad for miners' health and safety.[14] Yablonski was determined to do something about Boyle, and he would before another year passed. But first there was the need to address black lung and miner safety in the next Legislative session.

Legislative Session--Black Lung Bill and Miner Safety

To whose benefit is it to violate coal dust regulations and resist black lung benefits for miners?

Coal production has long been notorious for the associated health, safety and environmental issues. In southern West Virginia, where there is little alternative economic opportunity, young coal miners have long understood their destiny. A third generation coal miner knows his grandfather died from black lung; his father, who still works in the mines, has black lung, and his destiny, if he continues to work in the mines, is much the same. What does a coal miner do? In a democracy the coal miner talks to his representative who may understand, but the representative is just only one out of a body. The young Delegate McGraw was determined to represent the interest of his coal miner constituents.

In the aftermath of the Farmington disaster, Warren's first Legislative session in January, 1969 was challenging. The session was also the first one for Governor Arch Moore, a Republican, who won the 1968 general election to succeed Democrat Hulett Smith. Black lung legislation was a major issue, and debate was intense and controversial. Industrial interests were opposed to any increase in health and safety regulations including black lung compensation.

In the wake of Farmington disaster, mine safety and health issues like black lung became a preeminent legislative issue for miners, activists and doctors who treated black lung patients. In early January, 1969 Doctors Donald Rasmussen, Isadore Buff, and Hawey "Sonny" Wells, members of the Committee of Physicians on Mine Health and Safety, along with Arnold Miller, later UMWA President, and other reformers established the West Virginia Black Lung Association (BLA), a grassroots organization advocating for the addition of black lung disease to the workers' compensation law.[15] Members of the BLA traveled the state speaking to miners, organizing rallies and lobbying legislators to garner support for legislation that would properly compensate black lung victims. The BLA found a champion for their cause in the young legislator Warren McGraw. McGraw drew frequent speaking invitations from local union leaders. As full of character and charisma as his voice and tone were, the real magic of Warren's speaking ability was that he ardently believed in what he was saying, and when he spoke it was as if he were speaking to each person individually.

On Saturday January 12, 1969, at a rally in Cheylan, West Virginia designed to draw public attention to the lack of appropriate compensation for miners with black lung disease, Dr. Hawey "Sonny"

Wells told miners, "You are sick in the head if you and other miners don't make the legislature extend coverage of 'black lung disease' under worker's compensation."[16] He said, "The blame has been placed on Vista, the communists, the Reds, the Castrites, and on 3 of us medical bandits." This brought laughs from the crowd. He went on to point directly at the state legislature whose members "Sits on their hands to squash this legislation of humanity."[17]

On January 26, 1969 over 3,000 coal miners rallied at the Capitol and Charleston Civic Center demanding the enactment of legislation to provide compensation for miners with black lung. Delegate Warren McGraw along with Arnold Miller, Congressman Ken Hechler, Senator Paul Kaufman, Dr. I. E. Buff, Dr. Donald Rasmussen and Dr. Hawey "Sonny" Wells accompanied thousands of miners as they walked Charleston's Kanawha Boulevard in what was coined "The Black Lung March" to the Civic Center. Inside the arena the speakers passionately advocated for passage of worker's compensation legislation to cover black lung disease for an estimated 50,000 disabled miners.[18] It was there that Warren announced to the agitated crowd a bill he proposed to modify the worker compensation law to include life time black lung benefits for the disabled miner based on the percent of disability. The proposed bill went far beyond then current maximum of 208 weeks of pay.[19] Tony Boyle, UMWA President was invited to the rally, but he didn't show up.[20] After the rally, one of his union supporters sent a threating letter to local UMWA members warning them against donating any money to the Black Lung Association. "Dual association," the letter said, could result in expulsion from the union.[21]

Warren, with the support of his close friend Del. Robert Nelson, introduced the House bill to modify worker's compensation to include increased black lung benefits for miners currently suffering from and for those acquiring pneumoconiosis in the future. Sen. Paul Kaufman introduced a similar black lung bill on the Senate side. Both bills were stalled in committees. Coal companies knew that if black lung were recognized as a "work related disease," it meant increased cost for the company. Leaders of the Coal Association fought to keep any black lung bill from leaving the committees for a floor vote by the membership. If a black lung bill came to the floor, the increased interested in the community related to miner health and safety could result in a majority of representatives siding with miners.

One major issue of contention related to whether a bill could authorize "retroactive designation" which meant coverage for miners already diagnosed with the disease. The West Virginia Black Lung Association, which included past and present coal miners, lobbied to make black lung designation retroactive and increase compensation payments and benefits. Legal experts, including one from the national UMWA, were concerned with bills that contained the retroactive clause because of the additional cost to fund.[22]

Dr. Jethro Gough, World Health Organization consultant, testified at a legislative hearing and implored the legislature to take action to provide compensation benefits for all those miners who had suffered for decades: "The move to compensate West Virginia miners for black lung disease is 40 years late……coal dust, resulting from mechanization, causes pneumoconiosis or black lung disease and a special kind of emphysema."[23]

Hearings on black lung schlepped on. The hearings, packed with miners, were moved from committee rooms to the House Chamber. Miners filled even the spectators' gallery. Medical experts hired by the industry testified to the alleged benign nature of pneumoconiosis (black lung), claiming it was "compatible with reasonable health,"[24] and to smoking as the sole cause of problematic lung disease.[25] When Warren questioned Dr. Rowland Burns, expert medical witness for the Coal Association, Warren asked, "How much are coal operators paying you to testify?" Burns caught off guard, admitted to having been paid and replied, "I have not been paid near enough. I can't tell you exactly what I've been paid."[26] Jeers and shouts reverberated throughout the chamber from the Black Lung Association spectators in the gallery.

The UMWA is a brotherhood. Part of the creed of the union, of course, is not to cross a picket line. Another is not to go into a mine after a brother dumps his water out of his dinner bucket. When a miner dumps water out of his bucket he is saying to other miners not to go into a mine because it is not safe. "The strike's the onliest weapon the rank and file has," said one miner, Robert Payne.[27]

And so it was that shortly after Warren's deposition of Burns at the legislative hearing, that on Tuesday, February 18, 1969 a miner did just that. He dumped his water out of his dinner bucket. All of his brothers on the shift left the mine.[28] "Why?" asked the press. "Because we want the Black Lung bill to pass," said the miners.

The next day, 14 mines were shut down. By the end of the week, 12,000 miners were on strike. Then there were 30,000 on strike. [29] "If necessary we will stop every lump of coal in the state until we get this legislation through," one miner said.[30] Reaction to the strike was divided in the Legislature, with many legislators demanding miners return to work before legislative consideration and action. Legislators were concerned about the next election and feared the industry's power and money in supporting other candidates. But Warren encouraged his fellow legislators towards a greater level of compassion for the coal miners' plight. Warren rose on the floor of the House to implore action, "Some of us take the attitude that we won't be bulldozed, we won't be pressured by the action of the people of this state…I propose that each of us reassess our position and that we should be moved by the plight of these people."[31]

Warren was in his element. If he weren't working on the House floor, he was in committee re-reading each line of the Black Lung Bill. Keeping tabs on Steve Young, lobbyist, President of the Coal Association, was part of Warren's daily drill. While Warren worked his end of the Black Lung Bill, Steve was doing the same thing from the other end against it. Warren wanted to know who Steve had been talking to and what he was telling them and what he was promising them in exchange for support.

Those in midst of the black lung struggle understood big coal companies didn't want the liability associated with legislation that validated coal dust as the cause of black lung and silica dust causing silicosis. Such confirmation would require substantial financial outlay for increased mine safety processes to negate the inhalation of coal dust and silica; i.e. ventilation systems, protective equipment, rock dusters, fan powered scrubbers, water spray systems, shearer deflector plates and other expensive systems.[32] It also meant increased Workers Compensation charges as miners became eligible for benefits. The coal industry created diversions to cover the real reasons for their resistance. The industry contended the black lung legislation would result in lost miner jobs-and increase the cost of coal, which would be passed on to the consumer in increased electricity rates.

Warren was one of two brave state legislators who attended a rally near the Affinity mine in Raleigh County. The meeting was held at Midway Elementary School. When Warren arrived at the jam-packed rally, it had already begun. Warren started to enter the rally, but four loyals of "President" W. A. Tony Boyle guarded the door. "Meeting's closed," said one. "Closed to you," said another, twirling the handle end of a baseball bat, resting the thick end on his shoulder. "We were told if either of McGraw boys showed up and wanted to go in there, they might stir up the crowd."

After some protest, Warren pretended to leave but instead went around to the side of the building and crawled through an open window. Warren received a warm reception, warmed, perhaps, by his odd entry. Warren, the Legislature's youngest member said, "I'm not advocating the strike be continued, but you never get anything without flexing your muscles." That night, the miners vowed to march on the Capitol. The rally concluded when one aged miner stood on his chair and shouted, "Some of these legislators say we're finks and rabble-rousers, but we're coal miners and the only thing we ever got was when we went out and fought for it. So I say let's all get to Charleston tomorrow and show them what a fight we can give them."[33] On February 26, 1969 thousands of miners returned to march on the Capitol demanding passage of Black Lung Legislation.

Even though Warren was outraged when the chairman of the House Judiciary Committee again stalled the black lung bill in committee without bringing it to the floor for a vote, Warren used his leadership skills to calm striking miners who filled the House gallery awaiting the bill. He talked with the miners, shook their hands, discussed the intricacies of parliamentary procedures that can be used to stall bills but vowed to keep the struggle moving forward with all his legislative might.[34]

The strike spread like kudzu vine to other states. By early March over 40,000 miners were on strike and coal production had ceased in southern West Virginia. The strike combined with the Black Lung

Association's intensive campaign was effective in pushing the Legislature into action. On the House floor, Warren announced perfunctorily into his microphone, "House Bill number 1040 provides the coal miners and other industry workers of this state with a very, very excellent piece of legislation," and with that, the House Speaker called for a vote on the floor. [35] Even though tensions remained high and the debate intense, the House passed the black lung proposals sought by coal miners. The bill was sent to the Senate.

Warren was elated with the passage of the bill in the House and saw the legislation as a major victory for miners' rights: "The bill is the most important piece of labor legislation in this state in this century. With the bill, West Virginia has become the first state to reverse the traditional principle that a worker accepts the hazards of his job as the price of his employment."[36]

On March 8th the Legislature passed an agreed upon version of the House's Black Lung bill.[37] Minutes before midnight, the Senate bell rang, and the vote went live. Red or green lights beside the names of each Senator lit up one by one to indicate yay or nay. The Senate clerk tallied the votes. Down clicked the President's gavel.

Warren was ecstatic and wanted to share the news with his brother. It was well after midnight when a jubilant Warren reached Darrell, "You awake?" Darrell V. mumbled an answer. "Brother? It's over," said Warren. "It passed. The Black Lung bill, it passed." Darrell, with that news now wide awake and equally pleased, offered, "Brother, that is pretty amazing—'good work my brother good work,' as our Grandfather Zekany would say." They laughed. Both of the brothers' thoughts reverted back to Logan County, the grape arbor and their Grandfather's blacksmith shop where he told the brothers stories of life in the coal mines and the importance of good work. "Get some rest, the fight's not over," Darrell said as he thought about mine safety, the poorly regulated strip mines and the need to protect our resources for the benefit of local communities.

The success of the West Virginia Black Lung Association led to similar movements in Ohio and Kentucky to pass workers' compensation laws for black lung victims. The states' success to secure needed benefits at a local level was heard by Congressional leaders. Warren said to his

44

brother, "people know what black lung is now." This enhanced
awareness coupled with the passage of state black lung bills encouraged
action on the national level which ultimately resulted in the passage of
the 1969 Federal Coal Mine Health and Safety Act: "The Coal Act also
included specific procedures for the development of improved mandatory
health and safety standards, and provided compensation for miners who
were totally and permanently disabled by the progressive respiratory
disease caused by the inhalation of fine coal dust pneumoconiosis or
"Black Lung."[38]

Black Lung Disease—A Present Day Struggle
*If Black lung caused by inhaling coal and silica dust is preventable then
why are black lung rates higher than 50 years ago?[39] To whose benefit is
it to have inadequate rules and enforcement of coal and silica dust
regulations?*

The 1969 West Virginia Black Lung Bill and the Federal Coal
Mine and Health Safety Act were major milestones in instituting
regulations to reduce the impact of coal dust on miners and compensation
for those who were its victims. After the Black Lung legislation passed,
Dr. Donald Rasmussen, the outspoken doctor and advocate for miner
safety, prophesized "that the disease would go away before we learn
more about it."[40] Unfortunately federal and state regulators enforcement
of regulations to prevent excessive inhalation of coal and silica dust
remain inadequate, and the coal industry, their lawyers and medical
experts, often lock deserving miners out of black lung compensation.
In the 2010 the Upper Big Branch Mine Disaster killed 29 miners.
Seventeen or 71 percent of those miners were found to have black lung.
The disaster was attributable to inadequate ventilation necessary to
prevent black lung disease and ultimately disastrous combustion.
Investigation found that Massey Energy routinely falsified dust sampling
which was used by regulators to enforce air quality standards to protect
the miners. In 1998, twelve years before the disaster, miner Bruce
Vickers who worked at Upper Big Branch testified before a federal grand
jury of the dust pump falsification but "court records and government
documents don't show any charges ever being brought."[41]

In the decades following passage of the 1969 black lung laws, black lung diseases dropped significantly. However in the late 1990s things began to change when the lack of safety regulation enforcement within the mines negatively impacted miners' health. By 2012 black lung, the deadly coal disease was on the rise. The Center for Public Integrity reported that from 1968-2007 black lung disease caused or contributed to the death of 75,000 miners nationwide, and the incidence of the most deadly kind of black lung jumped significantly.[42] The report concluded: "The disease's resurgence represents a failure to deliver on a 40 year old pledge to miners…The system for monitoring dust levels is tailor-made for cheating, and mining companies haven't been shy about doing so. Meanwhile, regulators have sometimes neglected to enforce even these porous rules."[43] In 2012 when Dr. Rasmussen was asked about his 1969 prophesy that black lung would disappear, Dr. Rasmussen lamented, "I was dead wrong."[44]

Thomas Jefferson said the "execution of the laws is more important than the making of them."[45] West Virginia's governor takes an oath of office "to faithfully discharge the duties of the office" which includes state laws and regulations regarding mine health and safety. The governor's responsibility is to execute the law made by Legislature. The execution of public policy whether coal mine health and safety regulations, equality of educational opportunity, workers compensation, road construction, collective bargaining, health cost containment, etc. remains with the integrity of those elected or appointed officers charged with enforcement of the law.

Certainly mine health and safety regulations must be rigorous but even the most rigorous requirements without enforcement is grossly insufficient. With whatever inadequacy exist in the mine safety rules the "enforcement of those rules hasn't been adequate, and the sanctions for mine operators who violate rules are not adequate."[46] Control of coal and silica dust, the cause of black lung, is plagued by weak enforcement by regulators and by the loopholes company officials exploit.[47] Analysis of decades of federal regulatory data on dust-collection monitors in coal mines reveal a disregard by regulators to enforce air quality regulations. Regulators failure to recognize and respond to clear evidence of excessive and toxic coal and silica dust exposure results in the escalating numbers of miners suffering from black lung.[48]

As the thick seams of coal are "worked out," the coal industry mines thinner seams of coal that require cutting into the surrounding rock. The silica dust from the pulverized rock damages lungs faster than coal dust alone and results in miners acquiring an even more devastating black lung disease known as progressive massive fibrosis (PMF). In February, 2018 federal regulators reported the largest cluster of advanced lung disease (PMF) ever recorded.[49]

"Having miners die at such young ages…I mean this is such a gross and frank example of regulatory failure. It's an 'epidemic' and clearly one of the worst industrial medicine disasters that ever been described. We're counting thousands of cases. Thousands and thousands and thousands of black lung cases. Thousands of cases of the most severe form of black lung, and we're not done counting yet."[50]—*Scott Laney, epidemiologist at the National Institute for Occupational Safety and Health*

State and federal laws established the right for miners with black lung to receive compensation. However for decades miners suffering with black lung face a tragic trajectory as they struggle to receive appropriate compensation and health care. In a year long study the Center for Public Integrity unraveled and claimed the unethical behavior of 1.) the coal industry's go-to law firm, Jackson Kelly, who withheld evidence resulting in the denial of compensation claims to miners suffering from black lung; 2.) a small unit of John Hopkins professors and physicians, who for forty years were sought-after readers of chest films on behalf of coal companies, rarely found evidence of black lung resulting in the defeat miners' claims, and 3.) the coal industry who denied emerging scientific evidence of a new and more severe form of black lung disease in order to limit liability and lock multitude of miners out of benefits.[51]

Miners seeking compensation often find themselves without legal representation. Less than one-third of miners seeking black lung compensation have a lawyer in the initial stage of their case. Miner's attorneys are legally barred from charging the claimant any fees, and the often meager compensation if claimant wins means lawyers avoid representation of the sick miner. Time and money are on the side of the coal industry and their lawyers who often hire a multitude of experts and drag cases on for years.[52]

Jackson Kelly, named by U.S. News and World Report as the nation's top firm in mining law, has represented the interests of coal companies for a century. Jackson Kelly, perhaps not the only law firm, but the most prominent, frequently represents the coal industry against miners' claims for black lung benefits. A Center for Public Integrity investigation uncovered that for decades attorneys in the federal black lung unit of Jackson Kelly engaged in practices of withholding evidence that supported miners' claims for black lung compensation.[53] Withholding evidence is a violation of the ABA's Model Rule 3.3 regarding a lawyer's duty of Candor to the Tribunal. A lawyer "shall not knowingly…fail to disclose a material fact to a tribunal when disclosure is necessary to avoid assisting a criminal or fraudulent act by the client."[54]

The Center's investigation cited many cases involving the practice of withholding pertinent evidence. In one such case Gary Fox, a miner, was examined by a doctor certified by the U.S. Department of Labor and diagnosed with the most severe form of black lung. The government ordered his employer, a subsidiary of Massey Coal to begin paying him monthly benefits. As is custom the company appealed the decision. Jackson Kelly was retained by the coal company. Two years earlier Fox had removed a suspicious mass from his lung. The hospital pathologist ruled out cancer but there was no evidence the pathologist even looked for black lung disease. Jackson Kelly obtained the hospital slides of Fox's lung tissue for its two pathologists to review. The pathologists wrote reports that the mass was complicated black lung. Jackson Kelly did not submit those reports to the administrative law judge but rather only the hospital's pathologist report that ruled out Fox had cancer. In 2001, without knowledge of the withheld pathologists' report confirming black lung, the judge denied Fox's claim. Fox, unrepresented by counsel, and increasingly sick returned to the mines until 2007 when he again tried to garner worker's compensation for his black lung disease. This time with the assistance of counsel and numerous court orders, Jackson Kelly's hidden away evidence was uncovered. In 2009, Judge Burke entered a decision granting Fox's claim and admonishing Jackson Kelly:

"Despite knowledge of the role pathology evidence played in the case, Employer continued to conceal the more probative reports of Drs. Caffrey and Naeye while emphasizing, and encouraging reliance upon, the report of [the hospital pathologist]. When Claimant's counsel attempted to bring evidence of Employer's conduct to light, Employer engaged in a course of conduct designed to conceal its actions; first denying the presence of the reports, then conceding liability to prevent their disclosure."[55]

Judge Burke awarded benefits dating to 1997 after it was discovered Jackson Kelly withheld "an X-ray reading by one of its radiologists finding complicated black lung on an X-ray taken the year before Fox's first biopsy."[56] It was too late for Gary Fox.

Two months after Judge Burke's decision Gary Fox died from advanced stage black lung.

Judge Burke determined Jackson Kelly's behavior amounted to "fraud on the court." Jackson Kelly appealed Burke's decision. In 2014 the 4th Circuit Federal Court ruled in favor of Jackson Kelly. Despite Jackson Kelly deliberately withholding medical evidence that showed Gary Fox had complicated pneumoconiosis and was entitled to black lung benefits, Jackson Kelly's actions were ruled not sufficiently egregious to constitute a fraud on the court.[57]

The Center for Public Integrity uncovered numerous documents showing that Jackson Kelly in its representation of coal company interests withheld unfavorable evidence and only showed their reviewing doctors what they wanted them to see. It was part of a cutthroat approach to fight miner's claims for black lung benefits.[58]

For decades coal miners attempts to qualify for black lung have also been thwarted by a cadre of doctors with prestigious affiliations, including John Hopkins radiology unit led by Dr. Paul Wheeler. In more than 1,500 cases decided since 2000, Dr. Wheeler never found a case of complicated black lung and in only 2 percent of the cases did Wheeler identify early stages of the disease. The opinions of these prestigious doctors often negate whatever positive interpretations a miner produces.[59]

As a result of the Center of Public Integrity and an ABC investigation, John Hopkins University School of Medicine shut down its black lung unit. But coal companies engagement of doctors with prestigious credentials to rebuke black lung claims continue.[60]

49

Finally, as new and more devastating types of black lung are identified by doctors and scientists, coal companies devote resources to resist their classification as black lung. In actuality black lung is not just one disease but a term used to distinguish a variety of lung diseases caused by breathing coal dust, silica and a combination of coal dust and silica. Science continues to show that inhaling coal and silica dust involved in coal mining reacts differently in each person; i.e. different types of scarring within the lungs and different levels of severity. With each scientific advancement in understanding the complexities of black lung, coal companies mount well financed legal responses in opposition. Coal companies hire pathologists, pulmonologists and radiologists in order to maintain the narrowest qualifications for black lung compensation and avoid the liability of compensating more sick miners.[61]

Take the case of Ted Latusek, a miner with Consol Energy, who was identified in the Center for Public Integrity investigation. It took Ted Latusek 24 years to finally earn black lung benefits.[62] Even though Mr. Latusek breathing was so bad he was considered totally disabled for that entire time, Consol and its legal counsel, Jackson Kelly resisted his claims. Latusek's scarring in the lungs was different than simple black lung disease. Research increasingly confirms the pattern of scarring in Latusek's lungs is a previously an unrecognized form of black lung. The National Institute for Occupational Safety and Health (NIOSH), the National Institutes of Health (NIH) and independent doctors link the scarring pattern evident in Latusek to black lung caused by coal mining. As coal companies have done in over 380 cases identified by Center for Public Integrity that involved miners with similar scarring, Consul disputed that Latusek's particular pattern of scarring was a type of black lung.[63] Finally in January, 2018 the U.S. Court of Appeals of the Fourth Circuit upheld black lung benefit claims for Mr. Latusek, a case which was originally filed in 1994.[64]

Coal company denial of scientific advancements in understanding the complex varieties of black lung disease is representative of the longstanding war between companies and miners—coal company desire for containment of liability versus miners' right to black lung compensation.

Jock Yablonski, Union Reformer, Murdered

When W.A. Tony Boyle led the UMWA, power was an end unto itself. By 1969 Boyle maintained a system that allowed him to achieve the appointment of 19 of the 23 district presidents, rather than democratically elected by union members.[65] Jock Yablonski was of the idea to change that and make every local office an elected position. Yablonski wanted the officers at every level more responsible to the membership. It was part of his platform when he ran against Boyle in 1969 for President. Yablonski had proven himself with the rank and file by way of his work with McGraw and Senator Paul Kaufman in the passage of the Black Lung Legislation. For the same reason, he gained disapproval of the W. A. Boyle's union hierarchy.

On May 30, 1969, Jock announced his candidacy for UMWA President by saying, "When ye be an anvil, lay ye very still. But when ye be a hammer, strike with all thy will." It was a quote from John L. Lewis. Jock then said, "Today is the day I cease being an anvil."[66] Yablonski's aggressive campaign accused Boyle of running a "dictatorship" and labeled him a "crook and embezzler."[67] He further accused Boyle of nepotism and misuse of funds, while pushing for greater voting rights for rank and file members in union affairs.[68]

Boyle felt the need to take drastic measures. He enlisted Albert Pass, a Boyle appointed officer from the notoriously violent District 19 (Kentucky). Boyle told Pass, "We're in a fight…Yablonski ought to be killed or done away with."[69] Boyle then funneled $20,000 of union money to Pass in order to carry out the deed.[70]

On Thanksgiving Day, 1969, the same Mr. Pass who had taken $20,000 for the Yablonski assassination asked W. A. Boyle's secretary if she wanted to know what the final vote would be in District 19. "It's going to be 3723 votes for Mr. Boyle and 87 for Joe Yablonski," he said. District 19 results turned out just as Mr. Pass said.[71] The national election for UMWA president on December 9, 1969 found Boyle winning by 80,577 to Yablonski's 46, 073 votes.[72]

Yablonski reported to Federal officials that Boyle had won by fraud, prompting an investigation into the electoral process.[73] Yablonski gave immediate notice that he would contest the election in Court. Three

weeks later Yablonski was murdered. At one post-election rally, when
the hit on Yablonski's life was alive, in Welch, West Virginia, Boyle-
hired thugs attended and milled around wearing guns. They wrote down
license plate numbers from the cars in the parking lot.[74] At Yablonski's
side was Warren McGraw.[75] Yablonski's pilot told McGraw their plane
was making a funny sound. "Like there's sugar in the gas tank."[76]

In mid-December, 1969 Paul Gilly and Claude Vealey, two of the
gunmen ultimately hired to carry out the murder, went to Yablonski's
house in Pennsylvania but lost their nerve at the last moment. They
returned around midnight on New Year's Eve, a little over a year after
Farmington disaster, with Buddy Martin. The three assassins arrived at
the Yablonski house in a blue 1966 Chevrolet with Ohio plates. First,
they drank beers on the hillside across from his house. They cut the
electricity to the house, and then snuck upstairs to the bedrooms where
the family lay sleeping. They shot Yablonski's 25-year-old daughter,
Charlotte, twice in the head. They shot his wife, Margaret twice; one of
their bullets cut through her pulmonary artery. Lastly, they shot Jock
Yablonski. He was 59 years old. From the foot of his bed, they shot him
three times, but still he wasn't dead. Finally, one killing bullet hit him in
the back of his head.[77]

Darrell knew Jock Yablonski and his family. Jock's wife attended
graduate school with Darrell's wife Marie at WVU, and Darrell worked
with Jock's daughter Charlotte in President Johnson's poverty program.
After the tragedy, Darrell went to see Jock's son Chip in Washington. It
was an incredibly sad time for the family and the union.

In the wake of their family's brutal murders, Jock's sons Chip and
Ken Yablonski led the *Miners for Democracy* organization. The
Yablonskis, Jack Perry, President of District 17 and Arnold Miller,
President of the WV Black Lung Association, thousands of West
Virginians, miners and non-miners alike, supported *Miners for
Democracy* efforts to oust Boyle and elect a new president. Some of
those non-miner supporters included Warren and Darrell, Davitt
McInteer, an activist lawyer from Fairmont, Congressman Ken Hechler,
Senator Paul Kaufman, Senator Robert Nelson and Dr. Fred Barkey,
labor historian and professor, and many other community leaders. The

first meeting of *Miners for Democracy* was held in the basement of the church after Jock Yablonski's funeral.

A few days after the news of the Yablonski deaths, 20,000 West Virginia miners walked out of the mines on a one day strike. The miners were convinced Boyle was responsible for the deaths. "We all knew in our bones at the time that the union hierarchy was behind this but we couldn't prove it," said journalist Brit Hume, later a Fox News political analyst.[78] Three years passed and another election for UMWA president occurred before the miners' convictions were vindicated, and Tony Boyle was brought to justice.[79]

Two years after Yablonski's charge of election fraud and after a federal investigation, a U.S. District Judge ordered a new election to be supervised by the US Department of Labor.[80] In 1972, Arnold Miller defeated W. A. Boyle for President of the UMWA.[81] Much needed reform of the UMWA organization continued under Miller's leadership.[82]

In 1973 Boyle was convicted on embezzling union funds for the 1968 election, and in 1974 he was convicted of murder in the Yablonski killings and sentenced to prison. The conviction was overturned and Boyle was re-tried in 1978 and convicted again.[83]

The UMWA is a tight family culture, a brotherhood. They refer to each other as "Brothers and Sisters" in their constitutional union obligation: "I further promise to help and assist all Brothers and Sisters in adversity, and to have all workers join our union that we may all be able to enjoy the fruits of our labor; that I will never knowingly wrong a Brother or Sister or see him or her wronged if I can prevent it." Into this tight and loyal brotherhood, the McGraw brothers fit right in. An iron-clad, lifelong allegiance between the UMWA and the McGraws formed, as strong, perhaps, as the very one between the McGraw brothers themselves.

Struggle for Better Strip Mining Regulations

Mountain-top removal mining destroyed or damaged nearly 2,000 miles of streams and threatens to destroy 1.4 million acres of our forests and mountains by 2020.—Sierra Club

As a freshman Delegate in the Legislature, Warren established a record of speaking out for working men and women. Warren continued to introduce bills each year designed to better address the working conditions of miners. Warren and his friend, State Senator Robert Nelson, introduced legislation to improve Workmen's Compensation benefits to include fair compensation rates and the establishment of an Occupational Disease Board. Miners rallied at the State Capitol in support of the legislation as issues related to black lung and strip mining continued to raise intense reaction.[84]

On the Senate side, Sen. Si Galperin introduced a bill to abolish strip mining. The UMWA was against the bill, as were the coal operators. Even though deep coal miners were losing jobs to the more machine operated strip mines, the UMWA leadership feared the abolition of strip mining would result in a negative impact in the number of overall mining jobs. And with any reduction in overall production of coal in union mines, the UMWA lost revenue to the health and welfare fund.[85]

The introduction of the strip mining bill in the Senate intensified the convictions of the three camps related to the strip mining. First there were those who favored the abolition of strip mining (abolitionists /environmentalists); second those who were fine with only increasing regulations on strip mining and reclamation (regulationists) and finally those who wanted no interference (big coal). With the introduction of the bill to abolish strip mining, each camp became more entrenched and passionate about the righteousness of their stance. Allegations of threats including intimidation and physical harm to supporters within each camp occurred.

Intimidation and threats were not effective with the McGraw brothers and generally served to make them more determined in their convictions. Warren knew the Senate bill that completely abolished strip mining was not likely to pass, but believed it provided a vehicle for compromise that could result in increased environmental regulations for the industry. When Warren heard rumors and experienced actual threats he became more hard-nosed in his reaction, "If threats of physical harm weren't being circulated, I would have abandoned my intention to introduce a bill calling for abolishment of strip mining, but they are and I won't."[86]

The controversy over abolition of strip mining continued to escalate throughout the 1971 session with UMWA concerned that complete abolition of strip mining might be detrimental to miners. Coal miners returned to the Capitol and confrontations occurred. The strip mine abolition bill eventually died, but others followed. The Senate continued to author bills to regulate strip mining and reduce the negative environmental impact. However, when the bills reached the House they were often 'stripped' of any value despite Del. McGraw's efforts to build support for common sense strip mining regulation. While Warren worked to protect the people and the land he loved from strip mining, some coal operators promoted strip mining, and its more aggressive counterpart, mountain top removal. Coal operators pooled their money and worked to promote favorable laws and regulations. They vowed to use their collective power and money to campaign against Warren McGraw.

Coal operators noticed Warren was an exhilarating politician; in him, they knew they had a problem. Coal and strip mine operators stood against him, but two of them with him would monumentally tangle. Those two were Senator Tracy Hylton, a strip mine operator, and Don Blankenship, future CEO of Massey Coal. At this time, Blankenship was building his personal wealth while propagating strip mining and mountain top removal.

The McGraw brothers are not anti-coal mining. Members of their family mined coal. Peggy's grandfather was superintendent of mines at Itman Coal, and her father owned and operated a mine. The McGraw brothers understand that coal mining brings good jobs and respectable wages to homes throughout West Virginia. But being for coal mining did not negate the McGraw brothers' duty to express concern and resist improper practices as it related to miner health and safety, environmental protection, fair taxation and community responsibility.

Strip-mining, especially in irresponsible hands, is detrimental to Appalachia. Not just the mountains and the streams, but the people, too. Strip mining requires fewer workers. It only takes one man to operate a dragline excavator, a mechanized $100 million dollar destructor of mountains. Big Muskie, the largest single dragline digging machine ever created was 22 stories tall with a bucket that could hold two Greyhound buses. Consol's Big Muskie was across the river in Ohio doing its work, but similar machines in WV exposed seams of coal, loaded the coal into rail cars and hauled it away as their mother used to say.[87]

Warren only had to look around the counties he represented to know the impact of strip mining. As mining companies stripped the trees and scraped away the earth to get to the thin coal seams, the landscapes, forests and wildlife habitats were destroyed. The result was often barren, unsightly lands that stand in stark contrast to the mountains' original majesty. Washed away by rain, the sediments from strip mining pollute the waterways. The upturned minerals and heavy metals become mine wastewater, negatively impacting the water table for local residents and causing flooding.[88] This mine wastewater or coal slurry is toxic, containing arsenic, lead, cadmium, manganese among chemicals and other acids. With each strip mining regulation bill passed by the Senate, Warren struggled to get it approved through the House scrutiny. He had little success.

Early in his career, Don Blankenship ran "Rawl Sales," a coal mine near Matewan. The mine was located close to his home. Blankenship "decided it would be simpler and cheaper to inject the coal slurry into old coal mines underground"[89] instead of properly disposing of it. The company dumped over 1.4 billion gallons of the slurry into the worked out underground mines. Members of the surrounding community and students at the nearby elementary school began getting sick.[90] According to the community, Blankenship's company knew that the ground was cracked where they dumped the slurry which allowed the toxins to leak into the town's drinking water. When his neighbors started to get sick, the company paid for a pipeline to bring clean, treated drinking water from miles away to Blankenship's home, but not to the neighbors.[91] Years later, Don Blankenship was quoted as saying, "The very idea that they [Washington's EPA] care more about coal miner safety than we do is as silly as global warming."[92]

Warren worked to pass a statutory regulation that required coal operators to provide notice of intent to apply for a strip mining permit. The notice required coal operators to provide information on the potential location of a new site and allow opportunity for the community to raise concerns before any permit was issued. It took longer than Warren hoped, but he eventually achieved success: "The House adopted an amendment sponsored by Del. Warren McGraw, D-Wyoming, which would require strip mine operators to advertise application for a permit and which would require that a public hearing on the application be held on petition of 50 residents or 5 percent of the registered voters in the magisterial district in which mining operations will be undertaken."[93]— *Charleston Gazette*

During the time Warren served in the House, he attempted to increase the tax rate on coal. Estimates of revenue lost to the state on existing property tax assessments practices ranged from 150-300 million annually.[94] It wouldn't be until years later, when Warren was in the Senate, that he was able to successfully increase the tax on coal.[95]

The 1971 session ended with a watered down bill that placed a two year moratorium on stripping, applicable only in the 23 counties where there was no current strip mine operation. Environmentalists hoped the bill might deter the expansion of strip mines.[96]

Bad mining practices and inadequate enforcement of mining regulations often leads to disaster and death.

Buffalo Creek—An Act of God

To whose benefit are coal company officials' disregard of coal mining regulations and state officials' negligence in enforcement of regulations at impoundment dams result in one of the country's largest disasters? To whose benefit—not the 125 people killed, 1,100 injured and 4,000 left homeless.

On Saturday, February 26, 1972 the Buffalo Creek Flood occurred. The Legislature was recessed for the weekend. The Sunday morning paper described the disaster where a slurry impoundment dam no. 3, located in Logan County, West Virginia burst, just four days after having been declared "satisfactory by a federal mine inspector. "At least 37 people were reported killed Saturday...A [Pittston Coal] slag heap collapsed and released thousands of gallons of water onto communities along Buffalo Creek downstream from the Logan County coal camp of Lorado."[97] By Monday the death toll increased to 60 and over 300 people were missing, and an estimated 400 persons were homeless.[98]

In 1960, Buffalo Mining, acquired by Pittston in 1970, constructed the first gob dam near the mouth of Middle Fork hollow, a tributary of Buffalo Creek. In 1966 a second dam was built 600 feet upstream. Dam No. 3 was under construction and about 50 percent complete when Pittston acquired Buffalo Mining. Pittston officials later testified to the safety of dam no. 3, even though it was being built on top of coal slurry sediment rather than solid bedrock of earlier dams nos.1 and 2.[99]

"Buffalo Creek consists of 3 branches. As part of its strip mining operations, the Buffalo Mining Company, a subsidiary of the Pittston Coal Company, began dumping gob into the Middle Fork branch as early as 1957. Buffalo Mining constructed its first gob dam, or impoundment, near the mouth of Middle Fork in 1960. Six years later, it added a second dam, 600 feet upstream. By 1968, the company was dumping more gob another 600 feet upstream. By 1972, this third dam ranged from 45 to 60 feet in height. The dams and coal mine waste had turned Middle Fork into a series of black pools."[100]

State officials knew of problems with the dams. In March, 1967 a partial collapse at one of the dams caused some flooding. Area residents were alarmed. State officials responded by only requesting a few minor alterations to the impoundment dams. That same year, federal officials warned "state officials that the Buffalo Creek dams—and 20 others throughout West Virginia—were unstable and dangerous."[101] One resident wrote to the governor asking him to do something about the dams before we are all washed away. In February, 1971, dam no. 3 partially failed but dam no.2 held and halted the water. State inspectors cited Pittston for safety violations, but failed to follow up with inspections.[102]

After several days of heavy rain, mine officials were aware of the significant rise in water levels behind the dam. Pittston never advised the community of any concerns related to the safety of the dams. On the morning of February 26, dam no.3 collapsed overwhelming dams no.2 and no. 1 and sending 132 million gallons of water rushing down the Buffalo Creek Hollow. The thick murky torrent of water killed 125 people, injured 1,100 and left over 4,000 people homeless.[103]

The black wall of coal wastewater was estimated 30 feet high and 550 feet wide and moved at a rate of seven feet per second smashing through a dozen small villages in the narrow creek valley. As the slurry wave descended it accumulate trees and rocks, gouging out the land and increasing in lethal force. The rushing debris filled water swept away homes, cars, bridges and rail lines in its 17 mile path of destruction that ended at the Guyandotte River. Buffalo Creek was deemed one of largest disasters in the United States.[104]

"Immediately after the tragedy, (Governor) Moore's first response was to seal the area off with National Guard troops and to try to prevent reporters from gaining access to the area. He viewed the disaster as twofold...beyond the obvious tragedy for those who lived there; it was a black eye upon the face of the Coal Industry and occasioned an unwelcome spotlight upon the relationship between state lawmakers and the coal barons they served."[105]

Reconstructed view of the 3 dams above Saunders, Geological Survey Circular 667

Warren, Darrell and many others were in overdrive to reach the disaster area and find ways to help, but they found the area blocked by the National Guard: The brothers' access was restricted, but they saw enough to be overwhelmed by the devastation to so many families. Warren arranged for a helicopter from the National Guard to fly into the area. Warren invited a few key news reporters, including Jim Kincaid,

ABC national news correspondent. The National Guard pilot flew them in and landed. Rotors still roaring, Warren scanned the area and said, "This is not the place. This is not the dam site." The pilot said, "I've been told not to take you there." "Take us there," Warren demanded, over the roar of the rotors, and the pilot did. Jim Kincaid secured the footage he needed to produce a Peabody Award winning documentary about the Buffalo Creek Flood.

As anticipated by many, there was resistance from coal companies to delay investigations into the cause of the flood. Warren introduced a resolution in the House to require an immediate study by state agencies to determine the cause of the Buffalo Creek Flood. The House adopted the resolution and required submission of a report to the Legislature in time for necessary action during the session. Warren explained, "Without a preliminary report, the legislature would have to wait another year. This is of special importance to the people in my area…noting there are three impoundments in Raleigh County and several others I know of personally which drain the Guyandotte basin. I went to Lorado on Sunday and God knows there are not words to describe what I saw there. Some people had only 10 minutes notice."[106]

The Senate resisted the House resolution and instead supported Governor Moore's recommendation for a long-term study. Governor Moore assembled an *Ad Hoc* Commission, consisting of coal operators and associates, to study Buffalo Creek disaster. Pittston's public relations office in an attempt to absolve the company from legal responsibility issued a press release calling the Buffalo Creek Flood an "Act of God," noting the dam was incapable of holding the water God poured into it. [107] At the time of the disaster Pittston reported $44 million in profits.[108]

The "Act of God" defense outraged residents. At a protest meeting, an elderly woman stood up and shouted, "I've lived up at the top of the hollow for a long time. I ain't never seen God Up there driving no bulldozer dumping slate on that dam."[109] A climatologist, Robert Weedall, attending the meeting explained that "Act of God" is a legal term but that perhaps more apt legal terms were "involuntary manslaughter" or "criminal negligence."[110]

Miners for Democracy leader Arnold Miller objected that the *Ad Hoc* Commission did not include coal miners or community residents.

After Governor Moore rebuffed Miller's request for miner participation a Citizen Commission was assembled.[111] After completing an investigation which included public hearings the Citizens' Commission issued a report, *Disaster on Buffalo Creek: A Citizens' Report on Criminal Negligence in a West Virginia Mining Community,* that found officials of the Pittston Company were "guilty of murdering at least 124 men, women and children living the in Buffalo Creek Hollow."[112]

Perhaps appearing to show a callous disregard for human life, Governor Moore objected to the media reports blaming the coal industry for the Buffalo Creek disaster: "The only real sad part is that the state of WV has taken a terrible beating that is worse than the disaster."[113] It was also reported that when Governor Moore's own Commission issued its report that he tried to suppress the findings. The Governor's Commission called for new legislation to regulate impoundment dams and further inquiry by the local prosecutor.[114]

Six hundred survivors and families of victims sued Pittston for $64 million. The litigation was settled for $13.5 million. Families received a paltry $13,000 each. The state sued Pittston Coal for $100 million in disaster and relief damages. However, Governor Moore, just days before he left office in 1977, settled the suit for just $1 million dollars."[115]

Promises by Governor Moore to build community buildings, and provide housing for the victims never materialized: "Gov. Moore, then in the midst of a reelection campaign, pledged to build 10 redevelopment projects for Buffalo Creek. Few were either completed on time or even materialized. ...A few model homes were constructed upon former gob piles, but the 750 new homes promised were never completed...only some taciturn apartment buildings...."[116]

"Long time Robinette resident Jack Vernatter later observed to reporters: 'If either one of you all would've told me that I couldn't have got anything from my state, or if my government would've lied to me, you would've had to fight me ....I'll tell you—they'll all lie to you, everyone of 'em."[117]

During 1972 Legislative session Warren again offered a strip mining referendum bill that was postponed indefinitely through a roll call vote.[118] Carl Baggie, President of the National Coal Association in the

70's responded cryptically to the environmental impact of strip mining, "I never promised you a rose garden in Appalachia."[119] In the final days of the session, George Wallace, Alabama governor and presidential candidate, spoke to a joint Legislative session in the House Chamber. Wallace's remarks lashed out at liberals for destroying the state and national economy. Warren claimed Wallace was looking directly at him while he spoke.[120]

Coal Waste Legacy Remains

Since the initiation of strip mining in the United States 5.9 million acres of natural landscaped have been altered.[121] It is estimated that coal companies buried over 2,000 miles of streams through mountain top removal. The environmental damage from mine sediments, including acid mine drainage, pollute the water ways and negatively impact land, wild life and health of inhabitants long after the coal is removed.[122]

Today there are hundreds of coal waste dams built from coal mine refuse to hold the slurry from the washing plants and the polluted water from the mines as well as more than a 1,000 coal ash impoundment ponds that take ash from the burning of coal in coal fired power plants. In addition to impoundments that hold coal wastes, these wastes are often dumped into abandoned mines and used to reclaim strip mines all of which are safety and environmental risks.[123] According to the industry's own data 95% of all coal ash ponds are unlined which means leaks or breaches when they occur—and they do—send toxins into groundwater.[124]

The struggle for adequate coal mining regulation and enforcement continues. There remains much resistance to more stringent coal and strip mine removal regulations. At a recent West Virginia Coal Association meeting an attorney fighting against the EPA's regulations to restrict mountaintop removal defended the practice by quoting Scripture: "Every valley shall be lifted up, and every mountain and hill be made low; the uneven ground shall become level, and the rough places plain."[125] —*Isaiah 40:4*

In the "Trump era" resistance to environmental regulations on the industry increased. President Trump's administration targeted the elimination of 80 environmental rules viewed as burdensome to the fossil fuel (coal) industry.[126]

Almost 50 years ago Jack Vernatter, the Buffalo Creek resident, expressed frustration with his government failure in its responsibilities to the people where he lived. Today polls show that, like Jack, people's faith in their government is diminishing. At the Federal level public trust in government has been on a steady decline with only 3 in every 10 people expressing trust in their federal government.[127] People's trust in state government, which has never been high in West Virginia, to handle problems has also declined by 4 percentage points falling well below the national average.[128]

Could another Buffalo Creek happen in West Virginia? Appalachian Voices, an environment group, thinks so, in fact just over two mountains from Buffalo Creek. Appalachian Voices warns of a massive Brushy Fork coal impoundment pond, owned by Alpha Natural Resources, just 40 miles south of Charleston, West Virginia. A 950 foot dam, taller than the Hoover Dam, restrains billions of gallons black coal waste water dense with mercury, arsenic, lead and cadmium. According to Erin Savage with Appalachian Voices, if the Brushy Fork dam fails a massive surge of coal waste slurry would overwhelm local residents and people would almost certainly die.[129] Emergency Plans in place in the event of a dam failure note that a 100 foot wave of sludge could reach Sherman High School, where over 400 students attend, in 17 minutes.[130]

Chapter III   West Virginia State Senate

Grassroots Campaign for WV State Senate

Warren's time in the House built his name recognition; allowed him to hone his public speaking skills, and grow his network of support. During Warren's time in the House, the brothers began to explore Warren's possibilities for higher office. The state Senate was the logical next move. Senator Tracy Hylton, a strip mining operator and a Democrat, represented Wyoming and Raleigh Counties. An increased concern for unregulated strip mining might enhance Hylton's vulnerability in the next election. In the spring of 1972 Warren filed his candidacy for the Senate seat. Warren, the poorly funded opponent, needed a strategy. The May primary was the first hurdle. Without sufficient financial resources, a strategy that took the opponent by surprise—a low-key, grassroots campaign, was determined to be the road to success.

Darrell, having worked as counsel in the Legislature, then managed Warren's campaign. Southern West Virginia needed a senator focused on enacting legislation to regulate the strip mining industry, including extraction and reclamation and strengthening all mine health and safety requirements. Some saw the senatorial election between Hylton and McGraw as a vote on future regulation of the strip mining industry: "Strip mining versus abolition wasn't put to a vote of the people, but the 11th Senatorial District race is as good as a referendum

64

with the voters having a choice between an abolitionist and a surface mining operator. Strip mining is the main issue in the district composed of Wyoming and Raleigh counties. But there are other factors—black lung, opponents' political machines, big business, versus the little man and the American way of life which has slightly different shades rooted in both candidates' ancestors. And money or a lack of it may ultimately be the key to the outcome on Election Day."[1]

This was my first up close and personal encounter with grassroots campaigning. Darrell mobilized family members and supporters into active engagement to promote his candidate including dissemination of mailers, posters, writing letters and making phone calls. This grassroots outreach extended beyond the two county area. For example, there was a parade, in St. Albans, WV, located in Kanawha County, a 60 mile drive from Raleigh and 100 miles from Wyoming. Darrell insisted the McGraws, spouses, aunts, uncles, kids and cousins, go the St. Albans. Everyone made their own Warren McGraw for state Senate hats and carried posters as they marched in the parade. I had no idea why this was a good thing to do. For Darrell, the answer was clear. Politics is personal. The presence in the parade demonstrated a broad base of support for Warren. People in southern West Virginia might hear about it.

Warren won the primary election. It wasn't supposed to happen, but it did. Both brothers worked every event they could find. They liked taking with people. They were the last to leave any event they attended. They would still be talking to people next to cars in the parking lot. Not just, "Hi will you vote for me," but engaging conversations. They not only listened to and heard these personal stories; they really liked people, and they wanted to help.

The grass roots campaign strategy used by the McGraw brothers in this and a multitude of future elections was based upon the work of Matt Reese, a Huntington, West Virginia native. Reese, recognized as the "godfather of professional political consulting business" honed his organizational skills in John F. Kennedy's presidential election. Reese went on to establish a political consulting firm engaged in more than 450 elections, for clients including Senators Robert F. Kennedy and Edward M. Kennedy.[2] Darrell worked for Matt Reese Associates in several political campaigns, and it was there that Darrell acquired the valuable grass roots skills of targeting likely supportive voters to ensure every positive constituent voted.

In the primary campaign their grassroots effort organized a bevy of volunteers who made thousands of calls on behalf of Warren. The volunteers were charged with taking the time to establish a relationship with the voter on the phone and conclude the call by asking if they "could help our family and community by becoming a precinct leader." The charge then given to precinct leaders simply involved getting five or so of their closest neighbors and family out to vote for Warren.

For whatever reasons, perhaps Warren's youth and lack of money, Hylton didn't take his challenger seriously. Warren won through a system that pre-dated robo calls where the caller in a real person to person conversation empowered the voter to get involved in the campaign.

Celebration of Warren's primary victory was short lived. After the primary, it was now Hylton's turn to surprise his opponent. Hylton switched from Democrat to Republican. The coal industry insider and associate led Republican Party, comfortable with Hylton's representation and confident in his primary win, didn't identify a Republican to run in the general election. Now with Warren's unexpected success in the primary, the Republicans needed a candidate. Hylton, clearly aligned philosophically, was a natural choice. It was now evident that McGraw was a serious contender.

Charles Peters, a former West Virginia legislator turned political commentator, Peace Corps administrator and founder and former chief editor of the *Washington Monthly,* watched Warren's primary upset with interest. Peters, interested in the politics of his home state, understood the issues at stake in the McGraw-Hylton election. Charlie Peters thought the state Senate general election was a good fit for a young filmmaker he knew named Wayne Ewing. Ewing was looking for a project related to election reform. Charlie, a mentor to many journalists, encouraged Wayne to go to West Virginia and talk to the McGraw brothers.[3] Wayne did just that, and after conversations with Warren and Darrell, determined to document Warren's senatorial campaign. Wayne saw an opportunity to record political reformers taking on environmental issues in a campaign funded with little more than hard work and enthusiasm.

Wayne and Darrell were in agreement with the filming, but Warren was much harder to convince of the virtues of the endeavor. Warren was an advocate of moving politics from the shadows and conducting it in the open.[4] However, Warren, 33 years old, a husband and a father of three young children, didn't like the idea of a camera filming inside his home. He wanted assurance that his children and wife's privacy were protected. Warren accepted that what he did publically was open for analysis; he was not so sure about the public critiquing his private activity. Warren agonized for two more days but finally agreed to allow the filming to go forward.[5]

Warren at the Formica Counter—Election Night 1972

Prior to the 1972 general election, Warren and Peggy were in the process of building second floor bedrooms and bath addition onto their house in Pineville. Wayne and his crew moved into this unfinished second floor. Wayne and the videographer became part of the McGraw family, joining the family around the orange Formica counter at dinnertimes and breakfast. They went where Warren went.

Warren's wife Peggy was a rock for Warren in his life's quest to address injustice and make a difference for working people. Peggy, educated at Mary Washington College, was personable, pretty, smart and hardworking; she embodied the family-first southern culture. Peggy was long suffering, but stayed positive during Warren's extended absences while he served in the Legislature. Charleston was two and half hours away from their home in Pineville. Peggy kept the family, her teaching job and the logistics of Warren's law practice all in order. Some months she had to pay the law office bills out of her teacher's salary, as Warren was rarely in Pineville working as a lawyer. He was in Charleston working in the Legislature. Her commitment to Warren remained unwavering through many trials and tribulations. The family refers to her as Saint Peggy.

The filmmakers filmed the highs and lows the brothers' experienced during, the hotly contested election. Wayne captured the spirit of their humanity and their sincerity as well as the conflict between the brothers. In one telling scene, an argument between the brothers drags on for some time. Warren rests his ankles on his desk, and Darrell V. sits across from him, and they begin to bicker. As the argument progresses, they move about the room in a blur of stormy gestures and raised voices. By the end of the argument, their voices calmed, they have changed seats with Darrell V. now behind the desk, and Warren across from him sitting with his ankles propped up on the desk.

The race itself made for compelling material. Warren stayed on the road giving passionate speeches in school gymnasiums before crowds and reminding them of the destruction that strip mining was doing to their land: "90% of the land Hylton strips has not been reclaimed. Hylton says he is a native son who stayed home to take care of state, yet nearly all of the work he does is for the benefit of non-resident land owners who reap the profit at our destruction and leave us with what is left for our children and our grandchildren."[6]

Warren tried to focus attention on Hylton's record as a state senator voting against strip mine regulations and as a strip mine operator his inadequate reclamation efforts. Hylton had slick brochures that countered any assertion that he wasn't reclaiming the land and denied any special interest influence on his vote record in the state Senate. The brochure claimed: "Throughout eight years in the legislature Hylton has consistently refrained from voting on legislation involving surface mining—although surface mining is his livelihood. Conflict of interest isn't part of Tracy Hylton's style."[7] The evidence contradicted these claims: "In the two instances in which strip mining interests were in danger of suffering a setback, particularly at the time of the Brotherton

Amendment to the 1971 Surface Mining Act, Hylton conveniently forgot his 'principles' and cast the vote that enabled stripping forces to tie and thus defeat the legislation."[8]

Hylton touted his record of reclaiming land that was stripped by his company: "since 1967 Hylton has reclaimed 4,724 acres of previously surface-mined land." The *Raleigh Register* noted evidence to the contrary: "Hylton has in fact reclaimed only 450 acres even under the Department of Natural Resources' generous definition, no more than 10 per cent of the acreage his firms have stripped in the last 10 years."[9] Warren's assessment of Hylton's reclamation efforts was bit more descriptive: "The man who is running against me is engaged in the business of devouring our land and flushing it down the Guyandotte River to New Orleans."[10]

Financing was a challenge in this election, as it was in every subsequent election for the McGraw brothers. Effectively communicating with voters required money the McGraws didn't have, but they had a strategy.

Their strategy, as it often did, involved family and friends. They encouraged people to write letters to newspaper editors expressing their concerns about Hylton's claims. The letter-writing technique was based on the premise that a reporter, after reading the letter to the editor, might do a follow-up article or, even better, an editorial might be written. It worked. Local newspapers received letters to the editor from Ellis Bailey, Frank Flanagan and others who spoke out against Hylton's record:

Tracy Hylton has out a brochure in which he said 'conflict of interest isn't part of Tracy Hylton's style.' Is that why he voted against Labor Relations Act, for a high interest rate, and against the people knowing what goes on in the Senate Committees? In the last session of the Legislature, Senator Susman tried to save 'the sunshine law' which provided for records being kept of what happens in Senate Committees

Hylton voted against Susman's Amendment because he doesn't want the people to know what he does behind the scene. Is the Senator Hylton, who says in his brochure, that he would rather be called 'Tracy' that 'Senator' the same Senator Hylton who is passing out bumper stickers that he paid for, which say, 'Re-elect Senator Hylton' they don't say 'Tracy' Hylton. Maybe the reason is that Tracy Hylton is the guy in the song that says, 'Strip Away Big D-9 Dozer, Coming For To Bury My Home.'

> *Sincerely yours,*
> *Ellis Bailey*
> *P.0. Box 36*
> *Clear Creek, W. Va.[11]*

Frank Flanagan's letter, similar to Bailey's received an editorial response:

Frank Flanagan, a resident of Helen, objects to Hylton's political brochures touting his reclamation efforts: 'Not The Kind Of Man To Represent Us'—a brochure mailed to voters in the Ninth Senatorial District claims undue credit for State Senator Tracy Hylton. The way Frank put it was, 'It's a damn lie.' What he was referring to was a paragraph in the brochure that claimed: 'Tracy Hylton's equipment crews have played a vital part in cleanup activities at local disaster areas. The recent emergency in Helen is a case in point There, in addition to cleaning up mud and debris, special new culverts and underground pipeline are being installed to help control runoff and prevent any such reoccurrence in the future--all at the expense of Tracy Hylton.'

It turns out that Hylton did not do all of this out of the goodness of his heart at all. He did it under contract to the Chesapeake and Ohio Railway and admitted Saturday that he hadn't yet figured the bill he would present to the C 0. That wasn't the only part of the brochure that made extravagant and untrue claims about Hylton. The brochure claimed that since 1967 Hylton 'has reclaimed 4,724 acres of previously surface-mined land.'

A Charleston Gazette story reprinted in Friday's Register points out that But the most bare-faced of all the claims in the brochure is one that says: The fact of the matter is that though Hylton did refrain from voting on legislation dealing with strip mining in a number of instances, he only did so where his vote did not mean anything.

A man who can so easily forsake principle for personal gain, a man who will violate the State Senate's code of ethics so readily, and then calmly lie to HIS constituents in a brochure that says in effect 'I wouldn't do anything like that, folks' is not the kind of man Ninth District voters should want to represent them in the State Senate. [12]

Wayne Ewing's documentary, *If Elected*, captures the passion of the McGraw brothers as they struggle against political odds in favor of the incumbent and the well-financed Hylton campaign. As the documentary begins, *Happy Days are Here Again* is heard and one sees coal-dust covered miners crawling out of steel conveyers (mantrips) at the end of their shift. How is this happy days? Warren greets the miners, who are acutely aware the quicker, more efficient strip mines are taking away their jobs. He asks for their help, "Hi, McGraw's my name, and I would appreciate your vote." Warren says as he hands the miners a matchbook. As Warren and Darrell drive in the Barracuda to the next campaign stop, they look at all the hardship just outside the car window, and Warren sings:

> *Oh those West Virginia Hills, how uneven and rough with their*
> *summits bathed in rock which make farming mighty rough.*
> *Is it any wonder then that my heart with anger fills as I try to*
> *make a living in those West Virginia Hills.*

The fight for the Senate seat steams through the fall. Darrell and Warren try to figure how to combat Hylton's heavily financed campaign and do more with less? Warren remains concerned that miners only remember Hylton from when he operated a deep mine at Itmann in Wyoming County. At a shift change at another stop, the brothers shake miners' hands as they come out of the mine. One miner says, "I heard of you, brother. My family's already voting for you. But my brother-in-law works at a Hylton strip mine, and Hylton requires his workers to make a $20 contribution to his campaign. My brother-in-law was one of them."

Later in the car, Warren rails, "Did, you hear that, brother? For God's sake $20 dollars from guys who work for him. That's against the law."…"Ah, Warren, you don't know that is true. The fact is Hylton is rich and can finance his own campaign," Darrell offers. Warren argues, "Hylton's signs are everywhere; you can't go a mile without seeing another sign."[13]

At another shift change, Warren mills around, approaches a group of off-shift miners, and when they don't acknowledge him and keep talking amongst themselves, he walks away unassumingly but most self-conscious of his dismissal.

In *If Elected* Warren's enormous frustration with raising campaign money and the frequent demand from others for a donation are apparent. Warren complains, "I'm being hit up for money from someone every day." As typical of 20th century politics, people call the campaign to get money for their own purposes. Warren says of one such caller asking for money, "I just told him to go to hell and hung up."

For decades, political campaigns offered direct handouts. George Washington used whiskey on Election Day. Today there exists a more disguised method for securing votes. Out-of-state corporations and political action committees provide millions of dollars to buy ads with messages to sway the electorate and tell the listener to "vote against the scoundrel."

Warren's campaign consisted of low cost phone banks, letters to the editor, mailers, radio commercials and daily personal campaigning throughout the countryside and towns. Warren and Darrell often exhorted voters of their "duty" during their tenure on earth to protect it for the future—words extracted from their parents' admonishments to them. It was a message that spoke to the hearts of West Virginians in the 70's who still maintained much hope for improving the lives of the next generation. The McGraw brothers were betting on Lincoln's "better angel" theory of Appalachians' nature to stand up against strip mining for their children's future.

The campaign was truly a family effort. The communications and media were designed by Darrell. Peggy, her sister and Warren's mother, Julia, addressed "mailers," and little Randolph had stamp duty. Darrell thought the idea of a campaign song would lend some spirit to the enterprise, and suggested Merle Travis' *Dark as a Dungeon*:

> *Where the rain don't fall;*
> *Where the sun don't shine;*
> *It's dark everyday down in the coal mine.*
> *Where dangers are many;*
> *Where the pleasures are few;*
> *It's dark everyday down in the coal mine.*

Darrell's own deep voice, rich and inviting, is recorded for an ad designed to let miners know Warren McGraw is fighting for them against big coal: "It takes a special kind of man to mine coal. It takes a special kind of man to fight for coal miners. Coal miners and Warren McGraw are special friends."

Darrell, working with friend and folk singer David Morris, modified the lyrics of Merle Travis' song *Sixteen Tons* for a radio commercial. David accompanied Darrell on the guitar as Darrell sang:

Some people treat men like he's made of mud;
McGraw knows a man is muscle and blood;
Works very hard for the children he rears;
But a man can get hurt and suffers for years;
That's why Warren McGraw fights for Worker's
Compensation for men who work in the mines;
That's why Consol is fighting Warren McGraw.

At the top the Democratic general election ticket was George McGovern for President and Jay Rockefeller for Governor. The McGraw brothers supported both, but knew both candidates were in an up-hill struggle to secure a win. Would their vulnerability have a negative impact on the down-ticket races? Political pundits considered McGovern's grassroots efforts to secure a victory a long shot. The Democratic Party was badly split in the primary, when McGovern secured the nomination over Sen. Hubert Humphrey, who was the first choice of many West Virginians in the southern coal fields.

McGovern's selection of a running mate was problematic. His first Vice Presidential pick, Thomas Eagleton, resigned when news of his bouts with depression and hospitalizations became public. McGovern then selected Sargent Shriver, John F. Kennedy's brother-in-law, to replace Eagleton, but critics continued to see the combined ticket as weak.

Rockefeller moved to West Virginia in 1964 as a Vista worker in Emmons, West Virginia. He was elected to the House of Delegates in 1966, and elected as Secretary of State in 1968, the same year Warren was elected to the House. Jay, Darrell and Warren worked together as aspiring young men in state government and were allied in the fight against strip mining.

After winning 1972 Democratic primary nomination for governor, Jay faced incumbent Governor Arch Moore in the general election. Arch Moore, a Republican in an overwhelmingly Democratic state, was a decorated World War II veteran who served in the House of Delegates and won a congressional seat in 1956. A charismatic personality and great speaker, Moore never forgot a name and was polite to most everyone. Besides his dynamic personality, Moore's success in 1968 was assisted with the indictment of Wally Barron, a Democratic governor, on bribery and conspiracy charges, and the public's sympathy when Moore survived a helicopter crash a few days before the election.

In 1972 election Moore focused on Jay's opposition to strip mining and labeled Rockefeller as a transplant from New York and a carpetbagger. He ran television ads asking New Yorkers if would like to have a governor of New York from West Virginia. It was effective. In the final weeks Moore traveled the state accusing Rockefeller of "seeking to destroy the [coal mining] industry in an effort to help his family's oil interest."[14] The McGraw brothers to supported Rockefeller, but worried Moore's allegations that Rockefeller was destroying the coal mining industry might negatively impact the state Senate campaign. Many coal miners believed opposition to strip mining jeopardized their jobs as illustrated by one miner's rejection of Warren's brochure, "I don't vote for people who are taking away my job."[15]

Election Day, November 8, 1972 brought reports of various election misconduct: campaigning too close to polls; destruction of signs; missing ballot boxes and vote buying. In *If Elected* Warren is seen in a phone booth outside the Cowshed Motel precinct and talking to his brother. "It's bad," said Warren. "Real bad." Not knowing what else to do, Warren hangs up the phone and puts a bumper sticker amidst the Tracy Hylton signs on the glass phone booth.

It was until 11 a.m. on Wednesday the 9th of November before victory was Warren's. McGovern and Rockefeller were less successful. McGovern lost to incumbent Richard Nixon in one of the biggest landslides in American electoral history, which included the Democratic stronghold of West Virginia.[16] Rockefeller lost to Arch Moore.

In 1976 Jay again ran for governor, this time spending $3 million and toning down his opposition to strip mining. He handily defeated his

Republican opponent, former Governor Cecil Underwood.[17] In 1980 Rockefeller's reelection campaign, he faced his nemesis Arch Moore, but this time Rockefeller out spent Moore by a 20 to 1 margin. Narrowly achieving victory over Moore, Rockefeller spent an estimated $12 million dollars. When Jay ran for U.S. Senate in 1984 against businessman John Raese, he spent another $12 million. Ronald Reagan led the Republican ticket and carried West Virginia by a considerable margin, making Jay's $12 million expenditure only enough for a narrow victory.[18]

Over the course of three campaigns, Rockefeller campaigns' spent almost $30 million. Such expenditures were in stark contrast to the poorly funded McGraw campaigns. The McGraw brothers knew the difference that money made in election outcomes, but it was never in the cards for them. They weren't wealthy in their own right, and were generally unpopular among big donors. In the absence of generous financing, the McGraw brothers depended on their intellect and strategy; the heavy support of labor organizations, United Mine Workers, AFL-CIO and the Teamsters, and grassroots efforts to reach out, meet and engage the voters.

If Elected—Ewing's Acclaimed Documentary

Wayne Ewing's film *If Elected* released on April 24, 1973 to a national audience as a feature documentary on *Bill Moyer's Journal*. The film received critical acclaim for portrayal of the campaign's struggle against power and money. A *New York Times* review described the one hour show as "thoroughly absorbing," and revealed the inner conflicts of the sincere politician:

"The candidate is seen walking up to miners and shaking hands. ('McGraw's my name and I'm running…') and then privately admitting: 'I feel like an ass…' In public speeches he is the would be statesman. ('We will not be bought.') In private, he is the young politician, given to salty language and nagged by a gut feeling about getting beat, despite evidence to the contrary."[19]

The *Times* applauded the film in exposing the honesty of Warren's nature: "The point of the film though, is not his victory but his campaign, which is as inspiring as it is ludicrous. For all of his wheeling and dealing, he is decent, and in a curious way, his story is reassuring. As Mr. Moyers puts it, 'the subject is politics, but the theme is human nature'."[20]

The *Washington Evening Star* found "*If Elected* as a fascinating and rare glimpse into how the least reported-on level of government actually operates and fails to operate…[*If Elected*] although obviously tied to a specific election, that of 1972 for the West Virginia seat for two counties, is also a documentary for the ages. It could be placed tomorrow in the civics visual library of any educational system in the land and still be of immense value a decade from now, probably a century from now."[21]

The *Washington Monthly* recommended that college and high school students see the film: "[*If Elected*] is a penetrating look at politics the way no textbook can. *If Elected*…a documentary film of one man's campaign for a seat in the West Virginia State Senate, gets behind the handshakes and the rhetoric to reveal the complex and tawdry realities of American politics. If Elected follows a young reform minded lawyer in his struggle against an incumbent backed by powerful corporate interests."[22]

If Elected was screened and discussed in political science classes across the country for decades, sometimes still showing up in syllabi at West Virginia University. Wayne Ewing became a nationally recognized filmmaker who produced and directed over thirty documentaries for American television networks, as well independent feature documentaries. Family reaction to the film was impacted by the community and particularly the people in the local church who were chagrined with Warren and Darrell's 'colorful language'—cussin in the film.

State Senator Louise Leonard, Republican from Jefferson County, filed a complaint with the Federal Communication Commission because of the language used by Warren and Darrell. Others thought differently: "We recommend the film not only to Sen. Leonard but also to State Commerce Commissioner Lysander Dudley and other West Virginians concerned with the state's "image." The film, an episode in Bill Moyers' Journal, does more for West Virginia's 'image' than all the whoop-ia and funny hats at the various athletic extravaganzas in which West Virginia teams participated. It was easy to imagine viewers throughout the United

States envying the people of West Virginia's Ninth Senatorial District for their thoroughly honest and thoroughly human representative."[23]— *Charleston Gazette Editorial*

Darrell acknowledged that he regretted the "language wasn't always pure," but when asked if Warren would be hurt politically by the "colorful" language in the film he offered: "Well, if politics continues to be a vicious, phony exercise where people try to portray themselves as something they are not and try to sell people something that really doesn't relate to their lives, it could be politically destructive."[24]

Warren R. McGraw, 1973

Years in the WV State Senate

Warren R. McGraw moved through the giant Corinthian porticos of the State Capitol in January 1973 from the House of Delegates to take his seat as a state Senator in the West Virginia Legislature. The Capitol is built from Indiana limestone, Vermont marble and Italian travertine. Its massive gold covered dome connects the wings of the building which house the three branches of government. The years that followed Warren's election to the state Senate often found Warren, exhausted from some bitter struggle over taxes, miner safety or strip mining regulations, escaping for a smoke outside on south portico steps. As he looked at the Kanawha River Warren was fascinated with loaded coal barge tows that were their way to electric power plants and steel mills in nearby states, or sometimes even on their way down the Mississippi to New Orleans for export to Europe and China.

The Senate Chamber, housed in the west wing of the Capitol, has 34 wooden desks and chairs arranged in a semi-circle of four rows, the first three rows with eight seats each and the fourth row with ten seats. Freshman Senator Warren McGraw's assigned seat was on the last row where other senators of a progressive persuasion, like Robert Nelson, Bill Moreland and Ralph Williams, found themselves.

Warren was eager to begin work on his long agenda of problems faced by his constituency including worker safety, health benefits, strip mining regulation, and developing proper infrastructure. But sitting in the back seat, literally and figuratively, meant securing action on a bill was a struggle, and good committee assignments were hard to achieve for Warren and other like-minded progressives. There were times when he really wanted to throw in the towel and return to Pineville to practice law full-time. His kids were growing up, and he was missing out on Randolph's touchdowns, his youngest child Rebecca's first words, and dinner table conversations about their school days.

Democratic National Charter Convention

In 1974 Senator Warren McGraw was a delegate to the Democratic National Charter Convention held at the Kemper Arena in Kansas City, Missouri. Warren was "jumping around excited," as Darrell described his brother, with the opportunity to engage in writing a charter, (a constitution of sorts) for the Democratic party. It was the first time a major American party determined to write a charter. At this convention, Democratic reformers further "democratize" the inner workings of the party, including the adoption of Article 10. Article 10 of the Charter required full participation for all and admonished "discrimination in the conduct of the Democratic Party affairs on the basis of sex, race, age, religion, economic status or ethnic origin is prohibited, to the end that the Democratic Party at all levels be an open party."[25]

During a break at the convention, Warren started talking with a man, who Warren said, "Sounded like home; he talked like my family in Pineville." Warren and the man were talking about the various aspects of the Charter when another delegate walked up and said, "I see Warren you met the Governor of Georgia?" Before Warren could reply the delegate continued, "Governor Jimmy Carter is going to be the next President of the United States."

A surprised but somewhat doubtful Warren patted Governor Carter on the back said, "If you are the party's nominee, I'm going to vote for you." A confident Jimmy Carter confirmed the delegate's assertion and said, "I am going to be President, and I'll invite you to the White House when I get there." Of course Jimmy Carter did go on to win the presidency, and he did invite Warren to the White House—twice.

Coal Severance Tax

To whose benefit is it for coal resources not to be equitably taxed. If Coal is King why are its subjects in such bad shape?

Warren knew the meaning of "coal is a stingy tyrant;" as Harry Caudill asserted in *Watches of the Night*.[26] He knew the perils, but he was determined to secure adequate taxation of West Virginia's greatest resource, coal, in order to help the state and its people. It was not until the 1975 Legislative session that a major coal tax bill was passed. This controversial tax created a revenue stream from extracted resources for the benefit of communities and schools throughout the state.

Warren, a student of West Virginia history, knew the story of Governor Marland's attempt to pass a coal tax; it was labeled a political suicide. Darrell, experienced as a lawyer in the Legislature, encouraged Warren to call the bill the Coal Severance Tax. Darrell contended that people understood the coal severance term because many knew that coal in place or severed was not appropriately taxed; i.e. the state placed inadequate tax value on the coal in the ground and the value when mined. However the idea of a coal severance tax was controversial, particularly with those who would have to pay: "A coal severance tax bill, with a potential of turning into a $23 million bonanza for counties, caused caucusing and general turmoil Friday in the State Senate."[27]

Warren sponsored the original Senate bill to tax coal companies and return the revenue to the counties that produced the coal: "The concept of the bill, meaning return of the money to the counties that produced the coal, is considered unique in West Virginia history."[28] Warren in advocating for the bill said, "Millions and millions of tons of coal have gone out of these counties. It is time that these coal cars change direction and head back into the counties and bring something with them besides empty cars."[29] Coal companies sent a different message, claiming the Coal Severance tax bill was unconstitutional; cost jobs and results in more cost to taxpayers.

The coal industry-friendly senators did not want another Black Lung hullaballoo on their hands. So one day, when the rotunda between the House and Senate teemed with coal miners, and miners filled the Senate gallery, the Senate officers locked the doors to the Chamber. Warren objected, "If my friends are not permitted in the gallery, then I want you to open the doors. I want to be with my friends." Spare "yeah's" and clapping arose from the miners who made it in before the lockdown.[30]

The fight against the coal severance tax bill in the Senate was grueling, with one session lasting seventeen hours. Defeat of the bill was looming, and senators supportive of the tax sought to extend the debating, aware that an early vote could be fatal to their effort. Issues that divided industrial and working class interests were always narrow—often decided by one vote. Senators supporting the coal tax knew they needed the vote of Senator Bill Sharp, who often supported pro union issues. As the debate went on, senators opposed to the severance tax lobbied Senator Sharp to vote against the bill.[31] With the loss of this one vote, Warren and the other pro-tax senators knew what they had to do—stall.

Darrell V. offered a strategy to generate more "yes" votes. Senators and delegates from the non-coal-producing counties, particularly the eastern panhandle, were generally thought of as "no" votes, as their counties were not positively impacted by the coal tax revenue. Often whether a senator or delegate voted for a bill depended upon its impact on their district. Past coal tax bills focused on funneling all of the money from the tax back exclusively into the coal-producing counties. Darrell suggested reworking the bill to distribute the tax revenue to all West Virginia counties, not just the coal producing ones, thus incentivizing representatives from non-coal producing counties to vote for it. The new bill also contained a caveat that less than 25% of the money from the tax could go to personal services which ensured funds were spent for community needs including schools.

Reworking the bill required time including time needed to explain the changes and convince more senators. Opponents of the bill wanted the vote to go down now, while they knew they had enough votes to defeat it. A Senate vote requires a "quorum." This means that a majority of the Senators must be present in order to take a vote. So, knowing they were one vote short, Warren and six of his pro- severance tax senators headed out of the Capitol to a close by sandwich shop in a last resort effort to try to save the bill. One of the seven, Senator Si Galperin, told the *Charleston Gazette* the next day, "We felt that all we had done was going to be undone."[32]

The seven left their colleague and fellow coal tax supporter Senator Lafe Ward, Democrat from Mingo County, behind to press the issue of the required quorum. Opponents pressed on, too. At 2:15 a.m. opponents demanded a roll call vote understanding that the coal tax supporters lacked the necessary votes for passage. Senator Ward objected noting the lack of a quorum. Senator Judith Herndon, Republican from Ohio County, who opposed the bill, called for the invocation of Senate Rule 1. This Rule authorized the Sergeant-at-Arms to search for the seven missing senators. Unable to find the missing senators, the Senate was forced to recess until Monday morning.

The strategy worked. The pro-tax Senators were gaining ground. But then, another problem arose. Senator Pat Hamilton, a dependable yes vote, was worried about his wife who was scheduled to go into the hospital on Sunday. Senator Hamilton's wife encouraged him to be present for the vote. It was important for the school children of Fayette County. Pat did just that on Monday morning.

On Monday morning, the missing Senators regrouped with the necessary votes to ensure a positive outcome. The Senate passed the coal severance tax bill by a 22 to 11 vote. It was a huge victory, greatly attributable to the changes in the bill to provide funds to all counties and the delay tactic. Opposition in the House was the next obstacle to overcome. Timing was important to the bill's ultimate success or failure in the House.

Warren wanted to deliver the bill to the House in order to avoid any potential delay that might result from the normal delivery process via the Senate clerk. The bill had to be read three times on three different days prior to a vote. During a session recess, Warren ran to the House with the Bill in his pocket. On his way he passed his friend Delegate Joe Albright in the loud, crowded rotunda. When Warren informed Joe of his mission, Joe told him, "The only way to success is to have the first reading immediately when it gets to the House." He also told Warren that he would make sure it got out of his committee. When Warren arrived in the House, he milled around in the red-carpeted entryway to the chamber until the House Speaker Lewis McManus could no longer ignore him and inquired, "What does the Senator from Wyoming want?" Warren said, "The Senator from Wyoming wants this Senate Bill to be read now." It was then read, just as the session ended for the day. This put them up by one day. It now went into committee for the first time.

After the first round in committee, Sen. Albright brought the marked-up bill over to Warren in the Senate, and smacked it down on Warren's back-row desk. House Judiciary Chairman Ned Watson's Committee had butchered the bill. Ned Watson of Fairmont came from a family with deep roots in the coal industry. Watson was a descendant of James Otis Watson (1815-1902), known as the "Father of Coal Industry." James Otis Watson's Fairmont Coal was a predecessor of coal giant Consol Energy.[33] The coal companies were working hard to kill the bill in the House. Warren called upon the public for support: "(the bill's) prospects in the House depend upon how much public attention it is given through the news media and other available means."[34] Industry-friendly Senators and lobbyists were encouraging the House to reject the coal severance tax. Sen. Carl Gainer, Democrat from Nicholas County, in speaking against the coal severance tax bill said, "[the measure] was one of the most unconstitutional bills that anyone has ever tried to run through this body."[35] House minority leader Roy H. Rogerson, Republican from Marshall County, said, he "served on a legislative subcommittee which they decided, above all else, not to impose a severance tax on coal. [It] would cause industries to look elsewhere for low sulfur coal."[36]

82

The coal industry aimed to frighten voters that any tax increase on coal would be passed on to the consumer. Ed Wiles, president of the Coal Association, threatened, "In an inflationary period, nationally, with the problems of rising electric utility rates, and with West Virginia's unique surplus financial position, it certainly seems ill-advised to add to the operating costs of an industry which—by necessity, will have to pass them on to the consumer."[37] It was a smokescreen. Coal was concerned about their bottom line. Coal didn't want to pay.

The Coal Severance Tax Bill was read again on the last day, and the Speaker put it up to vote. Because of the media attention, West Virginia's eyes were on the vote. On March 8, 1975 the House passed the Coal Severance Tax Bill: "This act added an additional 0.35 percent to tax previously imposed. "Seventy-five percent of the net proceeds of this additional tax are distributed to the counties where coal is mined in proportion to the total coal production of the county. The remaining 25 % of the net proceeds are deposited in county and municipal funds."[38]

The proponents of the Coal Severance Tax Bill acknowledged Governor Marland's courage in proposing a coal severance tax so many years earlier: "[The bill], a major alteration in state finances and a memorial to the late Gov. William Marland whose career was ended when he proposed a coal severance tax in 1953."[39]

The coal severance tax benefits all school systems. The tax provides a revenue stream used at the local level to support teacher and service personnel salary supplements, instructional materials and supplies, equipment, maintenance and designated county projects.

Fast Forward to Today

Unfortunately in 2019 the legislature passed House Bill 3142 which provides for a "three-year phase down on coal severance tax on coal from 5 percent to 3 percent, ultimately costing the state about $60 million a year in tax revenue".[40] In March, 2019 Governor Jim Justice signed this law into effect along with a companion bill to provide 35 percent tax credits for the cost of new coal mining equipment. Big coal continues to exert major influence on legislators and governors in keeping profits for themselves.[41]

Back to 1976---Warren is debating whether or not to seek reelection. The years in the State Senate were difficult not only because

Warren was so disillusioned with his "sentencing to outposts of the Senate," but because he was hours away from his growing young family. His children were now 13, 9 and 6, and he knew he was missing an increasing number of their activities. Randolph, his oldest child, was now heavily involved in sports and making the games was a continuing challenge. When he was home, family time was commonly interrupted with phone calls.

Warren thought running for circuit judge in Wyoming County instead of the Legislature addressed many family concerns. However, his strong supporters wanted him to stay in the Legislature, especially since Tracy Hylton filed to reclaim his Senate seat. Warren decided to let fate take its course. He filed to run for circuit judge and state senator. Hylton, determined to win, poured money and resources in the campaign. In the judicial election, Warren's opponent was Judge Arthur Kingdon, a Republican appointed by Governor Arch A. Moore. Kingdon was from Mullens, the largest town in Wyoming, and was heavily supported as the hometown son. Warren could potentially lose both races.

Ultimately, Warren lost the judge's race to Kingdon, but retained his Senate seat and returned to the West Virginia Legislature in January, 1977. Warren's name recognition as a coal taxer; an advocate for mine safety regulations and proper strip mine reclamation and a supporter of black lung benefits as well as the heavy assistance from the labor movement were all instrumental in again defeating Hylton. Warren, as a true local boy, wanted to be judge in Wyoming County, but that would have to wait.

In 1977, President Jimmy Carter did invite Warren to join him at the White House in recognition of Warren's work in the WV Legislature in securing black lung benefits for miners. President Carter acknowledged that securing benefits for miners suffering from pneumoconiosis through West Virginia's Black Lung legislation was instrumental in the passage of the national landmark Mine Safety Act. On August 4, 1977 Senator Warren McGraw stood next to President Carter as he signed the Federal Mine Safety and Health Act of 1977, which amended the Coal Mine Safety and Health Act of 1969.

President Jimmy Carter and Senator Warren R. McGraw
Federal Mine Safety Act of 1977 in the Rose Garden, August 4, 1977

That same year, Warren's brother Darrell V. found himself in very public disagreement with the President. The story, detailed in Chapter Ten was featured on the *Today* show and in a national magazine, *Penthouse*.

As a Senator Warren secured funding for libraries, fire stations, parks and of course coal severance tax that helped schools in his district. For this, the coal industry labeled him as a "pork-barrel spender" and a "tax-increaser." They wanted every day, working class folks to believe the taxes Warren McGraw raised were their own.

But most knew that Warren was for the people. Dutch Short, coal miner from Metheny, Wyoming County, spent his life mining coal, which allowed him to provide for his family and even proudly put his son Randy, through college. Randy was now in medical school, and Dutch could finally retire. Dutch traveled two hours to Charleston alone to attend and represent himself in his Black Lung retirement benefits hearing. Warren McGraw happened to be in the Charleston hearing room, awaiting a procedure on an entirely different matter. The administrative judge pressed Dutch on whether he was represented by counsel. The hearing officer looked at the members of the retirement board, then back to Dutch. "Mr. Short," he said, "Do you have a lawyer?"

Dutch, his face looking relieved, said "Oh, no. No I don't. But

over there's Warren McGraw," and he pointed to Warren. "And he, he'll
be my lawyer if I need one." He looked at Warren who looked back and
bowed his head at Dutch and blinked his eyes in agreement. Dutch was a
miner, a working man. Dutch knew Warren McGraw was on his side.[42]

State Senate President

In 1980, Senate President Brotherton lost his re-election bid for
state Senate to Bob Wise, who later become the state's 33rd governor.
Wise, with the endorsement of the West Virginia Education Association
(WVEA) and numerous other labor organizations, defeated the long time
Kanawha County State Senator in an upset that left the Senate Presidency
open. After the 1980 general election, Warren began working in earnest
to win the support of his fellow "out posters" to run for Senate president.
These out poster senators were all good Democrats who all wanted the
same thing—the betterment of the working community.

The vote for Senate President took place in December, a month
before the new legislative session began. On December 7, 1980, in the
west end of the Capitol, the Legislative caucus for Senate president was
taking place. At our house, which was just across the street from the
Capitol, preparations for the first birthday of our son, Darrell III, were
taking place. Darrell and Julia were there as well as my parents. We
were all anxious waiting for news on how the caucus was progressing.
As everyone was finishing dinner and getting ready to present the
birthday cake and gifts to young Darrell, Warren and Senator Robert
Nelson came bounding through the front door. I knew immediately by
the levity of their voices that another celebration was in order.

Seven years in the Senate under his belt, and with the hard work
of fellow senators, Warren secured the needed votes for election to West
Virginia Senate President. Warren and Nelson were elated, stepping all
over each other's words as they described the rough and tumble process
to secure the needed votes. Warren was exhibiting a trick he mastered as
a youth—literally jumping into the air and clicking his heels together.
Sen. Robert Nelson had initially vied for the Senate president himself, but
bowed out and cast his support for Warren. They both wanted the same

things, after all. Warren's election meant the progressive faction in the Legislature now had opportunity to make changes.

"Hey, young man what do you think, your uncle is going to be Senate President," Warren said as he lifted Darrell III out of the high chair and tossed him up in the air. Putting aside his own victory for a little while, Warren and Robert joined in lighting candles, singing Happy Birthday and opening presents.

But then the conversation returned to the Senate President race and the years since Warren first ran for the House. They discussed the fight for black lung legislation; the 1972 Senate election which gave voice to efforts to fight strip mining; the years of isolation as back bench progressives in the Senate; Darrell's election to the state Supreme Court in 1976; Warren's 1976 re-election to the Senate and the circuit judge loss, and now the opportunity for Warren to lead the Senate.

The caucus vote was the final and most important step to the formal nomination on the opening day of the Senate: "Liberals united at the last minute Sunday to nominate on a first ballot labor-backed Sen. Warren McGraw for President of the State Senate."[43]

"Darrell & Warren talk about family heritage in a clearing near the spot where their great great grandfather John McGraw built his home."—*Sunday Gazette Mail*

Less than a week after the caucus, a feature newspaper story stated "people" were concerned that a liberal, labor backed Senate President was elected. The coal industry and other big business interests

87

were fearful of the change. Darrell laughed as he recalled Warren's early efforts to bring about change. "He was involved in hanging a sign on Men's Hall at WVU, calling it 'Ptomaine Hall'…It was during a food protest. It made the University authorities very unhappy. They made it unpleasant for him, so he transferred to Morris Harvey."[44]

Conservative business leaders were concerned about Warren as Senate President, and they were already forming their messages for public consumption: "[they are] aghast that Warren, a labor-backed liberal lawyer, will turn the Senate into a Pinko camp for leftists and labor. Many think Darrell, the state Supreme Court's leading liberal, is already there."[45]

Warren called the charge absurd while Darrell offered a more philosophical reply: "All political offices are supposed to be used for the benefit of the people, and Warren and I are really interested in serving the people. We want to do as Mother said to do and that is to make the world a little better because we were in it. I know that all sounds trite and phony, but it's true."[46]

Darrell scoffed at concerns as he described the brother he knew and loved: "We see ourselves as mountain people, and when people talk about radicals, I smile when I think of Warren McGraw, who went to school at Tipple; was reared in a fundamental Methodist house; went to Morris Harvey, formerly a Methodist school, and Wake Forest, a Baptist law school, and he was elected by coal miners and their families. I look at all those things and think this is a guy who is going to destroy western civilization? Our Daddy was sensitive to a lot of social injustice he saw in southern West Virginia. Daddy wanted Warren and me to be lawyers because he thought we could do something about it."[47]

The formal nomination and election of Warren as Senate President occurred on January 15, 1981. Sen. Odell Huffman, a Democratic senator from Mercer County and Wyoming County native who knew Warren's father from school, added a second to the nomination and remarked that even though they had different philosophical views, he respected Warren's leadership and sincerity: "I have a sincere affection for him and admire his courage, his fairness and his honor."[48] Warren officially became Senate President.

88

Warren was forty-one years old when he was sworn in as the 44th president of the West Virginia Senate. Darrell, as a Justice on the West Virginia Supreme Court, administered the oath to Warren in the midst of cameramen and microphones.

Warren affirmed, "I do solemnly swear that I will support the Constitution of the United States, and the Constitution of the State of West Virginia, and faithfully discharge the duties of Senate President according to the best of my ability."

Justice Darrell McGraw said, "Congratulations, brother."

Senate President Warren McGraw replied, "Thank you brother."[49]

Senate President Warren R. McGraw, Peggy McGraw and Justice Darrell V. McGraw, Jr.

Warren's acceptance remarks as Senate President included his philosophy of government and reflected the McGraw brothers' life-long commitment to protecting the environment and West Virginia's resources for the benefit of its citizens. He acknowledged that under his leadership the securing proper taxation of natural resources was a priority:

As one who considers himself to be one of that new generation of West Virginians, I would like to share my philosophy with you for a few moments...a philosophy which will guide me in the discharge of my responsibilities. As my colleagues, you have a right to know that philosophy and to judge my performance by it. Simply stated, I believe in democracy, not in the word alone, but in reality. It will be my purpose to make the deliberative process in Senate as open , as participatory, as fair and as responsive as it can be.

Rather than repress our differences by whatever method, I would hope that this floor will be a free marketplace of ideas. Those ideas should be vigorously debated and stand or fall on their own merits. To insure this end, it will be my commitment to see that the rules are applied, not to cripple dissent, but to foster it. Democracy can serve no higher or better purpose than to invite the fullest possible debate before public policy is made. You have my pledge that I shall not deviate in this charge.

We are possessed of great natural wealth in West Virginia. We must develop it. But we in the Legislature have the responsibility to see that after the coal is mined and the oil and gas extracted that we have left an endowment for our own people. If the price of energy development is a ravaged environment and exploited people, it is a price too high to pay. But this need not be our path. It is up to this Legislature to require by law that West Virginians benefit from what West Virginians produce. The results of our leadership need to reflected in a better way of life and improved opportunity for the people of this state.

As surely as you will judge me by the philosophy that I have defined, we will all be judged by the people of West Virginia on how we respond to their needs.[50]

Warren's speech was referred to as "certainly one of the more thoughtful and literate legislative speeches in recent memory."[51] He expressed the importance of taking measures to ensure that West Virginians benefit from what West Virginians' produce. McGraw's election brought a wave of progressives into leadership positions including Senator Bill Moreland from Morgantown, the new Majority Leader, Ralph Williams, Greenbrier, Finance Chair, Si Galperin, Kanawha, Education Chair, and Robert Nelson, Cabell, Banking and Insurance Chair. The progressives moved from the back bench to the front row, where they hoped to better focus on their priorities.

There were issues this new leadership wanted to address including proper taxation of coal, revenue enhancement, worker safety, health care, educational opportunity, retirement and workers' compensation system solvency and collective bargaining. Making progress on these issues proved difficult for a number of reasons.

First, although the official vote for Senate president was unanimous, Warren secured the nomination in the caucus by only a few votes. The passage of any bill proposed by this new progressive leadership required the votes of senators who were not necessarily supportive. Any substantive progress required the leadership to reach across the aisle and effectively engage and work with other senators who perhaps had different priorities.

Second, and perhaps the most looming reason that made progress difficult, was the bleak economic situation in the United States and West Virginia. In 1981 the national economy was bad, but West Virginia was worse. Like counterparts in other parts of the country, the industrial cities along the Ohio River—Wheeling, Parkersburg, Huntington and Weirton—were hit hard by the recession. The major industries of steel, foundries, metal fabricating and machine manufacturing were all in substantial downturn. And the all important chemical plants in the Kanawha Valley, including Dupont, Carbide and others, were experiencing decline in production and revenue. But it wasn't just chemical, steel and manufacturing that were impacted by the recession. In the east of the state the lumber mills were closing. In Webster County, the Pardee and Curtin Lumber Company shut its hardwood mill for good—the only private industrial employer, outside of coal, in the county. With the collapse of the metallurgical coal market in 1982 West Virginia spiraled into a true economic disaster. In one year 18,000 miners lost their jobs which led the state's economy to be called the most depressed in the nation.[52]

The economic downturn actually started in 1979 and by 1983 West Virginia's non-agriculture employment dropped 13.9% as compared to the nation's drop of 2.4%. The unemployment rate was above 20 percent in nearly a fourth of the counties.[53] The overall state unemployment rate hit 17.8%. In two years, child poverty in the state increased from 19 to 35% and overall poverty increased from 15 to 25%, an increase of 122,000 people.[54] Unemployment benefits in West Virginia reached $40 million in one month.[55] The need for public

91

assistance was more than government entities were able to meet. Signs at the Kanawha-Charleston Welfare Office read, "We have less workers and more cases...you may need to wait longer than usual please be patient...You will be seen as soon as possible."[56] It was not an easy time to be a leader in the state. The impact of a nation in recession on an already depressed West Virginia economy continued throughout Warren's Senate presidency.

Even thought it was difficult economic times, the 1982 and 1983 Legislature passed senate bills that improved quality of life in the community. Early in the 1981 session Senate Bill 81 established the public defender system. W.V. Code Section 29-21-1 would define the responsibility of the state to administer the provision of legal representation to indigent persons. Another bill established a grant program to fund local domestic violence shelters and programs. And still another bill passed that advanced social service assistance to incapacitated adults and another mandated equal opportunities and rights for individual with handicaps. Senate bills also advanced more stringent safety protection for surface miners as well as requiring better safety protection for construction workers.

The 1981 and 1982 legislative sessions saw advancements in health care protection and quality including bills that required 1.) alcoholic treatment benefit inclusion in group accident and sickness insurance policies; 2.) consumer representatives must constitute the majority on boards of directors of hospital and dental service corporations, and 3.) examination, and subsequent collection of that data, of newborns for physical and mental impairments. Senate bills passed the legislature that addressed educational issues including: 1.) establishment of a daily planning period for all teachers; 2.) requirement of a minimum number of instructional days in a school term; 3.) remuneration for extra duty pay for teachers; 4.) supplemental benefits for retirees in the teacher retirement system and 5.) expanded seniority rights for school service personnel. Minimum wage requirement was also increased.

The recession continued to impact anticipated revenues essential for the operation of government services. The Legislature needed to increase state revenue in order to meet the state's obligations. Senators knew the correlation between tax increases and public dissatisfaction with elected officials, but the depressed state tax revenues also meant the inability to provide competitive salaries for teachers and quality education opportunities for children. Even with the associated political liability, progress on a tax plan that increased state revenues had to occur.

In 1982, a Tax Study Commission was convened by the Governor to study and generate recommendations for securing increased state revenues. A year after its formation, the Commission requested another $306,000 and more time to study tax issues. Warren resisted the request, "What a farce. After $456,000 is spent on the study, vested interests probably will kill any proposed tax boosts. The only tax change will be that the Legislature must raise an extra $456,000 in taxes to cover the tax study bill."[57]

Determined not to wait for the Tax Commission, the leadership asked now Senate Finance Chair Robert Nelson and Vice Chair Senator Tom Loehr to design a tax plan with the potential to raise $100 million. During the 1983 legislative session Senators Nelson and Loehr developed a tax package that Senator Loehr described as "some of the most significant tax legislation this state has undertaken in many years." The plan phased out over a five year period the antiquated Business and Occupation (B & O) tax that often unfairly burdened small businesses.[58]

There was resistance to the tax plan. Warren, dismayed with the attempts of big business lobbyists to shelf the proposed tax package, lamented, "It doesn't do any good to say that the Senate leadership has come up with a damn good tax plan." The lobbyists and their clients portrayed the Senate leadership as public enemy #1 to which Warren retorted, "and if you don't believe it ask your lobbyists."[59] The senate leadership continued to work to convince enough legislators that the tax plan was essential.

William Wheaton, economics professor at MIT, reviewed the tax plan and provided evidence that the overall tax burden of state business was one of the lowest in the nation—15th from the bottom. Wheaton's report helped to garner support for the tax bill by relieving concerns regarding the existing level of taxes on business and industry.[60]

The tax package provided relief to the manufacturing and other large industries whose production cutbacks and the weak national

economy resulted in declining profits. FMC, a major chemical plant,
reviewed the tax package and commented that "it provided an innovative
approach to change the tax law." The proposed tax bill moved the
Business and Occupation tax imposed on gross sales to a structure that
taxed the profits. The bill shifted the tax burden to a corporate net
income tax and provided a $1,000 tax credit to business and corporations
that hired and trained unemployed workers.[61]

The Senate tax package was estimated to increase revenue by
$100 million. The tax package established major modifications to the
antiquated Business and Occupation Tax structure, including reducing
B&O taxes for manufacturers and various tax credits for employers who
rehired unemployed workers. It was a progressive piece of legislation.[62]
"McGraw's plan gives a jobs credit against corporate taxes to
manufacturers who rehire laid off workers and decreases the business and
occupation tax for manufacturers. The plan also increases taxes for West
Virginians in the higher tax brackets, and it removes the B&O liability for
thousands …"[63] In the waning hours of the session, a compromised tax
package passed both the House and the Senate. The tax plan would result
in an estimated $92 million in revenue in future years.[64]

However there remained a projected revenue shortfall that had to
be addressed. Governor Rockefeller requested, and received approval
from the Legislature, to borrow $50 million from the State Board of
Investments. Fortunately the revenue shortfall at the end of the year was
less than anticipated thus reducing the loan to meet obligations to $20
million.[65]

Peggy McGraw, Sen. Pres. Warren R. McGraw, Justice Darrell McGraw & Gov. Rockefeller

There were other attempts by the leadership and the Governor to raise revenue. One such bill proposed to raise revenue through a utility tax rate restructuring bill that increased taxes on electrical power sold to out of state entities. With an estimated seventy percent of the state's electrical power going out of state under a cheaper tax rate, the state was losing approximately $18.3 million in revenue each year. The utility rate restructuring bill simply increased taxes on electrical power sold to out of state entities. The bill was described "as the least painful tax because it would cost out-of-state customers millions of dollars, but hardly affect state consumers."[66] Senate Bill 117 finally passed both Senate and House adding public representation on the board of directors of public utilities; lowered utility rates for residential consumers and established a life line of service and reduced rates for recipients of supplemental social security income.

Another measure passed by the Senate was Governor Rockefeller's request for a five cent per gallon increase on the price of wholesale gasoline. This tax was designed to support essential funds for road construction and repair. This major revenue tax hike on gasoline and diesel fuel raised about $54 million in new yearly revenue for the ailing state road fund.[67]

During the same period the Legislature passed a bill to amend the state's Constitution to allow for the establishment of lotteries in the state.[68] The Lottery Amendment, placed on the ballot in the 1984 general election, was approved by 67% of the voters. Since its inception the Lottery has generated over $9 billion in revenue which provides funds to public education, senior services and tourism.[69]

The 83 session saw appropriations to the Teacher's Retirement Fund. Monitoring its solvency was a priority for the leadership. Unfortunately this priority fell to the wayside in sessions beginning in 1985 when the Legislature and the Governor failed to appropriate necessary funds creating a substantial deficit in the Teachers' Retirement Fund.

In 1983 bills were passed to protect the environment including one that authorized the air pollution control commission to set requirements for determination of emission offsets related to intrasource pollutants. Also a bill protected municipalities from the expansion of an industry to adjacent land areas that were contrary to zoning ordinances.

There were also set backs during Warren's term as Senate President. The State Constitution provides people with the right to associate, assemble and petition the government; i.e. join a union. But there were many who resisted this Constitutional notion and desired the passage of a statute that specifically authorizes and defines governmental participation of state and local workers in unions such as AFSME. In order to address the concern the Senate leadership supported a collective bargaining bill for government workers. The collective bargaining bill passed the Senate with a vote of 20-14: "The bill allows public employees to organize and requires government units to talk with them. It provides for binding arbitration and a board to help facilitate talks between the two sides."[70] The collective bargaining bill was defeated in the House of Delegates.

In 1983, the Governor sponsored a bill designed to weaken the tenants of the 1978 *Mandolidis* decision which recognized "a distinction between negligence, including gross negligence, and willful, wanton and reckless misconduct" in workers compensation law.[71] The business community lobbied for the bill and despite the efforts of labor unions, Warren and other like minded senators, the bill passed both the House and Senate. The Governor, surrounded by members of the business community and the WV Chamber of Commerce, signed the bill limiting an employee's right to sue when the employer's misconduct resulted in employee injury.[72]

In1983 a controversial bill made its way through the 55th Legislature. The Hospital Cost Containment Bill was written to establish a commission to control rising hospital rates, assist doctors' ability to compete in a competitive health care environment, and provide patients with greater access to healthcare. The bill ran into problems when hospital lobbyists engaged legislators to reject the bill. Selected legislators raised over 22 objections to the bill during the last 24 hours of the session. Del. Joe Manchin was "dead set" against the bill.[73] Manchin referred to the bill as a "bureaucratic noose around the heads of hospitals."[74] But something was about to change Del. Manchin's mind.

Some 30 years later, Dave, Lieber, a journalist with *Watchdog Nation,* wrote about the events of the last night, the last hour of the 55th Legislature on March 12, 1983 as he described the newly elected U.S. Senator Joe Manchin's special interest maneuvering skills. A WV statehouse reporter in 1983, Leiber described the closing hours of the session in what some refer to as "how sausage is made;" that is how deals are made and how cheating occurs in order to achieve an end. The following narrative summarizes what Lieber observed:

It's after 11:00 p.m. and Delegate Manchin and a small group of senators gather in the Senate Chamber around the desk of Health Committee Chairman Senator Jean Chase to make modifications to the Health Containment Bill.[75] They reach agreement on the changes and "at 11:20 p.m. Delegate Manchin's signature suddenly appears on a conference report supporting the bill—clearing it for passage."[76] The hour is late and important jobs bill are awaiting a vote, but discussion is overheard that places a Physical Therapy Bill up next for a vote. The Physical Therapy Bill allows patients to see physical therapists without a doctor's referral. Why is this happening? Interestingly Manchin is the nephew of a physical therapist in Fairmont, West Virginia. The PT bill belongs to Manchin. Throughout the session senators fought against the bill, but as the vote is taken the senators affirm support. Senator Larry Tucker, who later serves prison time for taking a bribe from gambling lobbyists, explains Del. Manchin's change of heart, "They're paying Manchin off. Not with cash, though, but with votes."[77] Lieber asks Manchin, "Why are they running your PT Bill right after the hospital cost containment? Was there some kind of arrangement? Lieber asks as his tape recorder captures Manchin reply, "No, no, no." he says. "No, no, no." But the truth Lieber says is yes, yes, yes. Manchin's P. T. Bill passes as does Hospital Cost Containment Bill.[78] Lieber looks at his watch. It's much past midnight. The rule states that all bills must pass before midnight or they are lost. But that night in West Virginia someone stopped the Senate clock at 11:59 so the work continued.

The 55th Legislature passed three of Senate leadership priorities: the modified tax package, utility rate restructuring and hospital cost containment bills. The hospital cost containment bill was a step in the right direction, but Warren was concerned that without continued diligence by future Legislatures, hospitals and insurance companies would gain control of this Commission.

Warren actively supported the establishment of the West Virginia School of Osteopathic Medicine in 1976, and during the 1983 session he worked to secure needed funds for the Southern West Virginia Community College in Wyoming County. The Community College located in an old funeral home building in downtown Pineville was not an aspirational place, nor one conducive to learning. In 1983, the Legislature actually appropriated $1.5 million for the Community College, but the Governor vetoed the line item to build a new building in Wyoming County. In 1984 the Legislature re-appropriated the money for a new building. Many Wyoming County residents seldom see a sunrise because the mountains obstruct their view. Warren lobbied for the school location on top of a high knoll near Twin Falls State Park. "I wanted something that reflected our ancestors. I wanted something built on a mountain top. I wanted the students to enjoy the beauty of their surroundings. I wanted them to appreciate that view of the world."[79]

Southern West Virginia Community and Technical College, Saulsville, West Virginia

Even with the tough economic situation, the Senate passed a pay increase for teachers during the 1983 session, but it was less successful in the House. Speaker See promised teachers to take up the Senate pay raise bill in the House prior to the end of the session, but it never happened. The teachers stood outside the chamber on the final night of the session, but the Speaker never brought it up for a vote. The teacher groups were outraged, "We took the speaker at his word, and it was a mistake."[80] A teacher pay increase was approved during the 1984 session. The revenue generating 1983 tax package eased the passage of a pay raise.[81]

The 1984 legislative session was productive and resulted in the passage of a number of progressive bills including 1.) establishment of a children's trust fund for child abuse and neglect prevention; 2.) implementation of compulsory hearing vision speech and language screening tests for all children entering kindergarten or first grade; 3.) mandate for the state department of human services to develop a plan for comprehensive system of adult protective services; 4.) requirement that state contractors hire at least 50% state residents, and 5.) enactment of tax credits for employers who hired veterans. Pay increases for teachers and state employees and annual pension percentage increases for members of the teachers and state public employee systems were approved during the session. Other bills established a hazardous waste emergency fund and enhanced authority of public service commission to regulate hazardous liquid pipelines.

The years as Senate president were long and hard. Warren routinely made the two and half hour trip to Pineville to see his family and maintain his law practice. Balancing the duties of Senate President, father, husband and attorney were tough. Often upset when he was unable to make a family event, Peggy continued to encourage and reassure Warren that everything on the home front was alright. She never wavered in her support. She was always there for the kids as well as Warren. Even when the Legislature wasn't in session Warren frequently needed to be in Charleston. Sometimes as he was racing back to Pineville to make his son's football game, he ran out of time and just stopped on the top of Saulsville Mountain, where service from WWYO, Wyoming County's local radio station was available, and just listened to the game. Sometimes there was something to compensate for his absences. As Senate President, Warren was officially issued the #2 license plate he so coveted as a youth. Warren's son Randolph was now driving, and so Warren, like good fathers everywhere, placed the # 2 license plate on the car Randolph drove.[82]

Paul Rusen, U.S. Steelworkers, Sen. Pres. Warren R. McGraw and Joseph Powell, Pres. WV-AFLCIO and the #2 license plate.

Entranced with the Statehouse since his first visit as a child, Warren served 16 years in the Legislature as a Delegate, Senator and the Senate President. From day one, when he was a back-row maverick, Warren championed underdog causes like black lung benefits, civil rights, teacher pay raises, coal severance taxes and open government. In a recent reflection on his years in the Legislature Warren said, "I still have that same wonder about it all...If I have any talent whatever-it has to be as an advocate."[83]

Labor Unions and the McGraws

Guarding the Capitol, Justice Darrell V. McGraw, Jr. and Senate President Warren R. McGraw
—*Taylor Jones, Charleston Gazette*

Warren McGraw was serving as Senate President concurrently with his brother's Darrell's tenure as Supreme Court Chief Justice. Labor was happy. The coal industry was not. There often exists a tense relationship between coal operators and their union employees. Don Blankenship, long time CEO of Massey, once said "The UMWA is trying to take away our freedom,"[84] It was said that Blankenship valued production over all else which meant there could be long stretches without breaks for the miners. One of Blankenship's miners told a story of how he brought the same sandwich to work 3 shifts in a row because he was unable to take his dinner break.[85] Another fellow miner complained that his supervisor told him to suck on a peppermint when the miner complained about having to skip meals during his work shift..[86] **UMWA**—Cecil Roberts, a sixth generation coal miner and current President of the UMWA, knew Blankenship's feelings on unions. Cecil is a masterful, spellbinding speaker, who pulls people in through powerful and sometimes heart wrenching stories. Roberts grew up in Cabin Creek, West Virginia where his dad worked in Shamrock Mine and belonged to UMWA Local #720, with activist union leader Arnold Miller. Cecil served in Vietnam, went to college and then went underground in Carbon Fuels' No. 31 mine in Winifred, West Virginia where he was a member of Local #2236. In 1977, Cecil was elected vice president of District 17. In 1982 Cecil was elected as UMWA International's Vice-President and served for 13 years with President Richard Trumpka.. When Trumpka was elected Secretary-Treasurer of the International AFL-CIO, Roberts became the UMWA's International President, a post to which he would be re-elected over and over, serving for 20 plus years and counting.

Cecil is known for an all work and no play outer steeliness coupled with an inner fire and dedication to his membership, each of whom he considers as family.[87] Cecil leads by strong and down to earth example. He doesn't ask anyone to do anything he wouldn't do. His International Vice-President James Gibbs described Robert's leadership during one strike by saying, "Every time he was getting arrested, I was getting arrested or some of the other folks around us were getting arrested."[88] President Roberts was arrested 9 times during one strike alone, and he was arrested in front of Massey mines too many times to count. At the Pittson strike, of 1989 and 1990 the Judge fined Roberts $13,000 a day, then raised the number to $50,000 a day and ordered that the money was to be paid by Roberts personally, not by the union. Ultimately, the United States Supreme Court said the fines were illegal.[89]

Roberts once said that Don Blankenship has caused more misery to more people in Appalachia than any other human.[90] Roberts is known for his commitment to advancing the rights and quality of life of the union's brotherhood. Cecil and Don Blankenship were once interviewed on the same WV Radio show. Host Hoppy Kercheval asked Cecil, "Do you hate Don Blankenship?" Cecil replied, "I don't hate anyone. I hate what he stands for. Hoppy posed the same question to Don Blankenship in reverse. "Do you hate Cecil Roberts?" Blankenship replied, "I hate him."[91] Cecil was born on Halloween night in 1946; perhaps the reason he frightens Blankenship.

UMWA consistently supported the election efforts of the McGraw brothers. According to Cecil the support of the McGraws was "because they were good friends to start with, and they had similar philosophical views as the unions' as far as what West Virginia and the USA could be. They have always stood for the rights of working people and their safety, especially coal miners."[92] Joe Carter, long time District 29 UMWA

President and International Vice says, "Because you always knew you could trust them [the McGraw brothers]."[93] Joe Carter became the first UMWA member to serve in a top leadership position as executive secretary of the WVAFL-CIO and Cecil Roberts is the Vice President of the International AFL-CIO. The unions are all of one brotherhood.
WVAFL-CIO—The WVAFL-CIO was created in November, 1957 after the national merger of the AFL and CIO. Miles Clark Stanley was elected the first president of the merged organization and served as president until 1974. The WV AFL-CIO created the Committee on Political Education (COPE) a powerful political organizations in the state expressing the voice and views for thousands of West Virginias. The McGraws' connection with the WVAFL-CIO was strong. In every election the McGraws went before COPE to ask for and receive their endorsement and support.

Friendships based on mutual respect and common values were developed with the bright competent men and women of the WVAFL-CIO who work to advance workers' rights. Glen Armstrong, secretary treasurer of the WV AFL-CIO under the newly merged organization, and Miles Stanley bolstered support for Warren in his first state Senate election in 1972. Joseph Powell, a glasscutter from Clarksburg, became president in 1974 until 1997 and right beside him for 20 of those years was Secretary Treasurer Jack McComas. These men offered unequivocal assistance to Darrell as he ran for the state Supreme Court and Attorney General and for Warren in his bid for Senate President and for Governor. Jack, who carried Darrell's son on his shoulders in the Labor Solidarity March in the 80s, spent his life in advocating for progressive reform of working conditions for all union members. It was under Joe Powell's leadership that the union adopted a change in their logo to reflect and in honor of its diverse membership. The WVAFL-CIO was the first federation to add a woman's hand to its log. The logo now depicts a woman's hand descending from the top in support of her male brothers.

In 1997 Jim Bowen, a steel worker was elected President. The WVAFL-CIO championed the efforts to elect Warren to the state Supreme Court in 1998 and again in his reelection bid in 2004. In both of these elections B. B. Smith, a Building Trades staff representative, crisscrossed the state with Warren to turn out the labor vote. Kenny

Perdue became President in 2004, with Larry Methany as Executive Secretary. Methany was active in Darrell's races for Attorney General. W.Va. labor unions, with limited funds to spend on campaigns, worked to positively impact election outcome through their membership's efforts to support the McGraw brothers.

The 1984 Legislative session was the last for Senate President Warren McGraw. It was time to accept another challenge.

Chapter IV   Warren McGraw for Governor

'I'm a child of the '50s in West Virginia, where they taught the three R's in school: readin', writin' and Route 21 to Cleveland, where I went to work in the steel mill. While it was a good job, the truth is that we had a great outflux of our population. We will continue to have that every time we have an economic downswing until such time as we are able to have an educational system that will cause industry to be attracted to West Virginia."
— Warren McGraw

"Finding New Coal Uses Top Priority for McGraw," *Sunday Gazette Mail,* May 17, 1984

From the time Warren was elected Senate President in 1981 there were rumors of Warren running for governor. In January 1984, Warren believed the time was right and announced his candidacy for governor. The successful Democratic nominee would face Arch Moore, the popular Republican candidate and previous two-term governor (1969-1977). Private polls showed Warren as the only Democratic candidate who could beat Arch Moore in the general election, but there was a major first hurdle—defeating the conventional Democratic slate candidates in the June 3, 1984 primary election.[1]

Warren's primary election opponents, House Speaker Clyde See, Jr. and Attorney General Chauncey Browning, Jr., shared many of the same supporters as Moore. This shared base made neither Browning nor See likely to beat Moore in the general election. All three primary candidates, See, Browning and McGraw, had high name recognition. However, with insufficient campaign funds and the party split three ways, Warren was considered the underdog in the primary race.

Clyde See, Jr., a lawyer from Hardy County and current Speaker of the House, was the business-backed Democratic candidate. See led the defeat of the 1983 collective bargaining bill in the House after its passage in the Senate. Governor Rockefeller, as the titular head of the

Democratic Party, did not make an endorsement for governor, but his staff supported and worked for Speaker See. David Callaghan, the Director of Natural Resources during the Governor Rockefeller's administration, managed See's campaign.[2]

Chauncey Browning, a lawyer from Charleston, was in his fourth term as the state's Attorney General. Browning was Commissioner of Institutions in Governor Wally Barron's administration. In 1968 Barron and members of his administration were indicted on bribery charges and all were convicted except Governor Barron. Browning refused to testify before the federal grand jury, invoking the 5th Amendment. No charges were ever brought against Browning.[3] In 1972 Governor Barron was convicted of on jury tampering related to the 1968 trial and served prison time. Browning candidacy for governor received the support of Democratic county and state elected officials, and his name was on most of their slates.

Warren, a lawyer from southern West Virginia, was the labor party candidate and endorsed by labor organizations including the UMWA, AFLCIO, and WVEA. Warren's record of performance included progressive actions that addressed strip mining, black lung legislation, workers compensation benefits, collective bargaining rights, human rights and public education.

Richard Brisbin, a political scientist, notes that West Virginia's Democratic Party consists of three factions. The gubernatorial candidates in the 1984 primary were representative of those factions. See represented the "conservative faction" of the party consisting of the traditional economic business entities and large corporations; Browning represented the "non-ideological statehouse and courthouse faction" consisting of the county and state officeholders (good ole boys club), and Warren represented the "progressive faction" of the party consisting of organized labor, teachers, advocates for women's rights, trial lawyers, environmentalists and opponents of the abusive power of large corporations.[4]

In a speech before the Contractors Association, Warren voiced concern that the federal government's recent attempts to reduce inflation through job cuts were negatively impacting state business and revenue: "West Virginia businesses shouldn't have to repay the hundreds of millions the state has had to pay for unemployed workers caused by federal gov't efforts to reduce inflation."[5]

If elected governor Warren promised to create jobs and build a stronger infrastructure of roads. He proposed to increase state revenue for roads which suffered disrepair from overweight coal trucks and harsh winters. Warren stated that his plan to build and improve roads would not only create jobs but increase commerce revenue. Warren's proposal to increase appropriation of state revenue for road construction and repair were a sharp contrast to his opponents. See and Browning advocated trimming government spending in other areas and redirecting to infrastructure problems such as roads.[6]

Warren believed a starting point for progress in government was acknowledging the cause of the problem that needs addressed; i.e. coal dust causes black lung; strip mining causes environmental damage; inadequate mine safety regulations causes mine accidents and death, and inadequate taxation of coal negatively impacts the availability of needed community services. As it pertains to road construction and repair, inadequate revenue causes access problems that resulted in an inability to attract new businesses. Reducing-the size of government was not the answer to generate enough revenue to fix roads throughout the state. Building roads that provided good access and enhanced commerce required a greater source of revenue, and for that Warren proposed a comprehensive road bond. Warren, never one to retreat from his philosophical beliefs, concluded his appearance before the Contractors' Association acknowledging that he supported collective bargaining.[7]

With the Senate President and Speaker of the House both running for governor, the 1984 Legislative Session was even more politically charged than usual. However the Senate with House agreement passed a long needed pay raise for state employees and teachers. But there was a politically orchestrated attempt to roll back the prior year tax bill developed by the Senate leadership. Interest groups opposing Warren candidacy, including big business and coal operators, galvanized low income tax payers, including the elderly and minimum wage workers. These unknowing citizens were told the tax legislation that Warren spearheaded was responsible for an increase in their individual taxes. In actuality the legislation increased taxes on the highest income brackets.

Hundreds of protestors descended upon the Senate to demand the repeal
of the new personal income tax. The protest attracted media attention.
Warren and other members of the Senate Finance committee tried to
correct the misconceptions of the crowd: "...several hundred taxpayers
came to the Senate to repeal the personal income tax increases and surtax
passed last year...people at higher end of tax spectrum were getting
people in which the tax change wouldn't effect to protest...amid all the
hysteria, it was clear that many of the citizens did not understand the tax
changes in Senate Bill 310...affects high income brackets substantially
but has little or no effect on people earning less than 20 thousand dollars
(the equivalent of $47,000 today)."[8] The protest and associated media
campaign focused on Warren as raising people's taxes negatively
impacted Warren's gubernatorial efforts.

   As is often the case political campaigns can become vicious.
Warren received the usual intimidating phone calls and viewed these
occurrences as, par for the course. "Hot car," one phone call to his home
said, after accusing him of running coal and business out of the state.
Warren, perhaps too familiar with anonymous, threatening calls, thought
little of it. However, one day on his way home from a usual grueling day
of campaigning, as he neared the top of Saulsville Mountain, he pulled
over and jumped out of the mint green Buick Skyhawk. The dashboard
was on fire.[9]

   The campaign struggled to secure funds essential for a state-wide
gubernatorial race. In an interview less than a month before the election,
Warren acknowledged his campaign was yet to run any radio or
television commercials, and his campaign was primarily operated with
volunteers. Warren, a great campaigner who enjoyed meeting people and
speaking before crowds, resisted asking people to contribute to his
campaign. "I don't like asking people for money—I know the people
who are for me are struggling to make ends meet. I am a populist. I
accept that definition [of a populist] for the reason that, as Webster
defines it, "it is one who is representative of the people."[10] As a populist
Warren believed in the rights of the common people.

   The bulk of Warren's campaign contributors were laborers,
teachers, hospital employees and so on. Not wealthy people, not poor
either, but dignified working people. A run down on his financial

statement showed individual contributions of "$26, $50, $127," and so.
But overcoming the formable odds of opponents with money and
corporate support was a challenge even for the most enthusiastic
candidate. Warren expounded on the differences among the candidates,
"...My legislative career has been primarily concerned with issues that
have a substantial impact on citizens...hospital cost containment, utility
cost control...consumer legislative proposals. Mr. See ...has a tendency
to be more representative of what I consider special interests...and Mr.
Browning is representative of old kind of politics in WV."[11]

Warren responded to allegations by his opponents that he was
anti-business: "Essentially that is a myth that has been perpetuated by a
number of business lobbyists who have not been successful in programs
that they have advanced for their own special interests."[12] He continued,
"I was the person who, after 50 years of history of the business and
occupation tax, caused the B&O tax to begin to be rolled
back;...promoted...a program that pumped $50 million into the housing
markets...to pump up the building industry trade...sponsored the
program that gives a tax credit, a write off, against corporate net income
tax for people who are willing to employ unemployed West Virginians...
and sponsored the program to see that Weirton Steel continued to operate
as a functional corporation in this state."[13]

A realist about existing high tech industries moving to West
Virginia, Warren said, "I doubt seriously that we are going to begin to
attract the people who make microchips and put radios together from
sunny southern California."[14] Instead, Warren proposed to develop
industries which included new uses for coal: "What we West Virginians
have to do in my judgment is to begin to deal with the industry of the
next century in this state. My proposal is that we get into the high tech
industry and that we do it with what we West Virginians' possess and
that's our natural resources. We can get into the high tech industry and
diversify the industrial base of this state if we will commit ourselves to a
course which provides for massive research in coal development."[15]

Gubernatorial elections often include a question and answer
session with the editorial boards of major newspapers. In one such
interview an editorial board questioned Warren's support for the
establishment of a third medical school, the West Virginia School of

Osteopathic Medicine in Greenbrier County. Warren first acknowledged that educational opportunity was the foundation for all improvement in the community. Then Warren explained his rationale for the new Osteopathic school by relating a family story: "Shortly after World War II [the state] imposed a penny tax on pop. I lived in the country at the time at McGraws, and every day or once a week or so my brother and I would trot down to a little country store about twice the size of this room we're in here and buy a bottle of pop for a nickel. One day we went down to the store and our cousin who ran the store said the pop is now six cents. He explained to us why it was important that we pay an extra penny on pop for the WVU medical school. He said, 'it's so we can have more doctors here.' "[16] Warren concluded, "We've paid the extra penny, but we've had no physicians from West Virginia University come to Wyoming County. They are simply not there. It hasn't provided for all the medical needs of this state."[17] Warren concluded that his support for a new Osteopathic School was to enable more West Virginians to have the opportunity become doctors and hopefully work in southern West Virginia where the need for medical care was great.

Another question from the editorial board related to Warren's support for collective bargaining. Both McGraw brothers supported collective bargaining and never deviated from their stance which was based on the tenants of freedom of association and the right to contract found within the U.S and State Constitutions. Warren explained his position on collective bargaining, "…collective bargaining at this point in the state's history is a matter of fact. It's already the law of this state. We've had a long series of attorney general's opinions, Supreme Court cases, which permit collective bargaining in West Virginia. It is already a fact."[18] Warren noted his attempts to pass a collective bargaining bill to assuage those who doubted the Constitution. The collective bargaining bill passed the Senate, but Speaker See defeated the measure on the House side.

Warren concluded the editorial interview by reiterating his proposals for the establishment of business innovation, research and development centers; research focused on reconstituting existing coal and manufacturing industry purposes and define comprehensive initiatives to increase jobs opportunities. Without "sugar coating" his position on two hot topic issues, Warren stated, "I'm opposed to right to work… Of course, I'm opposed to capital punishment, I don't believe in people killing each other as a policy of the state."[19] Warren went on to say that "hot topic" questions were often a way to divert the voters from the issues that were his true focus—jobs, revenue enhancement through taxes on coal and oil and gas, and increased support of public education.[20]

Neither the *Charleston Gazette* nor the *Daily Mail* endorsed Warren. Don Marsh, editorial writer, chastised the *Gazette* for endorsement of Clyde See. Marsh contended that people like Warren McGraw and Justice Sam Harshbarger, who was running for re-election to the state Supreme Court, pay a heavy price for resisting the political power brokers. Marsh defined the power brokers as "those groups which have benefited historically from the very kinds of acts which have caused people like my father to accept economic and political inequities with the same passivity they accepted death in the mines and expropriation of their land."[21] Marsh went on to write that his father, like decent hard working men and women throughout West Virginia, had long suffered from political exploitation: "…[their] ability to have government provide a legitimate service was dependent upon supplicating a local power broker for a favor…an arrangement that assured the continued political exploitation of people like my father." [22]

Despite the lack of major newspaper endorsement, public polls showed the three candidates were neck and neck. Perhaps many agreed with Ned Chilton, publisher of the *Charleston Gazette* description of Warren, "You're a nice guy and you're an honest guy—of all the candidates running, I think you're the most honest; you run an honest campaign."[23]

Election Day on June 12th revealed the impact of money on elections. Warren and Peggy were personally invested in working the campaign. They often traveled together, expressing their sincere concern for West Virginians and detailing Warren's plans to address the issues facing the state. As was their Election Day tradition, Warren and Peggy took a ride in their car going from poll to poll. Back at home, Peggy prepared dinner and the family filed in and listened to the results as the numbers were announced. The television blared, and Warren lay on the floor next to the radio, his head propped up with a small stool. As the results became clear, the mood became gloomy and Warren and Peggy knew they would have to do what they dreaded—make the trip to the Charleston headquarters to say thank you.

Warren did his duty, loyally thanking his campaign helpers. He left the campaign headquarters late on election night holding Peggy's hand to make the long car ride back home. With tears streaming down her eyes, Warren's Aunt Jackie offered, "They worked so hard and are such good people."[24] Warren and Peggy walked to the parking lot with Bob Miller, Warren's campaign manager. Before he got into his car, he shook Bob's hand and said, "I'm sorry."

Warren lost the primary election for governor to Clyde See. Warren received 101,950 votes compared to See's 143,480 votes. Browning received 98,653 votes. The expenditures of See and Browning were around $500,000 each. Warren spent $69,453. "Interestingly enough, McGraw spent only about $70,000 but was able to run second."[25]

"Oh but for the money," Warren said. Joseph Powell, president of WV AFL-CIO said of Warren's funding dilemma, "It's known as lack-of-moneyitis."[26] Dr. Lowell Johnson, president West Virginia Education Association said that quite simply volunteerism is trumped by money every time: "The obvious thing is that money and the TV media apparently made the difference. Those were the two key essentials that the volunteer effort was unable to combat."[27]

Clyde See lost the general election in November 1984 to Arch Moore. The Chamber of Commerce achieved what they really wanted—the re-election of Arch Moore. Moore, accused by federal prosecutors in 1976 of extortion but acquitted, returned to the Governor's office for the third time in 1985. This time after Moore left office, he faced an extensive federal investigation resulting in five felony guilty pleas tied to taking illegal payments during his 1984 election campaign. Moore lost his law license and was sentenced to prison and served more than two years.

Warren's passion and understanding that state level decision makers greatly impact the quality of life in the community was not dimmed. He was, for the moment, out of the state arena and out of law-making—and perhaps out of the coal industry's hair.

Meanwhile—Blankenship Was Rawl's President

The same year that Warren was running for governor, an UMWA strike occurred at Rawl (Coal) Sales, a mine operating in Rawl, Mingo County. Rawl Sales was an A.T. Massey mine, and Rawl's president was Don Blankenship. An often used Massey strategy to break union holds by treating each of its different mines as a separate company. This allowed Massey to re-open its mines as non-union. Blankenship was familiar with the Massey strategy and perhaps was a skill that led to Blankenship's eventual selection as CEO of Massey.

In its strike-busting efforts, Blankenship's Rawl Sales not only hired non-union replacement workers, but also installed a two-mile chain link fence, complete with barbed wire around the property. Blankenship himself tried to recruit at least one retired miner to spy on his own union.[28] Rawl hired a security company that specialized in strike breaking. The security guards tried to incite violence from the miners, including by mooning them. The company brought in armed guards. They brought in the attack dogs.[29]

Staging violent events and blaming it on the union was a company tactic that came to light through the years[30]. The headline of the *Charleston Gazette* on February 3rd, 1991 told the story, "Massey Terror Tactics Detailed in NLRB Affidavit."[31] One Massey-hired security company guard testified: "To prove that the pickets [picketing union employees] shot at them [a guard] took a shotgun and shot the tool truck in the windshield and the door panel maybe three times and [another guard] also shot the tool truck in the windshield. They blamed this on the pickets. Sometimes the company would film the violence so that the coal company could get an injunction."[32]

Back at Rawl Sales, Blankenship claimed to be afraid, despite having hired armed guards. He slept in a different bed each night during the Rawl Sales strike. The Rawl Sales building was shot up with bullet holes it. The picketing miners blamed it on the company. "There is no one who would ever convince me that a United Mine Worker did that. These (non-union) drivers will be driving along shooting (guns). And then they start hollering, 'Need a trooper here, somebody's shooting at me,'" said Bill Davis, of UMWA Local 1440.[33] "Those boys that were

113

picketing, they had a little old table sitting on the side of the road there and they played rummy all day long. He (Massey) hires a police force, barricades the fence," said an observer.[34]

The UMWA had a strong newly elected executive team at the time in President Richard Trumpka and Vice-President Cecil Roberts. Union stalwart and Roberts' confident Don Barnette ran the strike at Rawl Sales. "Were you scared?" he was asked. "We weren't easily scared," he answered without a smile or a flinch.[35]

One day the miners sat down their picket signs and put up a makeshift pulpit to ask for help from the divine. Ballard Yates, a preacher and a member of the UMWA Local 2248 said to company guards, "All you're doing is protecting a man that's full of evil. How can you call yourselves Christians and treat a bunch of men like you do?"[36]

The company sought an injunction which was granted by the local Mingo County Judge Spike Maynard. When the UMWA continued their strike, Judge Maynard fined them $200,000. The fight over the injunction was appealed to the state Supreme Court. Justice Darrell McGraw was part of the majority that held "the circuit court had no authority to impose a prospective penalty in an indirect criminal contempt proceeding whereby a specific fine was imposed payable to the State for each subsequent violation of the court's order." Darrell, in writing for the majority, admonished the actions of the trial court: "its motivation was retaliation and not remediation. This exercise of raw judicial power without benefit of proper lawful safeguards was properly rejected by the majority."[37]

Ten years after the strike at Rawl Sales, Blankenship became CEO of Massey. 1985 was only the beginning of the relationship between Don Blankenship and Spike Maynard. That relationship became national news in 2006 when Maynard was then a Justice on the state Supreme Court.[38]

Nyden Factor—The Massey Doctrine
To whose benefit is it for corporations to have secret documents that place profit before the interest of employees?

In the early 1980's, an energetic Columbia educated journalist landed at the *Charleston Gazette*. Dr. Paul Nyden relentlessly pursued wrong actions by coal companies. At that time, the top of the coal food chain in West Virginia was A. T. Massey, a Virginia based company that operated numerous West Virginia mines and was then the nation's fifth largest coal producer.

Brave soldier of journalism, Nyden uncovered an internal Massey company document called, The Massey Doctrine. The front page of the Doctrine underscored its secrecy.[39]

> **THE**
> **MASSEY COAL DOCTRINE**
> *CONFIDENTIAL*
> **THE ENCLOSED MATERIAL IS CLASSIFIED AND RESTRICTED TO SENIOR MANAGEMENT OF A.T. MASSEY COAL COMPANY, INC. AND ITS MINING SUBSIDIARIES. DISTRIBUTION AND/OR DISCLOSURE OF ALL OR PART OF THIS MATERIAL OUTSIDE OF THE COMPANY WOULD BE ADVERSE TO OUR BEST INTEREST.**

Massey operated as fifteen separate entities, and therefore required separate (and by their requirement non-union) negotiations with each. The Doctrine's "Code of Ethics," outlined Massey's expectations for all of its subsidiaries and provided guidance for employee conduct as it related to:

1. *Bribes or contributions to politicians, union officials, labor organizations and other illegal payments of corporate funds*
2. *Undisclosed accounts or funds*
3. *False entries on the records*
4. *Prohibited payments for services unsupported by invoice*
5. *Bribes or kickbacks to employees*
6. *Antitrust or other prohibitive competitive practice*
7. *Gifts and gratuities*

115

8. *Conflict of interest*
9. *Disclosure of proprietary information*
10. *Disclosure of prohibited funds or acts*[40]

The doctrine was endorsed by E. Morgan Massey on September 27th, 1982. It was not made public until 1985. Its corporate objectives stated that in "a hedonistic society, self comes before society at large."[41]

Throughout the course of his career, Nyden uncovered millions of dollars of outstanding fees owed by coal companies to the Department of Energy (now DEP) and the federal office of surface mining. Once, when a publically elected political official called a DOE higher up and requested the Department immediately issue a mining permit that had been put on hold pending concerns about the damage that the mine might cause, the DOE higher up immediately acquiesced and told the official, "I'm going to have to put a note in our files that we issued it on your orders. You know the files I mean… the ones that Nyden looks at all the time." The politician said, "Just forget it," and hung up.[42]

Dr. Nyden's dissertation, which he wrote in the same era when the John Prine song *Paradise* was written, echoes the song: "Today, thousands of railroad cars leave the mountains every day, loaded with coal. When they return, they are empty. The people of Appalachia have nothing to say about how that coal is used, nor about who reaps the harvest of riches from their mines. Someday, the vast riches of Appalachia will no longer flow into the hands of a few powerful individuals, but into the hands of Appalachian and American peoples."[43] Nyden saw that hope systematically hauled away coal train by coal train.

Many years later, Nyden, by then entirely gray, ran into Don Blankenship in southern West Virginia's Boone county courthouse during the recess of the 2002 *Caperton v. Massey* trial. In the hallway during the trial's recess, Nyden, as usual, said, "Hey, Don, can I get an interview?"

Blankenship responded, "You are one of the two biggest assholes I've ever met."

"Who is the other?" Nyden inquired,

"Cecil Roberts."

Nyden considered the comment a badge of honor.[44]

Back Home

After the 1984 gubernatorial election, Warren was ready to return to Pineville and spend more time with his family. For the 16 years he was in the Legislature, it had been difficult to keep up with the demands of a law practice and family while zealously representing his constituents. Warren did not give up on his duty to his community upon his return. In 1986 he ran for and was elected to the Wyoming County Board of Education, where he was known to be a forceful advocate for children and teachers. In 1996, Warren was elected prosecuting attorney of Wyoming County. He stayed in the arena working to improve his community, but frequently thought of venturing back to the Capitol.

Chapter V   Justice Warren R. McGraw

Justice Warren R. McGraw

Election for the WV Supreme Court

In December, 1997 Warren was finishing his second year as prosecutor in Wyoming County when Justice Thomas McHugh, a Democrat, announced his retirement from the state Supreme Court. Governor Cecil Underwood appointed a fellow Republican, John McCuskey, to fill the unexpired seat until the next statewide election. Warren determined it was the right time to tackle a statewide race for a seat on the state Supreme Court. Warren, like Justice McHugh, was a Democrat and a progressive. If elected to the unexpired six-year term, Warren would join Justices Larry Starcher, Spike Maynard, Margaret Workman, and Robin Davis on the state Supreme Court.

Justice Larry Starcher, a Democrat and long-time Monongalia County circuit judge,was elected to the Court in 1996. Born and raised in rural Roane County, Justice Starcher has special affinity for kids and a well-grounded understanding of how difficult life is for underprivileged children. As a circuit judge he addressed the needs of juveniles through the establishment of alternative learning centers for at risk youth and the use of work release and community service programs for non-violent offenders. As a circuit judge Starcher presided over the trial of thousands of asbestos injury cases. Justice Starcher, a progressive and hard worker, is a people person and an individual known for his quick wit and ability to tell great stories.

Justice "Spike" Maynard, a Democrat, was born and raised in Mingo County and served as prosecuting attorney and circuit judge in his home county before election to the state Supreme Court in 1996. Justice Maynard, a former director of the Tug Valley Chamber of Commerce, was known for his pro-business bias. While circuit judge, Maynard issued the injunction restricting UMWA picketing at the Rawl Sales mine and fined the union $200,000. Justice Maynard was a longtime friend of Don Blankenship.

Justice Margaret Workman, a Democrat, was appointed Kanawha County circuit judge by Governor Jay Rockefeller in 1981, successfully running in 1982 and 1984 for circuit judge. In 1998 Workman defeated Justice Darrell McGraw in his primary reelection bid for state Supreme Court. Justice Workman became the first woman elected to a statewide office and to serve on the high court.

Justice Robin Davis, a Democrat and Boone County native, joined the court alongside Justices Maynard and Starcher in 1996. Even though Justice Davis wore bibbed overalls to campaign events and touted herself a coal miners' daughter, her opinions were often markedly less progressive than her supporters had hoped. Over the years Justice Davis's vote often aligned with Justice Maynard's.

Warren faced two strong Democratic opponents in the May primary, Joseph Albright and William Forbes. In 1995 Joseph Albright, a Wood County lawyer, was appointed by Governor Gaston Caperton to fill a vacant seat on the state Supreme Court. Justice Albright ran to secure the seat in 1996 but was defeated by Larry Starcher in the primary. After his defeat in 1998, Justice Albright returned to his law practice in Parkersburg, where he was also the proprietor of Albright's of Belpre, Inc., a family owned furniture company. Justice Albright had a long history of public service including as prosecuting attorney, city attorney, a six-term member of the House of Delegates, and as the 52nd Speaker of the House.[1] Justice Albright and Warren were friends and colleagues who served together in the state Legislature.

The third candidate was William Forbes, a longtime Kanawha County Prosecutor with a record of action to curb violent crime and political corruption. His public service record included time as an Assistant Kanawha County Prosecutor and Special Assistant U.S. Attorney. In 1989 Forbes pursued the prosecution of Attorney General Charlie Brown and Circuit Judges John Hey and Joseph Troisi.[2] A tough prosecutor, he was built as solid as a linebacker and was as hard to knock over. Indicative of Forbes advocacy for those who were victims of injustice was his investigation into a West Virginia State Police lab serologist Fred Zain. The Zain case received national media coverage when Zain was found to have falsified lab results leading to numerous wrongful convictions.[3]

In a poll of Democratic voters a week before the election, Warren was leading with 34%, followed by Forbes with 16% and Albright with 9%. Albright, Forbes and McGraw were all hardworking public servants who would bring a progressive philosophy to the Court. It was a positive campaign with all candidates showing much respect for one another. Pat Maroney, a state and community leader, general counsel to the WVAFL-CIO, and state Democratic Party chair, acknowledged the quality of the Democrat candidates. Ultimately Warren prevailed and secured the Democratic nomination.

Justice John McCuskey, the appointed incumbent, won the Republican primary. Justice McCuskey, a Republican from Harrison County, was first elected to the House of Delegates while in law school. He was then appointed by Governor Arch A. Moore to serve as his Commissioner of Finance and Administration. Four years later, he joined the Huntington defense law firm of Campbell, Woods and Bagley. Justice McCuskey's campaign was heavily funded by the Chamber of Commerce, health insurance companies, and the coal industry among a multitude of other business and corporate entities. Justice McCuskey pledged to accept no money from lawyers or their families in his bid for the Court, stating he wanted "to restore the public confidence in the integrity and independence of the judiciary. The problem is money. The problem isn't road signs or speaking at Rotaries. The problem is large amounts of money given by lawyers to judges they appear before."[4] Justice McCuskey's logic regarding lawyer contributions did not extend to contributions his campaign received from doctors, insurance firms, coal companies or other large corporations with cases that might appear before the Court.[5]

Having served for less than a year, Justice McCuskey's record on the Court was limited. However Justice McCuskey's demonstrated a concern for rights of state pensioners when he dissented in an original mandamus proceeding brought by the relator, West Virginia Regional Jail and Correctional Facility Authority and supported by Governor Underwood. The Authority requested the Court evaluate the constitutionality of House Bill 4702 (1998). The Bill directed the respondent, the West Virginia Investment Management Board, the group charged with investing the funds of the Public Employees' Pension System, to invest $150,000,000 of the pension system funds in the West Virginia Jail and Correctional Facility Authority. The pension funds were designated to complete the construction or renovation of certain jails and correctional facilities in West Virginia. Justice Maynard writing for the majority found House Bill 4702 met Constitutional standards and granted the writ of mandamus sought by the relator. [6]

During the campaign, attacks against Warren were centered on his record of support for working people. The state Republican Party chairman said of Warren, "He's a true liberal and true liberals aren't very popular right now."[7] Warren, like his brother, were familiar with those who sought to derisively label them as liberal, populist, anti-business, or an activist in order to create or enhance a bias within a population. The McGraw brothers simply saw themselves as advocates for the people. Darrell's progressive decisions as a state Supreme Court justice were used in the attacks against Warren. The *Daily Mail* endorsement of McCuskey referred to Darrell "as one of the most lamentable Supreme Court justices in memory."[8] They editorialized that Warren would bring the same type of liberalism to the Court. Years later Darrell received WVU School of Law's highest honor the *Justicia Officium Award* for many of those decisions the *Daily Mail* criticized.

Elections were always tough for the McGraw brothers, and this time was no different. Special interests that stood to profit from Warren's defeat poured money into McCuskey's campaign. McCuskey's campaign received $347,880 in contributions compared to Warren's $214,176

during the May-November reporting period.[9] The McGraw campaign
was much dependent on the grassroots efforts of labor and volunteers.

Warren's kids, now adults, and Peggy joined him on the campaign
trail. There were many 14-16 hour days that frequently involved 300 plus
miles of driving, with multiple stops to give speeches and shake hands
with hundreds of people. In one such day of campaigning, Warren
started in Morgantown with a speech to the Democratic Executive
Committee, and then moved on to Ravenswood for lunch with local 5668
Steel Workers. After lunch, Warren drove to Charleston to meet voters
and campaign volunteers. After another two and a half hour drive,
Warren arrived in Lewisburg for a Meet the Candidate evening. Warren
was allotted the usual two-minute speech in his turn, but skipped it.
Warren preferred to make sure he met and shook the hand of everyone
there. It was 10 p.m. before he reached the drivers' seat of his dark gray
Oldsmobile. It was long after midnight before Peggy and Warren walked
into their home in Pineville. Home was out of the way considering the
next day's stops, but Warren and Peggy liked their own bed. When
Peggy couldn't join him, Warren's traveling companion was B. B. Smith.
Warren walked the parade routes, smiling, shaking hands, and speaking
to people. B. B., a construction worker member of the Construction
Trades, was on staff at the AFL-CIO. Bebe, a great campaign companion
for Warren, was a genial activist whose picture could be next to
"likeable" in the dictionary. Warren's grown children went wherever
their father couldn't make it. They were all over the state, all of them, at
any given moment for many months of this campaign—but it was a good
kind of hard work.—*Recollections by Rebecca McGraw Thaxton*

Hope for a Progressive Supreme Court

In November 1998 Warren won the election for the unexpired six
year term on the West Virginia Supreme Court of Appeals. Warren
received 52% of the vote compared to McCuskey's 46%. Legal
observers opined, "[Warren] represents a more forward thinking,
philosophical addition to the court. He could very well be not just a
swing vote but might actually create a liberal majority."[10]

On January 5, 1999 Warren left his home before 6 a.m. to reach Charleston for his first day as a Justice on the West Virginia Supreme Court. Unlike his old Legislative chambers, the Supreme Court's offices on the third floor of the Capital's east wing were eerily quiet. Red carpet covered the corridor floors. White Vermont marble walls encompass the courtroom itself, which boasts a thirty-foot ceiling and an awe-inspiring rectangular skylight of stained glass, bordered by bronze carvings depicting the "Scale and Balance" and the "Book of Law." An intricate compressed cork floor laid in a checkerboard pattern sets the tone of majesty for all who enter. Behind the massive walnut bench, designed by Capital architect Cass Gilbert, are four imposing white Imperial Vermont marble columns with black marble bases.[11] Behind the columns stretch twenty-foot high burgundy velvet curtains where Warren entered the Chamber as his brother had done for the first time in 1977. There the McGraw brothers read the words of Thomas Jefferson written in gold in the frieze along the top of the wall, "The true foundation of republican government is the equal right of every citizen in his person and property and in their management."

It was so different from the noisy Legislature where people roamed freely. Here there were hushed conversations. But underneath the subdued surroundings were real tensions among justices. Justice Larry Starcher and Justice Robin Davis were openly antagonistic to each other. For example, one day in judge's conference, Justice Starcher said, "I get so tired of your bullshit, Robin." Justice Davis countered, "If you cuss at me again, I'm going to file a complaint."[12]

And there were controversial cases.

Affiliated Construction Trades v. Vieweg
*To whose benefit is it for Big Coal not to pay their Workers'
Compensation premiums to the state?*

In the 1999 case *Affiliated Construction Trades v. Vieweg,* [13] the Affiliated Construction Trades (ACT) asked the WV Supreme Court to prevent the Employment Program Commissioner William Vieweg from dismissing more than $200 million in lawsuits against 18 large coal companies.[14] Commissioner Vieweg determined to dismiss the cases against the coal companies alleged to be liable for missed workers compensation payments.[15] The Commissioner's decision meant the large coal companies did not have to pay a significant amount of past due workers' compensation premiums. The missed payment claims stemmed from large coal companies' practice of contracting with small local operators to mine the coal. This contracting model was straight out of the Massey Doctrine, which outlined the plan for keeping employees—the miners themselves—at arm's length from the big coal company. By hiring small mining contractors to pay the miners' wages and benefits, the large coal company avoided the cost of worker compensation payments to the state. After large coal companies bought up the coal, they often stiffed the small contractor, which sometimes put them out of business. When the smaller company inevitably bankrupted, they were excused of their debts, including workers compensation claims. The employees then looked to the larger company for recovery and usually come up dry.[16]

In 1993, Massey and Island Creek Coal contractors owed $120 million to the West Virginia workers compensation system.[17] These same two companies owed tens of millions of dollars to the UMWA for workers' health care and retirement fund.[18] From 1978-1993, the two companies hired 750 small contractors, and by 1993, most of the contractors were out of business.[19] These contract mines were often notoriously unsafe. From 1980-1993, 38 men were killed in Massey and Island Creek affiliated mines, 27 of whom died in contract mines.[20] Altogether, large coal companies owed $200 million to the state. Commissioner Vieweg determined to let these companies off the hook at a time when the workers compensation system needed money to pay for medical treatment and benefits to injured workers. Stuart Calwell, lawyer for the ACT, filed a petition with the state Supreme Court arguing that Commissioner Vieweg violated his fiduciary obligation to the workers' compensation fund set forth in WV Code. The lawsuit claimed that large coal companies were responsible for paying the compensation payments, which their defaulted contractors owed to the system.

Stuart Calwell, prominent Charleston lawyer, wears Sperry glasses and a tweed sport coat. Suede patches cover the elbows. His vintage white saddle oxfords lace up tight with black shoestrings.

Perpetually trendy, he dons this haircut worthy of a prep schoolboy—wisps and all—and somehow maintains a boyish quality in his grown man face and the bodily proportions of a fit young man. He was tight with the Affiliated Construction Trades group "ACT."

Like the McGraw brothers, Stuart's parents attended Berea College. They taught Stuart he had a duty to regular folks, the working class. He knew and lived by the motto, "God has made of one blood all the peoples of the earth." He often said he shared an unshakable affliction with the McGraw brothers which he called, "Berea-itis."

He never stops working for working people against exploitive corporations and industries. In his young years, Stuart went around to local construction trades unions in the evenings after working all day at his law office. He spoke to plumbers, pipefitters, sprinkler fitters, sheet metal workers, boilermakers, carpenters, millwrights, laborers, operating engineers, painters, cement masons & plasterers, electricians, ironworkers, roofers, and many other Teamsters. These were the working men and women who made West Virginia industries go. Their unions were founded on the theory of strength in numbers and solidarity against large industry employers. Many of these industries were run from out of state.

Mr. Calwell explained to the union men and women how the working people were captive of these huge corporate employers (giant industries, mind you, not small businesses) in that the big industries were often more worried about their own profits than about the workers' safety and long-term benefits. He said the big companies were not interested in improving safety because that cut into profits, and that, for these big companies, "No amount of money to be saved is too small." He explained how companies took their profits, ravaged the people (some of whom were left injured from their toils) and their environment and left the people's "trail of tears." It was an eternal push-pull: big corporates' profit vs. the people. It was a constant back and forth, year after year throughout history.

Mr. Calwell managed to prove to these workers who move our industries just how these big companies were contributing to unsafe work environments. He managed to explain to them how the corporations with their high paid lawyers and fancy legal maneuvers and their big money connections took away the people's voices in court. "They lobby, they change laws, they duck out, and, at the same time," he said, "they demonize the good guys. The people's judges and the senators and delegates that would be friendly to us, and good they take out. They smear those people to get rid of them. And you?" he pointed, "They shut the court house door on you guys." The key to that door? He asked. "It's green. It folds. It's money."

These respectable union workers were on board and wanted to stand up for themselves and fight against this. They needed something to fight with: money. The union workers agreed to each contribute money out of their wages to set up a fund. Within 6 months, they had hundreds of thousands of dollars. "ACT" was born, and ACT did a lot of very good work through its years thanks to this Berea son. One particular example of this good, was ACT v. Vieweg[21]—Contributed by Rebecca McGraw Thaxton

Two of the lawsuits Vieweg sought to dismiss were against Island Creek Coal for $47.5 million in unpaid workers' compensation insurance premiums. Both Vieweg and Governor Underwood had connections to the company. Vieweg was an Island Creek Coal lawyer and executive for ten years. Island Creek's Worker's Compensation debts to the state began accumulating during Vieweg's employment at Island Creek. Governor Underwood, Vieweg's boss, was a former executive with Island Creek. Vieweg openly supported Justice John McCuskey in the 1998 Supreme Court election.[22]

ACT, in *Vieweg,* wanted the coal companies to pay their compensation premiums. The coal companies wanted the taxpayers to swallow the debt. The Court received "solicited responses from the West Virginia Chamber of Commerce and the West Virginia Manufacturers Association on behalf of the respondents (Vieweg), and from the AFL-CIO West Virginia Labor Federation and the United Mine Workers of America on behalf of the petitioner (ACT). The Court also received amicus curiae briefs from Attorney General Darrell V. McGraw, Jr., the West Virginia Trial Lawyers Association and the West Virginia Citizen Action Group on behalf of the petitioner (ACT), and from the West Virginia Coal Association, West Virginia Mining & Reclamation

Association and the West Virginia Business & Industrial Council on behalf of the respondents (Vieweg)."

The weight of those siding with the respondents, Chamber of Commerce, Manufacturers Association and the Coal Association, was substantial. The WV Supreme Court ruled in favor of *Vieweg* with Justices Workman, Davis and Maynard all voting to excuse the large coal companies' debt. The Court held that the Commissioner did not act with "partiality" even though the Commissioner and the Governor had both worked as executives at Island Creek Coal. "After considering this rationale, we are unable to find that the Commissioner acted with caprice, passion, partiality, fraud, arbitrarily, with some ulterior motive or misapprehension of the law."[23]

Justices McGraw and Starcher both wrote dissents expressing outrage with the majority decision. The dissents questioned why large coal companies should get away with not paying workers' compensation premiums for the people who were doing their work? Justice Starcher's minority opinion stated: "What a blow to West Virginia workers. What a sweet deal for coal companies that made a fortune using contract mining companies! And what a sour deal for the West Virginia businesses—including responsible coal companies—that played by the rules and paid their fair share of Worker's Compensation premiums." Warren, agreeing with the minority opinion, wrote, "the Court's decision was reminiscent of the time when Governor Moore, three days before leaving office, settled a $100 million lawsuit for $1 million against Pittston Coal. In that action Moore let the coal company off the hook for its responsibility in the Buffalo Creek dam collapse in 1972 that killed 125 and left 4,000 homeless, and in the words of Paul Nyden, 'depriving the people of West Virginia of their day in court against a coal company that had betrayed the public trust and ignored its obligations to society.'"[24] The *Vieweg* dissent provided fodder for Warren's opponents within the coal industry, fueling their fire to get rid of him once and for all.

Others desire to rid the Court of Justice McGraw was heightened when Warren wrote the opinion protecting citizen's from the harm of exposure to big industry toxic chemicals.

Bower v. Westinghouse

To whose benefit is for a company to knowingly expose the community to toxic hazards and then not pay for medical tests to detect resulting diseases prior to their onset?

     Bower v. Westinghouse, often referred to as the "medical monitoring case," was brought as a certified question from the US District Court for the Northern District of West Virginia.[25] The question before the Court was whether an industry that has knowingly exposed residents to a toxic substance must pay for medical testing to detect disease before those exposed have any signs or symptoms of a disease. The case emanated from residents who lived near a hazardous waste site created by Westinghouse Electric. For 40 years Westinghouse dumped hazardous waste including aluminum, arsenic, barium, leads, PCB (polychlorinated biphenyl), and mercury without informing residents of the danger. It was only when Westinghouse sold the property to American Philips that Philips held a hearing to inform the residents of the presence of toxic wastes. The residents were angry that Westinghouse, a rich and profitable company, hid the level of toxicity of the waste from residents who were being exposed on a daily bases. The residents, fearful the exposure to the hazardous wastes would eventually make them sick, wanted the company to pay for medical testing to identify any symptoms or abnormalities that might indicate a health problem.[26]

     The state Supreme Court's answer was unanimously "yes." Warren wrote the unanimous opinion that held "West Virginia law recognizes a cause of action for future medical monitoring costs where such necessary expenses are incurred as a proximate result of a defendant's tortious acts."[27] The precedent for medical monitoring existed in other states such as In New York where the Love Canal litigation provided for medical monitoring of residents who lived near the chemical dump. [28] But the Court's opinion was met with resistance from specific sectors.

     One of West Virginia's leading business executives and philanthropist, James Thomas, wrote an op-ed in the *Charleston Gazette* stating the "ruling creates a superhighway for personal injury lawyers to haul West Virginia businesses and private citizens into court on behalf of victims who have not yet been victimized and may never be victims."[29]

Mr. Thomas was a member of the West Virginia Chamber of Commerce, and one of founders of Citizens Against Lawsuit Abuse (CALA) in Southern West Virginia, a politically active pro-business group.[30] CALA is an organization whose message focuses on the alleged proliferation of unnecessary lawsuits: "CALAs are grassroots [special interest] groups created by industries and businesses to give the appearance of a groundswell of public desire to alter the legal system to make it harder to bring lawsuits for injuries and illnesses caused by hazardous products."[31] CALA, generally funded by large corporate donors including tobacco, insurance, oil and gas, chemical and pharmaceutical companies—largely Fortune 500 companies, has a direct financial stake in restricting lawsuits.[32]

The Westinghouse case was a unanimous opinion. Justice Maynard's vote was recorded as part of the unanimous decision to allow cost for future medical monitoring. However, after attending a business summit sponsored by the state Chamber of Commerce at the Greenbrier, Justice Maynard wrote a dissent closely reflecting the Chamber's views.[33] One session at the Chamber summit featured a pro-business panel of lawyers discussing the state Court's opinions considered "anti-business"– including *Bower v. Westinghouse*. Panel members asserted that *Bower v. Westinghouse* opinion "created a new species of lawsuit that adopted the most liberal standards for plaintiffs to receive monetary awards in the United States."[34] In actuality, the state Court's ruling required a specific multiple step standard to determine eligibility for any medical monitoring which included the following:

- "evidence that exposure must be to a 'proven hazardous' substance;
- exposure must be proved to be the fault of the company;
- people must be at an increased risk of contracting a serious latent disease relative to the general population because of exposure;
- risk must make it reasonably necessary for the people to require a medical exam besides routine checkups, and
- medical exams must be able to detect the disease early."[35]

The opinion defined the establishment of strict limits in determining any application of eligibility for medical monitoring.

Justice Maynard's change of mind validated his allegiance to those who funded his election and who stood to profit from the absence of medical monitoring requirements—members of the Chamber of Commerce and big businesses.[36] Maynard repeated his public attack of the medical monitoring opinion when he spoke in 2000 before the Federalist Society, a national network of conservative lawyers funded in large part by Pittsburg billionaire Richard Mellon Scaife. Justice Maynard spoke to the prejudices of the audience and their extended network of corporate clients when he said, "The court's July 19th ruling could allow West Virginians to sue if they take zinc in their vitamins or if their car tires contain magnesium. The real winners though are aluminum and iron. If you are exposed to iron in my state, you have been exposed to a hazardous substance."[37]

Bowyer v. Westinghouse fomented the aggression of corporate entities, CALA, and the Chamber of Commerce against Warren during his next re-election bid.

The *Bowyer* case was decided in July 1999. In August Justice Workman retired from the Court in order to explore other political office, including a run for governor. Securing a progressive majority on the Court became even more difficult.

Sert Rist v. Underwood

On September 9, 1999 Governor Cecil Underwood announced his appointment of House Speaker Robert Kiss, a Democrat from Raleigh County, to replace Justice Workman. Kiss was first elected to the House in 1988 and became Speaker in 1997. During his time as Speaker, Kiss secured passage of a self-audit bill in the House that allowed the chemical industry to mask problems from regulators and coal companies to double the size of valley fills (like the Pittston damn on Buffalo Creek) without making restitution for damage.[38]. This self-audit bill was defeated in the Senate.

Although Gov. Underwood was a Republican, he chose to appoint a Democrat who perhaps had greater likelihood of winning the 2000 election.[39] In their capacity as citizens and taxpayers John F. Rist, III and Richard A Robb each filed petitions asserting Robert Kiss was disqualified from serving as a Justice on the Court pursuant to Article VI, § 15 of the West Virginia Constitution.[40]

In *Sert Rist v. Underwood* the Court was asked to decide Kiss's eligibility.[41] The issue before the Court related to Constitutional prohibition on appointments: "No senator or delegate, during the term for which he shall have been elected, shall be elected or appointed to any civil office of profit under this State, which has been created, or the emoluments of which have been increased during such term, except offices to be filled by election by the people."[42] The Court, in a 3-2 decision written by Justice McGraw, held that House Speaker Robert Kiss was not eligible to accept Governor Underwood's appointment to the state Supreme Court. The opinion stated that language within the Constitution prohibited Delegate Kiss from being appointed to the Court because during his last legislative session Kiss voted to increase the justices' annual salary.[43] Justice Maynard dissented with the majority opinion, comparing the majority opinion to "a cruel act of human slaughter, like the Japanese attack on Pearl Harbor." [44] The decision was not popular with members of business groups and executive and legislative branches government who supported the Kiss appointment to the Court.

In November, 1999 Governor Underwood appointed George Scott, a Republican circuit judge from Roane County, to fill Justice Workman's vacated seat. Justices Starcher and McGraw remained the staunch progressive voices on the Court.

Attempt to Run for Re-Election

In the spring of 2000 there were 2 twelve year seats on the Court to be filled in the upcoming year's elections. Warren, currently elected to a 6 year term as Justice, determined to run for one of the seats and Justice Davis was running for re-election to the other seat which she presently held. With Justice McGraw's announcement to file, the swords of opposition began to rattle. George Carenbauer, a lawyer with Steptoe and Johnson, and longtime McGraw nemesis, filed suit to prevent Warren from seeking the twelve-year seat on the state Supreme Court. Chief

Justice Maynard assigned the Republican appointee Justice George Scott to chair a panel to review the case.

In *Carenbauer v. Hechler,*[45] the Court held Justice McGraw was ineligible to seek the twelve-year seat while serving as a justice. Justice Starcher objected to the Court's ruling in his dissent: "The majority opinion unconstitutionally steals from the voters of West Virginia the right to decide whether or not they, the voters, would elect a qualified, eligible candidate—Justice Warren McGraw—to a twelve-year seat on our Supreme Court of Appeals."[46] Justice Starcher noted in his dissent the majority opinion sharply criticized his remarks in oral argument regarding the selection of the members of the panel who "had preconceived political leanings."[47]

There was a significant history of conflict between Carenbauer's law firm Steptoe & Johnson and the McGraw brothers. Around the time Carenbauer filed his legal action against Justice Warren McGraw, Darrell, as Attorney General, was threatening legal action against Steptoe and Johnson for conspiring to conceal the misconduct of State Police forensic crime analyst Fred Zain. Ultimately the AG's office filed suit in 2002, contending that Steptoe and Johnson' awareness that Zain, a forensic chemist for the State police falsified DNA evidence, resulted in innocent people remaining in prison.[48] Further, as AG, Darrell refused the School Building Authority's request for Steptoe and Johnson to serve as bond counsel without competitive bidding.[49] In 1993, Carenbauer himself, a lobbyist engaged to represent clubs and taverns in the expansion of video lottery, worked against the Attorney General Darrell's efforts to restrict expansion of gambling.[50] In addition Steptoe & Johnson represented many large coal companies, including Massey Energy. Steptoe and Johnson was the law firm who would spend more than a decade defense of Massey Coal for fraudulent misrepresentation and concealment that damaged a small union coal company and put miners out of work (*Caperton v. Massey*[51]).

Although Justice McGraw was thwarted in his attempt to run for reelection, Justice Joseph Albright, a like-minded progressive was elected to the Court.

Chief Justice W.R. McGraw and Medical Malpractice

In 2001, Warren became Chief Justice on the WV Supreme Court. That same year, hundreds of families in Wyoming County and surrounding areas lost their homes to a massive flood. Seventy-five percent of the businesses were damaged or destroyed.[52] The heavy rain accumulation was exacerbated by the impact of increased runoff from under-regulated mining and timbering operations into watersheds.

The testimony of residents was all too familiar to that heard from residents in the aftermath of the 1972 Buffalo Creek disaster:

There were no warnings of an anticipated flood. We had four very hard rains in a six hour period but no harder than we had many times in the past. I heard something and looked, and it looked like a tidal wave coming. That thing was thirty feet high and looked like a surfer could be underneath it, an ocean wave. This resident spoke of a chemical smell in the air and a sheen that could be seen on the water. The resident commented that she smelled this same chemical odor when they de-gassed the holes on her property and that it burned her throat and caused her difficulty with breathing. The resident also stated that a "mine blowout right below the Hilton Strip caused a big tidal wave which never touched the ground until it hit the creek in Indian Creek. There it met one just like it coming down Indian Creek and it was just unreal, and it will happen again."[53]—Resident Public Meeting 4, Wyoming East High School, Wyoming County, WV., November 26, 2001.

Warren was doing his work on the Court but helping his neighbors as was his brother, the AG, who was assisting in deliveries of needed supplies from Charleston to Wyoming County. The residents of Wyoming County were the victims of unregulated mining and timbering while those who benefited the profits from coal and timber lived somewhere else.

The Supreme Court of Appeals of West Virginia 2001

Justice Elliott E. Maynard   Justice Joseph P. Albright

Justice Robin Jean Davis   Chief Justice Warren R. McGraw   Justice Larry V. Starcher

In 2001 the Court addressed appellate convictions, writs of prohibition, and certified questions and rendered over 180 opinions. Some of the decisions had far-reaching ramifications, such as *Verba v. Ghaphery*[54], where the insurance industry had an interest in ensuring a $1 million cap was maintained in medical liability awards.

Verba v. Ghaphery
To whose benefit is it to cap the value of a life when doctors are negligent?

Verba, the plaintiff, died shortly after she was prematurely discharged from a hospital following a surgery in which a laceration of her stomach occurred. The circuit court found for Verba, and awarded her $1 million, the cap on recovery in medical malpractice cases established by W.V. Code Section 55-7B-8. On appeal, the Court upheld the constitutionality of the $1 million noneconomic damages cap in a 3-2 decision. [55]

Justices McGraw and Starcher wrote dissents that questioned the constitutionality of a statutorily imposed cap. Justice Starcher called the cap "a patent violation of the equal protection and certain remedy provisions of the West Virginia Constitution." He continued, "This discriminatory statute arbitrarily treats similarly situated persons differently and unfairly, and often deprives severely injured plaintiffs a remedy by due course of law."[56]- Warren's dissent also questioned the Constitutionality of the cap: "It is highly doubtful that § 55-7B-8 would pass constitutional muster. As other courts have observed, statutes imposing a "one-size-fits-all" limitation on damages (economic or non-economic) create classifications based upon severity of injury, and then proceed to penalize those who are more seriously injured by denying them compensation beyond the statutory limit."[57]

Importantly, the *Ghaphery* appeal presented evidence the state insurance commissioner's office failed to comply with a state law requiring insurance companies to report how much they charge West Virginia doctors for medical malpractice coverage. Evidence showed the commissioner levied no fines on the insurance companies for failure to report their premium rates. The record in the appeal showed there was no evidence the imposed legislative cap had reduced either malpractice insurance premiums or health care costs.[58]

Later, big insurance companies used Warren's dissent in *Ghaphery* to target him in the next election, claiming increased medical malpractice rates were driving doctors out of the state.

WV Physician Mutual Insurance

At the time of *Verba v. Ghaphery* was in the courts, medical malpractice premiums in the state were undoubtedly increasing, and there was concern for the escalating insurance costs for doctors. Existing state statute provided the authority to establish professional liability insurance if an identified need was determined. The law was there; the need was there, but still there was no state supported professional liability insurance for doctors.

As Justice, Warren wasn't in a place to do anything to assist doctors. But as AG, Darrell was able to influence the establishment of a physician mutual insurance. Beginning in 2001, Darrell's office reached out to the Governor's office and key legislators advising that law existed to support state assistance for doctors through establishment of professional liability insurance. "The Legislature finds and declares that there is a need for the state of West Virginia to assist in making professional liability insurance available for certain necessary health care providers in West Virginia to assure that quality medical care are available for the citizens of the state."[59] The law was in place but it was not used to address the escalating malpractice rates that doctors incurred. Darrell also proposed way to fund a physician insurance program through the recently acquired tobacco settlement monies. The Governor and Legislature remained resistant. The insurance lobby was strong.

For two years the AG office advised and promoted the creation of a Physician's Mutual Insurance, and the utilization of the work product of the AG office to provide implementation funds. Finally in 2003 the Legislature authorized the West Virginia Physicians Mutual Company Act. The statute also identified the West Virginia Tobacco Settlement Medical Trust Fund to provide the $24 million for seed money for what is now called West Virginia Mutual Insurance Company.[60] It was a milestone that helped doctors throughout the state. It was difficult to achieve because private insurance companies did not want it to happen.

The legislative cap did not reduce malpractice insurance premiums or health care costs.[61] It was the state established malpractice insurance, promoted by Attorney General Darrell McGraw, which significantly reduced the insurance costs paid by doctors. So why did so many doctors dislike McGraws?

White Coat Day—A Secret Deal
To whose benefit is it for the public to be told, over and over again, there is a medical malpractice crisis caused by meritless lawsuits and bad judges?

Medical Assurance, an Alabama-based large insurance company, teamed up with the West Virginia Medical Association, which represents doctors, to allege that meritless malpractice claims were causing insurance rates to increase and drive doctors out of the state.[62] Lawrence Messina, an award winning investigative reporter, uncovered a secret document which Medical Assurance was required to file with the SEC.[63] The document was stamped, "Confidential" on each page, and carefully outlined a circuitous arrangement between Medical Assurance and the WV Medical Association. The arrangement worked like this—Medical Assurance made annual payments to the WV Medical Association which

totaled more than $690,000 in a 6-year period, and in return the WV
Medical Association agreed to lobby legislators on the company's behalf.
There were more benefits for those doctors who purchased their policies
from Medical Assurance: "Association members [doctors] can reap a
share of the $208 million of the company's annual profits, as well as a
series of breaks on their premiums—provided they buy their policies
from Medical Assurance."[64]

Medical Assurance provided the talking points for the Association
and the Association's doctors, in turn, convinced legislators, WV
Chamber of Commerce, and deans of medical schools that there was a
medical malpractice crisis. Lobbyists dutifully passed on the medical
malpractice misinformation, which was used by a disturbing number of
newspapers, television stations and paid political commercials "to place
the blame for increased premiums on meritless malpractice lawsuits."[65]
This comprehensive and long term campaign of misinformation included
in 2003 a "White Coat Day," a media circus act where doctors from
across the state, donning white coats "descended on the state capitol, in a
litany of distorted public statements, and distribution of literature that
consistently exaggerated the frequency and severity of jury awards in
medical liability cases."[66]

So what were these talking points and what were the facts? First
of all, the Medical Association claimed that increase in malpractice
premiums was driving doctors out from the state. In fact, over a five year
period the number of doctors in West Virginia increased by 9.6%. Five
hundred more doctors practiced in 2000 as compared to 1990, and the
number of doctors grew at a rate 20 times greater than the population. At
the same time West Virginia had the 7th highest average physician
income in the nation. An average income higher than all surrounding
states which was perhaps the reason West Virginia was actually retaining
doctors.[67]

The Medical Association also claimed that malpractice insurance
rates were increasing primarily because of "frequency and severity of
lawsuits." The truth was that the number of malpractice claims decreased
in the previous eight years. The increase in liability premiums was
actually caused by the insurance cycle (when the economy falters and

interest rates fall, companies increase premiums) not by any increase in malpractice awards.[68]

Finally, the Medical Association claimed that one out of every two doctors have been sued for malpractice. In actuality fewer than 4% of doctors were sued each year.[69]

In a 2001 a *Gazette* report series analyzed West Virginia malpractice claims over an eight year period. The report found the "talking points" Medical Assurance gave doctors and lobbyists were not supported by facts. In 2003 a study by *Citizen's Watch* found that "medical malpractice awards have remained steady, despite claims of the medical lobby."[70] The report described how insurance cycles, not jury verdicts, were causing an increase in medical malpractice premiums. The report did not support that medical malpractice claims were frivolous but rather described how malpractice claims were very expensive for plaintiff's lawyers to bring and certainly not always successful. The report blamed any "crisis," real or otherwise, in West Virginia and three other states on insurance companies:[71] "The insurers don't want to admit they are manipulating rates to compensate for the reduction in profits from a poor investment market and thus look for a scapegoat, and have thus created the current 'crisis.'"[72] The report concluded the assertions "that it [the malpractice crisis] has been caused by 'many frivolous lawsuits,' an 'out-of-control legal system,' an 'irrational lottery' or 'astronomic jury verdicts' have no basis in fact.'"[73]

Chapter VI   *State v. Arbaugh*

To whose benefit is it to victimize an already victimized youth?

In early 2004 the state Court heard a case about Tony Arbaugh who since the age of seven was sexually assaulted by family members and then was sexually assaulted by a teacher for four years. The record showed Tony Arbaugh was a victim of inhumanity and abuse by adults and of a system that did not afford him protection from his abusive family and teacher. When Arbaugh was fifteen years old he was accused of "acting out sexually against his younger half-brother." Arbaugh was convicted for molestation and sentenced to thirty five years in prison. [1] The decision of the circuit court was appealed to the state court.

Justice Robin Davis, in writing for majority, reversed the lower court decision noting the failures of the system to provide basic protection to a young Tony Arbaugh: "Having read the briefs, reviewed the record, and heard oral argument, we reverse and remand with directions to the circuit court to grant Mr. Arbaugh probation to follow his proposed rehabilitation plan. We further direct that the rehabilitation plan proposed by Mr. Arbaugh should include specific provisions that Mr. Arbaugh undergo both sexual offender counseling and substance abuse counseling."[2]

In the opinion Justice Davis described the abuse that had befallen Arbaugh:

Mr. Arbaugh has led a long and painful life. He endured a long history of sexual assault at the hands of two of his adult male family members, beginning when he was seven or eight years old. These assaults included oral sex, sodomy, mutual masturbation, and 'dry humping.' Mr. Arbaugh was also sexually assaulted by one of his teachers for a period of four years… As a result of these attacks, Mr. Arbaugh began acting out sexually against his younger half-brother…a delinquency petition was filed on February 28, 1997, when Mr. Arbaugh was fifteen years old. After a hearing, Mr. Arbaugh was transferred to adult jurisdiction on April 7, 1997.[3]

Justice Davis' opinion summarized Arbaugh's years spent bouncing in and out of juvenile facilities, rehabilitation centers and the court system:

- On September 4, 1997, the court sentenced Arbaugh to an indeterminate term of fifteen to thirty-five years and restitution, but suspended his sentence due to his age and contingent upon enrollment in the Chestnut Ridge Treatment Center, and then once he finished at Chestnut Ridge enrollment in a secure juvenile facility.

- On August 20, 1998, the court placed Arbaugh in Stepping Stones, Inc. Group Home, but his behavior digressed, and the state filed a motion to reconsider disposition. The circuit court transferred Arbaugh to the Eastern Regional Juvenile Facility.

- After he turned eighteen, the circuit court transferred Arbaugh to the Anthony Center under the Youthful Offender Act and determined to review the sentence once Arbaugh was released from the program.

- Arbaugh successfully completed the youthful offender program, and the court placed him on five year probation.

- On December 11, 2000, the state petitioned to revoke Arbaugh's probation based on his admission that he had used marijuana and alcohol; failed to seek on-going counseling, and did not pay his five dollar a month probation fee. The circuit court revoked Arbaugh's probation.

- February 1, 2001, Arbaugh filed a motion with the circuit court to reduce his sentence and grant probation conditioned on participation in another rehabilitation program, Youth Systems Services (YSS). Paul Flanagan, a volunteer with the Marist Brothers, a Roman Catholic religious community and an employee of YSS, explained on the record that the organization chose Arbaugh to participate in their free program because they believed Arbaugh "can be saved and brought around to a pro-social life."[4] Flanagan explained that Arbaugh's YSS program would include relocating him so as to remove him from the influences that initially caused his conduct. He would reside in community apartments; participate in a variety of skill development programs to prepare him for independent living; be provided with supportive services through the Marist Brothers, and have round-the-clock access to designated YSS staff for crisis situations. YSS would provide required reports to the circuit court.[5]

- The circuit court denied Arbaugh's request to reduce his sentence. It was from this order that Arbaugh sought appellate relief.

Justice Davis authored the majority decision in the *Arbaugh* case and then authored a dissent objecting to the majority decision. This was a step beyond what Justice Maynard did in *Bower v. Westinghouse.* (In *Bowyer,* Maynard in a unanimous opinion that he did not author, later issued a blazing dissent.) In this instance Justice Davis wrote the majority opinion in *State v. Arbaugh* and then issued an emotional dissent that scorched her fellow Justices.[6] Justice Davis's dissent attacked her own opinion and concurred with her fellow Justice Maynard's dissent: "the majority has bent, stretched, ignored and distorted law and facts to afford Mr. Arbaugh yet another opportunity to avoid prison."[7] Justice Davis used descriptive words in her dissent that cast the majority opinion as releasing a "rapist" to work with children in schools which was contrary to the facts in the case. Justice Davis wrote, "Mr. Arbaugh not only repeatedly raped his younger half-brother from August 1, 1995 through April 22, 1996, but he also sexually assaulted a number of other victims ranging in age from four to thirteen, including two brothers, two sisters, two peers, two nephews and two cousins."[8]

"In all the courtrooms in which Arbaugh's case had been heard and in the entire voluminous public record, this was only the second time anyone had called Arbaugh a rapist. The first occasion was in the state's brief to the state Supreme court, which attempted to justify Judge Cookman's refusal to grant Arbaugh probation."[9]

Justice Davis's description of the Arbaugh's assaults was taken from the record of Arbaugh's therapist. Arbaugh confided the information to his therapist in the confidential environment of his therapy

141

sessions, and they were placed as evidence that Arbaugh's ability to articulate these occurrences was indicative of his rehabilitation. Justice Davis' descriptions, obtained from Arbaugh's treatment and therapy sessions, if legal, were at the very least insensitive to Arbaugh's rights to privacy.[10]

Justice Starcher, in a concurring opinion, expressed amazement and displeasure with Justice Davis's dissent that attacked "articulation of the facts and law and the conclusions in the *per curiam* opinion. Justice Starcher wrote, "A decent society is where a child who has been sexually victimized for years, and who becomes seriously disordered—but who does work in structured situations to improve—gets our help, not a thirty-five year prison sentence."[11]

Unfortunately there was also particular factually erroneous passage in the majority opinion. In that opinion Justice Davis wrote: "He [Arbaugh] would be employed as a janitor at a local Catholic high school..."[12]

This incorrect statement was used in the next judicial election to portray Arbaugh as child rapist who the court (Justice McGraw) allowed to work in around children. The court record actually showed that Arbaugh was not going to be employed by a school but by the Youth Services' Offender Job Skills Program. Arbaugh was to work under the supervision of a Marist brother cleaning a school at night when there were no students present.[13]

In what the Brennan Center for Justice called one of the most vicious judicial campaigns in the country, the *Arbaugh* case was exploited by those with special interests who wanted Justice McGraw off the court.[14] Unfortunately, the political attacks during the election further compounded the problems of young Arbaugh's already difficult life.[15] The exploitation of the *Arbaugh* was associated with a case on its way to the state Supreme Court, *Caperton v. Massey.[16]*

Chapter VII   *Caperton v. Massey*

To whose benefit is it to put small companies out of business?

Widely criticized for his union busting skills, Don Blankenship was also criticized for putting other companies and their workers out of business.[1] As was the case in 2002 when a Boone County jury awarded Harman mining $50 million in damages to be paid by A.T. Massey.[2] Hugh Caperton owned Harmon Coal, a small coal company in Virginia that produced elite quality metallurgic coal. Caperton bought Harmon Mining in 1993, hiring 125 union miners.[3] In 1998 Caperton filed suit against A.T. Massey for actions which resulted in Harmon's bankruptcy and ultimately closed the mine and put 150 people out of work.[4] Blankenship was Massey's CEO.

The Harman Mine—A Story of *Force Majeure*

In law, *force majeure* is a clause that frees both parties from obligation. It refers to unforeseeable circumstances that prevent someone from fulfilling a contract. According to Don Blackenship Massey spent $1 million a month on attorneys. Certainly Massey lawyers were skilled at the intricacies of *force majeure.*[5]

Harman mine produced a costly high grade metallurgical coal used for making steel. This prized Harman coal was bought by Wellmore Coal Company, who processed the coal and shipped most of it to LTV Steel. Wellmore had a long-term contract with Harman. Wellmore and LTV Steel were quite happy with Harman coal. Competitor A.T. Massey had tried for years to win LTV's business, but LTV preferred the higher quality Harman coal. After failed attempts to take LTV's business from Wellmore, Massey decided to buy Wellmore. Massey knew this was a risky purchase. A memo showed that Massey executives were aware LTV might no longer purchase its coal from Wellmore if they began supplying Massey coal instead of Harman. LTV Steel had no long-term contract with Wellmore. LTV Steel was reluctant to buy the inferior Massey coal, but Massey provided them with price quotes for their coal undercutting Harman coal prices. Blankenship insisted that LTV buy only from Massey mines. They negotiated a long-term coal contract establishing this.[6]

A cost analysis determined that if now Massey-owned Wellmore declared *force majeure*, Massey profits would increase. Wellmore declared this *force majeure*.[7] During the notice period, Massey entered into negotiations to purchase Harman Mine. Through the negotiations, Blankenship acquired confidential information regarding Harman's intent to mine adjoining Pittston reserves. Blankenship used the confidential information to purchase a narrow band of Pittston coal reserves surrounding Harman which decreased Harman's value and blocked its sale to another buyer.

Blankenship delayed the termination of the Wellmore-Harman contract until late in the year. Blankenship kept it a secret that the Harman coal no longer had its buyer, aware that the delay kept Harman from finding any alternate coal buyers. When Wellmore stopped buying Harman coal, Harman was unable to stay in business and was forced to file bankruptcy. Harman's miners lost their jobs.

The owner of Harman mine, Hugh Caperton, told *Rolling Stone* that Blankenship paid him a visit after he ran Harman out of business. Caperton said, "It was one of the strangest conversations I've ever had. He just walked into my office, and if I would have had a couch, he would have laid down on it. Blankenship said, 'I don't understand why people don't like me anymore. In high school, I played ball. I was really popular.' Then, Caperton said, Blankenship just stood and left."[8]

Caperton filed a lawsuit against Massey, and in 2002, a Boone County jury found in Caperton's favor and awarded Caperton and his Harman Mining $50 million in damages. This $50 million was to be paid by Massey. Much of the $50 million was needed to pay debts, some of which were to the miners who'd lost their jobs. One of Harman's former miners was Jeff Coleman from Grundy, former member of UMWA local 7025. He came to the state Supreme Court in Charleston the day it heard the Caperton appeal because he needed money. He said he needed thousands of dollars. He owed bill collectors, including doctors and hospitals, money. With interest, by 2008, when the case was still ongoing, Harman owed the UMWA $13 million plus interest to cover costs of displaced miners benefits.[9]

Caperton was a coal operator, too. But he was playing by the rules. He was hiring union workers. He didn't abide by the *Massey Doctrine*.

The Appeal—Massey Needed a Positive Verdict

Prior to the 2004 election Massey's lawyers were in the process of constructing an appeal to the West Virginia Supreme Court. Blankenship and his lawyers knew the importance of who sat on the state Court and were concerned of the outcome with the current construct of justices. Justices McGraw, Starcher and Albright were viewed by some as positive votes to uphold the lower court ruling. Justice Spike Maynard, a personal friend of Don Blankenship, and Justice Robin Davis were considered as possible votes to reverse the ruling. The numbers weren't there for a successful outcome.[10]

In 2004 when Warren was up for re-election, the opportunity presented itself to utilize money and power to influence the makeup of the state Court. Blankenship spent $3 million in personal money in the 2004 judicial election, but a positive outcome from the state Court was worth $50 million to Massey. As CEO Massey Blankenship earned millions of dollars a year, so he could easily afford a personal outlay of $3 million.[11] Legal scholar Kenneth Karst described Blankenship's motivation and strategy for involvement in the judicial election:

Blankenship is accustomed to throwing his weight around. If this means supplying money for a campaign to remove a justice who seems likely to vote against Massey when the company's $50 million liability for damages comes before the state supreme court—well, that is all in a day's work.

The target justice is Warren McGraw, a former tough prosecutor and classic pro labor politician, who had been elected to the state senate and eventually became president of that body. In the ordinary course, Justice McGraw could expect to pass through a ho-hum electoral season to the customary re-election.

145

But Blankenship decides to provide funds for McGraw's opponent in the Democratic primary. McGraw wins, but his adversary gets enough votes to give encouragement to Brent Benjamin, the Republican nominee. Blankenship now turns the money spigot to full force.

Blankenship's political consultants included specialists in political "opposition research," who can almost always find something that can be used to rouse voters' wrath.

The campaign against McGraw follows this pattern. Anti-McGraw radio messages, television spot announcements, and direct mailings are supplemented by recorded phone messages telling voters to be "scared" of McGraw. Of course, these campaign ads do not refer to the case that Massey is taking to the state supreme court.[12]

Caperton v. Massey, in the process of being appealed to the West Virginia Supreme, was never heard by Justice McGraw, as was the intent of Massey CEO Don Blankenship: "By the time this brief is filed, Blankenship has the first of his objectives in hand: the elimination of McGraw from his company's case."[13]

Massey lost a $50 million fraud verdict to the petitioners, Caperton, at the circuit court level, and Massey's CEO Don Blankenship determined to prevail at the Supreme Court: "[Blankenship] contributed (both directly and indirectly) $3 million supporting the 2004 campaign of Justice Brent D. Benjamin for a seat on the Supreme Court of Appeals of West Virginia. These campaign contributions, representing more than 60% of the total money spent on Justice Benjamin's campaign, were made at the very time Massey was preparing to appeal that verdict." [14]

In 2008, Justice Robin Davis authored the majority opinion in *Caperton v. Massey* that reversed the lower court ruling and held for Massey. Justices Davis, Maynard and Benjamin voted together and by so doing voided the Boone County jury verdict, then estimated at $75 million. Justices Starcher and Albright dissented.[15]

Caperton v. Massey was ultimately appealed to the U.S. Supreme Court. *Caperton v. Massey* became the backdrop to the blatant buying of a seat on the state Supreme Court; the rebuke of sitting Justices; the scandal involving Justice Maynard and Don Blankenship; the release of books, documentaries, articles and commentaries, and for some the lost of jobs and financial ruin.

Time Line of Major Events Related to *Caperton v. Massey*

1998

- In October, 1998 *Caperton v. Massey* was filed alleging that "Massey had tortuously interfered with Harman and defrauded it, destroying the company in the process."[16] Steptoe and Johnson law firm represented A.T. Massey against Harman Mining. (*Caperton v. Massey).*[17]

2000

- Warren McGraw, whose term expired at the end of 2004, filed to run for one of the two open seats on the state Court. George Carenbauer, attorney with Steptoe Johnson law firm, filed a law suit contending Justice McGraw was not eligible to run for the open seat. Chief Justice Maynard assigned the Republican appointee Justice George Scott to chair a panel to review the case. The panel held Justice McGraw was not allowed to run.

2002

- Boone County jury awarded Hugh Caperton and Harman mining $50 million in damages caused by the acts of Massey Coal.

2004

- Brent Benjamin, candidate for WV Supreme Court, drove to Kentucky early in the election process to meet with Don Blankenship, Massey president.[18]
- Steptoe and Johnson's George Carenbauer's advised Don Blankenship to establish a 527 organization through which he could spend unlimited money in the state Supreme Court election. Blankenship established "And for the Sake of Kids," and hired right-wing political consultant Gregory Thomas to manage it. Blankenship personally donated $3 million dollars to the organization to attack Justice McGraw and elect Brent Benjamin to the West Virginia Supreme Court.[19]
- Blankenship's "And for the Sake of Kids" ran ads attacking Justice McGraw for letting a rapist loose to work in schools: "Week after week, ["And for the Sake of Kids"] pays for advertising hammering away at McGraw for being soft on child molesters."[20]

2005

- Beginning in 2005 and through 2007, Justice Maynard voted in favor in 12 of the 13 cases involving clients of Scott Segal, a nationally recognized trial lawyer and husband of Justice Robin Davis.[21]

2006

- Summer, 2006 Justice Maynard and Blankenship vacationed in Monte Carlo, sharing meals and champagne, while the $50 million Massey verdict was on appeal to the state Supreme Court.[22]
- October, 2006 Justices Benjamin, Davis and Maynard prevented Justice Starcher from serving as Chief Justice. By negating the long observed Court process of rotation to Chief Justice, the majority justices ensured the Massey case assignment and judge selection in recusals was not handled by the progressive Justice Starcher.[23]

2007

- August, 2007, Justice Robin Davis stood at Justice Maynard's side when he announced he was running for re-election to the Court. Canon 5 of West Virginia's Code of Judicial Conduct states that a judge or judicial candidate "shall refrain from inappropriate political activity" and shall not "publicly endorse or publically oppose another candidate for public office".[24]
- Justice Davis' husband, Scott Segal, hosted a fundraiser at their home that raised more than $100,000 for Maynard's reelection campaign.[25]
- Justice Maynard frequently sent emails to Blankenship which confirmed a close personal and political relationship.[26]
- "Justice Benjamin, requested by the plaintiffs to recuse himself, does no such thing—and in West Virginia there can be no appeal to the whole court."[27]
- October 11, 2007 the justices met in conference and voted on *Caperton v. Massey* without any discussion. Justices Albright and Starcher objected to taking a vote without any discussion.[28]
- November 21, 2007 the West Virginia Supreme Court, in a 3-2 opinion written by Justice Robin Davis, ruled in favor of Massey Coal. Justice Davis was joined by Justices Maynard and Benjamin in reversing the Boone County decision award that with interest was now at $76 million. Justices Starcher and Albright dissented.[29]

- "When Benjamin won, he three times refused requests that he disqualify himself from ruling on the case [*Caperton v. Massey*].[30] "Justice Brent Benjamin, elected in 2004 with the help of more than $3 million spent by Blankenship during the campaign refused to step down and voted in favor of Massey."[31].

2008

- January 15, 2008 a *New York Times* article featured photos that showed Chief Justice Elliott "Spike" Maynard in Monaco with Massey Energy C.E.O. Don Blankenship. "A justice of the Supreme Court of Appeals of West Virginia and a powerful coal-company executive met in Monte Carlo in summer of 2006, sharing several meals even as the executive's companies were appealing a $50 million jury verdict against them to the court."[32]
- February, 2008 Justices Davis, Benjamin and Maynard refused Justice Starcher's request to investigate the conduct of the Court related to Justice Maynard.[33]
- June 17, 2008 in *Deborah K. May v. Matte Securities* the state Court reversed a lower court ruling in favor of Don Blankenship's former maid's requests for unemployment benefits. According to Justice Starcher's diary, Justices Maynard and Davis stated they would support unemployment compensation for the maid if records of Blankenship's conduct were not part of the majority opinion. Justices Starcher and Albright agreed with their request but later wrote a concurring opinion exposing Blankenship's conduct.[34]

2009

- In March, *Caperton v. Massey* was appealed to the United States Supreme Court. Caperton's petition argued that Don Blankenship's campaign expenditures on behalf of Benjamin created an appearance of partiality and due process required Benjamin's recusal. Caperton was represented by former U.S. Solicitor General Theodore Olson. Within a week eleven briefs amici were filed in support of the petitioners appeal including a brief of the Conference of Chief Justices.[35]
- In June, the (U.S) Supreme Court ruled in *Caperton v. Massey* that Justice Benjamin had a major conflict of interest and returned the case for a rehearing. Justice Kennedy writing for the majority held: "We

149

conclude that there is a serious risk of actual bias—based on objective
and reasonable perceptions—when a person with personal stake in a
particular case had significant and disproportionate influence in
placing the judge on the case by raising funds or directing the judge's
election campaign when the case was pending or imminent."[36]

- The Supreme Court decision resulted in the case returning to the WV
Supreme Court. Justices Starcher and Albright were no longer on the
Court. Justice Benjamin was now forced to disqualify himself in
Caperton v. Massey's third appeal to the W.Va. Supreme Court.[37]
- Justice Davis, acting as Chief Justice, denied a request from Caperton
to submit a new brief.[38]
- On November 19, Justice Davis again wrote the majority opinion in
which *Caperton* was rejected for a third time.[39]
- Justice Workman dissented and wrote: "The majority not only
deprives the plaintiffs of the substantial damages awarded to them by
the rightful finders of fact, a Boone County jury, but also leaves them
with no legal recourse by which to address Massey's extensive
pattern of fraudulent conduct."[40]

2010

- In January in an administrative hearing court administrator Steve
Canterbury testified Justice Davis requested the firing of the three
female court employees who allegedly leaked the photos of Justice
Maynard and Don Blankenship to the press. "Justice Davis was very
annoyed about the pictures and in an emotional moment she thought
that it was time to clean house, I believe is what she said."[41]

During Warren's time on the Court, the majority sided with Justice
McGraw in 88% of the labor related cases.[42] *Vanity Fair* described
Justice McGraw as being, "Proudly liberal, [Warren McGraw] tended to
side with coal workers in injury cases. A popular figure."[43] Warren, like
his brother, Darrell, embraced being identified as a liberal. They
appreciated its history. Liberal, a Latin based word, defined during the
Enlightenment to mean "free from prejudice, tolerant not bigoted or
narrow." This enlightened definition of liberal emerged within the
seminal document of the Declaration of Independence and the subsequent
form of government established by the U.S. Constitution (1976-1981).[44]
The McGraw brothers saw the state Court as people [liberals] in a group

who should try to figure out the best thing to do without the influences of money, like those [liberals] who developed the Declaration of Independence and the U.S. Constitution. The McGraw brothers saw "liberals" as those who use their education to advance the progression of man, and they were honored to be so considered.

Warren's decisions related to workers' rights were based on the law including the West Virginia Constitution: "the courts of this state shall be open, and every person for an injury done to him, in his person, property or reputation shall have remedy by due course of law, and justice shall be administered without sale, denial or delay."[45] Warren's decisions adhered to WV Workers' Compensation law, at the time, which stated that determination of compensation shall be "liberally construed in favor of claimant."

Warren's presence on the Court was problem for those who were viewed in many people's mind as the antithesis of liberal. Don Blankenship, portrayed in *Vanity Fair* as ruthless, was described by Cecil Roberts', President of the UMWA, as an individual who "[Blankenship] caused more misery to more people in Appalachia than anyone else."[46] Blankenship wanted to rid the Court of the liberal, Justice Warren McGraw.

Chapter VIII   Most Vicious Judicial Election

Justice With A Target on His Back

In 2003 *Forbes* magazine placed a judge with a target on his back on the cover. According to Don Blankenship, "that judge was Warren McGraw."[1] The *Forbes* article forewarned of the upcoming 2004 judicial election for the West Virginia Supreme Court. The article describes how corporations are engaging in a highly financed "secret war" to elect judges favorable to their interests noting that "West Virginia Supreme Court Justice Warren McGraw will be among the targets."[2]—*Forbes*

Warren's campaign for reelection became the most brutal campaign of his career and was labeled as one of the nation's most vicious and costly judicial elections.[3] A jurist positive to Massey was needed on the Court to negate the $50 million verdict against Massey. Those in the Massey camp did not believe Justice McGraw was that jurist. In was said that Don Blankenship feared Warren was "unbeatable."[4] Blankenship determined, through his political action committee, to beat Warren McGraw even if it meant spending millions of his personal money.[5]

Twenty years earlier Warren, in one of his first interviews as Senate President, was asked about the growth of political action committees and whether he viewed them as a good or bad influence. His answer was prophetic of the 2004 election: "That depends upon which end of the barrel you look down. From my perspective, I perceive that the growth of political action committees in large corporate entities to be destructive to the public end, the public will. Large corporate entities tend only to have a primary concern about their own individual interests, as opposed to what the prevailing attitude might be in the community…So from my perspective, I see the corporate political action committees as being organizations who are primarily calculating to see that I don't hold office."[6]

The 2004 state Supreme Court election was a textbook example of utilizing national political strategist Karl Rove's mastermind tactics designed to shift state courts to the right. The tactics included assisting the Chamber of Commerce in identifying and then targeting progressive judges with negative ad campaigns. Rove's formula for electing pro-business judges was to demonize the sitting progressive judge as puppet of labor or the plaintiff's bar and then select a verdict by the judge designed to appeal to prejudice and outrage the voting public: "Rove brought to Alabama a formula, honed in Texas, for winning judicial races. It involved demonizing Democrats as pawns of the plaintiffs' bar and stoking populist resentment with tales of outrageous verdicts."[7]

Rove's formula was applied in West Virginia. First the WV Chamber supported the selection of pro-business candidates for the state Court—Jim Rowe, in the primary and Brent Benjamin in the general to run against Warren. Next, a case was selected to demonize the vote of the sitting progressive justice, Warren McGraw. The perfect case was located with the selection of *State v. Arbaugh,* through which Justice McGraw's majority vote was communicated to the public as resulting in the release of a rapist into the community.[8]

The Last Campaign DVD—A Film by Wayne Ewing

153

Wayne Ewing, producer of *If Elected*, returned to film the political miasma that enveloped Warren's campaign for reelection. The documentary film captured the angst, anxiety and disappointment of the brutal campaign.[9] For months, Wayne and his production crew followed Warren as he crisscrossed the state in his grassroots campaign efforts. The documentary called *The Last Campaign* was nominated in 2004 for "best documentary feature exposing the nastiest state Supreme Court race in history."

In the primary, Jim Rowe, a Democrat circuit judge from Greenbrier County, was backed by the Chamber, physicians, insurance companies, banks and big coal. The negative ads started in March with Rowe blaming Warren for the state's economic condition and lack of health care: "Folks don't take my word for it, ask your doctor, your insurance agent or your employer about the condition of our state and who's to blame" for rising insurance rates and unemployment related to decisions by the West Virginia Supreme Court."[10]

This effort to convince voters that Warren was "bad for your health; running doctors out of the state and costing money had legs. An increasing number of doctors, their patients and community began to fear the reelection of Warren. Time was on Warren's side in the primary with only a couple months of serious campaigning before the May primary, the McGraw name withstood the attacks. Warren and his immediate family were engaged in a grassroots campaign. Door to door, person to person, meeting upon meeting campaigning resulted in Warren winning the primary Democratic nomination for the state Court. Warren garnered 56% of the votes compared to Rowe's 44% of the vote.[11]

Warren's primary victory galvanized Don Blankenship's efforts for the general election. There was more time and opportunity to implement a heavily funded campaign. In conversation with Gregory Alan Thomas, a right wing political consultant who worked for WV Citizens Against Lawsuit Abuse (WVCALA), Blankenship committed to spending $1 million to defeat McGraw. Thomas presented a plan that cost $2 million, which Blankenship agreed to fund. In the end the cost was much more.[12]

Brent Benjamin, the Republican nominee, was a lawyer with Robinson & McElwee, a corporate defense firm that represents such

entities as American Electric and Power, Bank of America, Chesapeake
Energy, Marathon Petroleum and West Virginia Manufacturers
Association. Benjamin had no record of public service and never argued
a case before the state Supreme Court.[13]

Blankenship met with George Carenbauer, a lawyer with Steptoe
and Johnson, former Democrat party chair, and the longtime adversary of
the McGraw brothers. Carenbauer filed the legal action which ultimately
kept Warren from running for re-election in 2000. Carenbauer wanted to
help Blankenship succeed in his efforts to "get McGraw." Carenbauer
advised Blankenship that he needed to establish a 527 organization
through which Blankenship could spend whatever he wanted to attack
Warren. With Carenbauer's assistance a 527 was created. A 527 is an
entity created to "influence the selection, nomination, election,
appointment or defeat of candidates to federal, state or local public
office…There are no upper limits on contributions to a 527 and no
restrictions on who may contribute. There are no spending limits
imposed on these organizations."[14] It was a perfect vehicle for
Blankenship to surreptitiously achieve his purpose to defeat Warren.

Blankenship's 527 was strategically named "And for the Sake of
Kids." It was not about kids; its purpose was to deceive the voters; defeat
Warren McGraw and elect Blankenship's candidate, Brent Benjamin.
Perhaps Carenbauer realized that a heavily funded 527 focused on
defeating Warren would also negatively impact the other McGraw,
Darrell, who was running for re-election as Attorney General. It was a
twofer.

Blankenship's "And for the Sake of Kids" campaign exploited the
decision in *State v. Arbaugh* case to orchestrate a media campaign against
Warren. The Rove formula for getting a liberal judge was used: "Being
the street fighter that I am, I instructed my aides to find a decision that
would enrage the public."[15] When they returned with the *Arbaugh* case,
Mr. Blankenship said, "He knew he had hit pay dirt." A smiling
Blankenship added, "That killed him."[16] "The case [*Arbaugh*] allowed
Blankenship to develop one of the most vicious advertising campaigns in
any election in America. Those ads, on billboards and television sets
around the state, accused McGraw of being friendly to child molesters."[17]
The attack ads were designed to convince the public that Warren was

155

placing "rapists" in schools, but they also served to further persecute Tony Arbaugh who was working to recover from years of sexual abuse by his family and teacher:

Early one September morning Tony was walking downtown when he looked up and saw a billboard. There, 150 feet above the ground, was his mug shot and these words, visible a block away: 'Judge Warren McGraw let this child rapist out.' He wished he could get up there and take it down, but of course he could not...But soon, above the highway, he saw another billboard, with another mug shot, and another accusation of child rapist. As he looked up, he knew that his rehabilitation and any attempt at a decent life was ruined.

...Whenever he walked down the street, mothers grabbed their children and hustled them inside...Whenever he went to Alcoholics Anonymous, people left the meeting. Wherever he went, police officers watched him.—Leamer [18]

It wasn't just Blankenship's ads that were negative. Benjamin's ads left the impression that Warren sexually molested multiple children: "In West Virginia, an ad by challenger Brent Benjamin opened with a narrator saying: 'According to the prosecutors, he sexually molested multiple West Virginia children.' Until halfway through the ad, the impression is given that the sex offender and Benjamin's opponent, Justice Warren McGraw, are the same person."[19]

Warren was visibly upset by ads asserting he harmed children. It was character assassination, and it was most painful for the entire family: "I'm just a West Virginia country lawyer running for office. They say our court set a child molester loose in our schools. It's absolutely untrue. I'm embarrassed to go out in public. They've absolutely destroyed me."

Blankenship, in some perverted way, seemed to find amusement in the impact of the negative ads: "Mr. Blankenship cheerfully conceded that his real objection was to Justice McGraw's rulings against corporate defendants."[20]

Dark money, filtered from the U.S. Chamber of Commerce to the WV Chamber of Commerce, bought ads asserting that Warren was bad for business; driving doctors out of West Virginia, and losing jobs for thousands of West Virginians. The Medical Association propaganda, provided by Medical Assurance, the Alabama based insurance company,

156

was now seen in ads. It was an uphill battle to convince the public that Warren wasn't driving doctors out of state and jeopardizing health care for their families. Warren's financial resources were insufficient to counter the money spent from outside interest groups, including the national Chamber of Commerce, and Don Blankenship.

The *Last Campaign* captures Warren's daughter Rebecca, a doctor, trying to refute an angry doctor who tells her, "Doctors are leaving because McGraw has made it easier for doctors to be sued."[21] Rebecca lists facts that contradict the doctor's assertion. Her attempt is futile. The doctor, like so many doctors and their patients, believe the propaganda fostered in the ads, "Warren McGraw good for lawsuits; bad for our health."

The documentary films Warren on the air with Hoppy Kercheval, host of a radio show on a regressive station. Hoppy confronts Warren with what is now a most familiar mantra, "Your decisions are hurting doctors, and they are leaving the State." Warren, in an increasingly futile attempt tries to counter, "No one wants to hear the facts from the General Accounting Office and the WV Medical Licensure Board that the number of medical malpractice claims are actually down and the number of doctors in West Virginia has increased."

The Medical Association and Medical Assurance Insurance Company propaganda was effective in convincing doctors and the general public that Warren was "bad for their health." Doctors, through Doctors for Justice, contributed $745,000 to Blankenship's And for the Sake of Kids (ASAK) war chest.[22] ASAK spent $3.6 million, nearly $2.5 million contributed by Blankenship, against Warren.[23] Blankenship "spent another $517,707 in direct support of the Benjamin's campaign, mostly through payments to media outlets for television ads.[24] The Chamber funded $648,840 ads in support of Benjamin.[25]

"A West Virginia judicial campaign considered one of the nastiest in the nation ended with the defeat of a justice targeted by mining executives, business interests and physicians groups. Warren McGraw, a Democrat who spent five terms in the state legislature before joining the Court in 1998, lost to Republican Brent Benjamin, a Charleston lawyer and political newcomer with 20 years in private practice, much of it defending corporate clients. Benjamin received 53 percent of the votes, about 47,000 more than McGraw, who received 47 percent."[26] The national Chamber claimed "victory in 12 of the 13 state high court races that it targeted" which included West Virginia. [27]

Beth White with West Virginia Consumers for Justice, a labor and consumer coalition described Warren's defeat, ""It proves that West Virginia Supreme Court seats were for sale."[28]
US Supreme Court Justice Sandra Day O'Conner opined, "We put cash in the courtrooms, and it's just wrong. The perception that money is corrupting the courts would be damaging enough. But often, it seems special interests are finding that buying up judges likely to side with them in big-dollar cases is a good investment."[29]

Political scientist Richard Brisbin called the election "a threat to justice and democracy lurking in in the contemporary judicial section process... the nationalization of state judicial elections to elect judges who will actively shape legal rules to the benefit of corporate interests."[30] Brisbin cited the impotency of the organized bar [the State Bar Association, an agency of the state Supreme Court] to deal with the "nasty" big money campaigns that work against the selection of judges who satisfy the "ideal of a neutral and dispassionate magistrate."[31] This intentional effort to elect a justice for the benefit of corporations backed by abundant dark money overwhelmed the McGraw's grassroots campaign strategy:

"He thought he could get his message across if only he met enough people, shook enough hands, spoke on enough local radio talk shows and was interviewed by enough local reporters and editors."[32]

Blankenship's $50 million dollar lawsuit, *Caperton v. Massey,* was decided by a newly constituted Court. The new justice, Brent Benjamin refused to disqualify himself and cast the deciding vote in a 3-2 decision that reversed the $50 million dollar verdict against Massey.[33]

The West Virginia Supreme Court election of 2004 was documented extensively. Lawrence Leamer's *The Price of Justice* revealed CEO Don Blankenship's efforts to defeat Justice Warren McGraw and elect his own justice in order to overturn a $50 million dollar verdict against A. T. Massey. Wayne Ewing's *The Last Campaign* documents "one man's long journey fighting the corporate takeover of American politics." The election became a real life reflection within

Grisham's novel *The Appeal*. When Grisham was interviewed by Matt Lauer on the Today Show, Lauer "suggested that this particular story might seem a bit farfetched." Grisham replied, "It's already happened. It happened a few years ago in West Virginia."[34] Grisham's book was fictional but sale of justice was for real in the 2004 WV Supreme Court election:

> *Mr. Grisham may have written his latest book, The Appeal, on the sale of justice, but the fierce nature of judicial elections should give all of us pause to wonder whether – or how often – justice merely goes to the highest bidder. His descriptions of high-spending judicial campaigns are rooted in fact. The real-life analogy to Grisham's book: ...West Virginia. There, in 2002, Massey Energy, the largest coal producer in Appalachia, lost a $50 million verdict in the local courts. As in Grisham's fiction, the five-member Supreme Court of Appeals of West Virginia was severely divided. And before Massey's appeal reached the state's highest court, the 2004 judicial election would pit a 'liberal' incumbent against an unknown corporate lawyer who had never argued a case before the court.[35]*

The 2004 election and the resulting *Caperton v. Massey* decision are illustrative of "defining an issue that remains one of the most crucial concerns of American public life;" that is, the buying of justice in America.[36]

Returning Home—Present Day Service Continues

As a Supreme Court Justice, Warren McGraw interpreted the law to benefit its intended beneficiaries—the people. His opinions sought to render justice for disenfranchised, abused and neglected; protect individuals exposed to toxins; provide adequate compensation for injured workers and guard the workers' right to safe working conditions and fair and equal opportunities for employment. Warren was disappointed to end his service on the Court.

After his defeat, Warren returned to Pineville where he was elected and still serves as Wyoming County circuit judge, fulfilling a lifelong dream. Warren wakes up every day driven to continue his life mission of serving the people of West Virginia and living by the words his mother often spoke said to him, "of one blood are all people."

Peggy and Warren with kids and grandkids and Jorea and Darrell (far right)

Chapter IX   "The Dark Lord of Coal"

Deborah K. May v. Mate Creek Security
How one treats the least of us speaks to the value one places on all of us.

On May 4, 2001, a Massey affiliate, Mate Creek Security, hired Deborah May as a maid to clean Don Blankenship's house. She worked eight hour days as a maid and personal assistant to Blankenship. After her first year of work, she was given a thirty-cent pay raise to $8.86 an hour. This was her last pay raise during the course of her employment there. In 2002 Blankenship assigned her work cleaning cabins in Kentucky in addition to cleaning the primary house. She was assigned routine housekeeping tasks at these cabins such as cleaning and doing laundry for Blankenship and the guests he entertained, largely other executives. It was reported that at one such executive dinner party, Blankenship showed off the fine china at his mountaintop mansion. After going on about the fine tableware, he enjoyed his meal off of it. The dinner guests' meals, however, were served on paper plates, and they were given plastic cutlery to eat with.[1]

Because of the additional work and the driving to the various houses and cabins, Deborah May asked for a raise in July 2003. Blankenship denied the raise. Then, in 2004, Blankenship instructed her to clean the coach bus he owned every week and make sure it was stocked with food and beverages as he specified. She was now working 70 hours a week, cleaning four houses and a coach bus. He was paying her $8.86 per hour. In addition to the high workload, he had taken to throwing "fits" over the wrong ice cream in the freezer or the wrong McDonald's breakfast sandwich. After she brought him a McDonald's breakfast sandwich that included bacon he hadn't ordered, he allegedly "flung" the bacon from the sandwich. When she forgot to get ice cream, he made her write a letter explaining her actions.[2] When he saw stains on his carpet, she said he told her, "What I ought to do is take you out and stone you to death."[3] This comment was similar to his sharp tongue towards mine supervisors when urging them to run more coal and cut more costs. He threatened one mine president by saying, "I could Khrushchev you. Do you understand?"[4]

Deborah May repeatedly asked for pay raises during the course of her employment. The court record stated her goal as of her last request was "to get a pay raise and to get medical insurance for my daughter." She had been to the Welfare office to try to get medical insurance for her daughter, but the Welfare office told her she made too much money, $144.00 per month too much. She finally quit on November 18, 2005 when Blankenship bought a German police attack dog and expected her to take care of that, too. Her pay remained at $8.86 per hour.[5]

When she submitted her 2 weeks' notice, she said the company asked her what it would take to keep her from quitting. She told them it would take a wage of $12.00 per hour, a company vehicle, and medical insurance for her children. The company never answered her. Ms. May applied for unemployment and was denied. In 2008 May appealed this decision, and the matter reached the WV Supreme Court. In conference, Justices Maynard and Davis offered they would support unemployment compensation for the maid if records of Blankenship's unkind conduct were not included in the text of the majority opinion. In perhaps a calculated maneuver, Justices Starcher and Albright agreed with their request but later negated their agreement and wrote a concurring opinion exposing Blankenship's behaviors.[6] One plaintiff's attorney represented Ms. May. Three corporate attorneys represented the Massey affiliate.[7]— *Contributed by Rebecca McGraw Thaxton*

Upper Big Branch Disaster

"At approximately 3:02 p.m. on Monday, April 5, 2010, a powerful explosion tore through Massey-owned Upper Big Branch mines, killing twenty-nine miners as the enormously powerful blast rocketed through two and one-half miles of underground workings nearly 1,000 feet beneath the surface of the rugged mountains along the Coal River."[8]

After the disaster, Don Blankenship testified before a Congressional committee that "Massey does not place profits over safety. We never have and never will."[9] An independent investigative team, led by longtime safety advocate Davitt McAteer, disagreed with Blankenship and "placed the blame squarely on Massey Energy." The team concluded "that a corporate culture that put coal production before safety allowed serious violations of basic safety practices to become common and accepted at Upper Big Branch."[10]

In the "Massey Way" section of the investigative report Massey, led by Blankenship since 1992, was described as creating a long standing culture based on the *Massey Doctrine,* uncovered years before by investigative reporter, Paul Nyden. The report described this Massey culture as "causing incalculable damage to mountains, streams, and air in the coalfields; creating health risks for coalfield residents by polluting streams, injecting slurry into the ground and failing to control coal waste dams and dust emissions from processing plants; using vast amounts of money to influence the political system, and battling government regulation regarding safety in the coalmines and environmental safeguards for the communities."[11]

On that April day in 2010, miners Jason Stanley and David Farley, who were part of the "pump crew," reached the mine earlier in the day and realized there wasn't much air flowing underground. Over the weekend the pumps had broken down deep inside the mine, and the pump crew spent the day wading in waste deep water to try and get the pumps to work. Water build up in the tunnels between the mine's working section and its main ventilation fan meant that crucial airflow was greatly reduced.[12] Massey did not keep the miners from going underground.

Leo Long testifying before a Congressional hearing expressed the grief surrounding the men who died at Upper Big Branch, "It just tore us apart, broke our hearts. I cry every day and every night. I can't help it."[13]

In 2016, six years after the deadly incident, Blankenship was sentenced to a year in prison.[14] Don Blankenship's conviction on safety mine violations was of little comfort to family members. Their husbands, sons, and friends were never coming back. Blankenship, however, was released from prison in May 2017.

Don Blankenship escorted by Homeland Security officers after being sentenced.
Federal Courthouse, Charleston, WV—*F. Brian Ferguson, Gazette-Mail*, April 6, 2016

While behind bars Blankenship orchestrated the mailing of 250,000 pamphlets proclaiming his innocence. In the 67-page booklet, he bragged about his efforts to unseat Warren McGraw: "West Virginia Supreme Court Justice Warren McGraw was my first target because he was an activist anti-business Judge. There was a movie made about his first campaign for State Senate called *If Elected* and *Forbes* magazine had put him on their cover with the accompanying story headlined, 'Buying Justice'. McGraw came from a prominent political family—his brother Darrell had previously been on the State Supreme Court before becoming Attorney General—and he (Warren) was considered politically unbeatable. The first survey I had taken showed Warren leading his opponent, Brent Benjamin, by 50 percentage points (63-13) with the rest undecided. It shocked the West Virginia political establishment that the campaign I funded to defeat McGraw was so successful."[15]

Chapter X Darrell McGraw Begins His Journey

Berea Academy and the Army

As Darrell, Jr. grew into adolescence, a rebellious streak began to show. After a disagreement at school with his music teacher, young Darrell was given a "new opportunity" by his father. Darrell Sr. ordered his eldest son into his car late that evening and drove towards his alma mater in Madison County, Kentucky where early the next morning Darrell Jr. enrolled in Berea Academy, the College's preparatory Foundation school. Berea proved to be a life-altering experience. After just one year at Academy, Darrell returned home a focused young man with a renewed sense of duty and respect.

Thirty-two years later, Darrell, Jr. again made the trip to Berea. But this time he came with both parents to receive one of Berea's highest honors, the Berea Service Award, given to "individuals who rendered outstanding service to our society in achieving the ideals of Berea College's Great Commitments: Christ, liberal education, inter-racial brotherhood, Appalachian service and the dignity of work."[1]

His parents, who were the first of their generation to graduate college, were beaming as Darrell walked across the stage at Phelps Stokes Chapel. Berea, a school so important to his parents, was honoring their son for living a life of service to others. The celebration luncheon occurred in the school's dining hall where the young Julia and Darrell worked helping to prepare meals, clear tables and wash dishes—fulfilling their requirements of service in exchange for an educational opportunity that changed their lives. It was an amazing day.

Immediately after high school graduation in 1954, Darrell set off with his friend Jerry Wells hitch hiking to Florida with the fantasy of catching a fishing boat to Cuba. It was still Batista's Cuba where Hemingway, awarded the *Pulitzer Prize* for *The Old Man and the Sea,* wrote the story about an old Cuban fisherman who struggled to catch a big fish and bring it back to shore through shark invested waters. Darrell had read the book and was intrigued by the fisherman's perseverance and perhaps a premonition it might prepare him for his own shark infested waters. But more probably, the boys were taken with the stories of

Havana being the "mistress of pleasure, the lush and opulent goddess of delights."[2]

The plans included a stop along the way at the Briggs Cunningham sport car factory to see an American made sports car, the Cunningham. Darrell remains fascinated with cars and still takes a Sunday afternoon ride to car lots looking at "what's on offer," as he calls it. Longtime friend and car dealer David Saul, tells sales persons as Darrell pulls into his car lot, "don't get excited that's the Judge, and he's not going to buy anything—unless we are giving it away, and then he won't take it." Darrell's frugal ways were well known to family and friends. Co-workers later told of the "Judge" washing out Styrofoam cups to re-use in the office which prompted staff to come to meetings with their own cup in hand.

Darrell and Jerry had enough money to rent a room in Miami for a few days while they searched for a fishing boat. Failing in their effort and without funds to stay longer, the young men started hitch hiking back home. On their trip south the boys avoided capture by police for hitchhiking, which was illegal in many communities. But their luck ran out on their way north, when in Ft. Lauderdale, Florida the boys found themselves escorted to the local police station.
Out of money, Darrell called his father. "Daddy," as Darrell started to talk his father interrupted, "Son, Are you in jail yet?" Darrell answered, "No, But I am going to be if you don't send us money to get a bus ticket." The money arrived through Western Union, and the police took the adventurers to the bus station.

Thinking they could outfox the police, the boys bought a ticket to Melbourne, Florida with plans to save part of the money and hitch hike the rest of the way home. It was not a well thought out plan. The police met the young men in Melbourne and stood right next to them as they purchased two one way tickets to Bluefield, West Virginia. Darrell and Jerry, chagrined with their lack of success on many fronts, relented and stayed on the bus except for a change in Waycross, Georgia. It was at the bus change that Darrell and Jerry encountered the hurt of racism in the eyes of its victims

Growing up in Wyoming County everything was separate but not equal. The McGraw brothers' parents talked to the brothers about how bad racism was and later family members became active in the civil right movements. The African American families lived mainly in more remote Wyoming County communities like Wyco, McDonald Farm, Glen Rogers and Marianna and in the Goose Hollow section of Mullens. Black children attended Conley, the black school for the county. Mrs. Prince and a few other older black families lived in Pineville. On special occasions Mrs. Prince ironed clothes for the family. The brothers sometimes talked to Mrs. Prince as she fished under the bridge. Just like when she ironed, Mrs. Prince never talked much. She just cast her fishing line into the Guyandotte River, grey from coal mine drainage, and hoped for a fish. She had a great sadness about her that Darrell came to better understand that day in Waycross, Georgia.

Jerry and Darrell, tired from the trip, sauntered onto the bus and spotted the long empty seat that traversed the back. They saw the signs on the bathroom doors as they traveled—white only, but were naively unaware of racist bus rules as they made a dash for the seat. As they reclined their selves across the length of the seat with their eyes almost closed, the silhouette of the bus driver was reflected in the window, but he was in the aisle. They heard the bus driver's voice saying to a young man and his wife, "You all have to move to the back of the bus so these young white gentlemen can have your seat." Darrell whispered to Jerry, "What are we going to do?" The young couple stood up and gazed back at the boys. Darrell and Jerry, alert now, jumped up but not knowing what to do. The boys apologized to the couple. The young African American man replied, "It's not your fault." The bus driver added, "It's the law." Darrell thought to himself that it was his fault. He would not be so submissive in the future.

Darrell, Jr in the Army, Weisbaden, Germany

Darrell was expected to go to West Virginia University in the fall, but his trip to Florida made him think about his dependency on his family for money. For a young man eager for independence, it was not an appealing thought. In the 50's young men were subject to a compulsory obligation of eight years in the military, and Darrell contemplated how the GI bill might provide a path toward independence and needed finances for college. Darrell told his Daddy that he was thinking about joining the Army. His Dad was fairly non-committal when he replied, "that might be worthwhile" which was just enough encouragement for Darrell to conclude the Army was the right next step. Darrell and Julia resisted signing their permission for an underage volunteer, but they relented when it was apparent their son had made up his mind.

On his way to enlistment, Darrell passed by a classmate's house. Arnold Carl Ellison, already accepted in the Core of Cadets at Virginia Polytechnic Institute, yelled at Darrell, "Where are you going?" Darrell replied, "I'm going to join the Army." Arnold Carl said, "Wait a minute I'll tell my Mom, I'm going with you." 'Ellie', as most called him, must have been longing for independence because after one short exchange greeting, the Army was about to have two new volunteers.

Darrell and Julia, not particularly pleased with Darrell's decision to join the Army, were clearly dismayed that Ellie went along with him, as was Arnold's mother. Julia, in the many letters she wrote to her son during his service, always asked about Ellie hoping to learn something to soften his mother's dismay. Ellie's mother remained inconsolable. For their years in the service Ellie teased Darrell, "Mom wants you to come to eat when we get home—she has a special treat planned just for you."

Darrell turned out to be a gung-ho soldier and was ordered to Army Leadership School where he became an honor graduate. To this day he questions his decision not to stay in the Army and opines that had he stayed, he could have become a general. Darrell spent much of his service in Wiesbaden, Germany, where he was with the 4th Chemical Company, Seventh Army—a time he regarded as life enhancing. Darrell describes his chemical training thusly: "[we] learned how to 'smoke'em' but the mission also included, along with the related artillery "Atomic Annie" battalion, the ability to 'poison'em, infect'em or fry'em'—an idea he said was as ghastly as it sounds. His time in Germany saw a change in the United State military strategy in Europe. One night in early May, 1955, the soldiers were awakened and ordered to fall out in formation. Darrell still delights in telling others that they assembled as the *Army of Occupation* and when the clock reached midnight the company commander advised the troops they were now the *Ambassadors of Goodwill* in the U.S. Army.

West Virginia University—Bringing the Mast Home

Following his first years of duty in the Army, Darrell enrolled at West Virginia University on the G.I. Bill. During undergraduate school at WVU, he held a fulltime job as a manager at the Faculty Club, married, became a father and at the same time engaged in a multitude of student activities and scholarship.

In 1959 WVU's Dean of Men Rev. Joe Gluck, a former World War II Navy Chaplain, learned that the *U.S. West Virginia* was to be dismantled for salvage. Rev. Gluck brought the issue before interested student groups and raised the possibility of securing a part of the *West Virginia*, perhaps the mast, as tribute to veterans. At Gluck's recommendation, Student Body President Jack Bowman assigned the project to Darrell who was president of the WVU Veterans Club. The Veterans Club contributed the first funds necessary to move the mast.

The mast project was controversial with some of the faculty and students. They objected to bringing a symbol of war to campus. Herb Rogers, who later graduated Harvard Law School, was an active dissenter against the mast. The mast was transported by rail to Columbus, Ohio and then the Hume Trucking Company carried the mast through Huntington and on to the State Capitol in Charleston where the Governor and other officials acknowledged the importance of bringing the mast home. Then traveling north through various county seats, residents were able to pay respect to veterans who served under the flag the mast had held. When the mast arrived in Morgantown, picketers were waiting. Herb Rogers held a sign which read, "Let this mast stand as an eternal monument to the folly of man."

Darrell's leadership skills were recognized when he was elected Student Body President. It was Darrell's first time to organize a campaign. One of the smartest girls on campus, Sarah Brawley (Stebbins), a math major, was his vice presidential running mate. They ran on a 10 point platform which included equal rights for graduate students and greater student engagement in WVU government decisions.

The mast remains at WVU as a tribute to West Virginia veterans, who in significant and disproportionate numbers, answered the call to fight in every war. Young men in West Virginia, notwithstanding their cultural patriotism, perhaps internalize the paradox of their state's rich resources and the poverty of its people, know that military service offers an escape from the lack of good job opportunities or a destiny of working in the mines. Every year on Pearl Harbor Day a celebration honoring veterans is held at the Mast. For many years, Darrell attended the celebration, missing only two when a couple feet of snow made highway travel impossible and the day his son was born.

Darrell and Pearl Harbor Day at the Mast

After graduation Darrell entered West Virginia University College of Law where his outspoken defense of freedom of thought as an undergraduate left him at odds with a law professor. In undergraduate school Darrell served on the publication committee charged with the responsibility of selecting editors of the school's newspaper, *The Daily Athenaeum*. The committee consisted of journalism and law school professors and Darrell. The journalism school nominated qualified candidates for consideration, one of whom was an activist type whose writings were described as progressive. During the interview process a law professor "bored in" with a multitude of questions for the liberally inclined student. The frustrated applicant replied, "I don't understand your questions, professor." To which Darrell, most impertinently offered, "The professor is asking if you now or ever have been a communist." The student became the editor, and the law professor did not forget Darrell's McCarthy era cryptic remark. The result was Darrell needed to find a way to avoid the professor's course during law school.

So in the summer of 1963, a year before the Civil Rights Act passed ending segregation in public places and banning employment discrimination, Darrell, along with other WVU law school students, enrolled in courses at Washington and Lee. The Washington and Lee community, still enamored by Robert E. Lee who was buried at Lee Chapel next to the law school and Stonewall Jackson interred in the middle of Lexington, was a very "southern" place. The students lived at the Dutch Inn, a lodging house close to the law school and generally ate at the HedgePeth Restaurant but on occasion drove to a cafeteria at the Natural Bridge, a few miles down the road. Everyone liked their fried chicken. Hungry and in line, Darrell heard the cashier say to a black couple and their daughter who were in front of him, "Sorry we don't serve colored people here." Startled, Darrell turned to his friends and said, "Did you hear that?" Nodding agreement but standing still and quiet the boys listened as Darrell apologized to the couple and doubled down on the cashier, "I'm embarrassed that you would say that to another American. I'm embarrassed for my country. I refuse to eat here." Darrell following the black family out the door, turned to see his fellow students still standing in line to which he said, "I won't eat here and if you have a "hair on your ass"—a southern colloquialism from Pineville connoting sensitivity to resist injustice—you won't eat here." Standing up for what is right can leave you hungry and alone, but he did and he would.

In 1964Darrell fulfilled his promise to his father to become a lawyer.

Governor Hulett Smith—State Government

It was his last year of law school when Darrell found an application, posted on the bulletin board in Woodburn Hall, for a fellowship to study state government. The fellowship, through the National Center for Education in Politics at NYU Graduate School, was exactly right for Darrell. He applied. Hearing no response Darrell accepted a job with the Foreign Claims Settlement Commission at the State Department in Washington, D.C. The job involved the analysis and approval of meritorious claims from victims and heirs of victims of the Holocaust. The work was serious and emotionally stressful. While working at the Commission, Darrell received an unexpected call from the Dr. Bernard Hennesy, director of the NYU Center, who asked him to go to lunch and talk about his work and goals for the future. They talked about McGraws, "big coal," strip mining, poverty, jobs, educational opportunity, health care and Darrell's desire to make things better for West Virginians. After a long meal and good conversation, the director offered Darrell a Ford Foundation funded fellowship to study the operation of the executive branch of state governments' effectiveness in addressing public policy issues. As hoped, Darrell was assigned to the Governor's office in West Virginia where his hard work and enthusiasm as a Ford fellow ultimately earned him an offer of a full time position with Governor Hulett Smith.

In 1965 Darrell made his entre into state government as intern counsel to the Governor. It was here that he gained familiarity with major players in West Virginia politics and was viewed as successful in the administration: "It now appears certain that one of the brightest young faces in State Government in the 1960's is going to run for Congress. Darrell McGraw … is preparing to run against John Slack."[3]

The mid 60's was an awesome time to be in state government. President Johnson announced his commitment to an unconditional "War on Poverty," and West Virginia was a major beneficiary. There were abundant opportunities for the young legal counsel to assist the administration in implementing the maze of new federal programs including the Social Security Amendment which created Medicare and Medicaid; the Food Stamp Act which made the food stamp program permanent; the Economic Opportunity Act which created Job Corps, VISTA, Head Start and the Elementary and Secondary Education Act which established Title I. Those involved in government during the 60s gained an appreciation of the importance of federal dollars in improving the lives of children and adults throughout West Virginia. The War on Poverty took Darrell to D.C. on many occasions where he met with government officials and on one occasion with President Johnson in the White House. It was quite an honor to meet President Johnson.[4] He heard his grandfather's voice as he shook the President's hand, "Good work my son, good work."

173

Darrell V. McGraw, Jr., & President Lyndon B. Johnson, 1966

While in Governor Smith's office, Darrell met Don Marsh, a young state house reporter. Marsh and Darrell became lifelong friends, committed to make life better for the West Virginia they both loved. They were reserved people whose friendship was not that of lunch time buddies, but one based on mutual understanding and respect. Marsh was dedicated to exposing arrogance, corruption and hypocrisy, and he had gift for utilizing the right words to reach out and capture the reader to his point of view. Don was a bright articulate fellow, a WVU graduate and a child of a coal mining community in Logan County. They had similar points of views and attitudes and perhaps connected by their common types of origins. They were young professional men together. Marsh was a World War II veteran, older than Darrell, but his magnetism of intellect was compelling. They called each other by their last names and agreed that democracy was negatively impacted by elected officials who were poorly informed and lacked dedication to the common good. Marsh, who later 'became the editor of the *Charleston Gazette,* never gave up on a duty to portray things as they were and at the same time point out how they should be. It was a contradiction that was not relished by those described as disciples of the status quo or those who had much to profit from maintaining it.

Ned Chilton, owner and publisher of the *Charleston Gazette* for twenty-five years, gave encouragement to Marsh and other reporters to do their job no matter who it impacted. Chilton, a man to the manor born, a Yale graduate, with an incredible conscious, fully utilized Marsh's clever and succinct writing in ardent examination of "basic injustices and fundamental idiocies." Chilton developed a journalism philosophy that he called "sustained outrage," and Marsh, as well as fellow journalist, and later editor, James Haught were masters in its pursuit.[5]

Darrell admired President Lyndon Johnson's conviction to institute a focused program to end poverty in this country. Unable to eliminate poverty, but making gargantuan progress, Johnson had his share of critics. Darrell liked to paraphrase the President when he faced the unrelenting criticism from the *Charleston Daily Mail*: "If one morning I walked on top of the water across the Kanawha River, the headline that afternoon would read: "McGraw Can't Swim."[6]

While at WVU, Darrell married Marie Tyler, later a PhD and noted historian, author and distinguished professor and associate at the Valentine Museum in Richmond, Virginia. Darrell and Marie had two children, Julia Elizabeth, born in 1960, and Sarah Ruth, born in 1967. After eleven years of marriage they were divorced. It was a long lasting tough time for all.

During his time in the Governor's office, Darrell was asked by Chief Counsel to the Governor, Julius Singleton, of his interest in becoming the President of the WV Coal Association. Singleton, former Speaker of the House and one-time candidate for governor, was familiar with board of directors and knew they were interested in Darrell becoming their President. Darrell declined consideration. Upon reflection a McGraw brother, President of the Coal Association was a startling possibility.

Service to Governor Smith provided an in-depth knowledge of the inner workings of Democratic politics and state government that proved useful in the McGraw brothers' journey. Governor Smith was always good to Darrell, even tolerating some of Darrell's more contentious foibles and actions. When he first came to the Governor's office Darrell supported Ken Hechler in his 1966 re-election bid for Congress which engendered ill-will with the Democratic brass. Hechler was a people's congressman, and the Democratic establishment supported another candidate. Again, in 1968 Darrell found himself, an ardent, but albeit necessarily quiet supporter of Jim Sprouse for Governor when the establishment was for Don Robertson. Darrell left the Governor's office, several months prior to the end of Smith's term. But his service and commitment was recognized:

"He is dedicated to sincerely doing something to lift the state's poor above their almost forgotten depression and adamant in rejecting the old brand of political shuffling. For one whose job was politics, McGraw surprisingly couldn't stand politicians—at least the garden variety that usually grows in WV. Politics as it's played by both Democrats and Republicans play upon his nerves, and often you can see him visibly wince."[7]—*Register Post Herald*

However, it was time to move on. Others thought he shouldn't be gone long: "If he remains lost to West Virginia government, West Virginians will be the worse for it."[8]

After his tenure in the Governor's office and a stint as a staff member at the WVU Bureau of Government Research in Morgantown, Darrell worked as a political consultant for Matt Reese Associates, a D.C. firm affiliated with the Kennedy campaigns. One of his assignments was the 1968 primary campaign of Thomas Eagleton. Eagleton was running for U.S. Senator from Missouri. Eagleton, former Missouri Lieutenant Governor and Attorney General, was successful in unseating the incumbent Sen. Edward V. Long and True Davis, achieving the Democratic nomination for U.S. Senator. Eagleton won the general election and went on to serve in the U. S. Senate from 1968 to 1987.

In 1972 Senator Eagleton was selected as a vice presidential candidate. Darrell was well aware there might be issues. In the last hour of the Democratic convention George McGovern tapped Eagleton to be his running mate with little to no vetting of his personal record. Eighteen days after joining the Democratic ticket for President, Eagleton withdrew when it was discovered he was hospitalized three times for depression, in two of which he received electric shock therapy. In a time that pre-dated an understanding that depression could be effectively treated, Eagleton had little choice but to resign.[9]

As a political consultant Darrell worked as a grassroots organizer in campaigns in North Carolina, Indiana, Missouri, Rhode Island and Florida. With Matt Reese, Darrell honed many of the valuable skills put to use as he managed his own and Warren's early elections. Darrell's involvement with Matt Reese Associates was interspersed with periods of

working as counsel for the West Virginia Legislature and opening a
private law practice in Charleston, West Virginia.

A Life Together—Jorea and Darrell

Jorea and Darrell, March, 1972

It was during the 1972 Legislative session that I met Darrell. I
was 23 years old and a teacher at Kanawha City Elementary in
Charleston, W.V. After a Saturday morning shopping at the Diamond
Department Store, a long time landmark that succumbed to closure after
the Town Center Mall opened, I walked across the street to the Daniel
Boone Restaurant to eat lunch. It was noon and the restaurant was
packed with shoppers, businessmen, legislators and staff. As fate would
have it, my life changed when the hostess escorted me to a table where
four suited men, just finishing their lunch, were getting ready to leave.
Darrell and Warren were lunching with Leon Copeland and Robert
Nelson, all on break from work at the Legislature. Robert and Warren
were elected members in the House of Delegates, and Darrell and Leon
were legal counselors. The men, nice looking but older, introduced
themselves and stood to leave as each searched for their package of
cigarettes, the natural conclusion to any 70's business lunch. A few
minutes later, the rushed hostess returned to the table, smiled, winked and
told me, "You have a phone call at the receptionist desk."

"Hi, this is Darrell McGraw; we just met at lunch. I would like to take you to dinner tonight," a rather confident Darrell asked. I was unsure which one of the four distinguished men were speaking but hoped it was the nice looking man with specks of gray hair streaking through his dark hair. I accepted the invitation and was most pleased when I opened the door that evening. This chance encounter resulted in finding the love of my life and a marriage that has lasted for over 40 years.

Darrell's wonderful Aunt Jackie once described his charisma: "Women have always been attracted to Darrell. He is handsome and has an incredible ability to relate to anyone he meets. He seems to always know something about the person, their family, where they live or the place they were born. People, definitely women, love it."[10]

Darrell's Aunt Jackie was married to Leon McGraw, the youngest of Darrell's father's siblings. This Uncle was very special to the brothers. About a decade older than the brothers, Leon was the star performer in Mr. Hollinger's machine shop department at the Wyoming County Vocational School. One of Leon's first impressive projects in the program was designing and building a model airplane engine which he brought home to fire up on the front porch at McGraws. All were impressed when the engine ran. Leon's siblings wanted him to go to engineering school, but he wanted to marry Jackie so he went to work at the Kopperston Coal mine from which he was drafted into the Korean War. As a soldier he became a supervisor in repair shops for Korean railroad locomotives. After his service, he worked for Union Carbide Corporation and quickly became nationally recognized by the company as an expert in valve design, maintenance and manufacturing—valves, pumps and seals were the life devices of the chemical industry. Leon was an inventor and a creator.

The McGraw brothers believed their Uncle was an expert in implementia of mid-20th century civilization devices—valves, pumps, seals, cars, farm trucks, tractors, motorcycles, engines—everything that fascinated his younger nephews. So, much to Jackie's chagrin, her basement garage contained the McGraw brothers' implementia—cars, motorcycles and a BMW kabinetteroller. Warren and Darrell were doubly blessed when they went to Leon's because it always included one

178

of Jackie's incredibly delicious meals. Leon was a rock for the brothers. He was always available for a solid opinion.

During our courtship and the early years of our marriage we spent many evenings enjoying Jackie's wonderful dinners. The evenings were usually filled with much political conversation. Warren's 1972 campaign for State senate as was Darrell's 1973 campaign for Congress monopolized evening discussions.

Often asked what I thought made Darrell so determined to right perceived injustices, I sometimes relate the story of the first time I met his mother Julia who had a significant influence on her sons' character. Darrell's parents were in town and wanted to take me out to dinner. Julia inquired, "Where would you like to go eat." I replied, "I don't care, wherever you would like." Julia, narrowing those Hungarian eyes even more and pointing her finger at me said, "Young lady, the hottest place in Hell is reserved for those who don't know or don't care." I thought her statement spoke volumes about the man who would share my life. We were married on March 6, 1977 and became life partners in all the elections and public service to come.

Congressional Race—Building A Progressive Brand

Darrell, Jr. Democrat for Congress 1974

In late summer of 1973 the Watergate hearings were underway and President Nixon just told the nation "he wasn't a crook." Darrell determined it was the right time to run for Congress in the 3rd congressional district. The incumbent John Slack, Jr. seemed to agree with Nixon for he "refused to join the hue and cry demanding the ousting of President Nixon during the months before Nixon's resignation in August, 1974."[11]

Slack was member of an old line Virginia political family with strong influence on early state history as well as modern day Kanawha County government and politics. Director at Kanawha Banking and Trust, building contractor, coal mine operator and partner in two highway pavement firms, Slack was a conservative Democrat on issues ranging from the environment to unions.[12] Jim Dent's caricature depicted Slack's conservative leanings: "You may not actually Be a Republican or a Southerner, John – but You VOTE like one of us!"[13]

"John Slack the Republican,"--*Jim Dent, Charleston Gazette,* 1974

The first candidate to announce his candidacy, Darrell needed time to build name recognition.[14] Pundits gave Darrell a fighting chance against the veteran Congressman Slack:

At first glance, Darrell McGraw's announced candidacy for the Democratic nomination to Congress in this district appears a rash thing, taking on veteran Congressman John M. Slack Jr. But take another look. Liberal Democrats have had the head on Slack for a long time but could not come up with a candidate with half a chance of knocking him off. They were encouraged last year when Congressman Ken Hechler...defeated James Kee...In that same election Darrell McGraw's brother, Warren, won a State senate seat from Tracy Hilton...With signs like that it had to follow that someone would think about tackling Slack...By getting his name in early, Darrell McGraw is waving off other liberal Democrats who could split the vote...[15]

Darrell also thought his early filing might prevent others from entering the race. It did not. Paul Kaufman, who served in the state Senate from 1960 to 1968 and supported legislation for human rights, health care, pollution control and repeal of capital punishment, also filed for Congress. Kaufman led the charge on the Senate side for the passage of black lung legislation. In 1968 Kaufman lost the Democratic nomination for governor against Jim Sprouse. Kaufman was the organizer and director of the Appalachian Research and Defense Fund, a regional public interest, consumer oriented law firm.[16]

Darrell and Kaufman's strong philosophical alignment left little room to build a different base of voter support. They had the same constituency and commitments to improve working conditions, environment, tax reform and human rights. Kaufman announced for Congress in January, 1974, almost five months after Darrell began his campaign. Darrell liked and respected Paul Kaufman and certainly did not want to run against him, but he was obliged to continue. Kaufman's entry split the progressive vote, each candidate making a statement from their very act of filing: "Kaufman rode a bicycle from his office at Broad Street and Kanawha Boulevard to the Capitol to emphasize the stress he is putting on ecology and the environment. McGraw, also of Charleston, mailed his certificate from Boone County to emphasize the importance he is placing on coal mining and its related problems."[17]

Coal miners, who were part of the reform movement, were unhappy with Slack because of his inaction on coal miner issues including black lung. Slack was pro strip mining and was said to have partial ownership in a strip mine at Stickney, West Virginia. Darrell represented miners on many occasions and was well aware of the work safety and health issues miners faced. Darrell, like Kaufman, worked with miners who were part of the Miners for Democracy, a reform group established in 1970 in opposition to the leadership of the controversial president Tony Boyle. Reformers claimed that Boyle was corrupt and too closely aligned with mine owner's interests. They were right. Boyle was eventually convicted and sentenced for embezzlement and the murder in the Yablonski killings.[18]

Paul Kaufman's entrance into the race split mine workers' support. Darrell and Kaufman were both friends with Arnold Miller,

President of the UMWA. Kaufman received the important UMWA endorsement, but many rank and file members supported Darrell. Some union members blamed Kaufman for Jim Sprouse's failed gubernatorial candidacy in 1968 when he was defeated by Arch Moore. Kaufman ran in the Democratic primary against Sprouse and lost. There was some thought that Kaufman, who was very popular in Kanawha County, was reluctant in his support for Sprouse during the general election.

Darrell, true to form, never relented in addressing the negative impact of strip mining. In late 1973 there was a flood that impacted homes in Lincoln, Boone and Kanawha counties. Darrell visited with many of the families in the flooded areas; surveyed the damage from the air and took pictures. He knew what caused the flooding, and it wasn't an "Act of God." Department of Natural Resources claimed there were no strip mines along the Mud River and that "strip mines actually helped alleviate flooding."[19] Pictures of the strip mine and coal scattered on the flooded property confirmed a need for stricter regulation of strip mining.

Debate with Bob Brunner center to his left John Slack, Jr., Darrell McGraw & Paul Kaufman

An ABC-TV documentary on the coal industry in West Virginia aligned with the need for more strip mine regulations: "20 months after the Buffalo Creek disaster there are still numerous (gob pile) dams that could fail and kill again."[20] But Big Coal didn't buy it. Steve Young, president of the WV Coal Association and active in discounting the effects of black lung and opposition of black lung bills, had a different message for the public when he called the ABC program "dishonest in documentation."[21] Steve Young and Darrell were law school friends. Young, a handsome, ambitious fellow served in the service as a Navy seal. Both believed coal was an important part of West Virginia's economy. Even in law school, Young was a proponent of the coal industry. Darrell liked to tease Steve that Wyoming Co had real coal mines unlike the small mines where Young grew up in Upshur County. They were bright men whose careers took a different direction. After serving as president of the WV Coal Association, Young became an executive with Consol.

Warren's view on the film was different than Young's, "I think probably the most important thing that I observed in the film is the fact that we in West Virginia have been subjected to a great deal of abuse by an industry that is apparently controlled from outside the state."[22]

Darrell wanted to bring attention to the inadequate taxation of coal resources. He sent a request to Sen. Edmund Muskie asking that his Intergovernmental Relations Subcommittee hearing on taxation of coal lands in Appalachia be held in WV: "West Virginians are increasing concerned about taxation of coal feeling that large out-of-state land-holding corporations do not pay their fair share of tax and that county educational systems suffer as a result."[23] Sen. Muskie responded that at some point a panel would be invited to appear before the Committee but that never materialized.

The *Gazette* invited the candidates to develop a written response to the question, "Why I Should Be the Congressman?" Darrell's response was entitled "Tax Laws Give Rich the Benefit." Darrell noted that "the economic development of our natural resources in West Virginia has almost been entirely for the benefit of people who live outside the state. These people have not been concerned with our mutilated mountains and ravaged forest, our acid laden streams, our volcanic slate dumps and with the very air we breathe which has become a menace to health."[24] Darrell pledged to support efforts to reform the taxation of our resources; establish a national consumer protection agency; ban strip mining, institute stricter regulation of pollution emitted by manufacturing companies in the valley; invest more in quality education for all children including federal aid to supplement teacher salaries and school building programs; establish a national health insurance program; enhance social security benefits to cover cost of living increases and secure federal aid

183

for secondary roads. Darrell's campaign platform was reflective of doing what he believed was the culturally right action for all the community.

Darrell McGraw, Jr. candidate for 3rd Congressional District, *Charleston Gazette,* May 9, 1974

UPI writer Andy Gallagher accompanied Darrell as he traveled to coal mines, stores and schools. Gallagher documented Darrell's grass roots efforts reminiscent of Warren's 1972 state Senate campaign:

The miners in the lamp room reacted slowly. One man would peer at Darrell McGraw, blink once or twice and say: 'I've heard of you. You're runnin for Congress.'

After the initial break in, McGraw was greeted warmly by the men at Armco Steel Corporation's No 8 mine at Twilight, Boone County. He had arrived at the mine at 7 a.m. – two hours after his campaign hit the trail from Charleston – and just as the men were loading into the metal-covered, orange man-trip vehicle to take them underground.

If you're a Democrat, that's half the battle won, one of the miners told the 3rd District congressional candidate.

'Come here, Darrell,' another man called. 'This is the man who walked the picket line with us during the gasoline strike,' he told the other men on the man trip as McGraw stooped in the rain beside the vehicle. Passing out McGraw for Congress stickers to the men, McGraw asked them to remember him May 14 in the Democratic primary.

Loading back into his car, he drove back toward the main highway, visibly irritated that the rain had made him late in arriving at the mine. His car didn't resemble one owned by a candidate. Its only

184

campaign stickers are two on the rear that say: *Mine Safety...Or Else, UMWA.*

A miner driving the opposite way recognized McGraw and stopped him along the road. 'We change shifts at 7 a.m.,' he told McGraw, 'but our sister operation at No. 9 doesn't change till 8 a.m. I'm a Republican, but my wife's a Democrat. She'll vote for you.' He disappeared.

McGraw raced up the hill to the lamp house at Armco's No. 9 mine. He approached the men, asking for help. He chatted easily with them and joked.

'Where do you stand on strip mining?' one man finally demanded.

'I'm against it,' McGraw shot back, without hesitation.

'Well, you're the first man to say it like that.' That's good enough for me.'

He told the men he was also in favor of impeaching the President.

When the shift disappeared back underground, McGraw jumped into his cluttered car and headed for Eastern Associated Coal Company's Wharton No. 2 operation. He explained there was a slag dam there that he wanted to watch. He said he'd been keeping his eye on it all winter.

Driving up to the foreman he said: 'I'm Darrell McGraw – you know that pain in your ass. I'd like to see the dam.' The foreman smiled, assured McGraw that he wasn't a pain and sent some engineers with the congressional hopeful to the dam. Through the rain, the engineers assured McGraw that the dam was safe and was being drained.

Seemingly comforted, McGraw turned his campaign toward Madison. At Van, he strode into McCoy's Discount store.

'I'm Darrell...,' he started.

I know who you are, Darrell, old buddy,' Jim Foster cut in. 'I admire your stands and I'm going to vote for you.' McGraw, who later said he didn't know the man, stammered his thanks.

He shook more hands in the tiny hamlet of Van, then made his way to Madison. There he stopped at Harold's Barber Shop, tested the favorable political air, passed out signs and headed out for Lincoln County.

The rain fell in heavy sheets as he reached Hamlin. He stopped at Columbia Gas Co. to talk with his cousin – a Republican – who *introduced him around the building. The people laughed at the political differences of the two cousins, but reacted warmly to McGraw.*

Driving back toward Charleston, he stopped at a number of shops along the road. They were all operated by Republicans. 'Well, every good Republican had one good Democrat friend. Could you ask yours to help me on May 14?' McGraw would ask while passing our match books and fingernail files.

I've been picking up strength all across the 14-county district, he told a small group of teachers at Duval High School in Griffithsville. I think I've got a good shot of winning.

He said later he felt he would always win, or else I would never have gotten involved in the campaign. 'Well, one thing,' one teacher said, 'John Slack never campaigned in little old Lincoln County; so you've got my vote.'[25]—Andy Gallagher, Charleston Gazette

Darrell at a campaign party with his "Congressional Donkey"

Kaufman and Darrell were progressives who shared the same support base which was problematic for either's success in the election: "It's fair to assume that either Kaufman or McGraw would vote for the other, if only one were in the race, since their political philosophies are closely paralleled. Yet, by all indications, both are determined to run, in which case they will split the liberal vote and smooth the way for Slack."[26]

Darrell was elated when he received the endorsement of the *Charleston Gazette*: "He takes clear positions, unencumbered by advance assessment of how they will affect his standing as a candidate.

186

He recognizes the problems of West Virginia and he denounces the contempt for law and morality that is evident in Washington."[27] This newcomer's passion had won the hearts of the rank and file newspaper staff: "When the endorsement meeting started, I was impressed by the submission of a petition from the newsroom. It urged the board to endorse Darrell McGraw and had 12 or 13 signatures on it. The staff's presentation of a petition on behalf of a candidate was unique."[28]—*Don Marsh, Gazette Editorial Board*

Overcoming the entrenched establishment support for John Slack did not occur. The morning headline read, "Slack Runs Away with Nomination." Slack received 60% of the vote; Kaufman 23% and Darrell 16%: "McGraw, a former assistant to Gov. Hullett Smith, was endorsed by the Gazette, but had little other assistance and limited funds." In response to his defeat, Darrell simply said, "I had hoped to do better."[29]

While Darrell's bid for Congress was unsuccessful, it built his progressive brand and drew attention to the issues he came back to again and again throughout his career.

Chapter XI   Darrell McGraw Elected Justice

Darrell, Jr., 1976

Supreme Court Election

For months Darrell and Warren contemplated the 1976 general election and possibilities for the McGraw brothers. Warren loved being a state senator but found time away from home difficult. Warren was torn between filing for circuit judge of Wyoming County or for re-election to the state senate. He decided to do both. There was something bigger in the McGraw brothers' plan for Darrell. With Darrell's run for Congress and Warren's work in the Legislature, the McGraw name recognition was increasing. Perhaps it was time for Darrell to venture into a state-wide election.

There were an unprecedented three seats open on the West Virginia Supreme Court—two full-term twelve-year seats, and one unexpired eight-year term. The full term seats at stake were those held by Chief Justice Thornton G. Berry Jr., who was retiring, and incumbent Justice Donald Wilson. Justice Wilson, a Republican, appointed by Governor Arch Moore after Justice Charles H. Haden II resigned to accept a federal judgeship, was running for re-election. The unexpired eight year term was held by Justice Edwin Flowers, a Republican also appointed by Governor Arch Moore after Justice James Sprouse resigned to run for governor in 1974. Justice Flowers was running for reelection.

The McGraw brothers believed there was greater interest in the two full term seats which meant increased number of candidates might file. They thought the greater number of people in the race the greater the

188

chance of Darrell's success. So with limited finances but lots of
enthusiasm, Darrell filed to run for the twelve year term.[1]

The McGraw brothers were correct. Seven Democratic
candidates filed to run for the two full-term seats: Harry, G. Camper, Jr.
Welch, WV; Judge Charles L. Garvin, Jr., Fayetteville, WV; William
Jacobs, Parkersburg, WV; Thomas Patrick Maroney, Charleston, WV;
Darrell V. McGraw, Jr., Pineville, WV; Thomas B. Miller, Wheeling,
WV, and Edward H. Tiley, Charleston, WV. Three Democrat candidates
filed for the unexpired seat: Leo Catsonis, Charleston, WV; Sam R.
Harshbarger, Milton, WV, and Robert E. Magnuson, Charleston, WV.[2]

Miller and Camper were held to be the candidates with the
greatest opportunity to win. Camper, a former U.S. Attorney, had a level
of state-wide recognition, and Miller, a lawyer whose firm represented
big coal and insurance companies, lived in the populated northern
panhandle. They both were supported by individuals and corporations
with money.

Darrell's life time friend Thomas Patrick Maroney, a man of
strong Irish heritage from Cabin Creek, also filed to run for the state
Court. Pat was in law school with Darrell, and Darrell, like all who know
Pat, hold Pat in high honor and regard. Pat worked his way through
undergraduate and law school. Pat has continued to work advocating for
the rights of workers as general counsel to the AFL-CIO for more than 30
years. Maroney, a progressive, has never veered from the culturally right
action. Darrell knew they weren't running against each other. They were
for one another. The 1976 state Supreme Court race was the only time
Pat ventured into running for office. As the longtime Chairman of the
State Democratic Party, Maroney worked to assist others at the national
and state level seeking public office. In 2015 in recognition and in honor
of Pat Maroney's service to the AFL-CIO a new apartment complex for
persons with disabilities was named the Thomas Patrick Maroney Unity
Apartments.

The first hurdle in Darrell's campaign for state Supreme Court
was lack of money to finance a state-wide race. Without money
increasing name recognition was problematic. Darrell's after election
primary report showed a total of $14,609 in funds received, of which he
personally loaned the campaign $7,000.[3] The second major issue was

that two other candidates filed from southern West Virginia (Camper and Garvin) which would split Darrell's base of support. From his filing in late January, 1976, Darrell spent his time traveling to every part of the state. Darrell understood grassroots politics so when he spoke to voters regarding the 2 twelve year seats open on the Court he appealed to their local bias, "I know the candidate from your area is your first choice, so I am asking you to vote for me as your second choice." Darrell sensed that people liked his respect for their loyalty to a hometown candidate, and they liked the idea of making him their "second choice." So that became his message everywhere he went, except in southern West Virginia, where he asked to be their first choice.

Darrell didn't have funds to run ads in the local papers so as he traveled the state he stopped at every county marker and took a picture standing beside the sign. He then took the picture to the editor of local paper and said he just wanted them to know that he was visiting their county. Invariably they talked with him and ran a story with the picture. Still stored away in the family treasures are the 55 pictures of Darrell standing beside each county sign.

Darrell beside the Braxton County Marker

Darrell needed to secure television time in order to increase his visibility with voters. There wasn't money to purchase any significant level of commercials, but he had an idea. After researching television costs he learned there was a lower rate for preachers to run their shows at night and non-peak times. He asked Wayne Ewing, producer of *If*

Elected, to cut the documentary about Warren's 1972 state Senate election to 30 minutes. The stations were then contacted and asked if they would run the documentary at the preacher rate and without hesitation the channels agreed to show *If Elected.* It was a real coup. The week before the election the campaign purchased $10,000 worth of time on television channels throughout the state. *If Elected* was Darrell's "hail Mary pass." People watched the late night show and remembered the McGraw name.

The primary election day was Tuesday, May 11, 1976, but the final results were not determined until two days later. Election night was long and sleepless. On May 12th the *Charleston Gazette,* the morning paper, reported that with 40 percent of the precincts in, Miller led with 37,891 votes, followed by Camper with 34,214 and McGraw with 30,965.[4] Darrell did not despair and continued to call counties with outstanding votes to report. The day was tortuous, but the afternoon paper seemed quite final and disappointment was palatable. The *Daily Mail* cited the winners of the full term Democratic nomination were Harry G. Camper and Thomas Miller and declared that labor lost in a big way: "Both the UMW and AFL-CIO endorsed Darrell McGraw and Thomas Patrick Maroney for State Supreme Court. They lost. In fact, endorsements not only from labor, but from other groups, such as environmentalists, didn't appear to do special favors for the candidates."[5]—*Richard Grimes*

Darrell was not "throwing in the towel." It was another sleepless night as Darrell and Warren stayed on the phone checking the results with counties around the state. Thursday morning, May 13th, offered a glimmer of hope as the *Charleston Gazette* reported that with 92% of the 2,368 precincts in, Darrell was 200 votes behind Camper: Miller-89,195, Camper-88,120 and Darrell-87,921.[6] In the early afternoon the few remaining precincts came through with Darrell edging out Harry Camper by 1,276 votes. Thomas Miller and Darrell McGraw were the Democratic nominees and incumbent Justice Donald Wilson was the Republican nominee for the two 12 year terms.[7] Sam Harshbarger was the Democratic nominee and incumbent Justice Edwin Wilson was the Republican nominee for the unexpired 8 year term.[8]

If Elected was instrumental to Darrell's successful nomination. Warren's wife, Peggy, pleased with Darrell's success, lamented that

191

church members were talking again about the brothers' cussing in the film. However, the general election was next on the agenda and opposition remained: "It brings us to the primary just passed. The Democrats had Darrell McGraw winning over veteran lawyer Harry Camper and far out-polling a number of other lawyers held in esteem within the profession. The voters obviously liked McGraw. That's the test. Candidly many lawyers are fuming. They are plotting how to head McGraw off at the general election–the party disregarded."[9] *Charleston Daily Mail*

Republicans were unable to muster contenders to run against Sen. Robert Byrd or Congressman John Slack, and John D. Rockefeller IV exhibited a determination to spend whatever necessary to secure victory in the gubernatorial race against former Republican Governor Cecil Underwood. This was all good for Democrats in the general election running for the state Supreme Court. Rockefeller supported Miller, McGraw and Harshbarger, and he was spending millions on his election which helped the entire Democratic ticket.[10]

Powerful labor blocs worked to elect the Democratic candidates. Joseph W. Powell, president of West Virginia Labor Federation encouraged its membership to get out the labor vote: "We should all remember the importance of the Supreme Court, which is frequently called upon to make decisions regarding the law that affects the lives of all working people."[11]

Darrell was dependent upon small individual contributions to finance his campaign. He was delighted when the Huntington Labor Council organized a bean dinner fund raiser, and over 500 people attended. At $2 dollars a ticket the event raised $900, after expenses which—a variable wind fall for the campaign.[12]

Total campaign expenditure for the 1976 primary and general was $22,000 with $16,000 financed by Darrell. It was shocking little money compared to today's judicial elections.[13] Darrell McGraw, Thomas Miller and Sam Harshbarger were elected to the West Virginia Supreme Court on November 2, 1976 and with their success a "troika," of three strong horses, formed to take on injustice.

Progressive State Supreme Court

Oath of Office Chief Justice Fred Caplan and Darrell V. McGraw, Jr., January 17, 1977

Inauguration Day, January 17, 1977, was a bitter cold day, but family and friends stood on the steps of the north portico to watch with great pride as Chief Justice Fred Caplan administered the oath of office to Darrell.[14] John D. "Jay" Rockefeller, IV became the 29th Governor and people from the national stage came to watch. Vice President Nelson Rockefeller, U.S. Sen. Charles Percy (Sharon Rockefeller's father) Secretary of State Cyrus Vance and President Lyndon Johnson's daughter, Lynda and her husband Charles Robb, and President Jimmy Carter's son Jack were all there.[15] It felt like a new day for West Virginia—a better time was on the horizon.

Darrell was 40 years old. Young, but not as young as fellow justice, Richard Neely—"When [Neely] took office, he became the youngest judge of a court of last resort in the English speaking world in the 20th century."[16] Their youth brought a more contemporary view to the role of judges, and Darrell hoped the public was ready: "I have always been active in community affairs…I often thought I would like to be a judge but was reasonably sure I could not embrace the subdued lifestyle demanded of judges…I think the public now has a more contemporary view of judges so I have no qualms about serving on the bench. I am wary of judges who seem to have an inclination to set themselves above everyone else after they get elected."[17]

Justices Richard Neely, Fred Caplan, Sam Harshbarger; Darrell McGraw, Jr. and Thomas Miller
1977 West Virginia Supreme Court

Darrell saw the WV Supreme Court as a "people's" Court. His vision was realized as the Court granted more cases for appeal; litigants' grievances were heard, and the back log of un-reviewed cases cleared: "From 1976 to 1986 petitions filed increased from 789 to 1579 and decisions increased from 99 to 494."[18] This people's Court, in its duty, adhered to the WV Constitution Bill of Rights mandate, "the courts of this state shall be open, and every person for an injury done to him, in his person, property or reputation shall have remedy by due course of law, and justice shall be administered without sale, denial or delay."[19] Those interested in maintaining the status quo were not impressed with the Court's openness. The Legislature cut the progressive state Court's budget.

In an interview with Darrell, Don Marsh inquired of the ramifications of the Court's activism: "The Court in the last year or two has become more activistic. It has changed its posture on the kind of cases that it accepts and the kind of action it takes. Some people theorize that there is a group of lawyers and interests representing a desire to maintain the status quo–the establishment–and that this group is reserved and suspicious of the new directions of the court. Do you think that this is involved in this budget problem?"[20] In response Darrell said there was little question about the Legislature's motive: "Yes, there could be something to that…this has to be one of the more humorous of dilemmas in government. We on the Supreme Court are taking the brunt and receiving all of this criticism because we are doing our work. It is not often in government that people get criticized for doing their work. We are cleaning up our docket. This is what people are always complaining about in the courts, that the dockets are always clogged, that the work is never done, that it takes years to get a decision. We are doing our work and some people do not like it."[21]

This progressive Court was granting more petitions; rendering decisions and clearing up a back log of cases. "Prior to 1976 the Court was ranked one of the least progressive courts in the nation. By 1986 the Court was one of the 10 or 12 most progressive in the country. It is ironic that the Court's intervention in public policy disputes, deemed judicial activism, which caught the most "hell" were cases similar to those decided in Michigan, California and New Jersey 20 or 30 years earlier.[22]— *Patrick Hagen, UNC College of Law*

The cases decided by the WV Supreme Court during Darrell's tenure reflected the "people's court" intent to do what was culturally right for all people, and reflected the language as the law as written. (Chapter XII provides a more comprehensive list and brief description of the state Court's decisions.) The following cases, offered in more depth, are illustrative of many of the state Court's notable decisions.

Mandolidis
To whose benefit is it for an employer to not be liable when the employer intentionally creates a work situation that results in injury or death to the worker?

Justice Darrell McGraw, Jr. listening to *Mandolidis*

In 1978 the word *Mandolidis* became synonymous with Darrell's time on the Court. *Mandolidis* was actually three cases consolidated for argument and decision: *Mandolidis v. Elkins Industries, Inc., Snodgrass v. United States Steel Corp., and Dishmon v. Eastern Associated Coal Corp.*[23] Each case involved real people; real injury and real death. All the plaintiffs alleged deliberate intent by their employers which resulted in injury and or death. All were denied relief at the lower court level and all found justice in the WV Supreme Court.[24]

James Mandolidis was a machine operator at Elkins Industries, a furniture manufacturing business in Elkins, West Virginia. James lost two fingers and part of his hand while operating a 10 inch table saw not equipped with a safety guard. Five other employees, including the president and the steward of a union at Elkins Industries, said they complained on numerous occasions to the plant foreman and the plant manager regarding the lack of guards on the table saws: "The steward indicated that on one occasion when he complained about the lack of saw guards, the plant foreman just hee hawed around about it. Employees testified that the plant foreman removed the guards from the saws at various times. The former plant safety inspector said that he had shut down and placed an out-of-order sign on a guardless saw, but the foreman tore off the sign and placed the saw back in operation. Four of the former employees, including the plaintiff, indicated that the foreman's instructions via the plant manager were that anyone refusing to run a saw without a guard would be sent home or fired. One former employee indicated that he had been fired for refusing to run a saw without a guard."[25]

In *Snodgrass,* one employee died and several sustained series injuries when a temporary building platform used in the construction of a bridge collapsed. The plaintiffs alleged the employer violated safety regulations in the construction of the temporary "work-platforms and, therefore, rendered the platforms patently dangerous. Additionally, the plaintiffs alleged that the company violated numerous regulations by failing to provide safety nets and lifelines on the platform."[26]

In *Dishmon,* three miners were killed when the coal company "allegedly used explosives illegally to clear a rock fall in one of its mines. Shortly after the explosions, the plaintiff's decedent was sent to work in clearing the area. Soon thereafter, one of the rib roof supports fell into the area, killing the decedent and two others."[27]

The troika, Miller, Harshbarger and McGraw, joined by Chief Justice Fred Caplan held for *Mandolidis* in an opinion labeled by many as a landmark decision. *Mandolidis* was the right decision for workers who are intentionally put at risk of injury or death. In *Mandolidis* the issue before the state Court was whether an employer who knowingly requires an employee to do something exposing that employee to high risk of death or injury is liable beyond the typical recovery allowed under workers' compensation.[28] At the time West Virginia Workers Compensation law provided immunity to employers from law suits based on employment injuries if the worker was able to recover under Worker's Compensation. An exception in the Compensation law noted that when the injury is the result of an intentional act, not a negligent act, of the employer then the employee can sue for redress. "In each of the three cases, the Court found that the plaintiffs adequately alleged that the employers had deliberately acted to injure the employees. The state Court held that an employer loses statutory immunity from common law liability when his conduct constitutes an intentional tort or willful, wanton, and reckless misconduct."[29]

The backlash to the *Mandolidis* decision from business leaders, Chamber of Commerce and the Governor was immediate and continues to the present day.

Mandolidis is a landmark case because it greatly expanded a worker's right to sue an employer, even if the worker was covered by the workers' compensation program. In the decision, Justice Darrell V. McGraw Jr. said the court recognized 'a distinction between negligence, including gross negligence, and willful, wanton and reckless misconduct'. Such misconduct was interpreted as a deliberate intention on the part of the employer. This intention need not involve an actual desire to injure the worker, but rather an awareness of exposing the worker to a risk entailing a high probability of physical injury

The Mandolidis ruling came after three new justices were seated on the five-member court as a result of the 1976 general election. All three—Darrell V. McGraw, Thomas E. Miller, and the late Sam Harshbarger—were perceived as favorable to workers.

The president of the state Chamber of Commerce and other business leaders criticized the ruling and asked the legislature to pass a law to lessen its impact. Governor Rockefeller asked the 1982 legislature to consider a change in the law, but the legislature decided to appoint a study commission which made its recommendation in 1983.

That year the Mandolidis bill (HB1201) was enacted, modifying the seven-year old decision. The new law softened the impact of the court decision but provided more rights to workers than prior to Mandolidis.[30]

At the 1982 AFL-CIO Solidarity March, Bobby Thompson, Building Trades leader said, "the *Mandolidis* decision has done more for workers in one year that OSHA or state safety laws and regulations have ever done"[31] *Mandolidis* resulted in significant advancement for the protection of worker safety, but the push back from those who benefit from higher production output and lower costs remains a formidable adversary to progress. Governors and legislators responded by systematically resisting the rights of injured workers provided in *Mandolidis*. The *Mandolidis* bill of 1983 was only the first attempt to negate the state Court's ruling.[32]

In the 2015 legislative session *Mandolidis* was again addressed: "HB2011 significantly tightens the "deliberate intent" exception to employer immunity under West Virginia's workers' compensation law, imposing more rigorous standards for actions against employers by employees alleging intentional harm as a result of a workplace condition."[33] The Legislature passed the bill over the rightful concerns of those directly impacted by intentional actions of employers: "Caitlin O'Dell's husband was killed in a coal mine accident two years ago, leaving her a single mother of a young child. She testified that workers compensation, which pays workers for on-the-job injuries, would not have been enough to support her family. Workers compensation is not enough to make up for the death of my husband. Being able to sue the coal company to recover the damages is absolutely necessary. Without that I would lose my home in foreclosure."[34]

Stuart Caldwell, a leading trial lawyer and worker advocate in WV concluded that "*Mandolidis* remained the 'target' on Darrell's back for his entire political career."[35] Caldwell was right. In a 2016 election for the state Supreme Court *Mandolidis* decision was used against Darrell by the corporate community.

Teller v. McCoy
To whose benefit is it for landlords to not provide decent, habitable living quarters, no matter how low the rent?

The *National Law Journal* described *Teller v. McCoy* as landmark case in which the state Court was asked to make a determination of the landlord's contractual responsibility to maintain a habitable rental for the tenant.[36] In *Teller v. McCoy* the state Court held that landlords are required to provide, decent, habitable living quarters, no matter how low the rent. West Virginia became one of the 40 states to judicially recognize the implied warranty of habitability as it pertains to residential renter agreements. The state Court negated the traditional "no duty to repair" rule that developed out of "an agrarian economy in the Middle Ages when the land itself, not the residential structure, was the focal point of lease transactions."[37]

Darrell in writing the majority opinion held: "Landlords must provide decent, habitable living quarters, however low the rental. This Court, along with many others, has concluded that the harsh common law rules of property, riddled historically with numerous exceptions, no longer exclusively govern the residential lease in light of legislative enactments and intent. Since the rights and duties of the landlord and residential tenant must be viewed under contract principles, the tenant's duty to pay rent is dependent upon the landlord's fulfillment of the implied warranty of habitability."[38] The language in the opinion was perhaps complex but the intent was simple; landlords must fulfill their responsibility to ensure the house or apartment is habitable.

Justice Neely, owner of two large high rent apartment complexes, wrote a dissent condemning the majority opinion: "As with all populist pronouncements in the modern world the majority opinion has attempted to use a cudgel wielded by a cyclops to do work which can be accomplished only by a skilled athlete using a rapier...It is very much as if one were to write an opinion which implied that everyone had a natural right to a Rolls Royce, and that an action in warranty would lie against all

199

other automobile manufactures if they provided anything less elegant. There may be those who prefer less than habitable housing to more expensive accommodations."39

McGraw and Neely, frequently at opposite ends of the perspective, shared a common respect for each one's intellect. The *National Law Review* labeled McGraw and Neely the "West Virginia's Felix and Oscar Show." It was an apt description of the on-going banter between Darrell and fellow Justice Richard Neely. They served on the state Court together, but their varying backgrounds and lifestyles were conducive to spats "over the most basic questions of judicial philosophy between two members of the highest court."40 They were deemed the "Odd Couple:" "Associate Justice Richard Neely, 38, is the fastidious one – formal, erudite and slightly prissy. On a summer day when the court isn't sitting, he relaxes in his chambers in a three-piece suit, vest buttoned, with a billow of white poking out of the jacket pocket."41 "Associate Justice Darrell McGraw, 42, wouldn't be caught dead in a buttoned vest. He refers to himself as "the people's judge" and is a shirtsleeves kind of guy who is quick to tell you that his father was once a coal miner."42

Despite their differences, after their tenures on the court, the influence each had on the other was more apparent. Justice Neely embraced a more progressive point of view, often advocating and representing the disenfranchised and voiceless in his law practice. Darrell regularly applied Neely's analysis and prediction of human behavior whenever he was faced with how an elected official might react in a particular situation. Neely believed the preponderant of elected officials is to avoid conflict. They learned from one another.

McGraw-Neely War of Words – Jim Dent *Charleston Gazette*, 12/12/78

Interestingly, Charles Lopeman in an analysis of activists' state courts noted that: "Paradoxically Neely was the catalyst for his court's judicial activism, an activism that was more activist than his judicial philosophy allowed him to be."[43]

1979 was a tumultuous year—a year that tested focus and commitment to do what was culturally right. There were times when crawling into bed and pulling the covers over one's head was tempting. Darrell never did. There was criticism related to the state Court's attempts to make progress in education as well as the welfare and treatment of juveniles. First there was the appeal of *Pauley v. Bailey* to the state Supreme Court where the deplorable conditions in many schools were revealed, and finally there was an altercation that took place when Darrell attempted to inspect a jail cell where a juvenile hanged himself.

Focus and commitment to answering the basic question was tested: "Is this the right thing to do? If so, there was only one direction to move—forward, with the discipline and courage to put adversaries in a proverbial box to 'shelf.'

Pauley v. Bailey
To whose benefit is it to inadequately fund public schools?

Janet Pauley had just moved back to Lincoln County from Chicago when one of her son's asked her to come to a PTA meeting at McCorkle Elementary.

So I went down to the meeting, and I happened to look and the seats were broken in the school. You couldn't even sit down. I bet there were 21 windows broken out in that school. And, most of all, the smell, oh, you couldn't stand it.

The smell was coming from a sewer behind the school where a 'river of waste ran through the children's play area.' All of Mrs. Pauley's children attended that school.

The principal said, 'There's not anything we can do.' Janet Pauley said, 'there was plenty she could do.' But at the time she uttered that vow, Mrs. Pauley never dreamed that before she was finished, her name would be linked forever with the battle for better schools in West Virginia.[44]

Mrs. Pauley wasn't alone in her outrage over the schools in Lincoln County—so was Linda Martin. In 1975 Linda Martin, married to Julian Martin a high school science teacher who was in the Peace Corp in Africa and longtime activist, transferred her two older children into Lincoln County Schools.

It blew my mind to see the difference between Kanawha County Schools and the ones here. I couldn't believe the conditions: 47 kids in a classroom, ten-year-old textbooks, no written curricula, unqualified teachers, blatant discrimination against poor kids, better meals in the town school. The county ranked 54th out of 55 in the state in basic skills test scores'. My husband found that half his ninth graders couldn't read.[45]

At about the same time Pauley and Martin were struggling to bring about change in Lincoln County, Dan Hedges, a young attorney for the Appalachian Research and Defense Fund in Charleston, was fighting battles for school reform through the court system. Hedges, tall, lanky and determined, wanted to make a difference for the poor. He believed education was the key. Hedges carried in his pocket a well-worn picture of Millerville, a school in Roane County where his father and grandfather taught and where he returned to find a school he never forgot. Hedges' friends said he became obsessed with doing something about public schools: "Millerville touched him deeply with children who had never seen an orange or a toothbrush, who didn't have food or adequate clothing, who were taught by teachers not much older than they, who lacked books, equipment and supplies, who were a throwback to a different era and a different set of values."[46]

A perfect storm of likeminded advocates came together when Pauley and Hedges met. Shortly after that meeting Hedges filed suit in Kanawha Circuit Court on behalf of Janet Pauley, her sons and all other similarly situated plaintiffs alleging that, as a result of the existing property-based financing system for the State's educational funding, their children lacked access to the Constitution required "thorough and efficient system of free school."[47] Success was not immediately theirs. The circuit court admitted as a point of fact that Lincoln County schools were inadequate in comparison to wealthier counties in the state but denied the plaintiffs' motion for summary judgment and dismissed the action. The circuit court found that the equal protection guarantees did not apply because there was "no evidence that public school children residing in those counties are necessarily poorer than such children who reside in counties with higher overall property values."[48]

Four years passed before *Pauley v. Bailey (*originally *Pauley v. Kelly)* made its way to the WV Supreme Court. In 1979 Chief Justice Harshbarger, writing for the majority, reversed the dismissal of the action by the circuit court, holding the plaintiffs' complaint was sufficient and there were many genuine issues of material fact yet to be resolved. It was viewed nationally as the pioneering case in addressing infrastructure equalization in public education.[49] The state Court remanded the case "for further evidentiary development" which meant the need more information prior to a final decision. The state Court was very specific in its remand order, requiring the circuit court take the applicable constitutional standards as it pertains to public educations and then analyze and determine the level of the State's performance in its role and duty. It was not to be a simple task.[50] The state Court remanded the case to Circuit Judge Recht of Ohio County, to take testimony and provide findings back to the Court.

Pauley v. Bailey decision by the state Supreme Court almost went the other way. The troika stumbled. The Governor, the Legislature and the Attorney General were opposed to the *Pauley v. Bailey* case because of the funding implications. There was great political pressure. It was at the Governor's mansion when the intensity of interest as to what the Supreme Court might decide crossed the boundaries of propriety. An intense young lawyer pushed up against Darrell and advised "the decision needs to be the right one." The children were not on his mind.[51]

The day the Justices considered *Pauley v. Bailey* in their conference Darrell was adamant there existed substantial inequities in the public school system—not only from school to school but from county to county. Darrell wanted the state Court to stand up for the children's Constitutional right "to a thorough and efficient education". The conference became overheated when it was apparent there were not three votes to rule for the plaintiffs. It was only Darrell and Justice Harshbarger siding with the plaintiff. Prior to leaving the conference, Darrell said in a not so quiet voice, "the hottest place in hell is reserved for those who don't know or don't care. This case is why I am here, and if we don't have the strength to support the Constitutional mandate for the children there is no point in me being here anymore."[52]

Darrell was disappointed and believed the situation hopeless. He was distraught with the notion that he had failed the children. Later that evening Justice Miller, his face most lined with the struggles of day, walked over to our house. Miller, as Darrell called him, stayed for dinner. They talked and debated. The next day the majority was there, and the children won. The West Virginia Supreme Court held there must be equality of educational opportunity for all children in all public schools. But there was resistance ahead. Sometime later Miller in referring to that evening said, "My God his backbone never bends." Miller was a good guy.[53]

In the meantime *Killen v. Logan County Commission* came before the state Court in a certified question asking whether W.Va. Code Sec. 18-9A-11, which allows assessors to value property at 50 to 100 percent of its appraised value, was in violation of the state Constitution's guarantee of equal and uniform taxation. The trial court held the statute was unconstitutional which meant the Constitution required that property had to be assessed at its true and actual value.[54]

In was here in this decision the state Supreme Court held to tenants of the Constitution. Darrell wrote the majority opinion which upheld the lower court ruling that the statute was unconstitutional. The Governor, many legislators, business and industry leaders and the Chamber of Commerce all cried foul when the opinion was released citing that adherence to the Constitution placed an increased tax burden on property owners. Perhaps left unsaid was a fear that implementing the opinion was a political suicide for those in office.

The original drafters of the West Virginia Constitution understood the importance of assessing property at its true and actual value. In West Virginia, schools districts are dependent upon local property taxes and the state aid funding formula dollars to fund education. When local property taxes are insufficient funding of public schools is negatively impacted. Without adherence to the Constitutional provision to assess property at true and actual value, revenues for schools are lessened and inequalities in educational opportunities for children increased. But would the

Legislators act in the interests of children and the state's future? Would the legislators adhere to the admonition offered by Justice Oliver Wendell Holmes, "Taxes are the price we pay for a civilized society?"[55] Could legislators actually take umbrage from that long ago and far away advice of 1884 Tax Commission: "The question is whether we shall continue to sit with folded hands and witness other less favored localities outstrip us in the race of progress of whether we shall make some intelligent efforts to utilize our advantages?"[56] The answer wasn't long in coming.

"Gov. Jay Rockefeller's first reaction was to point out potential problems in the Recht decision and warn state residents about enormous tax increases. Then, he called a special session of the Legislature to consider a "Tax Limitation Amendment," calling for a reappraisal of property which would require all property to be assessed at 60 percent of market value rather than 100 percent as had been ordered in a court case [Killen] coming out of Logan County."[57]

Legislators understood increases in property taxes correlated with defeat in the next election. House Speaker Clyde See, who had aspirations to run for governor and later operated a coal mine in Logan County, led the Legislature to support placement of a measure on the upcoming ballot asking voters to approve a Constitutional amendment that negated the Killen opinion: "Property Tax Limitation and Homestead Exemption Amendment of 1982 provided that all property subject to ad valorem taxation shall be assessed at 60% of its value…based upon periodic statewide appraisal that considers: 1.) trends in market value over a fixed period of years prior to base year; 2.) location of property, and 3.) other such factors and as it determines."[58] Big Coal was happy and so was the state Chamber with curtailing any potential for increased property taxes. Op-eds in local papers asserted that the Killen decision might send inappropriately assessed and unassessed property taxes up as much as 500 percent and cripple taxpayers.[59] This message of exorbitant tax increases reverberated around the state, and taxpayers voted accordingly. A resounding 80% of the voters supported the passage of the Tax Limitation Amendment. With its passage the chance of securing a source of revenue to finance quality educational opportunities for children was severely crippled.

Back to *Pauley v. Bailey*

After 17 months of expert testimony, Judge Recht issued an opinion in the *Pauley v. Bailey* case which outlined high quality education standards and concluded the state education system did not meet those standards. In 1984 the West Virginia Supreme Court issued a decision, confirming the 1979 original ruling and embraced Judge Recht's findings. The Court held education was a fundamental, constitutional right; defined the parameters of a "thorough and efficient" educational system and held the Constitutional duty of the Legislature was "to provide a high quality State-wide education system."[60] It was a landmark decision.

The *Pauley v. Bailey* Master Plan (Judge Recht's decision) provided a playbook for quality education programs and services for all students including student-teacher ratios, highly qualified teachers, a comprehensive curriculum encompassing world language, art, music, vocational, higher education and counseling services and facility standards. The Master Plan defined what "should be" in place for all children in all schools in West Virginia. The Master Plan was to be fully implemented. It was the right thing to do. Adequate funding for the outlined Master Plan standards within the *Pauley v. Bailey* decision was essential. But no one wanted to pay.[61]

Activists Linda and Julian Martin knew the deterrents to their battle for school reform: "If we don't change the tax system so the corporations that own the minerals and profit from their extraction pay their fair share of taxes, then West Virginia children will never have the schools they deserve, and poor children from poor counties will continue to pay the highest price for this failure of leadership. The governors and the people who have controlled the Legislature have protected those corporations through the years and they have done so on the backs of our children."[62]—*Linda Martin*

"I think legislators and governors have all just ignored it. The Recht Decision wasn't enforced. We still have all these poor counties running operations off property taxes, and, in counties like Lincoln, there's not much income from property taxes."[63]—*Julian Martin*

Pauley v. Bailey led to improvements in public education: "While no school in West Virginia has ever met all of the standards established by the Recht decision or the Master Plan, the litigation led to sweeping improvements in public education. Hundreds of millions of dollars were spent on new schools, upgraded facilities, and improved curriculum."[64]— *Bill McGinley, lawyer WVEA*

Less than 60 percent of the Master Plan recommendations were implemented, and there have been no substantial changes in the state school aid funding formula or tax assessments to ensure future equality of educational opportunity.[65] In January of 2003, Judge Recht closed the case and relinquished jurisdiction. Continued opportunity to fully implement the Master Plan for the benefit of all the state's children was greatly diminished.

Chapter XII Socially Conscious Justice

Justice Darrell V. McGraw, Jr.

Darrell's approach to jurisprudence defied the expectations of those who believe judges live a conservative, conventional lifestyle away and separate from the people who elected them. The McGraw brothers' lives were about engagement with people which they believed brought about greater level of knowledge and understanding. Without that engagement, Darrell believed the judges' reasoning in interpreting statute and precedent setting case law was limited. Life in the McGraw house reflected what happens when one stays in the arena. It was not always a sixties sitcom of happiness and tranquility.

Fran Hughes, a young public defender attorney and later chief deputy attorney general, described the first time she met this new Justice:

I had just finished arguments and was standing in the hallway outside the Court. The area was packed with miners—union and non-union who were interested in a mine safety case being heard that day. The air was filled with tension—everyone wasn't happy. I turned and saw Justice McGraw, still in his robe, come through those imposing wooden doors—probably 12 feet high but the "Judge," as I always called him, held his own at a robust 6 feet. He started shaking hands. As I learned about the "Judge" years later, he liked everyone and knew the surroundings in the Capitol, the Court room or the attorney general office were intimidating, and he always made an effort to make people more comfortable—union or non-union, Big Coal or not. He was just about people. One non-union miner was having none of it—he looked anxious. The Judge smiled at the man, shook his hand and moved right on to the next person. The miner knew this wasn't an ordinary judge. I thought, 'My God, the stories are true—he's fearless.[1]*—Frances Hughes, Chief Deputy Attorney General*

It was in his first year as a justice that the Bituminous Coal Strike began. Darrell understood the coal miners' concern about safety. But as a justice what could he do?

Bituminous Coal Strike—110 Days, 160,000 Miners
To whose benefit is it when miners find themselves in an unsafe working condition that they don't have the right to walk away from the danger without losing their job?

The Bituminous Coal Strike started on December 6, 1977 and ended 110 days later. It was about the right for local unions to strike— referred to by operators as a wildcat strike. The strike was also about pay, pensions and miner safety. Miners were frustrated with the terms in the nationally-negotiated contract that took away their right to strike over local health and safety conditions. The contract provided no encouragement for employers to resolve disputes at the local level. The miners were left with little recourse to ensure their fair treatment and safety.[2]

Arnold Miller, the president of the UMWA, demanded the national collective bargaining agreement be modified to give each UMWA affiliate right to strike over local grievances/issues. The Bituminous Coal Operators Association (BCOA) rejected Miller's demand, and countered with demands which included the right of employers to fire wildcat strikers or any miner who refused to cross the picket lines. The BCOA knew what they were doing. The mechanization of mining technology enhanced output but also put miner's lives at greater risk and increased the infliction of black lung. With much of the mechanization complete, increased output meant increased health and safety incident rates. Strikes over safety shortfalls at the local level interfered with production. The BCOA believed maintaining control at the local level essential if it were to continue to increase its rate of profit

209

in the coming years. Years in which BCOA expected President Jimmy Carter's energy policies—which emphasized energy independence from Middle Eastern oil—to boost demand for coal."[3]

Unfortunately in 1978 the bargaining power of the UMWA was not at an optimum level. Power companies had a120 day supply of coal and the demand for coal was at an all-time low level.[4] The coal operators had the advantage and were determined to rid the contract of language allowing strikers to walk for any reason, including safety. On March 6, 1978, after two proposed contract agreements were rejected by UMWA membership, President Jimmy Carter invoked the national emergency provision of the Taft-Hartley Act. Hearings were held and a federal district court issued a temporary injunction mandating miners return to work on March 9th. Miners simply ignored the injunction and the federal government officials were reluctant to enforce the action.[5] Bringing out the National Guard to corral miners back to work was logistically impossible and a public relation nightmare. Darrell believed the administration lacked a complete understanding of the struggles miners faced. He thought he could help. Darrell wrote to President Carter discussing the far reaching implications of using the Taft Hartley Act. His letter did not go unnoticed.

Darrell McGraw, Jr. and Governor Jimmy Carter, circa 1974

Darrell understood the "highly independent, insular and macho subculture" of miners, who viewed safety and pension rights, including those of retired miners, serious issues to protect. "The problem is that the young men just aren't in a position to have to look at Daddy and Grandpa and say, we've left you out. It goes against the whole culture. You don't leave your family out. Your family and union are all you've got. You sure don't have government. The miners see themselves as fighting not only for their lives but their families."[6]

Darrell was a child when John L. Lewis, a legendary union leader, took on President Truman—but he remembered the stories: "John L. Lewis really taught us we were important people. And the only time we were important was when we wouldn't do what the government wanted. The President would raise hell, the Governor would raise hell, and John L. Lewis would tell them all to go to hell."[7]

Darrell described the miners' perspective, "As the miners see it, you always have the right to walk away from a place that may kill you. After all, the mines are just like any other independent enterprise that might ultimately take your life. If they don't mash your life out in an accident, then you'll cough the life out of yourself later on."[8] The *New York Post* described Darrell as a "hero to plenty of WV miners… with his sturdy, handsome looks he is the type a casting director might pick for the part of a crusading lawyer."[9]

Darrell's advocacy for the working people was apparent in his appearance on the *Today Show* on March 10, 1978 to discuss the problems with invoking *Taft Hartley*. Julia and Darrell were proud as they watched their son on the *Today Show* defending coal miners. Julia knew that Darrell remembered her admonition: "The hottest place in hell is reserved for those who don't know or don't care," and she knew her son didn't like the thought of going to hell.

On March 19, 1978, President Carter asked the district court to make the injunction permanent, but his request was denied. Carter was left with no choice but to back off invoking Taft Hartley. The miners were hungry and tired and voted to approve a contract. The miners returned to work on March 26, 1978. The concessionary contract did not include the union's primary goal of winning the right to strike over local safety issues. The miners also lost their standardized health and pension plans to those offered by employers, and the cost of living salary adjustments were eliminated. On the plus side for miners, the contract included a 37% wage hike and guaranteed payment of health and retirement benefits even if union's funds were depleted.[10] The strike and troubled contract took a toll on Arnold Miller who suffered a stroke 10 days after the contract was ratified. He never fully regained his health.[11]

Justice Darrell McGraw, Jr. *Charleston Daily Mail,* August 1, 1978

The final contract did little to improve the lives of miners and their families. The editor of *Penthouse* magazine determined to do a feature story on the strike through the eyes of Darrell McGraw. Editor Jim Good explained their magazine wanted interviews with "people who have something important to say but who, like McGraw, do not have a big name nationally…they were interested in the Darrell McGraws of the world"[12] In the article Darrell was described as the "one voice raised that defined the true nature of the struggle, in terms that the average American could understand."[13] It was a lengthy article that focused on the factors which resulted in the 110 day UMWA strike including the unethical and sometime unlawful corporate practices; the laws and policies that hurt working people and communities and the most difficult life of a coal miner. Darrell's forthright responses to the editor's questions were in his typical "no-holds-barred" way:[14]

- On the difference between President Truman and Carter invoking the Taft Hartley Act, Darrell said, "No difference, Truman went to the same bunch and they passed the Taft Hartley Act but he finally admitted it was a mistake. I certainly admire Truman for many reasons including that admission."
- On the miners' anger about the wildcat strike provisions in the first contract Darrell said, "That first contract took away the miners' right to walk away from a dangerous work place…It [contract] set up so that if a local union official were to confer with another to discuss some dangerous work situation, they could be accused of a conspiracy

to provoke a work stoppage. That's taking away the First Amendment right of association… It's crazy."

- On life in a coal town Darrell said, "Most remaining so-called coal camps or towns are inhabited by the older, retired men. As a result the younger men are living in trailers on any patch of ground they can find…The tax base is suppressed by the coal companies to avoid payment of decent tax on the mineral wealth. As a result, the school systems, which depend on local property taxes, are poor. Another big problem…is the lack of opportunity…and integrated community services."
- On who owns the land in West Virginia Darrell was clear when he said, "The big companies own all the land. I come from a county where 82 percent of the land is owned by Georgia Pacific, Norfolk and Western Railroad or the C & O Railroad."
- On the exploitive practices of extractive industries Darrell offered that: "West Virginia is an anachronism. It is a state of hard-working, decent, patriotic people, who have kept many of the traditional values: love of God and a desire for a better life for their children…Yet, with all this, its citizens have been among the most exploited people in this country by the outside businessman and politician."[15]

At the end of the interview, Darrell cautioned about corporate exploitation: "If we had listened to Thomas Jefferson we wouldn't be where we are. Jefferson had a lot of strong commentary on the private accumulations of capital by the corporations. As a matter of fact, Jefferson wrote some pamphlets on the regulation of the corporations, even 200 years ago."[16] Darrell expressed the importance of people's rights over corporations.

Concern about corporate power infiltrating the right of the people remains a current issue as evidenced by Sen. Sheldon Whitehouse remarks during Federal Court Circuit Judge Neil Gorsuch 2017 confirmation hearings. Sen. Whitehouse expounded on cases heard by Supreme Court of the United States that "pitted corporations against humans including:"[17]

- *Citizens United* helps corporate money to flood elections and boost Republican candidates;

- *Ledbetter* protects corporations that harm their employees in pay discrimination;
- *Gross* protects corporations that harm their employees in age discrimination;
- *Walmart v. Dukes* protects corporations from class action lawsuits;
- *Concepcion* helps corporations steer customers away from juries and into corporate-friendly mandatory arbitration;
- *Iqbal* supports big business against unions, and
- *Hobby Lobby* holds corporations have religious rights that supersede health care for employees.[18]

Senator Whitehouse concluded, "That's an easy 16-0 record for corporations and against humans."[19] Senator Whitehouse, in his recent book, contends government has been "infiltrated and disabled by corporate political power."[20]

Illegal Incarceration of Juveniles
To whose benefit is it not to speak out about injustice?

It was the first morning in October, 1979, and Darrell was reading the morning paper over coffee. It was a ritual. I was seven months pregnant. Darrell stood up and began pacing about the kitchen. He was visibly upset by the morning headline: "Youth, 17, Found Dead Hanging in Kanawha Jail."[21]—*Charleston Gazette*

Michael Jeffery a seventeen year old Cabin Creek youth ran away from the Dunbar Child Shelter and was placed in the Kanawha County Jail on a circuit court order. According to Sheriff G. Kemp Melton, Jeffery had been in the juvenile section of the jail since August 27th: "Jeffery apparently tied a sheet around his neck and tied the other end through a ventilation fixture in the ceiling, then climbed on a bunk and jumped off."[22] Darrell held his head and moaned, "Do you really believe he was being treated like the kid he was?" He couldn't stop, "The year I was born, 1936, the Legislature passed a law prohibiting the placement of youth in cells with adults. My God, they are still violating the law." Darrell left home that morning determined to find out what happened to

214

this child. He had no luck on that day or any other over the course of the week. Every evening, Michael's was on his mind.

By Sunday evening Darrell knew he was being stonewalled by the Sheriff's department. Darrell was relentless when seeking the facts in any situation, and when it involved the life of a child, Darrell was not going to back down. Darrell determined that he needed to do more. On Monday, Darrell, his clerks and two members of the press went to the Kanawha County Jail to inspect the cell where Michael died. He was met with resistance.

Journal Star, October 9, 1979

West Virginia Supreme Court Justice Darrell V. McGraw, Jr., said yesterday he was beaten and handcuffed by police in a confrontation that resulted from his attempt to tour a county jail.

Kanawha County authorities charged the jurist with battery and obstruction of justice for the fracas at a jail where a teenager hanged himself last week. McGraw 'vehemently denied' the charges at his arraignment last night.

A large splotch of blood staining the left side of his white shirt, McGraw, 42, stood grim-faced as Magistrate Herb Pauley read the two battery and three obstruction charges filed by the sheriff's department.

The magistrate once complained sheriff's deputies assaulted him at the same jail. He said he planned to step aside in the case. McGraw was released on $2,500 bail.

The charges stemmed from McGraw's attempt to tour the jail earlier yesterday. The justice said he went with his clerks and two members of the press to inspect the facility because of the incident involving the teenager.

215

McGraw said a State Supreme Court decision precludes youthful offenders from being jailed with adult inmates and he wanted to check the facilities.

'I asked to see the place, and they were willing to let me in and not my staff and press,' McGraw said. 'I took the position it doesn't do any good for me to go in there and say what I saw.'

According to McGraw, as he turned to leave, 'I said jokingly, 'okay guys, let's go in. My humor is not good humor.'

He said two sheriff's deputies in the doorway grabbed him and 'one guy in the back jumped across everybody and started hitting me in the face.' He said there were a 'bunch of deputies there, six or seven or eight.'

'It was all very quick,' McGraw said from the emergency room at Charleston Area Medical Center. "They dragged me in, handcuffed me, shoved me in an elevator and took me upstairs. I said I wanted a lawyer.'

'It's incredible, like these guys were laying for me. They really stuck it to me.'[23]—UPI

It was around 6 p.m. when the phone rang. It was not Darrell telling his me that he was running late, but it was his good friend, Sterl Shinaberry whose smooth and soothing voice I heard. Sterl's calm demeanor served him well. Friends knew when Sterl was upset as a red flush would move up his neck, but his words belied any consternation. Sterl and Darrell were friends since WVU. One of 12 children from Cloverlick, West Virginia, Sterl was a handsome sort with his rust colored hair and fair skin. He was the serious type who knew his success was dependent upon being brighter and working harder than others. As a lawyer he concentrated on labor and personal injury cases, which he won with great regularity. Even when successful, Sterl avoided the limelight. He was committed to fixing the "wrongs" of the world and helping the "underdog." On this day a Justice on the WV Supreme Court found himself in an underdog situation, and Darrell immediately turned to Sterl for help.

Sterl spoke in slow, deliberate but reassuring tones as he said, "Jorea, first and foremost there is nothing to worry about; it's all under control." Immediately wondering what was under control and knowing Darrell had gone to the Kanawha County Jail, but before I could respond,

Sterl, in his self-confident and matter of fact tone that he used with juries to convince them they should listen to him, said, "Darrell has been arrested. The magistrate has released him, and we are on our way over to the hospital to get him checked over."

Sterl, realizing the impact of his revelation on a pregnant wife went right on, "Jorea, Darrell is fine, except for a small cut above the eye. Listen, I am telling you that everything is going to be o.k." I gasped and my knees began to buckle but Sterl went on, "I know Darrell. I know what happened. There will be publicity. Don't answer the door or the phone. Watch for Michael Farber (a legal intern in Darrell's office) and let him in. He is on his way and will give you more details. One last thing, Jorea, I'm taking care of this,"…and he did.

Some people blamed Darrell, deeming his actions unnecessary and un-judge like. An editorial in *Beckley Post-Herald* on October 10th criticized Darrell's attempt to uncover the facts surrounding Michael Jeffery's death.[24]

Others were shocked by what happened: "There is no reason Justice McGraw should have announced his visit ahead of time, just as coal mine inspectors do not have to announce a mine inspection to the company before they arrive on the scene. And why shouldn't it be standard practice, moreover, for county jails to be open to judges and responsible news reporters. One wonders just what the Kanawha County sheriff's department was afraid of. The whole incident makes a person uneasy about any police system which has no real checks. If a State Supreme Court Justice can be beaten up, then how about all the rest of us?"[25]—*Paul J. Nyden, Letter to Editor, Beckley Post Harold*

The ensuing months were filled with investigations surrounding Michael's death and Darrell's attempt to tour the jail cell. Charges were filed against Darrell and the deputies. Life was most difficult. Front page stories described the mistreatment of Michael by deputies. Fellow juvenile inmates alleged that Michael was taunted by deputies and beaten by other inmates. According to witnesses, Michael was locked up alone without adequate supervision and often housed with adult prisoners.[26]

Other teenagers who were incarcerated with Michael described being housed with adult prisoners in what they called the "bullpen." They believed Jeffery's treatment by the deputies and adult inmates pushed him to suicide: "Mike couldn't handle all this man… He just couldn't take being in jail…just couldn't handle the situation'…Mike was deadlocked. He couldn't use the phone, get to stores, do nothing. We don't get any exercise except on Sunday. If you cell with somebody for so long, you know, in a little old place like that bullpen, things just get you upset…"[27]

Sheriff Melton and the Prosecutor James Roark confirmed the accuracy of the teens' statements and acknowledged that on occasion adults were housed in juvenile sections. They promised that Jeffery's death would result in "sharp restructuring of the sheriff's department." and the practice of deadlocking juveniles would cease.[28] The promise was too late for Jeffery.

The investigation revealed that police records were often falsified regarding the incarceration of juveniles with adults. Mrs. J.S. Batman, a deputy who worked at the jail, came forth with allegations of routine misconduct by the deputies. Deputy Bateman, suspended for neglect of duty along with two other deputies as it related to this incident, said that falsifying records regularly happened: "Nobody ever thought of it as falsifying records because the practice was so common. It would be humanly impossible for deputies to inspect the cell block areas every 30 minutes. After each shift is over, the deputies always put their initials on the inspection reports, regardless of whether inspections have been done."[29] Deputy Batman also confirmed the practice of housing juveniles with adults occurred: "You could subpoena any number of people and would find out that adult prisoners were placed in the juvenile section. Deputies made various excuses for placing juveniles in the adult section. At one time they said they did it so that an adult would supervise the juvenile."[30]

Mrs. Batman's husband, Sherman Batman was at the jail the day Darrell went to inspect the facility and described what happened: "two deputies held McGraw while a third deputy hit McGraw in the face."[31]

In a sworn statement the Deputy recounted a meeting where an officer alleged that she was threatened with her job if she didn't support the Department stance in the McGraw case: "If she, or any member of this Department told anything to the State Police or the news media that was detrimental to any member of this Department that they would be fired on the spot, and that they have put her in a position, her job description, that she could be physically hurt." The Deputy recalled the officer reported she told conflicting stories in order to protect her job: "She told me that she told the Sheriff's Department that [officer's name] did not strike him [McGraw] and when talking with the State Police she alleges that [two officers' names] were holding him [McGraw] when [one officer's name] repeatedly struck the State Supreme Court Justice. ...She alleges that there have been numerous cover-ups since she's been here...She would not allow this to be covered up, and she didn't tell the Sheriff's Department because she knew that this was what they wanted to hear."[32]

An outgrowth of the entire trauma was that the public became more interested in the treatment of juveniles by law enforcement and the judiciary. An award winning investigative series revealed many distressing facts related to child protective services, welfare, law enforcement and judiciary treatment of juveniles including highlighting the widespread illegal lockups of juveniles: "West Virginia circuit judges and sheriffs broke the law nearly 500 times in 1978, according to jail inspection data of the state Welfare Department. They're still locking juveniles with adults in county jails, or locking teen-age status offenders with teen-age criminals in youth cells—although both types of confinement have been outlawed since 1977."[33]—*James Haught, Investigative Reporter*

Letters from people and advocacy groups across this state including parents, youth advocates, school superintendents, the West Virginia Magistrate Association and many others expressed gratitude for Darrell's intervention:

On several occasions in the past I have been tempted to fire off a letter to the editor after having read of some particularly stupid or callous act of a politician or public servant. After reading the accounts of your struggle on Monday, the 8th, I finally overcame my fear of seeing my own verbiage in public print and fired off a round. I refer in this letter to you as a Gonzo jurist. I want you to know that amongst certain younger folk Gonzo is a term applied to people who, in their pursuit of truth and fair play, become outlaw figures to the sheep who comprise the silent majority and the wolves who own the land.[34]—Ed Seltzer, Charleston, West Virginia.

Eight months later, the charges against Darrell were finally dismissed with prejudice by Greenbrier County Magistrate Louis Longanacre, which meant they could not be filed again. The charges against the deputies were dismissed without prejudice; which meant that Darrell could continue to pursue legal action, but Darrell was ready to move forward. Darrell called the dismissal of the warrants against him "a victory for civilization."[35] Reforms in the juvenile justice system were taking place:

Have you noticed all the attention jails are getting...The jail at Beckley recently got a surprise inspection from a state-organized committee to see if juveniles are being properly housed. This is an outgrowth of the scuffle at the Kanawha County jail two months ago in which state Supreme Court Justice Darrell McGraw tried to inspect the cell area where a 17 year-old youth hanged himself.

In fact, McGraw's episode, for all the emotion it generated at the time has had an interesting effect throughout the state. Circuit judges all over the state are asking that local jails be checked. The Department of Welfare is going over its policies for dealing with juveniles. And legislators are busy proposing new legislation to further protect young people.

McGraw says, 'People are suddenly concerned with juveniles. Nobody wants to lock them up with hardened criminals anymore. Of course, this has been against the law for a number of years in West Virginia. At last, some of our judges have decided to obey the law.

It would appear that McGraw's swollen ear and bruised face may have been worth it. Out of crisis comes change.[36]*—Richard Grimes, Charleston Daily Mail*

In response to the incident the West Virginia Supreme Court established the first Juvenile Justice Committee to review and provide recommendations related to the treatment of juveniles within the legal system. It was important work which resulted in positive changes for juveniles including an original jurisdiction proceeding where the West Virginia Supreme Court was asked "for guidance to set standards regarding the pre-adjudication detention of juveniles who had committed acts which would be crimes if they were adults."[37] The state Court turned to the Committee for assistance.

The case involved the arrest and incarceration of two children, a seven and nine year old, who were charged with breaking into a school and taking approximately $12 worth of toys and candy. The children were placed in the Kanawha Home for Children where they were locked in a cell with barred windows, bare walls and a steel door for four days before a lawyer was provided. The Committee's investigation and findings were used by the state Court in the development standards of treatment for pre-adjudication juveniles including age minimums, appropriate detention facilities, bail standards, and a clear preference for release to parents over custody except in situations where the juvenile presents a serious threat to the community or self. These standards dramatically improved the requirements for care and treatment of juveniles even before adjudication.[38]

National Judicial Merit Award from the National Center for Juvenile Law was awarded to the West Virginia Supreme Court "in recognition of the court's outstanding knowledge and understanding of juvenile law and its sensitivity to the need for providing adequate and humane treatment for juveniles."[39]

Justices Miller, Caplan, Neely, Harshbarger and McGraw

Even though Darrell's black eye was memorialized by the talented Taylor Jones, Sterl was right—he took care of it.

221

Taylor Jones, *Charleston Gazette,* circa 1979

In an interview when he was asked to reflect on this most difficult year (1979), it was apparent that Darrell intended to continue to do what he believed was right and good for the people:

He said the judgeship has dictated a more reserved and a more contemplative lifestyle and that he misses the personal freedom enjoyed before his election to the court, 'but I wouldn't trade the duties and responsibilities of serving the court to bring that freedom back.'

No stranger to controversy, the outspoken justice said he has no regrets about his confrontation with deputies at the county jail this fall or about the candid opinions that frequently have placed him at odds with his colleagues.

Somebody has to stand up for civilization, he said. That's the way I have viewed the things that have gotten me into hot water. The things I would have done differently are personal, not professional.[40]

Darrell's comments on his more reserved, contemplative style of late probably appeared a contradiction to what was in the newspaper. But for family, friends and business associates the description resonated. Darrell, as introspective and thoughtful as they come, often takes a frustratingly long time to ponder a question before offering a response.

Family Food Fund—Our Brother's Keeper
To whose benefit is it to object to helping hungry families?

True to his word to "stand up for civilization," each year on the state Supreme Court brought additional decisions that advanced citizen's

222

rights and protections. The state Court's progressive actions and
Darrell's advocacy outside the courtroom provoked controversy and
resistance from those who preferred the status quo. And so it was when
Darrell became engaged in an effort to help hungry families in West
Virginia.

1983 found West Virginia on tough economic times. The nation
was at the peak of the recession with unemployment at 10.8%, the highest
since the Great Depression.[41] West Virginians were hurting too. By
March of 1983 West Virginia led nation with the highest unemployment,
with some counties exceeding a staggering 20%.[42] Many families had
exhausted their unemployment benefits and hunger was daily obstacle as
described in this story of Randolph County family's daily struggle to
secure enough food for their children:

*Like countless others who live in poverty across the country, the
three children of Jerry and Betty Elkins know all too well what it is like to
sit down to meager meals. 'We usually have bread and gravy the last few
days of the month,' Mr. Elkins, who is 27 years old, said while waiting
for a handout of Federal surplus food at Guyan Valley High School.*

*'This cheese and butter will really come in handy at our house.'
The Elkins glanced at their children, ages 5, 6 and 7, as they talked about
trying to stave off hunger in one of the most economically depressed
areas of the country.*

*'I just can't find work anywhere, not even odd jobs,' Mr. Elkins
said. 'We're living on welfare and just barely getting by. Things really get
tough at the end of the month, when the food stamps are used up.'[43]—
Branchland, West Virginia—New York Times*

Always "out and about" in the state, Darrell knew the level of
unemployment, poverty and hunger were escalating. People were
struggling to feed their families. He simply wanted to help: "We have an
immediate problem in West Virginia that requires immediate
action…There is a lot of suffering out there right now. It's really pretty
grim this winter for a lot of families and something has to be done."[44]

Without any significant state-wide initiative to address the
growing hunger in West Virginia, Darrell took "it on." Darrell reached
out to a lengthy list of organizations to assist in an effort to feed the poor.
Working with the Council of Churches, union leaders and his office staff

during non-work hours, he established the Family Food Fund. Over a two month period, these efforts raised over $57,000 in food contributions to assist in providing food to an estimated 80,000 unemployed West Virginian's and their families.

Family Food Fund Recipients

To jump start the initiative, Darrell secured a $20,000 personal loan (equivalent to $48,000 today) to purchase food for distribution to those in need. The Family Food Fund was an effort of love and commitment by a lot of people to address hunger in the state. Michigan and Maine provided dried beans and potatoes to the effort. The Teamsters Union arranged for the transportation to pick up and deliver the food. Working with the UMWA, Darrell loaded a sack of coal on the truck bound for Maine and Michigan as a symbolic thank you for their generosity. The Council of Churches, UMWA, and the Teamsters Union led the effort to secure private donations. The Department of Welfare coordinated the donation of surplus butter and cheese for distribution. And all the volunteers worked to spearhead a bean dinner at the State Capitol to raise funds.

People were engaged and pleased with the opportunity to help others, and they wanted to continue with the effort. After the initial start-up, the Family Food Fund was taken over by the Council of Churches and labor unions. Other organizations established complementary efforts, including the United Food Operation, which engaged in continual food

224

drives to feed the hungry.[45] Today there are two major food banks in West Virginia, and an estimated 1 in 6 people still struggle with hunger.[46]

Chief Justice Darrell McGraw, Jr. loading coal

It rarely occurred when the pain of doing the right thing was simply too much for the family. But when the Family Food Fund became controversial and Darrell's philanthropic efforts generated charges that his involvement violated the Code of Judicial Ethics, many family members were upset. A complaint was filed with the State Bar and an investigation was initiated. Consequences for violation of the Code can be severe and range from admonishment to suspension or even revocation of one's license to practice law. Darrell knew his family was concerned: "My father-in-law thinks I'm a fool for sticking my neck out this way...My wife is frightened for the family and my mother is frightened for me. My brother Warren is almost hostile to me...Brother Warren also told McGraw he didn't think it was his place to become prime sponsor for the organization."[47]

Even though the family was concerned, the effort was the right thing to do, and the family stepped forward to raise funds and contribute food. My father (S.G.Joe Marple) donated 1,000 pounds of onions to go with all the beans, potatoes and cornmeal distributed. The extended family, including Warren, attended and worked to make the bean dinner

225

fund raiser a great success. Letters to newspaper editors, personal letters of encouragement, editorials, newspaper smiley faces noted that Darrell's efforts to feed the hungry were worthwhile.[48]

Ultimately, the West Virginia Judicial Investigation Commission "found nothing wrong with Chief Justice Darrell McGraw's role in setting up a food fund for needy families."[49] Darrell was right when he said, "But whose place is it to be their brother's keeper? I'm not doing it as chief justice, but as an individual. I may happen to have that forum. I hope we're willing to assume that responsibility to our fellow man."[50]

Ethics Complaints—Never a Dull Moment in WV Politics
To whose benefit is to file an ethics complaint?

Ethics complaints are serious business. But an ethics complaint can be filed for political reasons, undisclosed but apparent to some. The Family Food ethics complaint fell into that category. The complaint was designed to embarrass Darrell and negatively impact future elections. However, Darrell believed duty to mankind "trumped" any politically motivated ethics complaint.

During Darrell's time on the Court there were other ethics complaints. There was always the possibility of a reprimand or worse. Each ethics complaint was taken seriously and involved the engagement of a lawyer, expense, consternation and upheaval. One such ethics complaint filed by state Sen. Walter Rollins was deemed as "dumb" by one commentator and "ultimate silliness" by another.[51] It was viewed by most as simply political. Rollins filed the ethics complaint because Darrell spoke out against the legislative cut in the appropriation for operation of the statewide court system. Chief Justice Fred Caplan also spoke out against the legislative cut but no complaint was lodged against him.[52] The Constitution stated the Legislature shall not cut the state Court's budget. Rollins' ethics compliant resulted in two years of contention and turmoil through reviews by the Judicial Inquiry Commission, the Judicial Review Board and the WV Supreme Court. Why was the complaint filed?

"For starters, McGraw's name is like waving a red flag in front of a bull as far as the Legislature is concerned. It just drives some of those guys up the wall. Faces turn purple and smoke fairly boils out of their ears. McGraw has been dubbed a liberal in West Virginia, because on occasion, he's thrown off the musty solemnness of the court and has spoken out on behalf of the people."[53]—*Andy Gallagher, UPI*

The Judicial Inquiry Commission recommended to the Judicial Review Board that Darrell should be "tried on one charge that he commented on a pending or impending case before the Supreme Court."[54] However, there was no case before the Court when Darrell spoke regarding the unconstitutional cut in the Court's budget: "Originating the Court system's budget is one of the Supreme Court's official duties, a duty assigned by the Constitution. McGraw's statements defended the court's performance of that [administrative] duty and criticized what he saw as legislative incursion onto the court's constitutional turf."[55]—*Herb Little, Columnist*

No matter the merits of Darrell's position, the Review Board's recommendation brought great consternation for the family. This time it was Jeremy McCamic, the dashing and most brilliant trial attorney from Wheeling, who came to Darrell's aid. McCamic, as Darrell called him, was a decorated combat Marine veteran who was schooled in the southern ways, graduating from Ole Miss and University of Virginia Law School. He brought the southern gentleman smoothness and the tenacity of former Marine as he set about to question the Commission members regarding the Rollins complaint and their process for investigation and review. As Jeremy said, "It then got really strange."[56] The Commission members refused to answer any questions and asked the Review Board to grant an order to prohibit McCamic from deposing members. The Review Board granted their request and an appeal was presented to the state Supreme Court: "Justice Darrell McGraw has asked that a complaint charging him with violating the code of conduct for judges be dismissed because members of an agency that brought the complaint refused to answer questions about it."[57] The state Court, without Darrell's participation, held "the action of the Review Board was improper."[58] The *National Law Review* noted the craziness of the Commission's recommendation: "Mr. McGraw is now facing what many say is a trumped-up ethics complaint for his public statements criticizing the state legislature's attempt to cut the judicial budget."[59]

The Commission members continued to refuse to answer any questions from Mr. McCamic. Finally, the state Supreme Court ordered the "Commission to appear and to show cause why the complaint against McGraw should not be dismissed."[60] The complaint was subsequently resolved. Darrell summed up the trivia, "There's never a dull moment in West Virginia politics. It's all political. I am the people's judge. I did what was right."[61]

Anytime people run for office there is opportunity for unregulated mudslinging. In this case the Republican prosecutor of Kanawha County was about to run for Mayor of Charleston. As Chief Justice, Darrell intervened in the Kanawha County practice of holding the grand jury in the prosecuting attorney's office suite. Darrell issued an order which required the Kanawha Circuit Court to move the grand jury. His order addressed a practice that might "make it appear that the jury was a tool of the prosecutor's office, rather than an impartial body."[62] This time it wasn't an ethics complaint, but a call by Prosecutor Roark to impeach Darrell.[63] A call for impeachment left the family distressed but Darrell's words rang true, "There's never a dull moment in WV politics." The grand jury was eventually relocated. Roark became Mayor, and many said a good Mayor, until he pleaded guilty to six misdemeanor counts of cocaine possession.[64]

Chapter XIII   Court's Decisions and Reelection

To whose benefit is it for special interests to influence who is elected to the state Court?

There were accolades and awards for the Court's progressive decisions, which included cases recognized nationally for their significance in advancing human rights, workers' rights and equality of opportunity.

"I think they are recognized as one of the best courts in the nation. In the past 12 years 30 of the Court's cases have been cited in the American Law Reports, a standard text on leading decisions while only 19 were cited during the years 1940 to 1976."[1]—*Becky Baitty, Charleston Attorney*

"Of the twenty-eight decisions of the Court selected for publication in the prestigious *America Law Reports*, twelve were written by Justice McGraw and eight by Justice Miller."[2]—*Beth Fountain, WV Supreme Court*

The Court was recognized for its leadership in interpreting its own Constitution which contributed to American constitutional jurisprudence: "As the result of an increasing reticence by the United States Supreme Court and a heightened sensitivity to civil liberties issues by state jurists, the cast of players molding our constitutional structure has been substantially expanded. The rulings of the West Virginia Supreme Court of Appeals which construe the provisions of the state Constitution, therefore, have special significance not only in the lives of West Virginians but in the development of a national constitutional jurisprudence."[3]—*Gene Nichol, William and Mary Law School*

The troika that joined the Court in 1977 brought with them a progressive philosophy creating a more diverse construct of justices. Until he retired in December of 1980, Chief Justice Fred Caplan joined the troika in many decisions advancing the culturally right action for the state's people. Justice Caplan's commitment to activism continued after his retirement. In 1982 Caplan's concern for the "New Right" (the right wing) in West Virginia and American politics led to his honorary chairmanship of the first conference in West Virginia, perhaps the nation, to educate people on the "New Right" which ultimately developed into a powerful influential factor in political elections. Twenty-nine organizations, including civil rights, labor, courts and religious groups, came together to inform others on the threat to individual freedom guaranteed by the Constitution by a right wing insurgence. Florette Angel, a dedicated community progressive and activist, described the urgency for the community to galvanize: "WV is a state perceived as being 'ripe for the picking, and we don't want to be picked."[4] Justice Caplan foresaw the influence of the right wing when he said, "We've had attacks on the Constitution from the beginning, but this group is so well financed."[5] He was dead right.

This philosophical diversity among the justices spawned discussion, argument, compromise and advancement. Darrell explained both the resistance to and importance of progressive change on the Court: "...we are being criticized really because we are taking cases and hearing cases. As the cases are decided, a new philosophy is prevailing with respect to the law and this is what is unsettling to the power elite, if you would, who have a vested interest in the status quo...But we believe that if we have unsettled the law and set it in a new direction, that it has been in the direction of redressing wrong and of providing a remedy where previously there was no remedy by due course [of] law."[6]

Other legal experts saw the Court's work in the same way: "The post 1976 WV court quickly established its role in modifying common-law principles and channeled WV's court generated body of law into the mainstream of progressive tort and workers' compensation doctrine and rules. The new court did not hesitate to create new causes of action if it discovered a right without a remedy."[7]—*Charles Lopeman, The Activist Advocate*

In 2016 Darrell received West Virginia University College of Law highest award, the *Justitia Officium Award* which acknowledged his contribution and service to the legal profession, and his role as a progressive jurist in authoring legal opinions which recognized the rights of injured workers to hold intentional violators of work place safety laws accountable; the mandating of proper funding of public education; the enforcing of human rights law, and the obligating of proper funding for public pensions. The following cases, in addition to the ones previously presented, are representative of the troika led state Court's decisions that reflected the belief: ***Of One Blood are All People.***

A Progressive Court's Opinions

State Ex. Rel. Harper v. Zegeer,[8]—The Court held jailing of alcoholics for public intoxication was unconstitutional under the cruel and unusual punishment in Article II, Section 5(3) of West Virginia's Constitution. The Court delayed the effective date of the ruling in order to allow local and state government officials time to develop more efficient and facile methods for detaining and treating alcoholics than presently available. Soon after this decision, a nineteen-year-old youth jailed in South Charleston on a public intoxication charge committed suicide in a South Charleston. In reaction to the tragedy, the Court granted *Harper's* petition for a rehearing and reaffirmed the incarceration of alcoholics unconstitutional, clarifying that existing programs must establish "clean and sanitary centers for publicly inebriated people."[9] Warren was Senate President when the *Harper* decision was issued, and he expedited the passage of a bill which provided law enforcement officers the option of issuing a citation against a public intoxicant rather than seeking the issuance of a warrant.[10]

Dadisman v Moore[11]—The Court held the state must recognize and carry out their responsibilities to properly fund and manage the State Retirement System. In this case the Governor and Legislature, for four consecutive years (1985-1989), did not appropriate money to the Retirement System resulting in $80 million dollars in lost funds. Darrell writing for the majority held actions of the Governor and Legislature were illegal and violated their fiduciary duties to pensioners. The opinion ordered the State to develop a plan to restore the underfunded appropriations and adhere to the code for future required appropriations to the Retirement System. This wasn't the last time that Darrell addressed the funding of public employee's retirement system. As a result of successful tobacco litigation settlement during the time Darrell was Attorney General, the Legislature subsequently allocated $807 million dollars to the unfunded liability in the retirement system.[12]

Dunlop v. Worker's Compensation Commissioner[13]–The Court held that an injured employee who returns to work, then finds that he or she still cannot work because of the injury in question, does not lose Worker's Compensation eligibility.

Harless v. First National Bank[14]—The Court held an employee cannot be fired for trying to follow a regulatory law, even if the employee has no contract.

Bradley v. Appalachian Power Co.[15]—The Court rejected the doctrine of contributory negligence which prohibited injured individuals from any recovery in accidents for which they are partially at fault.

Hurley v. Allied Chemical Co.[16]—The Court held a qualified person cannot be denied a job because he or she received mental health services.

Peters v. Narick[17]—The Court held the "separate maintenance statute must be applied in a gender-neutral fashion; thereby extending right to receive separate maintenance to both men and women."[18] The opinion won an award from NOW for recognizing women on the same level of equality.

Breeden v. Workmen's Comp.[19]—The Court held that a worker can be compensated for physical or mental disability resulting from stress brought on by continuing and intentional harassment.

Wayne County Board of Education v. Tooley[20]—The Court held that school service personnel cannot be fired without a hearing before the county board of education.

E. H., et al v Khan Martin, M.C.[21]—The Court held that patients at a mental institution received woefully inadequate treatment, and the conditions of their hospitalization were "shocking to the conscience of any civilized society". Known as the "Hartley case," the Court referred to the 'Dickensian' squalor of unconscionable magnitudes in West Virginia's mental institutions. The Court remanded the case to the circuit court to develop a plan (Hartley Plan) in accordance with the rights established by *Code*, 27-5-9 to be provided to every patient in mental health institutions maintained by the State of West Virginia.

Webb v. Fury[22]—The Court held that statements made by an environmentalist to the Environmental Protection Agency do not give rise to a cause of action. In this case the Court prevented a libel suit brought by a coal mining company against an environmentalist from going forward. The Court became one of the first in the nation to offer greater protection for the right of an individual to petition the government for redress than had previously been afforded under the free speech clause.

United Mine Workers of America v. Miller[23] —The Court held miners were not to be penalized by employers for exercising their right to accompany mine inspectors during inspections, and that West Virginia Department of Mines was under a duty to enforce the statutory requirements regarding respirable dust.

Hodge v. Ginsberg[24]—The Court held the Department of Welfare was required to provide adult protective services to incapacitated individuals including the provision of emergency shelter, food and medical care to the homeless petitioners and other similarly situated persons as required by W.Va. Code.

Pittsburg Elevator Co. v. WV Board of Regents[25]—The Court held that citizens can sue state agencies as long as they seek damages under the state's liability insurance, rather than damages to be paid from state funds.

Adkins v. CSC and PSC[26]—The Court held that civil service employees can't be transferred or demoted without notice, hearing and written decision.

Javins v. Workers' Compensation Commission[27]—The Court held where there is conflicting medical evidence about the degree of impairment in a black lung claim, the Worker's Compensation division must accept the highest estimate.

Hechler v. Casey[28]—The Court held that A.T. Massey Coal Company cannot block the Secretary of State from conducting hearings to find out whether their security company has illegally hired convicted criminals to guard Massey mines during a strike.

Crain v. Bordenkirchner[29]—The Court held the lower court's order that required the prison system to implement sweeping changes was final.

State ex. Rel. Board of Education v. Casey[30]—The Court held that Boards of Education must honor seniority rights of personnel when reduction of force results in the need to lay off employees.

Pack v. Van Meter[31]—The Court held that an employee injured on the job can sue the owner of the building if that owner's negligence caused the injury.

233

Dillon v. Board of Education[32]—The Court held that boards of education must consider the seniority of the applicants in the hiring of the most qualified applicant for a teaching position.
Frank's Shoe Store v. Human Rights Commission[33]—The Court held that pregnancy discrimination constitutes illegal sex discrimination under the WV Human Rights Act.
Wiggins v. Eastern Associated Coal Corp.[34]*, 357 S.E. 2d 745 (W.Va.1987)*—The Court held that a coal miner fired for raising safety issues can sue the company in court.

It was the "People's Court"—1977-1988

Judicial Re-Election Campaign—Case for McGraw

From the standpoint of history, the poor in West Virginia have suffered more, perhaps, than the poor anywhere else in the nation. If Darrell McGraw sees himself as a champion of people who have been dealt a dirty deal by the economic system, what's wrong with that? And if Darrell McGraw wants to make a political career of standing up for poor people and working people, what's wrong with that? Others in the system, and there are plenty of them are just as political as McGraw, but they represent prosperous interests and prosper more from their advocacy for the wealthy than McGraw does from being an advocate for those least wealthy and powerful...His views are very much like their own [the people], and he is a powerful intellectual champion for their cause, because he says things they would say if they could say them.[35]*—Walter C. Massey, Jr., Editor, Register/Herald*

In 1984 Justice Harshbarger, one the members of the troika, lost his re-election bid. In 1988 it was Darrell and Tom Miller's turn to seek re-election. Justices Miller and McGraw were not only associates but friends. Vaughn, Tom's wife, was poised and reflective with a great sense of humor who took everything in stride. She possessed an artful ability to change the subject when the two justices' conversation became intense. Vaughn just offered the arguing justices her latest appetizer, always delicious, and said, "Here, try this. I've worked so hard making these. Tell me what you think." Discussion ended and argument

234

delayed. Vaughn's diversionary tactic was reminiscent of the story Darrell told so many times about Governor Wally Barron: The Barrons were at a social function when a less than supportive constituent came up to the Governor and started berating him saying, "Wally Barron you are the most no account son of a bitch I ever knew." To which the Governor, as he turned toward wife, said, "Have you met my wife Opal." The intruder totally caught off guard by the introduction to the Governor's wife slithered away.

Some evenings when the friends were together, Miller, born in Buffalo, New York, spoke about his difficult childhood and how he understood why kids rebelled and got into trouble. Miller never rebelled instead he became more determined to be the best at whatever he attempted. He was a dedicated student; excelled while in the U.S. Navy in the Korean War, and became a successful partner in the prestigious Wheeling law firm of Schrader, Byrd and Companion before his election to the Court. He never saw himself as handsome and debonair, but he was that, in addition to being "scholarly, intelligent, compassionate, fair-minded, even-tempered, modest, self-deprecating and industrious."[36] But Miller was sometimes beset by the devils of ruling with his good heart or staying accepted by a more established segment of society. In more cases than not, Miller went with his heart.

Three sitting circuit judges filed to run in the primary against Darrell and Miller: Judge John Hey and Judge Margaret Workman, Kanawha County and Judge Fred Fox, Marion County. Darrell knew it would be a tough race. In one of the first polls taken in the high court race, Darrell was in the lead with 17%; Hey and Workman with 14%; Fox with 6%, and Miller was last with 5%.[37] Darrell was concerned for Miller. However Darrell also believed money and the female vote might change his own advantage. The Court was recognized for their rulings in favor of women and children, but Darrell knew Workman would draw the female vote. Even though Darrell received in 1981 National Association of Women's (NOW) first Susan B. Anthony Award, "in grateful appreciation for distinguished contributions to the advancement of women's rights in WV," Workman received the endorsement of NOW.[38]

The heavily populated northern panhandle and the more liberal part of the business community supported Miller. Darrell had labor support, but labor was not committed to the endorsement of Miller. At a large combined labor meeting where Darrell was the keynote speaker, Darrell spoke to the importance of maintaining a progressive point of the view on the Court in order that it remain responsive to working people issues. Darrell asked the group to support both he and Miller. Darrell followed up with visits to local offices of UMWA, AFL-CIO, WVEA and a multitude of other labor organization throughout the state. Labor endorsed Miller. Miller appreciated Darrell's assistance in getting the labor endorsement. They were a team.

Miller's business and home area supporters remained concerned he might lose to Margaret Workman. A January, 1988 poll showed Workman-12%, McGraw-11%, Hey-11%, Fox- 5% and Miller-4%.[39] In the final week before the election the poll showed Miller was still in trouble: Workman-38%, McGraw-27%, Hey-26%, Miller-19% and Fox-12%. There was also a large undecided vote.[40] Miller's supporters determined to focus on getting out the vote for only their candidate.

A few days before the election Darrell knew he was in trouble. Raising twice the amount of money as Darrell, Workman and Miller saturated television and radio with their ads..[41] Rumors were prevalent that Miller's supporters were promoting a single shot vote. Labor remained committed to voting for both Darrell and Miller.

A few days before the election Darrell read an article in which he was described as a controversial justice. When he read the description of himself as "a beloved and detested judge, crusader and accused demagogue," he saw it as a red flag for any success on Election Day.[42] Some viewed the election as a referendum on Darrell but he viewed it differently: "The race is not about competence, balance or scholarship, as some have said. Rather as I see it through an age-old WV prism…a struggle between good and evil, between coal miner and coal operators, believer in a progressive court and 'nowheresville.'"[43]

Justice Miller and Margaret Workman won. Darrell was third. Margaret Workman became the first female to serve on the West Virginia Supreme Court. An analysis of Election Day results verified the rumors that Miller's supporters simply "one-shot the vote."[44]

Miller felt the loss of the man he called brother, "McGraw is self-described 'people judge' who wrote important decisions…We have

institutionally lost something, for what may be the human side of law."[45]—
Justice Thomas Miller

Happy for his own success, Justice Miller lamented Darrell's defeat.

May 11, 1988

Dear Darrell:

I did not get in very early today and, when I stopped by your office, you were out. I also tried calling you at home but no one answered. As you may guess, all of these procedural details are just a way to try to say something about the election. I am at a loss to understand it, much less to talk about it. I cannot say that I was unhappy to win.

On the other hand, I can say that I am grievously sorry that you lost. There is an institutional loss as your opinions were a major factor in this Court's record over the past eleven years. Moreover, I am of the firm belief that in matters of conscience, particularly as to the school system, election laws and the workings of government, I have learned much from you.

You are in the words of those that I met on the campaign trial – a good and decent man. I shall remember that you were the only one on the public television debate who had the courage to say that you had a moral antipathy against the death penalty.

Permit me to say that I sorrow for your loss.

Sincerely,

Thomas B. Miller[46]

It felt like the end…but was it?

237

Chapter XIV   Years in Between Public Offices

Sarah, Darrell, Elizabeth, Elliott and Darrell III McGraw

Losing the election was painful in many ways. The morning after an election defeat is akin to really bad hangover; i.e. preferring not to get out of bed; resisting conversation with anyone, and a spinning head with thoughts of darkness and despair. A substantial personal loan of $32,000 to the campaign, young children and uncertain employment heightened the anxiety on the home front. The lost election found me the next morning with an irrational vigor to clean, sort, throw away "stuff" and pack. For the twelve years Darrell was on the Court, he just crossed the street and went in the north east entrance to reach his office. The house was a great location while in office, but not so much when not. I was packing boxes with no idea of where the family was going. It was crazy, but elections can make one that way. The campaign was bruising. Negative ads attacked Darrell's personal character: "McGraw mis-spent tax payer dollars; McGraw's a liberal who is bad for business, and McGraw's behavior is erratic."[1] Our two younger children watched the ads, and now they saw their mother packing. It was a difficult time.

There were many kind words and letters from friends and family and even letters to the newspapers.

"McGraw, you see, had taken his call seriously and to him (and any other Judeo-Christian believing in democracy) that meant at least listening to the weak and poor when they came before his court...In his wisdom, Justice McGraw realized that the only thing most Appalachians

238

had to trade was their bodies, and for giving those broken bodies the benefit of the doubt, he was called a special interest judge. And so it went and so it goes…"—*John H. Yevuta, teacher*

"McGraw's decisions have helped the little guy, and McGraw genuinely wants to protect people from powerful interests. "[2]—*William Pepper, former law clerk*

Justice Sam Harshbarger, one of the troika who established a nationally recognized progressive Court and provided freedom for Justice Fred Caplan to be who he really was—a jurist of liberal education and action simply wrote, "even the heavens weep."[3]

Harshbarger, a tall, lanky and definitely gentlemanly jurist, was a compassionate people's judge, sensitive to injustice, and straight forward in his commitment to the working people. Shortly after Harshbarger was elected to the Court he questioned the equality of justice for the poor. His response captured the greatness of his character: "I question whether the problem of unequal justice for the poor is one that the public really wants to solve. There's an attitude that if a man can't compete in the economic system, then he can't compete elsewhere, including the courtroom. Only when the same caliber of representation is available to the poor, as it to the rich, will there be equal justice under the law. [I believe] those who defend the rich in criminal trials should be the only lawyers allowed to defend the poor."[4]

Always with a cigarette close by, Harshbarger—the troika always called each other by their last names—was the son of a hardware merchant and banker who was in private law practice before his election to the Court. Harshbarger, knew the struggles of small business people, and contrary to election propaganda, was both pro-business and pro working people. Darrell often related Harshbarger's comment when someone in the family talked about starting a business. Harshbarger, grateful for his $50,000 income as a Justice, simply said, "You have to sell a lot of paint to make $50,000." Harshbarger, always thoughtful with his actions, sent a dozen yellow roses to our daughter Elliott on the day of her birth with a note, "I want to be the first man to send a beautiful young girl a dozen roses."

Harshbarger lost his re-election bid in 1984 and by 1988 was critically ill. The Legislature changed the judicial retirement statute, as payback for progressive decisions in which the state Supreme Court held the legislative and executive branches accountable to Constitutional, statutory, due process and human rights requirements pertaining to education, mental health, prison systems, juveniles, workers' compensation and hiring and work practices for public employees. Justice Sam Harshbarger, one of West Virginia's unsung heroes, was denied the right to a judicial pension. It was a sad turn of events for a man who did so much good. Harshbarger died in 1992. But forever in the mind of those who knew him, Harshbarger will always be one of the "good people justices."

Judge Larry Starcher, who was later elected to the state Supreme Court, wrote of Darrell's contribution as a jurist:

I feel that I must let you know the disappointment many of us who have fought the battles for the 'little people' feel. We have lost a soldier from the trenches. Quite frankly, your sometimes daring leadership in controversial matters has, from time to time, helped others of us muster the courage we needed to get out on the cutting edge of legal/social issues. I thank you for that direction. After the sting subsides, you will probably settle into something which will be less stressful than have been recent times; but the voters philosophical leader, and the 'little people' lose the most.[5] –Judge Larry Starcher, WV Supreme Court Justice 1977-1996

Then there was the note from the undeterrable Herb J. Rogers, Harvard law school graduate, divinity and legal scholar, who in 1960 protested the arrival of the Mast at WVU. Herb, whose actions viewed by some as more than controversial, has devoted a great part of his life to goading the established order. Throughout the years, Herb has sent Darrell notes of applicable scripture; this time he wrote: "We are sick at our very hearts and can hardly see through our tears, because Mount Zion lies lonely and deserted, and wild jackals prowl through its ruins. But you o Lord, are king forever and will rule until the end of time - *5:17-19*"[6]— Only Herb.

I have, for a greater part of my life, kept a journal. The following journal excerpts express the personal impact of the election:

May 9, 1988 (eve of primary election)

Darrell III is taking all this election to heart. He broke down and just sobbed the other afternoon and said, 'Mom I'm just so scared.'

He doesn't want his Dad to loose. I don't think he is afraid of the future; he just doesn't like the idea of being defeated. He reads everything—the brochures, newspaper accounts, surveys, polls. Wish I could keep it all from him, but he is just too bright and interested. He stayed home from school today saying he was sick. I know tomorrow it will even be more difficult for him.

May 16, 1988.

It's over, and we lost. Darrell III was very upset. It broke my heart when he said to me, 'It wouldn't be so bad if Dad were running for Justice for the first time–but I was born into it. I'm so very frightened.' Every day he asks me where will we go.

But I am most thankful for our understanding and supportive family. It is the family who is always there for you in lost elections. I'll never forget lying under the apple trees in Sutton this past Saturday. There was big Darrell, Darrell III and Elliott. Mom and Dad came out with a blanket and laid down with us in silence and support.[7]

Years of frustration and disappointment with what was I perceived as the lack of community support was reflected in this journal entry:

May, 1989

We went to church on Sunday, and I couldn't help but cry. I am so upset at people who are supposed to be living in adherence to the social principles of their church. Where have they been? Darrell has unequivocally led his life with the church principles close to his heart. He actually frequently carries in his pocket a small copy of the principles of the Methodist Church.

Where was one person to come to the defense of Darrell when he was beaten up by the Kanawha County Sheriff thugs in his attempt to find out why a young boy hung himself in the adult jail facility? Where were they when Darrell wrote the opinion saying alcoholics are sick and need shelter and care? Where were they when the Court said children throughout West Virginia deserved equal educational opportunities? Where were they when the court ruled in the Mandolidis decision that an

241

employer could be held accountable when he intentionally put an employee at risk of injury or death in order to maintain his job?

Endless decisions with endless criticism from the press and the establishment, but never any defense offered by those who are principled in religious ethics. Well that ought to do it.[8]

Joseph Campbell's books, including *Power of Myths,* and the 1988 PBS episodes of Bill Moyers conversations with Campbell were helpful to us as we struggled with the reality of losing the election. Campbell's analysis of what guides human behavior and why one makes certain life choices uplifted our understanding of those who resisted the Court's progressive opinions. We found comfort in Campbell's admonition: "Is the system going to eat you up and your humanity or is your humanity going to resist the system and benefit all of humanity?"[9] Campbell's advice remained pertinent to us in lots more of our difficult professional situations.

The system wasn't going to devour Darrell. Darrell was 52 years old, not old enough to retire, but faced with the difficulty of entering private practice after serving as justice on the state Supreme Court. He wrestled with the notion of representing clients before judges whose opinions he reversed or present appeals before a reconstituted Supreme Court? How does a young ex-justice make a living? A progressive justice, viewed as controversial by many, was not in great demand. The reality of what it means to be on the losing side with no inherent wealth to assuage the difficulties was very much a reality for us

Controversy that often enveloped Darrell as a justice at times impacted my professional life as I described in this journal entry:

May 26, 1988

With the arrival of Elliott in 1984, I took a leave of absence from my job as a central office administrator with Kanawha County Schools. I've completed my doctoral studies and am ready to return to work. I applied and was recommended by the administration for an elementary principal job in an up-scale neighborhood. Politics reared its ugly head today when the Kanawha County Board of Education denied my employment. One of the board members said it was simple, "the community was not in favor of Darrell McGraw's wife as "their" school's principal." This was the first time that I experienced politics manifesting itself into my professional life. I surely don't like it, but somehow I think there will be others.

However, as I noted in another journal entry, sometimes something good comes from a perceived unfairness:

June 8, 1992

Sometimes adversity provides an unexpected opportunity. In this time, it resulted in one of the best jobs I ever had. Eight months after Darrell left the Court and with family savings eroded, I became principal of an inner city low performing school in an impoverished neighborhood. Working with a great team of teachers and parents, Tiskelwah Elementary has now received national recognition as a National Blue Ribbon School and one of Redbook's Best Schools in America. It is the best of times.

Darrell was never one to live in the past; bemoan the present or fear the future. He always found ways to move forward. Darrell routinely retreated to books for guidance, solace and strategies to analyze criticism, controversy, campaigns and elections, whether won or lost. His reading often provided an unbiased perspective to analyze the circumstances that contribute to the actions of others. Darrell fought his personal depression with facts rather than emotion. Darrell never succumbed to pity or any notion of the "why me" concept. Whenever family or friends complain Darrell likes to quote Satchel Paige, "Don't look back they may be gaining on you." There were many times when money was tight; worthiness shaken and loneliness particularly debilitating, that I succumbed to self pity. Darrell was always there to lift my spirits. Sometime during those difficult years I tried to express in writing how much I appreciated my life partner. For the years we lived at 18 California Avenue, Darrell kept this note from me in his dresser drawer:

Since 1972 you've been my true love...
As you've come through the years conquering all adversity
you've given your all for this family's prosperity.
A little son we had.
You became committed to being number one Dad
One by one personal flaws were eliminated for your goal to be

a good dad, and I am so glad.
Your courage to right the wrongs and fight the good fight
            has made you a hero in my eyes tonight.
You've never compromised
            for the hopes of others to be realized.
You remained the daring defender of human rights.
Taunted and harassed you continued to fight.
Wealth and power held no gold
            for you are like a crusader of old.
Attacked for not being a soft spoken mouse
            you chose to put your efforts into righting the house.
Don't hurt the workers, comfort the sick, feed the poor,
            educate the children and throw the rascals out the door.
A little curly haired daughter came our way—
            a perfect family now through night and day.
You asked that all the workers (big and small) do their job
You held your head high and did not flinch nor say me, oh why.
On you will go doing what is right and just and you must know.
That God is with you and to the people you have been true.[10]

During these "in between years" Darrell spent time maintaining our family's 1911 home which was always in need of repair. Darrell never enjoyed the role of handy man. He was frustrated by lack of the right tools, and his own personal skill level which made most jobs complex and time consuming. Our California Avenue home provided glorious views of the Capitol dome and a ring side seat for all of the celebrations, ceremonies, protests, proms, weddings and parties that occurred on the Capitol lawn. Sometimes the frivolity that took place at the Capitol was disconcerting to family life as Darrell frustratingly described the activity as the "California Avenue Beach" scene. Even with the problems of living across from the Capitol, it provided a playground for children, family and friends and a gift for almost 37 years with ready access to work and the beauty of the Capitol. The State systematically bought houses on the street making the home an island within a commercial bastion.

Darrell continued to explore business opportunities including establishing a lawyer referral service and a marketing business for

attorneys. Neither venture came to fruition. Darrell's efforts seemed
negatively impacted by his history as a progressive jurist and financing
his ventures was a burden on top of the obligation to retire the campaign
debt. Darrell's schedule allowed him the flexibility to take our children
to and from school; increased his involvement in their activities. Darrell
regularly assisted with programs at Tiskelwah Elementary where I was
principal. Always the reader, Darrell routinely brought to my attention
interesting new programs and services for children. One morning on the
coffee tray, which he always delivered to my bedside, Darrell placed a
story about a summer lunch program for children in Texas. Great idea
for the students at Tiskelwah his note said. Sure enough Tiskelwah
offered the first lunch program in the state that summer for students on
the west side of Charleston. It was a hit and expanded to sites across the
district and state.
          A welcome outlet each year for the family was the McGraw
reunion which has been held annually for 65 years. Darrell and Justice
Miller sometimes discussed the loneliness associated with being a justice.
They viewed personal relationships with others as problematic because of
potential perceived or real biases in cases that might come before the
Court. Family was the mainstay for social interaction and that included
the McGraw reunion.

          McGraw Reunions—The McGraws love to eat. Food is the
cornerstone for the McGraw annual family reunion. For years the
reunions were held in the gym at the "ole" John McGraws School in
Wyoming County always on the third Sunday in July, and usually the
hottest day of the year. The McGraw brothers have 49 first cousins. For
decades hundreds of McGraws, from states across the country as well as
from "across the creek" made the annual trip to the reunion, and if they
were the youngest or traveled the farthest they received a silver dollar.
The 12 children and all the offspring of "Fud (mountain shortened for
Herford) and Mary McGraw (the brothers' grandparents) were in
competition with Fud's siblings, Aunt Gerte, Aunt Ruby, Aunt Ole,
Uncle Walter and Uncle John and all their offspring, to see who could lay
out the best spread. The "spreads," as they were called, required table
cloths, cutlery and bouquets of flowers. Mary McGraw, the brothers'

grandmother, was a renowned cook whose recipes were thoughtfully compiled in *Mary's Cookbook* by the most wonderful Aunt Jackie Burton McGraw.

They all brought food. It wasn't only simple food but gourmet delicacies. There was often a strawberry layer trifle in a glass pedestal bowl carefully wrapped in dry ice and Styrofoam to wait its unveiling. Peanut butter ganache candy rolls were sliced with a razor sharp knife and presented with great pride by 80 something Maxwell (Mac) McGraw. Lasagna layered with homemade noodles and sauce and a decadent variety of cheeses was one of the many dishes executed by Aunt Jackie. Aunt Buena Cook, if we were all lucky, brought the angel biscuits, a heavenly combination of yeast and biscuit bread that was rightly smeared with homemade strawberry jam that she prepared in her hot kitchen at Second Creek during the last months of every summer. Then there was Aunt Verna's twelve, sometimes fourteen, layer applesauce cake with each layer patiently baked and then covered with homemade applesauce or apple butter.

Of course, the cornbread was made with cornmeal Aunt Buena bought from Reeds' Mill on Second Creek—valuable and highly prized. As the family added to their already full plates a piece of the luscious, buttered cornbread someone would almost certainly offer, "Do you know the story of President Eisenhower trying to get Orb's cornmeal?" An uninformed or obsequies family member responded, "No, I've never heard that story and that spawned the opportunity for a gaggle of McGraws to strive to take the lead in telling the well-heard story.

The miller, Orb Reed, was known to be a man of few words and punctilious habits. His water powered mill always ground corn meal on Thursday. President Eisenhower was visiting the legendary Greenbrier Hotel, just a few miles down the road from Reed's Mill in Monroe County. Having enjoyed the cornbread at a brunch, Eisenhower dispatched an aide to fetch some of Reed's cornmeal. President Eisenhower wanted to enjoy cornbread made with that robust meal when he returned to the White House. The aide arriving at the Mill looked around and couldn't find any meal. The young suit clad man saw Orb and said he needed to purchase 5 lbs. of the meal. It was Saturday. Orb replied, "I grind meal on Thursday." The aide replied, "You don't understand the President of the United States has sent me for your cornmeal." Orb responded, "You don't understand I grind meal on Thursday." Those who never heard, and those who heard the story a hundred times before, all laughed uproariously.

Everyone brought their specialty to the reunion. Tables aligned around the walls and up against the bleachers generally held a deep pot filled Julia's Hungarian cabbage rolls, a favorite of her sons; Aunt Fern's coconut pie, devoured before the main course, and Jackie's mother Eileen's slow simmered roast beef that closely resembled Oso Buco.

Darrell, like most McGraws, couldn't get enough of the wonderful food. They ate until the sweat was dripping from their brows, and the heat was about to overcome them. But they generally saved room for just one more serving of whatever they deemed as there last opportunity for the delight until the next year.

The reunions were not handled as well by the children. It was always hot, and the food was too complex. Ah save for Aunt Peggy, that is Saint Peggy, Warren's wife who knew children. She was a teacher. The kids were dependent on what Aunt Peggy brought. Loaded to the brim was her large covered roaster where Peggy carefully placed crispy hot fried chicken. Now this wasn't any ordinary chicken cooked over a hot frying pan. No, this was chicken from the gas station in Pineville— the best ever according to every kid who was saved from the casseroles. Actually truth be known, Warren was often seen hanging around the chicken roaster.

Darrell was most partial to my cooking. Darrell told me that the McGraw clan knew I was a "keeper" when I arrived at Cedar Side on Second Creek, where some of his aunts, uncles and cousins retreated during the summer. I opened the trunk lid of my gold 1972 Grand Prix. Single, and wanting to impress the McGraw clan, I had managed to bake five pies—two butterscotch, one chocolate and two coconut cream pies— on a Saturday morning in Charleston. I loaded the pies in a box lined with dry ice and drove the two and half hours south to meet Darrell and his family. I fervently hoped the pies would survive the trip. As the lid opened, I sighed with relief at the intact meringues and Darrell beamed with pride at my success. So as I began to attend the McGraw reunions, pies were often my contribution.

During these in between years Darrell was an active observer of political events in West Virginia. He often made phone calls or wrote letters to those he believed were mis-treated in some way and needed a call of encouragement. In 1990 Darrell became involved in the first teachers' strike in the state's history. Teacher pay was 49th in the nation. There was a proposal to increase the teacher's cost for state insurance which would further reduce teacher take home pay.

Gaston Caperton, endorsed by the teachers in his 1988 gubernatorial campaign, vowed to address teacher pay. Perhaps a sign that Governor Caperton might waffle on the promise was his association with WV Taxpayers Against Union Control of Government and Schools, an organization whose membership promoted "right to work." In early 1990 Governor Caperton proposed a five percent teacher pay raise which he recommended financing through a minimum tonnage tax on coal. It was estimated that the state was losing $6 million a year because it did not tax 20% of all the coal mined.[11] The coal companies objected to any increase in the coal tax and clearly communicated their displeasure. The Governor reversed his position and reneged on his promise of a pay raise for teachers.[12]

Teachers were outraged and determined to act on their convictions. They left their classrooms for picket lines. Striking was an act totally foreign to them. However, teachers, increasingly unable to meet their financial obligations, felt betrayed by the Governor's withdrawal of the promised pay raise: "West Virginia ranks 49th in teacher pay, with an average annual salary of $21,904…'I'm not proud of what I'm doing, but what we earn is a disgrace,' Susan Coffman, a second-grade teacher, said this morning as she picketed on a spring-like, overcast day in front of the Piedmont Elementary School in downtown Charleston. On the school's bright green doors were tacked copies of court injunctions prohibiting the pickets from blocking entrances and exists."[13]

Hope was briefly rekindled when the Governor announced he planned to speak on March 7th to the Legislature. Teachers thought he was announcing a change of heart, but the address did not turn out as expected: "He delivered a 'there is no table and I will not bend' speech

248

almost identical to what Reagan delivered to the air traffic controllers and Pittston's Douglas delivered to the United Mine Workers."[14]

The Attorney General, appointed by Caperton to fill an unexpired term, issued an opinion stating the strike was illegal and teachers "could be fired, suspended, dismissed or charged with a misdemeanor for walking off the job."[15] The PEIA Director also issued a statement that any "rehired former strikers would be treated as new employees and would liable for paying a third of their health insurance premiums for three years."[16] Both opinions were meant to intimidate the striking teachers, but they continued in their efforts. The Governor remained adamant that the teacher's strike was illegal and teachers faced dismissal if they participated: "Gov. Gaston Caperton and West Virginia's largest teachers union are girding for a showdown today, with the union refusing to end its strike and Caperton warning that teachers who stay off the job can be dismissed. 'The law's pretty clear,' said Caperton, referring to a state attorney general's ruling that the strike is illegal. The West Virginia Education Association accused the governor of backing off a promise to call a special legislative session to discuss pay if teachers returned to work. Caperton said the union's contention that he promised to call a special session was "a total lie."[17]

Darrell did not agree with the threats to dismiss the teachers. Of course as an educator I encouraged Darrell to find a way to help. As a principal of an inner city school, I knew that teachers, who hold the primary responsibility for educating our children, must be provided competitive compensation. Teachers were struggling to make ends meet. I saw it everyday. I also knew it was difficult to hire and maintain high quality teachers with the existing low salary base.

Darrell determined to help, offered his legal opinion regarding the teachers' right to strike: "McGraw said strike-related activities, such as picketing, are protected under the Constitution and Bill of Rights. There is no federal statute which prohibits teacher strikes. There is no state statute that prevents teacher strikes. Thus, there is no law passed by a Congress or Legislature which makes teacher strikes illegal....Education, as a mandate of constitutional law, is supposed to come first, not last. It is not lawful in West Virginia to present a budget to shortchange education at the expense of other, non-constitutional

249

functions."[18] Darrell's comments were not well received by the Governor
or the State Superintendent of Schools.

The strike ended 11 days after it started. The strike provided the
impetus for a special legislative session in August of 1990 that secured
pay raises for teachers.[19] Decades later the West Virginia Education
Association honored Darrell with the Margaret Baldwin Friend of
Education Award for his life time commitment to public education. In or
out of office Darrell wanted to make a difference whether it was standing
up for teachers, coal miners or the next door neighbor, Darrell lived daily
his duty to others. Darrell was always in the arena.

Did another opportunity for public service await Darrell?

Chapter XV Attorney General Darrell McGraw

Attorney General—Perfect Fit for Darrell

Jorea Marple and Darrell McGraw
Inauguration January, 1993

Three years after Darrell left the state Supreme Court, life dramatically changed for us. It was the last evening to file for office in the 1992 election and potential candidates were in the Secretary of State's office. Darrell was there too.

For the past several years Darrell worked on legal issues related to the lock out of workers at the Ravenswood Aluminum plant in Jackson County. The workers objected to a proposed contract that changed the seniority rules; eliminated a cost-of-living adjustment and any immediate pay increase. The contract changes occurred at the same time that the high cost of aluminum was creating generous profits for the company. Board Chairman Emmet R. Boyle's response to the contract rejection was to lock out the 1,700 workers and hire new employees—a practice condoned under the Reagan and Bush administrations.[1] Boyle and another investor bought the company from the Kaiser Aluminum Corporation in 1989 and renamed it Ravenswood Aluminum. Many believed Boyle took his orders from Marc Rich, a billionaire who fled to Switzerland after being indicted for tax evasion, racketeering and supplying oil to Iran during the embassy hostage crisis.[2] Under this new leadership's watch, five men died in accidents at the plant before the

251

lock-out occurred. Charles McDowell, a leader in Local 5668, described the difficult work environment: "It's a tough enough job anyway, with outrageous temperatures. But they started raw-dogging you and working you like a mule."[3] After the lock-out the workers were left without income until the state and the National Labor Relations Board officially determined their eligibility to receive unemployment benefits. The lock-out, lasting 18 months, was financially devastating to many families.

The Jackson County circuit judge seat was open, and community members were encouraging Darrell to run for the office. Warren, who was now practicing law and serving on the Wyoming County Board of Education offered, "Look as you have said a half a dozen times, everything is local, and it is certainly a way to add an objective voice to what has happened in Ravenswood."[4] So on an unseasonably warm January evening in 1992, Darrell left the house and headed to the Secretary of State's office. At this point, it was only the family who knew what Darrell was going to do.

After submitting his forms to run for circuit judge, Darrell turned around and saw Attorney General Mario Palumbo arrive with political advisers, Nelson Sorah and Leslie Milam. As Palumbo walked to the front desk, Nelson and Leslie whispered to Darrell, "Mario is not running for Attorney General; he is running for Governor." Darrell immediately began to contemplate a change in plans. He was thinking about his duty to a lot of people—family, friends and the steel workers in Jackson County, as he walked back across the street to the house. Palumbo's late night decision to file for governor left the Democratic ticket without a candidate for Attorney General.

The phone started ringing at the house. Michael Burdiss, an UMWA official, Nelson and Leslie all called and offered the positives for making the run for Attorney General. They knew Darrell had labor support and name recognition and the late hour for filing meant there might not be other candidates seeking the Democratic nomination. It was approaching 10 p.m. when the doorbell rang, and Larry Bailey, state Treasurer from 1976 to 1984, and his friend and political advisor, Harold Berthy, walked into the house. They said they were there to escort Darrell across the street to file the necessary papers to run for Attorney General.

There were others monitoring the filings in the Secretary of State's office. Justice Richard Neely, who served with Darrell on the Court, learned that Darrell filed for Attorney General. Ed Rebrook described that night: "When I was told, about 75 minutes before the deadline, that McGraw was the sole Democratic candidate for Attorney General, I went knocking on doors in my condominium, asking my neighbors to help me scrape up the $504 filing fee. Then I went to the home of Justice Richard Neely at 11:15 p.m. to get him to witness my certificate of candidacy because I knew I'd never find a notary public at that hour."[5]

The race was on for West Virginia Attorney General and despite the opposition's negative ads, Darrell won the Democratic primary with 55% of the vote compared to Ed Rebrook's 44%. In the general election Darrell defeated Robert Gould, the Republican nominee and buffalo farmer, securing 52% to Gould 48% of the vote.[6]

"Son, you need to become a lawyer and help the community," his father said. As West Virginia's chief legal officer, Darrell would do just that.

Attorney General Darrell McGraw, Jr.

Sixteen years earlier Darrell took the oath to become a Justice on the West Virginia Supreme Court. Now on January 18, 1993, four years after he left the Court, Darrell stood on the south side steps of the Capitol steps, on a much more temperate day, and was sworn in as West Virginia's 33rd Attorney General. He was 57 years old. Darrell loved being attorney general. Attorney General was a perfect fit for his personality and life's goal of duty to others. Every day there was opportunity to help the community and enforce the law against "wrongdoers." No matter the travail that might be on the day's agenda, Darrell was never anything but enthusiastic to go to work for the people.

A true son of teachers who believed education was the answer to most of the world's problems, the new AG organized the work of his office around this belief. A love for learning and appreciation of the importance of education infiltrated both Darrell's personal and professional life. A voracious reader, learning was a joy to him and he wanted it be so for others: "In the most ideal of all worlds, I've thought about education as being not only the preparation of us to participate, but education ought to instill in us an excitement for the experience of learning…When I was a kid the most delightful part of the year was when school started. It was all wrapped up with autumn and chinquapins. School represented to me excitement that people generally have about civilization and education."[7]

This love and respect for education resulted in the encouragement of numerous staff within the AG office to return to school and further their education. It also fostered the establishment, through public information programs, a nationally recognized office of consumer protection. The success of the consumer protection office was built on first educating citizens to understand their rights as consumers, and then making sure the consumer knew who and where to call when they had a problem.

Rebuilding Consumer Protection

The reorganization of Consumer Protection Division was a conscious, deliberate effort to fulfill the statutory duties of the office.

Prior to Darrell's term there were very few consumer cases, with exception of the asbestos case, which was initiated by the Governor's office, being the most significant. It was apparent that we needed to develop an office that could effectively respond to the multitude of consumer issues. But how?

We knew we needed to bring people together to help us. A Consumer Task Force of bankers, teachers, defense lawyers, trial lawyers, prosecutors, agency representatives, senior citizens, advocates and a host of other advisers was formed. They basically told us we needed to start over and reconstruct the Consumer Protection Division into an effective entity.

The first step was to establish a significant consumer public outreach initiative which included advertisement, education programs and 800 numbers where people could call to report issues. And we needed a way to fund the outreach program.

Second, we needed to figure out how to fund complaint investigations and any follow-up legal action. Big time litigation often costs millions and can take years to resolve. It was unlikely the Legislature was going to appropriate money up front for a consumer case. For example, the tobacco litigation that brought in billions would never have occurred, if we had been dependent upon the Legislature to approve and appropriate the millions necessary to litigate the case. It was as the Judge often said, "If we had asked the Legislature for money for the tobacco litigation they would have laughed us out of the Capitol." He was so right. Litigations are always risky and success never guaranteed. Not a likely construct for legislative appropriation of funds. The AG office in order to fulfill its statutory responsibility to address consumer issues needed another way to fund litigations. We determined that in the large consumer cases it was necessary to appoint special Assistant AGs who were willing to take on the litigation on a contingency basis.

Consumer education and outreach and appointing outside counsel were controversial. Perhaps controversial is an understatement. It was a vicious cycle—we used settlement dollars to educate the public. I want to reinforce that statement—the consumer education programs were funded through settlements not tax dollars. Through the outreach, more people turned to us for help, and we were successful. Then the attack dogs said we were promoting the "Judge" through educating the people where to call; who to call, and what to do.

We appointed outside counsel as special assistant Attorneys General and won millions, actually billions for the state. Then the attack dogs said we were lining trial lawyers' pockets.

But the "Judge," (a name everyone called him) knew the changes in the operation of Consumer Protection were right ones, and he simply said let's do it. And we did.[8]*—Frances Hughes, Chief Deputy Attorney General*

Based on the recommendations from the Consumer Task Force and the AG staff, two major strategies were identified and implemented to restructure the Consumer Protection Division into an award winning and nationally recognized entity.

Strategy # 1: Consumer Education Outreach

We scraped together every dollar we could to begin the consumer outreach and then committed to securing additional funding through court directed settlements in successful litigations. It worked. We didn't use tax dollars but our successful cases afforded more opportunity to reach out to more people. We received national awards, lots of them, recognizing our success.[9]*—Frances Hughes*

Consumer advocates were employed in different regions of the state to work directly with citizens in the area. Consumer advocates were often individuals who were retired from other jobs in the community. They knew the people, and the people knew and trusted them. Julia Stevenson and John Grossi were representative of the many dedicated advocates who loved their work and relished in helping community members solve their consumer issues. Julia served remote Randolph County and adjacent communities. Julia grew up in Coalton a small coal mining hamlet where one of the largest fund raising spaghetti dinners in the state takes place each spring. With Julia's involvement, the St. Patrick Church annually serves a thousand or so hungry friends and family. Julia, in between preparing and serving meals, always took the time to listen to community members stories about some scam that had been inflicted on them, and the next day she had a mission.

John Grossi, a gentle imposing giant of a man, not in stature but in being, was described by Darrell in one word "outstanding." He was recommended by Judge Risovich as the perfect person for the job. Grazie was a retired school administrator and probation officer who knew almost everyone in the northern panhandle that he served. John was person who was devoted to improving the quality of life for his family, his students and the community. John was loved by his community, and he loved the community. People knew that John listened to their issues and then, as John would say, "by golly we will do something about the problem."

The AG, office staff and the consumer educators, through participation in spaghetti dinners, school fund raisers, parades, festivals, fairs, forums, conferences—whatever it took, reached out to constituencies in every part of the state. Darrell loved being "out there" in the midst of the action. He enjoyed the opportunity to meet the people he represented; learn their issues and determine how to help. Part of the outreach program was making sure people had a phone number to call when they needed assistance. The number needed to be readily available. Common practice at all these events was for a staff member to take Polaroid pictures of as many people as possible, often with the AG. A magnet placed on the back of the picture, and a sticker with the consumer hot-line number on the front. People did just what the consumer outreach program anticipated; they placed the picture on their refrigerator and when they wanted more information or needed help they called. And call they did. At times the nationally recognized Consumer Protection Division received as many as 11,000 complaints in a year. They successfully resolved more than two-thirds of the complaints received and annually recovered millions of dollars. Routinely, people reported that when faced with a consumer issue they only had to say, "I'll just call the Attorney General's Consumer Protection Office," and their problem received positive attention.

Strategy #2: Spec. Assist. Attorneys General

We identified groups of attorneys with expertise in consumer protection issues who were willing to take large financial risk to help others. And they did. They were often successful, and in a big way. But they took enormous financial risk. All of the appointed special assistant AGs were closely supervised by the AG office. We were at the table in every court room; during every mediation; every settlement and in every decision before any action was taken. There wasn't one pleading filed that didn't have the imprimatur of approval from the Attorney General in consultation with his management staff. In the end this strategy recovered over $2 billion for West Virginia.

The 'judge' said he was the people's judge when he was on the state Supreme Court, and as AG he was the 'people's lawyer,' and we were all there with him. And contrary to any assertion made, there were some appointed counsel that gave contributions to the 'judges' future campaigns—but many did not. There was absolutely never any quid pro quo. The attack dogs took what we did really well and then turned it into our Achilles's heel—the use of lawfully appointed counsel."[10]—Frances Hughes, Chief Deputy Attorney General

The AG office successfully used the strategy of appointing assistant attorney generals to recover billions of dollars for the state. The AG office, like so many injured litigants who must find legal representation, did not have the staff and financial resources or support in the government to fund prosecution of complex legal actions against corporate wrongdoers. So the AG office appointed assistant attorneys general based on their track record of success in prior cases and the lawyers ability to finance the litigation, which in large, complex cases is substantial. The AG office supervised the work of these assistant attorneys general and remained engaged in all aspects of prosecution. If the appointed assistant attorneys general were successful in prosecution of the case they then presented a petition to the presiding judge, a quantum merit claim, for a reasonable fee, but if the case were lost, counsel received no reimbursement and lost their monetary investment incurred in the development of litigation. This investment could be millions in complex litigations.[11]

Resistance to this strategy of appointing assistant attorneys general came from those who had much to profit from preventing litigation against wrongdoers. Center for Justice and Democracy concluded that: "[These attacks on Attorneys General] have become part of the so-called 'tort-reform' movements—attempts by insurance, tobacco, pharmaceutical and industries to limit their liability should their wrongdoings result in injuries or death."[12]

The Center for Justice noted the negative impact on pro-consumer AGs': "Over the last decade, these business groups have launched unfair, misleading assaults against state Attorneys General, even to the point of manipulating state elections to defeat popular pro-consumer candidates for state Attorneys General."[13] The Center acknowledged the duty of

Attorneys General to act as the "people's lawyer:" "State Attorneys General are among our country's most important public advocates. Charged with enforcing state law, they act on behalf of citizens in many diverse areas, like consumer protection, antitrust and utility regulation and environmental protection."[14] WV's AG staff was not deterred in their duty to be people's lawyers.

Enforcing the Law—Rocking the State House Sea

As AG, Darrell's office intervened in many questionable and often illegal practices and policies of those in charge of governmental agencies, business and industry. The AG's intervention often interfered with someone's perceived or real base of power. Roderick Harless, a scholar and researcher, studied the political structures in West Virginia and defined this base of power concept as, "the capability of doing something without anybody else being able to do anything about it."[15] Harless found the base of power in West Virginia is related to people's acquisition of land, jobs and money and their subsequent influence on mass media, education and politics: "Those, then who control considerable economic resources are a major, if not dominant factor, in determining what happens within the spheres of public opinion, the electoral process and government."[16] Harless noted that whenever corporate, business and government leaders place their practices and policies above the interests of citizens, problems often ensue. Such practices and policies often caught the attention of the attorney general's office and necessitated intervention. With each intervention, the list of corporate and government "wrongdoers" against the AG in the next election increased.

Perhaps Roderick Harless' interest in political structures and bases of power emanated from his brother, Larry Harless, who was a master at interfering with the base of power of others. Larry Harless, a brilliant non-conformist WV lawyer spent his life defending the underprivileged and disenfranchised. Larry often said of his life of service, "I try to comfort the afflicted and afflict the comfortable."[17] When Larry's life came to a tragic end, his family and friends knew that Larry had "devoted his life to right those things he saw as immoral and wrong. He had great faith in the capacity of the law to make things more right."[18]

Darrell, reared a Methodist, strives to live by the social principles of the Methodist Church, and apply them to his work including the principle: "We hold governments responsible for the protection of people's basic freedoms."[19] There were two broad categories in which the Attorney General intervened on behalf of the people. First, the Attorney General intervened with governmental agencies and commissions, including Department of Education, Department of Environmental Protection, Department of Highways, Purchasing Department, Board of Investments, School Building Authority, Lottery Commission and Department of Agriculture, in areas of contracts, constitutional issues and statutory enforcement. Second, the Attorney General prosecuted the illegal practices and consumer violations of various business and corporate entities including tobacco, credit card, pharmaceutical, insurance, advertising, pay-day lenders, telemarketers, coal, banks, technology, waste disposal, etc.

Chapter XVI   Governmental Entities

In some instances the awarding of state contracts and bonds are a payback vehicle for political allegiance. Such contracts were an on-going challenge for the AG office. Whenever there was a question of legality of a contract it often related to the bidding and awarding process. The AG review of contracts was an endeavor often fraught with difficulty and generally involved a substantial level of resistance. Who benefited from the awarding of a contract? In some instances the answer was not the people. For the vast majority of dedicated state employees the existence of a comprehensive review by the Attorney General's office of contracts afforded much needed personal protection and ensured a high level of government accountability.

Whenever the AG office questioned a contract, someone was not happy—vendors, department heads, the governor and/or members of the Legislature. In order to curtail the AG review process, the Legislature enacted statute to limit the Attorney General authority. And the state Supreme Court rendered a decision that restricted the AG to approving "contracts to form". The Court interpreted the definition of approving "contracts to form" as simply determining if the contract format was in proper order which restricted the legal review of all the contract procedures.[1] Even with the negative response from the Legislature and the state Supreme Court, the AG office remained tenacious in their duty to review contracts.

In Darrell's first term as AG, the office questioned administration contracts and actions including: 1.) Department of Environmental Protection's outside counsel contract and garbage and landfill practices; 2.) Lottery Commission's video lottery machine and advertising contracts; 3.) West Virginia Department of Education's IBM computer contract; 4.) School Building Authority's legal counsel contract and bond sale, and 5.) State Investment Board's practice of investing pension funds in risky stocks.

With each intervention into the legally questionable administration actions, the animosity increased. The intervention was not personal. It was about duty to the citizens and enforcement of the letter of law. Some of the AG interventions led to litigations, state and federal investigations, indictments and prison terms.

Because the AG office critically reviewed contracts to ensure that everyone played by the rules, Darrell was viewed as "rocking the boat on the Statehouse sea." Chief Deputy Frances Hughes described the magnitude of the problems the office encountered in their review of state contracts: "He's [McGraw] reviewing the contracts in accordance with procurement laws. The problem is so systemic that if you tried to stop all procurement contracts, you would bring the government down."[2]

Frances (Fran) Hughes, a hard charging, attorney, started in the AG office with Darrell in 1993 and was there to close the door and walk out the east portico of the Capitol with him for the last time in January, 2013. The angle of her chin and piercing brown eyes told the story to those lawyers who crossed her path—don't try to con a kid from a steel mill town in northern West Virginia. Her life was tough from the beginning. She was only 5 when her father died in an automobile accident. Her mother was married three times and raised 4 girls with Fran, not the oldest, but always the caretaker. Fran brought new meaning "to take no prisoners" in achieving her outcome in a multitude of successful litigations. She wasn't into sparing the resources of any vanquished opponent. Hers was an uncompromising approach, not diverted by any time wasting discussion from less prepared opposing counsel, in achieving the best possible settlement for West Virginians. Her stance was articulated by an armor of words carefully researched and chosen, only slightly softened by her slim skirts and Jimmy Choo stilettos. As Chief Deputy Attorney General Fran Hughes was a figure to be dealt with by wrong doers who quickly learned it was not an experience they would relish with fond memories—they knew it would cost them.

The AG viewed his questioning of the administration contracts as simply doing his job: "I'm merely going by the book."[3] However, after the AG office rejected a dozen of the administration's contracts one cryptic journalist offered, "[Governor] Gaston Caperton might be forgiven if thoughts of poison and McGraw intersect in his mind at least once or twice."[4]

When questioned about his relationship with the Governor, Darrell, always the historian picked up his *Oxford Companion of Law* and shared the story of Thomas Becket, chancellor to England's King Henry II, noting the conflict between the chief executive and lawyers was centuries old. With tongue firmly in cheek he said, "Becket said he could not do what Henry wanted, and the king said, 'Will no one rid me of this pesky priest?' Whereupon four knights set upon Becket and stabbed him to death. I sure hope nothing happens to me like it happened to Becket...But we are in the same line of work."[5] Thankfully Beckett's ending wasn't Darrell's fate, but sometimes it seemed the "knights' acolytes" were nearby.

Contract for Outside Counsel
To whose benefit is the employment of outside counsel?

All too often state agencies hire lawyers through contractual arrangements in contradiction to the West Virginia Code which details the responsibility of Attorney General to serve as counsel for all government agencies. However, in instances where the AG determines a need to appoint outside counsel, they are hired as special assistant attorneys general under the supervision of the AG. The statutory law is clear—the understanding of the agencies is not often as clear as evidenced by their continued practice of hiring outside counsel.[6] Negating the practice of agency executives hiring their own counsel is difficult to change. It is a power thing. Having in-house counsel is seen as a higher level of autonomy and power.

In one legislative presentation, Darrell reported that over $3.3 million was annually spent by agencies to engage outside counsel as "bureaucratic hand-holders" noting that "lawyers should not be hired to make administrative policy."[7] Holding up a stack of contracts that totaled almost $200,000 for just six-weeks of outside counsel Darrell asserted, "Approving the contracts was not consistent with the law. The work could be done by people in his office who make far less money... saving the state $2.3 million which could be used for so many other important services—like road repair or pension fund allocations."[8] The Legislature took no action to stop the practice.

The agencies paid outside lawyers two to three times more than lawyers within the AG office. The average range of pay for agency counsel was $45,000-$75,000 as compared to lawyers in the AG office who made at the time as little as $23,750.[9]

"Fran, why should anyone work for us—40 plus hours a week when they can contract with an agency; set their own hours, and make 2-3 times as much," Darrell asked. "Because we are the 'good guys,'" Fran teased.

Stopping outside counsel contracts by agencies was difficult. Routinely department heads found a willing legislator to sponsor a bill to give the agency authority to hire their own counsel. As was the case when Chairman of the Finance Robert Kiss sponsored a bill that allowed "the School Building Authority to have its own lawyer and bond counsel."[10] Taking away personal lawyers from executives interferes with their financial power base which is, for many, a priority worth protecting.

Agency contract lawyers sometimes have political connections as apparent in the Department of Environmental Protection's (DEP)contract to the Curry law firm in Charleston. Curry's founding lawyer and principal was Arden John Curry, Sr. The Curry contract was issued for the purpose of recovering approximately $18 million in reclamation costs owed by strip mining firms to the state. Two of the delinquent firms listed John Curry as an officer. The DEP contract permitted Curry to retain up to twenty-five percent of collected recovery—an anticipated benefit to Curry firm of more than $4 million dollars.[11]

Curry had connections with previous state government leaders who were ultimately convicted of various unlawful activities and served prison time. During Governor Arch Moore's administration, Curry was appointed to an environmental commission even though Curry was previously employed by garbage landfill operators,. Curry was identified as a 'co-schemer' in a federal indictment of state Treasurer John Kelly who was imprisoned in 1970's for taking bribes. Curry was also the campaign manager for former Attorney General C. Donald Robertson who served prison time for corruption.[12]

The AG office stopped the contract to the Curry law firm and hired Tom Rodd, an activist lawyer with a successful environmental law practice, to take on the litigation against coal operators. Rodd had just won a precedent setting case in Preston County where he represented citizens affected by water pollution caused by coal companies. In this case, the coal companies lost their bond forfeiture money, so Rodd turned to the insurance companies to secure recovery for treatment of the polluted streams. The insurance companies settled for $3 million. The money was placed in a 99 year trust for the state to fund water treatment of damaged streams in futuro. The case was significant for several reasons: 1.) Citizens, who could have benefited directly from the settlement dollars, chose to utilize the funds for current and future water treatment issues; 2.) It was the first time insurance companies paid for a bankrupt coal company's damage to the environment, and 3.) Insurance companies became less willing to provide coverage for coal companies that engaged in mining where the environment might be negatively impacted. Rodd was the right kind of lawyer to work with AG team. Employment of one $40,000 employee literally saved the state millions of dollars in outside counsel fees:

Attorney General Darrell McGraw may have saved the state more than $4 million dollars by putting a Morgantown lawyer on staff to sue coal and insurance companies, instead of contracting the cases out to expensive private lawyers.

David Callaghan, director of the Division of Environmental Protection, wanted to give a contract to lawyers Arden and John Curry to recover up to $18 million the state has spent reclaiming mines…

The deal stank…Considering the elder Curry's involvement with shady politicos in the past, the contract became even more dubious…

Maybe this will convince other agencies to use the attorney general's office instead of hiring expensive private attorneys, something McGraw has been pushing for with little success.[13]*—Charleston Gazette*

The administration and members of the Legislature were not happy with the AG's intervention. The Legislature came to the director's defense and passed a law to allow Department of Environmental Protection to hire their own in-house attorney: "Notwithstanding any provisions of this code to the contrary, employ in house counsel to perform all legal services for the secretary and the department, including, but not limited to, representing the secretary, any chief, the department or an office thereof in any administrative proceeding or in any proceeding in any state or federal court."[14] The statute was an attempt by the Department of Environmental Protection and Legislature to avoid the scrutiny of the AG in awarding contracts and enforcing the law. With time and the right opportunity the Director was able to file an ethics complaint against Darrell in a subsequent environmental case.

The state *Constitution* provides for one chief legal officer, the AG, in order to ensure a cohesive legal policy throughout government. Without that consistency of supervision from the AG, these "in-house" lawyers might respond to FOIA requests, legal representations and settlement decisions in a way contradictory to the best interests of the state. Or even worse an executive officer engaged in wrong doing had their own legal counsel to support their improprieties.

Garbage and Landfills

To whose benefit is it to not enforce environmental regulations that threaten the environment and adversely affect people's health and well-being

Sometimes when the rubber meets the road, the rubber doesn't hold. That phrase makes sense in its application to elected officials who lack the fortitude to resist political pressure from those who profit from actions that negatively impact the environment. West Virginia has a history of succumbing to political pressure related to environmental issues. Such political pressure was evident in the case of a landfill lawsuit where the state reversed its stance to protect the citizens of Berkeley County against the dumping of foul out of state garbage and sewage sludge. The state's action didn't meet the smell test. In a strange turn of events the state's reversal came after victory was achieved. The AG office, representing the Department of Environmental Protection in the Berkeley Circuit Court, won the case in which the constitutionality of West Virginia's garbage law establishing limits on landfill usage was upheld. The good guys won, but political pressure was about to change things.

In 1990 the AG's office representing DEP filed two declaratory judgement actions against LCS Services, a landfill company 1.) to prohibit LCS from accepting waste at the Hedgesville, Berkeley County landfill until it received approval from the Berkeley County Solid Waste Authority, and 2.) to restrict the monthly amount of solid waste dumped at the landfill, unless the Berkeley County Commission approved. Berkeley County did not want all the New Jersey garbage and sewage. Judge Christopher Wilkes of Berkeley County granted the summary judgement on July 29, 1993.[15] The decision was a win for the citizens of Berkeley County, the West Virginia Environmental Council, the Berkeley County Commission, the Solid Waste Authority, the Department of Environmental Protection and the Attorney General's office. It was not a victory for LCS, a subsidiary of Chambers Development Company.

Many believed that political pressure exerted on the administration occurred when after a favorable ruling and without informing the AG office, DEP Director David Callaghan and his deputy met with the vice president of Chamber Development Company and the owner of LCS landfill. Ed Wiles, Vice President of Chambers Development and former President of the West Virginia Coal Association, and David Callaghan were friends. Callaghan and Wiles managed House Speaker Clyde See's primary campaign when See ran against Warren McGraw for governor.[16]

The meeting between Callaghan and the vice president of Chambers Development and the owner of LCS was said to include discussion of the motion filed by LCS to amend Judge Wilkes order. A meeting between two opposing parties without their legal counsel from the AG office was not proper. After the meeting with Chambers and LCS, the DEP contacted the AG's office to advise that DEP wanted to join in the LCS' motion for reconsideration of Judge Wilkes' order "by granting to amend, alter, correct, clarify and or reconsider the circuit court's order the DEP's motion for summary judgement."[17] "What is going on?" Darrell wanted to know.

Everyone was appalled. The 'judge' was on his toes, which everyone knew was a sign he was really upset, when he announced, 'We aren't going to let this stand.' It was amazing. We won a long hard fight in in Berkeley county circuit court and now the DEP reversed its position on regulations pertaining to the garbage dump. We couldn't continue to represent them. It was outrageous to say the least. The determination was made to appoint alternate counsel to represent DEP and inform the trustees involved in the case of the closed door meeting between DEP and LCS and DEP's change in direction.[18]—Frances Hughes, Chief Deputy Attorney General

Darrell described the DEP's actions as "repugnant, immoral, unethical, and totally improper." Stating conflicts and adversity, he withdrew from representation and appointed a prosecuting attorney to represent DEP."[19] Judge Wilkes denied the AG's motion to withdraw from the case, but refused LCS and DEP's request to reconsider his ruling—which meant the original ruling against LCS stood.[20] It was victory, but it came at a personal cost.

Even though the AG appointed alternate counsel, DEP Director, David Callaghan filed an ethics complaint against Darrell. The ethics complaint resulted in investigations, depositions, reviews by the West Virginia State Bar disciplinary counsel, the Investigative Panel Committee on Legal Ethics, the Hearing Panel of the Committee on Legal Ethics, the Lawyers Disciplinary Board and the West Virginia Supreme Court. Of course the ethics complaint, the hearings and all the articles and editorials resulted in great levels of consternation and concern.

The State Bar Hearing Panel Ethics Committee charged Darrell with four ethical violations and embraced their counsel's recommendation of a three month suspension of his law license even though: "the committee's chairman heads a law firm that represents landfills, and also represents bond sellers who are at odds with McGraw."[21] Even with the apparent conflict, the Hearing Panel's recommendation was of concern to the family. Others, less emotionally involved people, viewed the Panel's decision as threatening in its potential to curtail future inappropriate actions of agencies: "If McGraw loses his license for disagreeing with a bureaucrat, it will set an ominous precedent saying the attorney general must obey agency chiefs and keep his mouth shut, no matter what improper action they take."[22]—*Charleston Gazette*

The Lawyer's Disciplinary Board did not concur with the Hearing Panel's recommendation for suspension, dismissing three of the charges and ruling "you cannot force a lawyer to go into court and take a position that is repugnant to him."[23] The Lawyer's Disciplinary Board recommended a "public reprimand for telling a Martinsburg environmentalist that the Division of Environmental Protection did a 180 degree flip in August 1993 on its long-held opposition to the expansion of a Hedgesville landfill."[24] It was a strange recommendation since the environmentalist represented the Berkeley County activists fighting LCS landfill. The Lawyer's Disciplinary Board's recommendation moved on to the state Supreme Court for a final determination. Some noted the interconnectedness of politics at the state Supreme Court level: "Callaghan's wife is secretary to Chief Justice Margaret Workman, and Workman beat McGraw when he ran for re-election to the court. Rumors also are making the rounds that if McGraw runs for governor, Workman will leave the bench and run too."[25]—*Sunday Gazette-Mail*

In 1995, the state Supreme Court adopted the Lawyer's Disciplinary finding of a public reprimand but reduced Darrell's fine to $1,713 for disciplinary cost.[26] The ethics complaint exemplified the conflict that existed between the AG office's commitment to enforce the law to reduce out-of-state sludge disposal and monitor landfills in order to negate enhanced environmental damage and the political order's effort to accommodate business interest to the detriment of the community.

Rumors of the possibility of Darrell running for governor encompassed the events related to the filing, review and disposition of Callaghan's ethics complaint:

While McGraw has always been controversial, he has a proven ability to pull in votes. In fact, his name has been mentioned as a possible candidate for governor in 1996. If that happens, it's a pretty sure bet that organized labor will get behind him. McGraw may be the last of a breed, as far as labor unions are concerned.

He has been a strong advocate of organized labor. There are a number of politicians interested in running for governor or the state Supreme Court in two years. They see McGraw as a threat for either position. They also know that if McGraw gets on the ballot, they likely aren't going to get a majority of the labor vote.

Thus, if he isn't on the ballot going for one of those high ranking jobs, the dedicated labor vote might be out there for other candidates to divide up. A way to prevent this situation of course would be to keep him

*off the ballot and one way to encourage that would be to taint his record
in his present elected position.*

*Politics can get real mean when the stakes get high.[27]—Richard
Grimes, Political Editor, Charleston Daily Mail*

The Berkeley County case reflected the AG's tenacity to uphold the law
even when there the potential for unwanted personal consequences.

Hazard waste disposal issues were taking place in more than
Berkeley County. Communities across the state were concerned and
demanding limits on out-of-state waste, sewage sludge and more
stringent land-fill regulations. Governor Caperton responded by
announcing that "he wouldn't tolerate the disposal of any unsafe solid
waste within our border…I am therefore today directing a thorough
review of waste regulations." Martha Huffman, a member of the Wetzel
County Solid Waste Authority, wanted to restrict J.P. Mascaro and Sons,
a waste disposal company, from hauling sewage into the county from
New Jersey. Huffman was skeptical of promises from government
leaders: "That is a good start. A moratorium would be a stronger and
better step. The wolves are knocking at the door as we speak…sewage
sludge can contaminate groundwater, soil and other water supplies with
pathogens and heavy metals…[which] can cause disease…cause toxic
poisoning in humans, particularly children."[28]

Contrary to the Governor's promise, DEP Director Callaghan
"allowed Pasquale Macscaro to import more than 100,000 tons a month
of New Jersey sludge to his Wetzel and Brooke county landfills. The AG
issued an opinion stating the state had a duty to enforce environmental
regulations and that sludge should be limited."[29] Huffman and the
Wetzel and Brooke County Solid Waste Authorities sued Callaghan.
Callaghan objected to the AG's intervention and filed yet another ethics
alleging, "McGraw's office worked for the other side in the lawsuit, a
violation of legal ethics."[30] This complaint was eventually dismissed.

Resistance to Mascaro's garbage and sewage disposal operation
was not a singular occurrence. It lasted for decades:

- In 1996 the DEP ordered Mascaro's Wetzel County facility
  not to accept more sewage sludge without addressing its
  environmental problems.

- In 2000 Brooke County Circuit Judge Fred Risovich II ordered the Mascaro composting site closed.
- In 2002, DEP inspector Mike Zeto attempted to shut down the operation but Chief of staff Mike Garrison and DEP Secretary Mike Callaghan in Governor Wise's office gave Mascaro more time to comply.
- In 2003 the Public Service Commission administrative law judge rejected Mascaro and his company's requests for permits citing lack of fitness.
- In 2006 the WV Supreme Court held against Mascaro directing the PSC to immediately issue a cease and desist order with regard to the Lackawanna commercial composting facility.
  - In, 2007 the Environmental Quality Board upheld a DEP order for Mascaro to cease and desist operations.[31]

Lottery Scandal—People Go to Jail
To whose benefit is expansion of video lottery?

Except for pandering to the poor's hope for a monetary miracle and the state's need for more revenue, one wonders why elected officials, who are supposed to lead us to a greater good, moved away from an early 20th century status of the illegality of lotteries: "It's the job of the state government to promote the welfare of citizens. Do we really think to encourage them to gamble is a good way to promote the welfare?"[32]— *Rev. Alvie Edwards, Eastern Greenbrier Ministers Association*

The late 50's and early 60's saw the reappearance of casinos and lotteries as a means for governments across the country to raise revenue without raising taxes. Lotteries became an avenue for political leaders to convince citizens they weren't being taxed for basic governmental services. In reality, it is the poorest who are taxed at a high level as they line up to buy lottery tickets and gamble away their meager earnings in casinos; while the richest continue to reap the benefits of low taxation rates: "Gambling hurts the poor."[33]—*West Virginia Council of Churches*

In 1984 West Virginia followed the national trend, and the public passed the Lottery Amendment making the sale of lottery tickets legal.

The amendment was eventually reinterpreted by the Legislature to include slot machines (video lottery) which were located in businesses throughout the state and in five lottery table game casinos. The state's awarding of contracts for advertising and gaming machines evolved into what was labeled the "lottery scandal."

Lottery, by definition, is a form of gambling. Perhaps it was inevitable that administration of the lottery in West Virginia succumbed to illegal activities. The "lottery scandal" that unraveled in 1993 actually began two years earlier as government officials conspired to give contracts to Falhgren Martin, an advertising company from Parkersburg, West Virginia and to Video Lottery Consulting (VLC), a company banned from doing business in Australia. "VLC's chairman, Larry Lippon, was a partner with two crooks one who pleaded guilty to felony fraud in a platinum scam, and one who was convicted of gambling offenses."[34]

The state wide lottery was under the authority of the West Virginia Lottery Commission, whose membership and director were appointed by the Governor. There were two major parts of investigation related to the lottery scandal: Part One included the actions which resulted in 1991 advertising contract award to Fahlgren Martin and the subsequent attempt to award a 1993 contract to Fahlgren Martin. Part Two included challenges to the legality of private companies owning the video machines, and the subsequent activities of awarding a contract to Video Lottery Technologies/Consulting (VLC).

During the lottery scandal there were alleged inappropriate conduct in the Governor's office, the state lottery and purchasing offices that resulted in investigations, grand jury hearings, indictments, convictions and prison terms, as well as lawsuits filed in circuit court and appealed to the West Virginia Supreme Court.

William Gaston Caperton, III was the governor during the Lottery Scandal. Caperton was a tall, some would say handsome sort, born into a family who owned coal and insurance companies. As expected after graduating college, Gaston returned to take over his family's insurance business and ultimately own a bank and mortgage company. When Caperton became governor he was married to Ella Dee Kessell, a former Miss West Virginia and second runner up in the Miss America pageant.

Ella Dee's father, Oliver Kessell, served as a justice on the WV Supreme Court in 1972. Ella Dee was a smart, talented lady who was elected to the House of Delegates in 1986 but didn't seek reelection in 1988 in order to help her husband run for Governor. Gaston was successful in his bid for governor, but their marriage ended in 1990. During her short stay as first lady Ella Dee focused on women's issues and education. After the divorce Ella Dee ran for State Treasurer but lost. Ella Dee moved to France where she died at 57 after a long bout with cancer in September, 2000.[35] West Virginia House Resolution No.26 was adopted to commemorate the work of Ella Dee. The resolution noted her accomplishments including attaining a Doctorate in Psychology from the University of Pittsburg; a practicing classical guitarist and pianist; teaching university level English in the People's Republic of China and establishing *Mas Mireille,* a small hotel in the medieval town of Saint Remy. In the last decade of her life, she reclaimed her family name, Dee Caperton Kessel.[36]

Shortly after Gaston and Dee were divorced, Gaston married Rachel Worby, a raven haired symphony conductor, who was often frustrated by political interference into her personal life. The marriage lasted until 1998.[37] In 2003 Gaston married Idit Ron Harel, born in Israel and a MIT and Harvard alumni. Idit founded Globaloria, a computer learning system company, that Gaston sought, with Sen. Joe Manchin and his wife's Gayle assistance, to expand through-out the state.[38] For those in the education world who experienced the "Idit" phenomenon, her tenacity was reflective of someone who had experienced the Six Days War, Yom Kippur War and the 1982 Lebanon War. As State Superintendent of Schools, I resisted efforts by Idit, Gaston Caperton, State Board Member Gayle Manchin (wife of Sen. Joe Manchin) to expand Globaloria in schools without following state purchasing requirements for bidding and awarding contracts. My resistance ultimately was personally costly to my longevity as State Superintendent. Gaston and Idit divorced in 2012,[39] which perhaps saved the state from an unnecessary expenditure of $22 million for Globaloria.

In 1990 Caperton appointed Butch Bryan as Lottery Director with the charge to expand video lottery state-wide. As any businessman knows, one has to first sell the product, in this case video lottery gaming.

The Lottery commission needed an advertising company to market video lottery gaming, which leads to part one of the lottery scandals.

Part One—Fahlgren Martin Contract

Since 1985 Fahlgren Martin, Inc., a Parkersburg advertising company, held the contract with the Lottery Commission. In 1991 the State, required to re-bid the advertising contract, again awarded the $2.8 million dollar contract to Fahlgren.[40] How the state awarded that contract wasn't questioned until 1993.

Governor Gaston Caperton had close ties to Fahlgren Martin. His associate and personal friend was Tom Graff who was the son-in-law of Fahlgren Martin's President H. Smoot Fahlgren. Tom Graff was also the registered lobbyist for Video Lottery Consultants (VLC/VLT), the firm who was to receive the video machine contract.[41]

In 1993 federal authorities began an investigation into 1991 advertising contract. Federal Prosecutors alleged that Lottery Director Butch Bryan "ensured that Fahlgren Martin maintained the contract with the Lottery in 1991, despite an evaluation team's higher rating of the Arnold agency, a Charleston firm."[42] Darrell, concerned about bid rigging allegations, refused to approve the extension of the 1993 advertising contract to Fahlgren Martin.

On April 23, 1993, the Grand Jury concluded things were not right and indicted Lottery Commissioner Butch Bryan for bid rigging and perjury related to the award of the Fahlgren Martin contract. Despite the indictment of the Lottery Director for alleged corruption, Fahlgren Martin wanted the 1993 contract approved and filed suit claiming they were being "victimized" by the Attorney General.[43] Darrell argued it was the public who were the victims.

The deputy director of the Lottery Commission, Tamara Gunnoe, testified before a Grand Jury that Fahlgren Martin had not received the highest score in the bidding process and the 1991 contract should not have been awarded to Fahlgren: "After it was determined that Arnold had received the highest numerical score in the bidding process, I was told by Director Bryan that he had met with the Governor, and we were going to have to give the contract to [Fahlgren Martin]…[Bryan] told me that he and Caperton thought the contract should stay with Fahlgren Martin. So I told lottery commissioners that the evaluation committee rated Fahlgren Martin the highest of the bidders."[44]—*Tamara Gunnoe*

Sam Kusic, a Lottery Commission member, testified that he voted against the 1991 contract award to Fahlgren "because commissioners were not given a standard evaluation…I voted against it based on the principle that it wasn't evaluated as other contracts were evaluated on a numerical basis."[45] Testimony indicated others knew of the inappropriate award. Gubernatorial Press Secretary George Manahan and Communication Director Bob Brunner testified that in spring of 1991 they told Governor Caperton that Fahlgren did not win the evaluation but was still given the contract: "Butch [Bryan] isn't doing the right thing in the selection of the advertising agency for the lottery."[46]

The Governor testified that he "cannot remember details of the conversation" with Brunner and Manahan.[47] On September, 1993 gubernatorial press secretary Bob Brunner announced that he was stepping down as the Governor's communication director.[48]

In September, 1993 Butch Bryan, the Lottery Director, was found guilty of bid rigging: "In 1991 he illegally threw out an evaluation committee's recommendation to give the lottery's $2.8 million advertising contract to the Arnold Agency and ordered his employees to tell the Lottery Commission the Fahlgren Martin firm won the bid."[49]

Also in September, 1993 Fahlgren Martin petitioned the state Supreme Court "to reverse Attorney General Darrell McGraw's 1993 ruling that took away a $2.8 million contract…" Fahlgren contended that the Attorney General only had the statutory duty to approve the "form" of the contract.[50] Notwithstanding the state's illegal awarding of the 1991 contract to Fahlgren, the state Supreme Court, with Justice Brotherton writing for the majority, granted relief for Smoot Fahlgren: "In this case, the Attorney General must send the Fahlgren Martin, Inc., contract, approved as to form, back to the Purchasing Division, if he has not already done so, and Purchasing must also approve the contract. We affirm the June 14, 1993, order of the Circuit Court of Kanawha County in total."[51] The Court interpreted Statute Sec. 5A-3-13 that "contracts shall be approved as to form by the attorney general" to restrict review of contracts by the AG in any meaningful way: "If a contract is legal, then he is required by statute to approve the contract as to form, **regardless of any perceived wrongful acts.**"[52]

The Court held the word "form" meant "matters contained in the contract document as it relates to the Constitution, statutes, and the contract law of this State, but excludes any matters extrinsic to the actual contract.[53] The ruling meant that even if the bidding and awarding of the contract were illegal, the AG could not decline approval. In essence the court held the state's chief legal officer was required to approve contracts regardless of any wrongful or even criminal conduct in the procurement process.

In 1995 the Arnold Agency filed suit against the Lottery Commission seeking damages for the award of the 1991 advertising contract to Fahlgren Martin. In the litigation Arnold sought to subpoena Governor Caperton to testify. Caperton's attorney successfully sought to block the subpoena: "Kanawha Circuit Judge Irene Berger quashed the subpoena…saying [the attorney] had failed to show he had exhausted all other means of obtaining information."[54] Judge Berger was appointed in 1994 by Governor Caperton to fill a vacancy in the Kanawha County Circuit.

The Arnold litigation against the Lottery Commission continued for several years in Judge Berger's courtroom. In 1999 Arnold sought relief from Judge Berger's rulings contending on an appeal to the state Supreme Court "that the circuit court erred in (1) determining that the Lottery Commission is an agency of the State and cloaked in sovereign immunity under Article VI, § 35 of the West Virginia Constitution; (2) dismissing its fraud count; (3) permitting the Lottery Commission to assert the absence of insurance coverage after the deadline for filing dispositive motions; (4) concluding that the State's liability insurance policy does not provide coverage with respect to Arnold's breach of contract claim; and (5) granting a protective order prohibiting Arnold from deposing then Governor Gaston Caperton."

The state Supreme Court upheld the circuit court conclusion that the Lottery Commission was immune from suit thus negating the fraud claim, but reversed the lower court ruling and held "the State's liability insurance potentially provides coverage for the breach of contract claim, thus permitting the present case to proceed to trial". As it pertained to deposing former Governor Caperton, the Court noted that "unfolding of the crucial issue regarding whether the alleged breach of contract was a consequence of fraud leaves no question but that evidence demonstrating Governor Caperton's involvement in such a scheme would be highly relevant to a determination of whether Arnold has a jurisdictional basis for recovery. The fact remains, however, that the circuit court specifically directed Arnold to resort to less intrusive means of obtaining the sought-after initial discovery…Because of the availability of less burdensome means of initial discovery in the present case, we see no reason to conclude that the circuit court abused its discretion in entering the protective order."

Interestingly, a footnote in the opinion referenced Linda Arnold's testimony in which she "related a statement made by the Governor's former wife, Dee Caperton. Dee Caperton stated there was a meeting occurred between Governor Caperton, Dee Caperton, and Smoot Fahlgren (a principal of Fahlgren Martin) in the parking lot of the Greenbrier Hotel. During the meeting Dee stated that an understanding was reached [t]hat if Smoot Fahlgren would support Gaston Caperton [for governor] and raise money for him, then it would be worth his while in terms of the State business going to his agency."[55]

Rather than continuing to trial the West Virginia Insurance Agency (BRIM) settled the Arnold case.[56]

Part Two—Video Gambling Machines

Gov. Caperton, a business man, saw the expansion of video lottery as a way to generate $50 million a year in revenue for the state. During his first term in office the Governor appointed Butch Bryan as Lottery Director and charged him with the responsibility of seeing to it that an estimated 5000 video gambling machines found their way into bars and taverns across the state.[57] There were hurdles to address: 1.) overcoming negative public opinion polls against video lottery; 2.) obtaining official approval of video machine expansion from the Lottery Commission and 3.) bidding and awarding of a contract to the successful contractor.

The polls showed voters were against the expansion of video lottery. Caperton was up for reelection in 1992.[58] There were no public efforts to advance video lottery until after the November, 1992 election. But there were things going on behind the scenes. Bryan understood his "boss's" marching orders to expand video lottery.

Months before the election, Vice President of Video Lottery Technologies/Consulting (VLC), Robert Babcock, met privately with Governor Caperton in his office to discuss the video lottery machine contract. Babcock promised VLC would build a manufacturing plant in WV in exchange for an exclusive $25 million dollar video machine contract. Babcock later testified, "In 1992, we spelled out our offer…to build our first plant in the East in West Virginia if they went for us."[59]

After that meeting, the Governor directed Bryan and Bill Woodford, Lottery's security chief, to go to VLC headquarters in Bozeman Montana to further "explore the deal." They spent several days in August, 1992 with then VLC Chief Executive Officer Larry Lippon and "discussed the details of giving the company the sole rights to sell video lottery machines in West Virginia."[60]

On October 19, 1992 at a dinner at the Tidewater Grill in Charleston, Woodford "gave a copy of the bid specifications to VLC computer chief, Jeff Boyle…Boyle took it to Montana and then mailed it back with suggestions in the margin."[61]—*Bill Wolford testimony*

"On November 6, 1992, three days after Caperton was re-elected, Woodford and Wilhelm [Lottery employees] went to the Statehouse to gather up the books that were to notify vendors of the bid [for video machines]."[62] They needed revision.

Bryan overcame the second hurdle when the Lottery Commission officially approved the expansion of video machines through-out the state on November 30, 1992. With the Lottery's approval, another major component was now in place for Bryan to achieve his boss's charge.[63]

VLC and others were concerned their might be attempts during the 1993 Legislative session to intervene into the administration's plans to expand video lottery. To protect their interests VLC hired "Gov. Caperton's aide, Steve Haid as its lobbyist and hired one of the governor's friends Tom Graff as its lawyer."[64] There were other lobbyists engaged to protect the expansion of video lottery including

Charleston lawyer, George Carenbauer who represented clubs and taverns.[65] Carenbauer, a lawyer with Steptoe Johnson, was later an adviser to Don Blankenship on how to set up a 527 to influence an outcome in an election.

The Legislative session was proving difficult as members heard objections from their constituents about the expansion of video lottery. House Speaker Chuck Chambers expressed concern about the administration's determination to press forward with such a rapid expansion of video lottery machines: "If members of the state Lottery Commission do not slow down the implementation of video lottery statewide, the Legislature will do it for them."[66]

The last hurdle to overcome was the awarding of the video machine contract. In a brazen act that he believed fulfilled his boss's charge, Lottery Director Bryan recommended to the Commission the selection of VLC as the singular manufacturer for the state's video machine contract. Two of the commission members, Sam Kusic and Fred Haddad, both prominent businessmen, objected and voted against awarding the contract to VLC. Kusic expressed concern that VLC was already paying for renovations at the Charles Town Races in anticipation of the track installing video lottery machines. Kusic believed something was not right.[67]

Fred Haddad, visibly angry after the "Commission voted 5-2 to have a single manufacturer provide all of the video lottery machines," tendered his resignation. [68] Haddad said, "These [video lottery machines' are not scratch-off tickets…video lottery was serious and I won't have anything to do with it if it is not right."[69] Haddad pointed out the potential for lost revenue and jobs with the selection of VLC: "[Haddad] predicted the lottery could make $25 million to $40 million more by having multiple vendors and hiring 200 to 400 people to run a system under which the Lottery Commission either leased or owned the video lottery machines."[70]

There was much to concern the administration. The Legislature was questioning the expansion of video lottery; Haddad resigned from the Lottery Commission, and "Bryan and his lottery counsel, Ed ReBrook, were questioned by federal investigators on Thursday."[71] Haddad, the influential businessman, told the Governor that "he would not reconsider his resignation."[72] Caperton had no choice—"[he] halted the expansion of video lottery, citing unanswered questions that jeopardized the integrity of the lottery."[73] Things were not going as the administration had hoped.

In April, 1993 Bryan was indicted on charges of mail fraud, wire fraud, insider trading and lying to a grand jury. This was at the same time and with the same Grand Jury that indicted Bryan for bid rigging related to the Fahlgren Martin contract. Rebrook, counsel to the Lottery Commission was indicted in June, 1993 on charges of wire fraud and insider trading.[74] A year earlier Rebrook, while counsel to the Lottery Commission, was the Democratic establishment candidate for attorney general.

There were more problems with the video lottery machine expansion. In 1990 the Lottery Commission granted Mountaineer Park a contract to "own and operate video lottery machines" on an experimental basis until June of 1993.[75] In May, 1993 the Lottery Commission voted to continue the contract with Mountaineer Park. An Attorney General opinion concluded the state Constitution required the state, not a private entity like Mountaineer Park, to own video lottery machines. The AG opinion threw a "proverbial wrench" in the already highly problematic actions related to video lottery: "Until that opinion was issued, lottery officials intended to expand video lottery machines statewide. The machines would have been owned by a 'middleman,' or existing companies that owned coin operated machines. One such company was owned by Sen. Earl Ray Tomblin, D-Logan."[76] Tomblin, Senate Finance Chairman and President of the Senate, became governor in 2011. The opinion had implications on the future of gambling expansions: "it will determine whether West Virginia can have casinos and riverboat gambling without Legislative approval."[77]

The Lottery Commission objected to the AG opinion and appealed to the state Supreme Court for relief. In September, 1993 the Court denied the Lottery Commission's and Mountaineer Park's request to override the AG's opinion which meant Mountaineer Park's contract for electronic video games was voided: "For the reasons stated herein, we deny both writs."[78] This was a major victory for setting boundaries on the wholesale expansion of gambling in the state.

Also in September, 1993 the Grand Jury was receiving testimony regarding administration's bidding process: "VLC officials were the only video lottery industry members who helped Bryan and his subordinates draw up the terms of a contract to give a statewide, $25 million monopoly in video gambling machines to one vendor, several witnesses testified Friday."[79] Ultimately 18 witnesses testified "of deals made over rounds of golf, meetings in hotel room suites, and pressure put on friends who were put on the public payroll."[80]

Lawyers for Bryan argued that Bryan "thought he was fulfilling the governor's wishes to secure a new manufacturing plant and an estimated $50 million a year in revenues from legalized video gambling."[81] Bryan testified that the Governor was aware of his actions, "Caperton was fully aware of his efforts to direct a $25 million video lottery contract to one firm and approved of his plans to rig the awarding of a $2.8 million lottery advertising contract."[82] Jerald Jones, one of Bryan's attorneys said, "Caperton seemed to suffering from selective amnesia…the longer this goes, the less he seems to know."[83]

At the end of an eight day trial Bryan was found guilty of bid rigging, insider trading and lying to a grand jury in the award of the Fahlgren Martin contract and the VLC contract. Bryan was guilty of the following:

- *Using inside information to buy stock in a company that had a multimillion-dollar contract with the lottery…*
- *[Throwing] out the evaluation committee's recommendation to give the lottery's $2.8 million advertising contract to the firm the Arnold Agency and ordered his employees to tell the Lottery Commission that Fahlgren Martin firm won the contract…*
- *[Spending] 1991 and 1992 fixing the state's $25 million bid to expand legalized video gambling to bars and restaurants throughout the state…*
- *Buying 200 shares of stock in Gtech, a company that had the state lottery's computer contract…[and buying] stock in VLC while he was lottery director.[84]*

Ed Rebrook, counsel for the Lottery, was convicted of insider trading and wire fraud.[85] Governor Caperton testified three times before the grand jury. The Governor remained silent on the convictions, only releasing a four word press release after Bryan was convicted: "The jury has spoken."[86] The Governor maintained his innocence: "Gov. Gaston Caperton said he is innocent of wrongdoing in the state video lottery scandal, [he] then stormed out of a new conference Wednesday after answering one question on the matter…I want to make one thing very, very clear. I've done nothing wrong."[87]

The state Supreme Court decision to uphold Fahlgren Martin restricted the authority of the Attorney General to question improprieties in contracts presented. Some thought it incredulous that the chief lawyer for the state was required to approve a contract even if there were perceived wrongful or illegal acts within the bid specification and award process. The Governor's office vented their disdain with the AG's intervention by requesting a bill in the Legislature to give control of Attorney General's budget to the Governor: "The House Finance Committee adopted a measure Tuesday that was requested by the governor and would give him budgetary control over the attorney general. Officials denied the move was retaliatory or an attempt to get political legal opinions." [88] Fortunately the bill failed to pass.

The Governor's philosophy regarding the awarding of contracts was perhaps reflected in the statements made by his then wife, Rachel Worby. Worby expressed her views on the 'machinations of government' to justify a promise she made to a Wheeling restaurant owner that he would get the first video lottery machine in the area: "How do you think people get things? Through friends. You have a friend in the Senate who's on the finance committee. Guess what happens? You get something. You have an enemy on the finance committee. Guess what happens? You get nothing."[89]

During a hearing before the state Supreme Court on the legality of video lottery machines, Justice Richard Neely commented on the unwholesome lottery practice: "It is awful, disgusting and loathsome, and it is a shame the state of West Virginia tried to solve its fiscal problems…by engaging in vice. It's too bad we don't open up whorehouses on the Ohio River and come up with some other scheme for levying stupidity taxes."[90] After the hearing Darrell, trying to contain his laughter, said, "That's Justice Neely, but he is right." Darrell always respected Richard's gift for words to drive home a point that might elude others.

Struggles over the expansion of video lottery and gambling continued. In 1995 a bill was introduced in the Legislature to legalize gambling. The AG office resisted the legalization of gambling through its education outreach efforts including the sponsorship of a state-wide conference on gambling. National speakers expounded on the negative effects of gambling on individuals, families and the community. After the conference, the bill died. Proponents to gambling were not happy.[91]

Years later in 2012 the Lottery Commission's method of awarding contracts was again at issue when Fahlgren Martin received the advertising contract. The Arnold Agency lost to a rating scale that gave Fahlgren 93.96 points and Arnold 93 points even though Fahlgren Martin's bid for a one year contract was $473,000 which was $80,000 higher than the Arnold Agency. Individuals who took exception to this process were placed on administrative leave; lost their jobs and subsequent legal action ensued.[92] Perhaps a pertinent question for the state's purchasing office might be why was Fahlgren Martin still an eligible vendor after the 1991 award led to two convictions and prison terms of lottery officials?

"It [the Lottery] is awful, disgusting and loathsome."—*Justice Neely*

IBM Contract
To whose benefit is it to award a 10 year contract for the purchase of discontinued computers to IBM?

In 1989 Governor Caperton, through legislative enactment and appropriation, established the Basic Skills Computer Education Program. The statute required that the State Board of Education develop a plan for a state-wide basic skills computer program, including specifications for hardware and software. The plan included an investment of $70 million dollars over a ten year period in computer technology for schools across West Virginia.[93] Vendors were invited to submit bids for the technology. In a 1989 letter, IBM branch manager Ann Johnson told state officials that "her company was looking forward to helping West Virginia become a national role model for education through computers." In mid-1990, Governor Caperton hired Johnson to head his West Virginia's economic development team.[94]

In 1990 West Virginia Department of Education (WVDE) established a committee to review the computer bids. The committee included Kanawha County Technology Coordinator Hilary Cowan. Hilary, a hard charging brilliant educator, understood the technology specifications necessary to meet the needs of students. She bowed to no vendor and was only interested in securing the lowest price for the best computers. The committee evaluated the proposals, and the Jostens and Tandy companies received the highest marks. IBM "received especially low marks for its computer hardware."[95]

In June, 1990 a Tier II evaluation committee headed by State School Superintendent Hank Marockie contradicted the work of the review committee and "selected IBM to put hardware in every elementary school" as the vendor.[96] To whose profit was it to award a 10 year contract for computers that received low marks by a committee of experts? Marockie offered the rationale for selection of IBM was based on its plan to "promote the West Virginia project to a national audience and boost the state's economy." In the bid document IBM indicated their "public relations campaign would be worth $2 million."[97] Hilary Cowan, along with other committee members, were unsuccessful in reversing the Tier II evaluation committee recommendation.

In May, 1993 Darrell, now Attorney General, received a request from WVDE to approve the annual renewal of the IBM's 10 year contract. In order to circumvent the statutory requirement that forbids multi-year contracts, State Purchasing practices allows agencies to submit an annual renewal request.

Thomas Hark, parent, activist, and computer specialist at East Bank Junior High in Kanawha County, sent a letter to Governor Caperton expressing concern about the quality and cost of the IBM computers. Mr. Hark noted the computers specified in the contract were discontinued IBM Model 25 computers; that is the computers were no longer manufactured. Mr. Hark sent a copy of his letter to the AG office with a complaint that, "the state shouldn't pay top-of-the-line prices for computers IBM wants to get rid of."[98] Mr. Hark wasn't alone in his concern. Other teachers and computer specialists contacted the AG office objecting to the state paying $575 for IBM Model 25 computers that were sold on the open market for $249.[99]

Chief Deputy Fran Hughes, responding to the concerns received by the office, sent a letter to Chuck Polan, Secretary of Department of Administration. Fran, in her predictable no non-nonsense fashion, anticipated that by bringing the serious cost and quality issues to Secretary Polan's attention the administration would take appropriate action: "It appears computer equipment is being purchased by the state in bulk at a cost which exceeds what an individual would pay on the general open market. Normally, a consumer would realize a discount when purchasing in quantities. Instead, the state has experienced the reverse."[100] Fran, as was not often the case, was rather shocked by summary rejection of her concerns. In her letter Fran hadn't even mentioned the questionable logic of the state committing to a single computer vendor for 10 years. Fran thought the obvious issues with price and quality of the computers would propel the administration into reconsideration of their commitment to IBM.

Both State Superintendent and the Governor's office defended the purchase price of the computers by listing the extras IBM provided within the contract including delivery, warranty and training. County technology coordinators disagreed with the claims regarding no-cost training and delivery: "some computer experts working in county school systems say the state pays too much for IBM's machines. They say many of the benefits touted by the state, such as training and installation, are billed to the state separately."[101]

The AG office continued to receive reports from concerned teachers regarding the discontinued computers and exorbitant prices: "The state Department of Education last week spent $987 on an IBM computer that can be purchased brand new from a California firm for $219 or refurbished from a company in Massachusetts for $139."[102] Fran paced the hall between her office and Darrell's. She was clearly outraged. Fran's young son, Ian, might be the recipient of one of these outdated computers, and that wouldn't fly with a mother clearly devoted to her son's education. Pressed by Fran, WVDE again cited the $2 million national media campaign that came with the contract to "promote" the West Virginia's Basic Skills Computer Education Program. But when queried further, the state Superintendent was unable to delineate any media benefits provided by IBM in the two years since the award: "I don't know yet if the state has gotten its $2 million worth. It's too early to tell. We're really just through the second grade. We have gotten articles in major publications, but at this stage of the game, how much that's worth, I don't know."[103]

Fran joked with Darrell, "Yeah, right…a national campaign touting that West Virginia buys out-of-date computers for its students—some press." She lamented, "I don't get the resistance to simply rebidding the contract. Why would anyone not want the best computers for the least money?"

The AG office continued to withhold approval of the 1993 IBM contract until a determination was made if WVDE adhered to proper bidding and award purchasing requirements, and of the legality of a 10 year contract. Teacher Tom Hark, equally frustrated by the state's resistance to re-bid the contract wrote another letter to Governor Caperton in which he implored the Governor to find a way to secure the best computers at the lowest costs for students: "Governor, please forget the Model 25 computers and use your well-known business expertise to obtain the best deal possible at this time. Without rebidding this contract, you cannot show that you have done this."[104] Hark's request was ignored by the Governor.

Marockie and Caperton were upset with the AG's refusal to approve the computer contract. Marockie claimed that Darrell's action of withholding the computer contract negatively impacted the education of children in West Virginia. Further the state Superintendent contended that switching computers was detrimental to consistency in software access.[105] In a private meeting with reporters, the Governor's anger rose, as did his voice, when he talked about Darrell withholding approval of the contract. "Those contracts should be approved by the attorney general. Whether they're correct or not, it's not his responsibility to second guess the Department of Education." As the state's chief legal officer, Darrell disagreed.

The computer contract issues occurred during first year that I was superintendent of schools in Kanawha County, the largest school district in the state. The animosity of Caperton and Marockie toward Darrell was perhaps increased when as a county superintendent I supported county level staff, including Hilary Cowan, Tom Hark and other teachers who were all highly frustrated by the state's resistance to acquire the most up to date computers at the lowest price. In a separate issue, which added fuel to the already burning fire, Kanawha County Schools, based on my recommendation as county superintendent, brought legal action against the Governor and state for withholding $1.4 million in school aid to the County. The Governor authorized reduction in funds to counties based upon a projected state budget deficit. The deficit did not occur, and the state ended up with a $20 million surplus. After trying to resolve the issue with Caperton and Marockie, who both denied Kanawha County's request to restore the funds, the Board voted to take legal action. [106]

Kanawha County Circuit Judge Kaufman agreed with the Kanawha County's position and ordered Governor Caperton to restore funds.[107] The State appealed Kaufman's decision to the state Supreme Court. Twenty other counties joined with Kanawha County in seeking restoration of funds. In January, 1994 Justice Miller writing for the Court, reversed the lower court decision based upon the timing of litigation: "Although the Appellees are to be lauded for attempting to re-garner funds originally appropriated for public education, because they did not raise the issue until after the 1992-93 fiscal year had expired, the governor was without authority to restore those funds due to their expiration by law."[108]

In an effort to negate the impact of purchasing high cost discontinued computers for WV students, the AG filed a declaratory judgement against the Governor and state Superintendent requesting a determination of the constitutionality and validity of the two state computer hardware and software contracts.[109] The case was filed in the Kanawha County circuit court. The case was assigned to Judge John Hey. Hey, who ran against Darrell in the 1976 Supreme Court election, was openly hostile toward Darrell. As predicted, Judge John Hey held that the Governor and WVDE were allowed to go forward with the IBM contract. Fran never doubted that Hey would rule against the AG, but knew it was useless to ask him to step aside. Judge Hey's conduct eventually led to disbarment by the West Virginia Supreme Court: "In

287

1995 Hey's admitted egregious behavior…related to sexual harassment as a manifestation of his alcoholism…subjected him to criminal convictions, civil liability…and disbarment."[110] The West Virginia Supreme Court reinstated Hey's law license on October 14, 2003.[111]

The AG office moved to appeal Judge Hey's decision to the state Supreme Court. The Court upheld the validity of the state computer contracts. Justice Brotherton, writing for the majority, concluded: "Since we have held that the one year contract with multiple renewals does not violate constitutional or statutory provisions, there is no need to rebid the contract every time a renewal occurs. Accordingly, we affirm the November 10, 1993, decision of the Circuit Court of Kanawha County and remand this case for entry of judgment in accordance with this opinion."[112]

Another troubling part of the decision was that the Court held the "Attorney General is not a person and therefore not entitled to bring a declaratory judgement."[113] The ruling made the AG the only Constitutional officer not able to request a declaratory judgement to define the legal responsibilities of someone. Even members of the Legislature can bring a declaratory judgement. The state Court's decision simply supported the Governor.

Great effort was expended by the AG's office to uphold the law in order to protect the interest of students and finances of the state. The AG office simply requested the rebidding of the contract to ensure the most current, lowest cost computers were placed in schools. The disappointment in the AG office was palatable. In this case the WV Supreme Court opinion did not align with the interests of children: "McGraw wants the state to rebid the contracts. Caperton wants McGraw to butt out. McGraw has the authority to hold up the contracts, but Caperton insists McGraw shouldn't second guess the Department of Education. Somebody needs to. Whoever negotiated these contracts for the state exhibited an appalling lack of savy."[114]–*Charleston Gazette*

"We will not be a party to sentencing a generation of West Virginia children to using inferior, obsolete equipment while gouging taxpayers."[115] *Chief Deputy Fran Hughes*
And they weren't. It was on the shoulders of those less compelled by duty and more concerned with maintaining their power base.

School Construction Bonds
To whose benefit is it for Bond indebtedness to occur without the approval of voters?

Bonds were a concern to the framers of the West Virginia Constitution. Virginia was heavily in debt from the overuse of bonds for financing its government and financial failure was looming when West Virginia was formed. The framers, specifically to avoid the difficulties Virginia faced, built into the West Virginia Constitution a stipulation that bonds required citizen approval.

In 1989 Governor Caperton proposed and the Legislature established the School Building Authority for the purpose of addressing the vast construction and repair issues of schools throughout the State. In 1993, the Governor and the SBA announced plans to secure a $328 million bond on their own volition; i.e. without any citizen approval. The AG office questioned the legality of the bond sale without adherence to the constitutional requirement that bonds be approved by the electorate. In addition the AG office denied the SBA's request for a bond counsel contract without competitive bidding. Jim Lees, a Charleston lawyer well known for pursuing reform battles, filed a law suit questioning the legality of the SBA's authority to borrow money without voters' approval. Circuit Court Judge Zakaib held the Authority could not issue the bonds.[116] It was a victory for the framers of the state Constitution.

Labor was opposed to the AG's questioning of the SBA's authority to issue the $328 million bond, but that did not deter Darrell from proceeding with what was a violation of the Constitution by the Governor and SBA: "I view union people as good people. But we here at the attorney general's office are trying to go by the book, and we have to do that regardless of our friends."[117]

Lee's litigation revealed that in 1989, as the SBA prepared to sell their first round of bonds, the Governor and SBA received legal counsel that the SBA funding structure for bonds was unconstitutional. Dennis Vaughan, a prominent Charleston lawyer and partner in the Vaugh and Withrow law firm, advised the SBA not to proceed with the bond sale: "We told them what they wanted to do wasn't anything but a general obligation bond in a mask. We said we wouldn't consider serving as bond counsel unless the statute had been tested at the Supreme Court."[118] The Governor and SBA proceeded with the $301 million bond sale based upon advice from Steptoe and Johnson, counsel for 1989 bond issue.[119]

The bonds sold in 1989 were revenue bonds, which unlike general revenue bonds backed by the state's good credit, were riskier for investors and more expensive. A seven page memo signed by Governor Caperton, School Superintendent Hank Marockie and four other state officials, also uncovered in Lee's litigation, promised to seek funding for the Authority in each year's budget and not to veto or cut funding to the Authority even if the Legislature earmarked too little money for the WVDE to distribute to public school districts.[120] Promises made without legal authority.

The discovered letter raised many red flags: 1.) the promises contradicted the Constitutional provision that public education has priority state funding; i.e. education gets preference over other agencies in potential state funding cuts; 2.) the promises contradicted the Code requirement that government officials were prohibited from obligating future funds past the given fiscal year; i.e. financial obligations must be considered for continuation each year, no guarantees, and 3.) the promises were perhaps the reason Governor Caperton actually reduced funds in a 1993 mid-year cut to the county school systems in order to maintain no reduction in the allocation to the Authority; i.e. prioritizing funding of the Authority before public education.

Judge Zakaib's ruling was appealed to the state Supreme Court, and the Court upheld the lower court ruling stating the SBA was not allowed to issue $328 million in new bonds without voter approval. Justice Miller, in the majority opinion, found the Executive branch actions wrong: "Finally, unless we are to abandon our logic and common sense, we cannot help but conclude that the statutory scheme surrounding these bonds bespeaks a legislative requirement that they be funded. To accept the premise that the Legislature is not bound to fund the bonds and would allow a default, thereby impairing the credit rating of the State, assumes a naiveté on our part that we simply do not possess."[121]

However, in order to avoid "financial havoc", the Court allowed the 1989 bond issue and financing to stand. Two more court cases and an extraordinary Legislative session later, a new funding mechanism was

290

created in which a special fund, the SBA Debt Service Fund, was formed. The special fund received money allocated from the net profits of the WV Lottery in order to liquidate the revenue bonds.[122]

The AG's commitment to adhere to the law in the issuance of bonds did not go unnoticed by the West Virginia Legislature. Senate President Keith Burdette, D-Wood said, "McGraw may be operating within narrower limits after the Legislature convenes in January."[123]

Pension and Investment Funds
To whose benefit is it to not properly fund and wisely invest pensions funds?

As a Justice and as Attorney General, Darrell was vigilant in his respect of the state's statutory and constitutional responsibility to properly fund and wisely invest public pensions. The law anticipates the protection of pension funds as a solid trust between the state and the people's investment in a state retirement fund. West Virginia has a history of elected officials neglecting their duty to protect pension funds.

In 1985 under a new, again governor, Governor Arch Moore's and Senate President Dan Tonkovich's repeated violations of the state's duty to fund the pension system took place. The Legislature and the Governor for four years engaged in the illegal diversion of pensioners' retirement funds which left the System actuarially unsound.[124]

From 1985-1989 the Governor did not budget and the Legislature did not appropriate sufficient monies. The money that was appropriated was actually used in a shell game maneuver for other endeavors than the pension fund. These actions resulted in an $80 million unfunded pension liability which increased with time.[125]

In 1989 Ira Dadisman, a retiree and the Chairman of the Public Employees Retirement Association, brought action in *Dadisman v. Moore* to request relief from the WV Supreme Court in order to insure proper funding of the Public Employees Retirement System. In *Dadisman v. Moore,* Justice Darrell McGraw, in writing for the majority, upheld the property rights of pensioners in the retirement system and concluded the Governor and Legislature violated their fiduciary duties to pensioners.[126] The Court held the state must 1.) immediately stop the unlawful diversion of retirement funds for other uses; 2.) determine if diversion of funds resulted in a System rendered actuarially unsound, and 3.) develop a plan to return the System to actuarial soundness and re-compensate for the four years of unfunded contributions. In addition the Court addressed the petitioner's concern that pension funds were invested improperly and that the speculative investments exacerbated the actuary soundness of the fund. The Court ruled that, in accordance with Constitutional requirements, all pension funds must be removed from speculative to secure investments and that all future investments be made with "competent, educated and trained financial managers."[127]

The actions of the Governor and the Legislature to divert and underfund the pension system and engage in illegal and ill-advised risky investments left the state's retirement system with an enormous unfunded liability. On separate issues but as an insight to character, in 1989 Senate President Dan R. Tonkovich pleaded guilty and was sentenced to five year for extortion and Governor Moore pleaded guilty to five felonies and was sentenced to five years and ten months in prison. Ironically Moore and Tonkovich were from the same county—home of the state petitionary.

The changing of the state house guard in 1985 with the election of Governor Moore and the election A.J. Manchin as state Treasurer did not bode well for adherence to statutory and constitutional fiduciary requirements related to state investments. Larrie Bailey, an investment professional licensed by the Securities and Exchange Commission, had been state Treasurer since 1976. In 1984 Bailey lost his reelection to A. J. Manchin, "a political fixture best known for judging beauty contests…who later testified that he did not even know that when a number was in parenthesis it was a loss…and who resigned from office in 1989 under threat of impeachment."[128]

Anticipating pending disaster with a less than qualified new state Treasurer and an Investment Board headed by Gov. Arch Moore, the astute Treasurer Bailey in one of his last official acts had the old Board of Investment Board, composed of Gov. Rockefeller, Treasurer Bailey and Auditor Gainer, "pass investment guidelines that among other things, prohibited the Investment Division from purchasing any security with a maturity in excess of 90 days without specific Board approval."[129] The resolution was specifically intended to prevent the new Treasurer's office from engaging in risky speculative investments without careful fiduciary advice.

Unfortunately, Treasurer Manchin, as one of his first official acts on the new Board of Investment in 1985, introduced a resolution to negate Treasurer Bailey's investment guidelines. Manchin's resolution "authorized the investment staff to buy and sell securities with maturities up to ten years without prior Board approval…(and) also enabled the staff to use a larger percentage of the Fund to trade longer term securities"[130] Manchin's resolution was approved over Auditor Gainer's objection. These investment changes proved disastrous for the state with Treasurer Manchin in charge of investments.

Beginning in 1985 and ending when the market took a downturn in 1987, the state engaged in illegal speculation with state funds.[131] The state's partners in this activity included Morgan Stanley, Goldman Sachs, Salomon Brothers and others with both the state and their financial partners making much money in the beginning. "The trading was active—in one three month period the volume of trades came to nearly $20 billion. In just one year Mr. Maher (Morgan Stanley salesman), then 32, took home $1 million."[132]

The risky and illegal investments caught up with Treasurer Manchin in 1987 when auditors found the investment fund totaled $200 million less than the principal. When all the losses were toted up, this winning streak turned sour, came to $280 million. This financial disaster spurred the Legislature to institute a food tax that certainly hit the poor the hardest.[133]

In a state where there is never enough money for essential services, the Treasurer, entrusted with a legal responsibility to invest prudently and in a secure manner, placed the blame on someone else: "Yet he [Manchin] insisted the only mistake he made was to hire Mr. Margolin [Associate Treasure] and pay him a higher salary than my own."[134] Governor Moore and Treasurer Manchin determined through their first vote on the Investment Board, to violate the state's fiduciary investment responsibilities to the people.

Fortunately for the state, Rudolph L. DiTrapano, a veteran litigator and one of only a handful of WV lawyers to argue and win an appeal in the US Supreme Court , served as lead counsel in an action filed against Morgan Stanley, Goldman Sachs and Salomon Brothers. The litigation was complicated and took years with recognition by financial experts, counsel and judges that those involved were either stupid or greedy:

- "You've got the stupidity of the state agency versus the greed of Morgan Stanley, said Rudolph L. DiTrapano, a lawyer representing the state.
- "Morgan Stanley is just like used car salesmen," said H. Craig Slaughter, the state's director of investments. "They don't think about truth and justice, just the American way of making money at any cost. Don't they have any responsibility to their clients?"
- "We've always been victimized by corrupt and incompetent government officials…We look back and see how fast we lost money in the fund. It was shocking and embarrassing. So a lot of people thought we deserved it because we were dumb," lamented Rudolph L. DiTrapano, a lawyer representing the state.
- "The state and Morgan Stanley together engaged in transactions prohibited by the law…Those transactions were prohibited and the beneficiaries of the fund, the citizens are entitled to protection," wrote Judge Andrew McQueen in his decision holding for the state.
- In a hearing before the state Supreme Court, Justice Richard Neely called Treasurer Manchin a "simpleton." "If you look at all of these telephone conversation, he told Morgan Stanley lawyers, "you see that these folks here were behaving like jackasses. They didn't understand when they would sell $100 million. They didn't know if they had sold a put or a call."
- As to Morgan Stanley Justice Neely said, "There is nothing you can say to convince that this was not speculation. This stuff is just for blow-dried Harvard Business School types who think they can beat the market."[135]

The litigation continued for years. But in the end Mr. DiTrapano's expertise and efforts resulted in the recovery of almost $85 million for the state.

In 1993 the state Board of Investment asked the Attorney General for a legal opinion to determine the Board's limitation for investing state employees' and the state's matching contributions in the stock market. In accordance with prior state Supreme Court decisions, the AG opinion was clear, "the state constitution does not allow the board to invest in the stock of private companies or associations."[136]

The Board of Investments voted to bring litigation against the AG. Prior to requesting the opinion, the Board had already invested $18 million and had plans to invest 20 percent of the pension funds in stock over the next several years.[137] The Board's actions were in direct contradiction to *Dadisman v. Moore* which held that pension funds must be removed from speculative to secure investments.[138] Ultimately the Board had second thoughts about the litigation and withdrew it, but the issues raised by the AG opinion regarding pension fund investments into stocks remained a controversial and undecided issue.

In another attempt to avoid the Constitutional requirement pertaining to investments, the Legislature enacted the West Virginia Trust Fund Act. The Act required the state treasurer to pay nearly $4 billion dollars to the Trust Fund for the purpose of investing of up to 60% of assets into corporate entities; i.e. stock market investments. State Treasurer Larrie Bailey, who had returned to the office 1990, filed litigation questioning the constitutionality of the enacted legislation. It seemed like another shell game was taking place to avoid the statutory Constitutional requirements of secure investments.

In 1997, the West Virginia Supreme Court agreed with Treasurer Bailey and declared the Trust Fund unconstitutional: "After careful consideration, we conclude that West Virginia Trust Fund, Inc. is, to a highly significant degree, a state actor and instrumentality of the State. Therefore, the West Virginia Trust Fund Act essentially allows the State to indirectly invest employee pension funds and the workers' compensation and coal workers' pneumoconiosis funds towards becoming a joint owner or stockholder in companies and associations.

Accordingly, we find that the Act is unconstitutional, and affirm the circuit court's decision in that regard."[139]

Later that same year (1997), the voters approved a constitutional amendment allowing the investment of pensions into stocks and other investments. Concurrently with the constitutional amendment, the Legislature established the Management Investment Board for the purpose of professionally managing the investment of state pension funds.[140] The Management Investment Board was a step in the right direction. The investment of state dollars into risky speculative stocks must be undertaken with due diligence that includes an intensive system of checks and balances to avoid outcomes like occurred under Treasurer Manchin in 1985.[141]

In 1998, the pension funds again became an issue when Governor Cecil Underwood secured the passage of House Bill 4702 to finance the construction and renovation of much need correctional facilities with pension monies. The Bill required the WV Board of Investments, charged with the duty of investing funds from the Public Employees' Pension System, to invest $150 million of pension funds into the WV Jail and Correctional Authority. It was described as a loan. Darrell believed the bill was an attempt by the Governor and Legislature to raise money for services without seeking voter approval to borrow money or enact legislation to raise taxes.

The Management Investment Board also questioned soundness of this bill: "…the board rejected it. We didn't think it was a…responsible thing to do, from a fiduciary standpoint. The Investment Board members were concerned about fiduciary liability."[142]—*H. Craig Slaughter, Board Executive Director*

The Management Investment Board refused the transfer of funds and filed a "friendly" lawsuit with the state Supreme Court asking for determination of the legality of the law to loan pensioners' funds to the Jail Authority. The AG joined the lawsuit in opposition to the loan "arguing that pensioner's rights were being violated and that such an agreement could render the system financially unsound."[143]

However, Justice Maynard in writing for the majority held the law was constitutional and the Board of Investments was authorized to make the loan. Maynard's decision was precedent setting and a concern for those interested in the protecting pension systems. This loan from a state pension system to the Regional Jail Authority was a first for the U.S. pension industry: "The loan opens a Pandora 's Box on what investment standards and polices the board should pursue…The state faces a convulsive breakdown in authority in managing the pension fund and protecting beneficiaries."[144]— *Pensions and Investments,*

Industry analysts, the State Treasurer's office, the Investment Management Board and the Attorney General's office all questioned the soundness of the loan design: "What happens if the Legislature comes back and does it again for some other purpose?"[145]—*Jerry Simpson, Assistant State Treasurer*

"It's a step on the slippery slope that you don't want to take."—*H. Craig Slaughter, Executive Director Investment Fund*

"The decision to tap the state pension system for operating purposes is fraught with peril. It's not good public policy; it's not good public finance."[146]—*Darrell McGraw, Attorney General*

To some the AG's actions were meritorious: "Attorney General Darrell McGraw is an unrequited hero in the matter. He unsuccessfully opposed the mandated financing."[147]—*Pensions and Investments*

In 2007 with the approval of the Governor and the Legislature, the work product of the AG office, $807 million in tobacco settlement dollars, was placed in the Teachers Retirement System. This major infusion of funds substantially increased the solvency of the pension system.[148]

In 2015 the Pew Charitable Trust Fund concluded because of strict adherence to the 1990 plan required by the *Dadisman v. Moore;* the passage of the Constitutional amendment to allow pension fund investments in stocks; the establishment of an Investment Management Board to professionally manage those stock investments, and the contribution from 2007 tobacco settlement dollars that the state's pension fund moved from one of the worst funded systems to one of the best in the nation.[149]

Chapter XVII   Business/ Industry Interventions

Telemarketer/Sweepstake Scammers

One morning when the "Judge" arrived at his office he was surprised to find that Tom Rodd and I were already there. The Judge was always the first one at work. Tom and I were working together to deal with the increasing number of calls coming in from senior citizens who were the victims of telemarketing and sweepstake scammers. It was horrendous. People were suffering all over the state. That morning we wanted to make a point with the Judge—a powerful one.

We knew taking on scammers with big pockets was going to be tough. We hatched a plan. We lined the parameters of the Judge's office with pictures of elderly people. They were 70, 80, 90 year old men and women and underneath each picture was their name and the amount of money they had lost. They weren't small amounts. Some had lost $15 - 20 thousand dollars. I'll never forget there was one woman who later testified at 92 years old how she had been scammed.

The Judge looked around the room. He went to every picture. He looked at every amount. He simply said, 'Guys today we do something!' And we did.[1]—Frances Hughes, Chief Deputy Attorney General

West Virginia filed the first large scale case against 102 telemarketers and sweepstake scammers in the country. These companies disproportionately preyed on older people and understood the human nature propensity to believe it is our lucky day when offered what seems like a great deal.[2]

The *State v. Imperial Marketing*[3] case against telemarketers was successful with all but one. As the phrase goes 101 of the 102 of the telemarketers "went quietly into the night;" refrained from their deceptive practices; paid settlements to the injured and clearly understood the office of West Virginia's Attorney General would remain diligent in monitoring their future practices.[4] Lindenwold, a division of direct marketing giant Suarez Industries, was the only company who refused to stop their deceptive practices in West Virginia. Suarez Industries, a $100 million a year Canton, Ohio sweepstakes operation, employed about 900 people and marketed such things as jewelry, exercise equipment and what they called "the excitement and adventure of sweepstakes."[5] Research litigation found"17,563 West Virginia consumers who were swayed by Suarez Corporation Industries' ("Suarez") solicitations to spend $975,389.02 on trinkets."[6]

In response to the legal action(s) brought by the AG, Suarez filed a multitude of counter claims and law suits over a four year period in state and federal courts. Suarez' resistance included a barrage of harassing actions against the AG and staff, including Fran Hughes and Tom Rodd. Attorneys general in other states were familiar with Suarez Industries. In conversations with Washington Attorney General Christine Gregoire, Darrell understood the fight to keep Suarez' from victimizing West Virginians was destined to be most difficult. In Washington, Suarez funded ads seeking "damaging information" about Christine Gregoire to use against her in the next election. The *Daily Mail* referred to Suarez as an "Ohio businessman." The tactics used by Suarez were not reflective of the good, honorable businessmen and women of West Virginia.[7]

Tom Rodd, head of the Consumer Protection Division, filed suit to obtain from Suarez Corporation a list of their WV customers. Suarez resisted, but Rodd prevailed in circuit court and the state Supreme Court. In the appeal Rodd noted_"20,000 West Virginians were taken from as low as 20 to many hundreds of dollars…they mailed money to the company because they believed they were big winners and needed to send money to gain their earnings."[8] Suarez countered with massive mailings, television ads and full page newspaper ads attacking the AG. The attacks were vicious. The law suits and ethic complaints against the AG and deputy attorneys general were frivolous but took time, attention and resources.

As a youth Rodd, a dedicated environmentalist and a Quaker who attended Berea College, refused to register for the draft during the Vietnam War. As a result Rodd served two years in federal prison. In 1980 Rodd was pardoned by President Jimmy Carter. Suarez went after Rodd. Suarez organized a protest, engaging veterans and homeless people who he allegedly paid, to picket a national attorneys general meeting where Rodd was in attendance:

We were representing WV at a national attorneys general meeting in Washington, D.C. when I looked out window and saw all these people milling around and carrying signs. I couldn't believe it. They were attacking Tom Rodd who was sitting across the table from me. I knew who was behind this, and I was incensed. Suarez was trying to divert attention from his scamming of the elderly to getting people riled up about Tom being a conscientious objector.

I knew this would make for negative press so I called the Judge who was back at the office. The Judge said he was more concerned about Tom, 'I want to talk to Tom; tell him to call me.' Suarez was sending a message to the AGs from other states who were attending the meeting— don't fool with me.[9]—Frances Hughes, Chief Deputy Attorney General
In addition to the protest, Suarez took out full page ads in newspapers across the state and distributed fliers in the mail attacking the AG and Tom Rodd: "Lindenwold Fine Jewelers has a 25 year partnership of Trust, but can you trust Darrell McGraw and Tom Rodd?"[10]

After leaving the Attorney General's office Tom Rodd, a brilliant guy with a beard and a kind, gentle heart, went on to work for Supreme Court Justice Larry Starcher, a progressive justice who authored many cases protecting human rights. Rodd also authored a book about the life of Carrie Williams, an African American teacher, who worked in a segregated school in the 1890s but argued for equal pay and education, and her lawyer, John Robert Clifford, the state's first African American attorney. Fifty years before the landmark *Brown v. Board of Education* case, Clifford won a landmark civil rights case, *Williams v. Board of Education of Fairfax District,* before the WV Supreme Court. The Tucker County Board of Education decided to shorten the school year for African American children attending a segregated school in the Town of Coketon. Williams, the African American students' teacher, continued to teach four additional months without pay. Williams went to Clifford asking him to help the students receive a full term of instruction and recover her pay. Clifford successfully sued on behalf of Williams and the children.[11] Williams and Clifford went before an all white jury at the local level and won. Tucker County appealed to the state Supreme Court for relief. Clifford prevailed again and won a "landmark equal rights case to secure wages and school terms equivalent to those at white schools.

Justice Marmaduke Dent, an early believer in human equality, regardless of race or sex, authored the opinion which is viewed as one of the most progressive state civil rights decision in its era. *Williams v. Bd. Of Ed. Fairfax District* laid the groundwork for national cases like *Brown v. Board of Education.*[12] Rodd viewed the *Williams* case as a testimony to "how progress comes from persistence in the pursuit of justice and service to others even when there are setbacks."[13] For it would take another fifty years before *Brown v. Board of Education* ruled that racial segregation in public schools was unconstitutional. Rodd remains persistent in his pursuit of justice as he now devotes time to educating and involving others on the environmental issues: "Yes, human-caused global warming and climate change are real, and their dangerous impacts are growing every year. And understanding and preparing for these changes and impacts are everyone's business."[14]

Suarez and his aligned and personally funded entity, the Better Business Bureau, were engaged in all sorts of intimidating and harassing behavior against the AG and our family including anonymous phone calls; ransacked trash, and mysterious strangers lurking outside our house and even in the garage. One night after a particularly long Board meeting, I pulled into our garage to find a well dressed man going through a box in the back of the garage. As he ran by my driver's door with some document in his hand, he just smiled and hit the side of my door. It was during the Suarez period that we began taking our trash over the state dumpster versus putting it out on our street for pick-up. There had been too many mornings where we found our garbage strewn about on the lawn. Suarez wanted to make life miserable for all the McGraws. For me, his efforts were working.

Ironically it was Suarez who asked Federal Judge Charles Haden to issue a restraining order against the AG. David Cleek, attorney for the AG, responded to Suarez's demand: "the Ohio organization have picketed a McGraw aide, have posed as concerned consumers who came to McGraw's office and then took pictures of staff members and the office layout. He also alleged McGraw's office trash has been search by the Ohio organization members."[15] Judge Haden ruled that "McGraw was not a threat to the groups' freedom of speech" and denied Suarez' restraining order request.[16] Suarez' seemed obsessed with "getting" the

AG and members of his staff: "We'd have to be blind to believe Suarez's absurd ad campaign. The personal attacks on our attorney general and his staff attorneys are despicable. Darrell McGraw has steadfastly, unremittingly and consistently fought for ordinary and disadvantaged West Virginians, and he is doing so now."[17]—*Charleston Gazette*

Suarez's intimidations and negative assertions were tough to tolerate. Suarez petitioned the court to videotape Darrell's depositions. Fran was concerned, "Can you just imagine how they will turn his words, his gestures, his facial expressions upside down and use it against him in a political ad?" Darrell tried to convince the judge not to grant Suarez' petition: "These people are experts in creating false images…in my judgment, what they want is to digitize me talking so that they can create computer images that will make me say whatever they want me to say for purposes of political ads they intend to put on, anti-McGraw political ads."[18] Unfortunately the federal magistrate granted Suarez's petition to videotape the depositions.

In the 1996 re-election campaign, Suarez ran ads against Darrell and in support of the Republican opponent, Charlotte Lane. "One of the ads Suarez ran depicted Darrell as a free spending airhead who thinks money grows on trees. It features a gray-haired man in a dark suit climbing a tree, plucking money from its branches, and then crashing to the ground."[19] After seeing the ad, our youngest came screaming into the kitchen, "They've just killed Daddy."

The Suarez ads were effective and the '96 election results were close: "Buoyed by an assault on McGraw by Ohio millionaire Benjamin Suarez, challenger Charlotte Lane netted 49 percent of the vote in a race that was expected to be a McGraw runaway."[20]

Sometimes it just got worse and that was the case when a U.S. 4th District Judge held that Darrell did not have personal immunity in the Suarez case. Apprehension was intentionally exacerbated when the lawyer for the Better Business Bureau told reporters, "I think anyone who looks at the law can find it's exceptionally rare that immunity is stripped from an AG , a Governor or anyone else in authority…he is going to use the decision to go after McGraw's own money."[21] The potential of losing personal property and money in addition to reading and watching personal attacks created strains in the family.

One of the personal attacks that Suarez used in 1997 had great shelf life. In Darrell's 2016 campaign for the state Supreme Court, the 1997 negative ads were enhanced, digitalized and broadcast on television and then internet. The ads in 1997 and 2016 stemmed from a contortion of the facts related to a long planned family trip. On June 6, 1997, Darrell was required to testify against Suarez in federal court; the trial ran late and Darrell missed his flight with the family out of Charleston to Dulles International airport. We were leaving on a planned trip to see our son, who was studying at the University of Madrid. In order to meet the international flight out of Dulles, the Governor's office authorized Darrell to take the state plane from Charleston to Dulles. Even though it wasn't necessary, Darrell reimbursed the state over a thousand dollars for the flight from Charleston to Dulles.[22] Suarez orchestrated attacks alleging Darrell misspent public funds for personal benefit. The facts did not stop the Republican National Leadership Committee in 2016 from spending millions in commercials that depicted Darrell utilizing a nonexistent "state jet" for a European holiday with his family. Negative commercials misconstruing the factual events were difficult in 1997 but even more challenging in the 2016 election. Unfortunately it was highly effective.

In just one of the state papers, there were 47 stories in 1997 and 76 stories in 1998 related to Suarez litigation and attacks.[23] But sometimes there was a ray of hope: "Another defeat Suarez should slink off...In yet another court attack against Attorney General Darrell McGraw Ohio sweepstakes hustler Benjamin Suarez has been handed his hat...yet Suarez continues to insist that McGraw is out to get him. It seems to us that he is out to get McGraw, simply because McGraw did his job protecting state consumers."[24]–*Charleston Gazette*

In November, 1998 Judge Haden threw out seven of the nine counts in the Suarez case related to improper conduct by attorney general office in prosecuting the Better Business Bureau and Suarez. Haden's decision was a major victory for Darrell and the AG staff, but it wasn't over.[25]

Four years into this barrage of law suits, counter law suits, ethic complaints and negative ads, Darrell was being cross-examined in yet another Suarez related case in federal court. This case involved a former employee, a paralegal in the AG office, who took privileged attorney-client documents and turned them over to Suarez:

This same employee had a voodoo doll resembling me that she kept at her desk. She routinely put pins in it to cast spells on me. One day while at lunch I was stung in two places on my leg. When I came back to the office I was limping and this employee looked at me and said, 'See what I can do—don't mess with me.' The worst part was that when I heard her words—I was actually afraid. After she gave privileged legal documents to Suarez, we had no choice but to terminate her employment. The termination was the basis for her legal action against the Judge. It was beyond crazy.[26]—

Frances Hughes, Chief Deputy Attorney General.

At times Darrell's lack of tolerance for the absurd got the best of him. Darrell's frustration resulted in an "outburst" during trial. The Judge admonished Darrell and declared a mistrial. This was the second mistrial for this case. [27] After 12 lawsuits and much harassment, the Suarez nightmare came to an end in December, 1999. For the most part, Darrell prevailed in the legal challenges: "In addition to winning the consumer protection action, a jury found in McGraw's favor in the lawsuit filed by the Better Government Bureau. The former secretary...agreed to settle the suit for no money."[28] It was reported the Board of Risk who represented the AG spent $1.6 million in legal fees. Suarez contended he spent $4 million.[29]

In 2015, Suarez was convicted of witness tampering in a federal case. Suarez was sentenced to 15 months in prison and fined $15,000.[30] Assistant U.S. Attorney Carole Rendon described Suarez's influence over elected officials: "the case against Suarez was all about 'the power of money' and 'the influence it can buy from politicians'... the evidence will show Suarez to be politically sophisticated, politically active, and politically savvy. He had the private cellphone numbers of a number of different politicians, and he used them."[31]

Suarez's conviction occurred in Ohio long after the tumultuous years of resistance by WV's AG. Justice for those with money can be infrequent and most certainly if and when occurs, it requires much time and persistence.

Big Tobacco—Taking on the Marlboro Man
To whose benefit is it to convince the public that smoking is not harmful?

> *This time was different. It wasn't a personal injury lawsuit. They weren't going to be able to get the plaintiff in a room and ask what kind of baby food you ate that caused your cancer or how many times did you drink or have sex or whatever the tobacco companies could dig up to show that something in your life actually caused your illness—it wasn't because we lied and told you smoking was good for you.*
>
> *This time there was no individual plaintiff who tobacco could tear apart. This was an equity case. We weren't representing individual smokers. We were representing the state. West Virginia PEIA, Workers Compensation and Health and Human Service had to pay out all this money for tobacco related illnesses. It was a winner!*[32]*—Frances Hughes, Chief Deputy Attorney General*

The tobacco litigation was viewed by many as a not viable case or in vernacular of many—it was a frivolous law suit. The word "frivolous," a scapegoat term applied to divert attention away from those who stood to profit from tobacco sales, was frequently used to describe the tobacco litigation. Tobacco litigation nay sayers offered, "People should know better than to smoke." The tobacco litigation required tenacity and perseverance. There were many setbacks. During the five years of the tobacco litigation Darrell was known to offer over-used phrases in encouragement to others: "It is not over until it's over," or "Everything works out in the end. If it hasn't worked out yet, then it's not the end." The AG and staff believed in the merits of the tobacco litigation. They all realized success in this litigation would positively impact the lives of West Virginia citizens.

In 1993 at a National Attorneys General meeting, Mike Moore, AG from Mississippi, and Darrell discussed taking on "Big Tobacco." Many remembered Darrell's response, "tobacco's time has come." He repeated those words often during the litigation years. The AG team stayed the course in the tobacco case from filing in 1994 to the arrival of the first settlement check in 1999 and beyond. The push-back in the tobacco litigation was enormous; work efforts substantial; travails ever present; setbacks frequent and emotional and political consequences significant. The ultimate outcome was completely worth it.

In 1993 over 434,000 Americans were dying each year from cigarette smoking and the health care cost exceeded $52 billion dollars annually. Cigarette companies remained without culpability in tobacco related deaths or health care costs.[33]

In 1965 the surgeon general said that smoking was a perilous endeavor. However it wasn't until 1969 that the tobacco companies began placing warning labels on cigarette packages. The litigious issue in the tobacco case involved unraveling the level of deceit and fraud the industry engaged in to conceal facts and falsify information about smoking. How much tobacco companies knew; when they knew it, and what they did were all part of the massive discovery involved in the tobacco case. To whose profit was it to conceal the detrimental evidence of smoking? To whose profit was it to market cigarettes to generation after generation of potential smokers?

In 1993 Justin Catanoso, a *Washington Monthly* reporter, presented strong evidence that tobacco companies were aware as early as 1946 of the potential lethal nature of cigarettes. Catanoso reported that an independent research commissioned by the tobacco companies in 1950 found a conclusive link between smoking and lung cancer. Another research authorized by tobacco companies called the "Mouse House" found a causative connection between smoking and emphysema. The tobacco companies continued to only mention flawed or inadequate or inconclusive research that showed any harmful effects. Catanoso concluded: "There is now compelling body of evidence that would convince dispassionate observers—fair minded jurors, for instance—that over…the past four decades, the tobacco industry engaged in massive fraud."[34]

In 1994 three Attorneys General became the first to file against tobacco giants: Mississippi Attorney General Michael Moore led the litigation along with Minnesota Attorney General Hubert Humphrey III and West Virginia Attorney General Darrell McGraw. Other states filed separately or joined the class action litigation over the next few years.

Florida and Massachusetts filed in 1995 and the remaining states filed in 1996 and 1997 when evidence of litigation success became more apparent. Filing dates were important because disbursement recovery recognized that early state action incurred the greatest risk and cost.[35]

The record showed that attempts to expose tobacco companies' deceptive and fraudulent practices; assign liability and recover damages were fraught with failure. In 1985 the famous litigator Melvin Belli filed a claim on behalf of Mark Galbraith for $100 million against R.J. Reynolds. Galbraith, a three pack a day smoker, died in 1969. Belli lost with the court holding that neither causation nor addiction was proven.[36]

In 1988 Nathan Horton, an African American smoker, lost his request for $17 million in damages against American Tobacco when the judge declared a mistrial. In a new trial in 1990 the attorney representing Nathan Horton won, but his client was awarded no damages.[37]

In 1994 *ABC* aired a series entitled "Day One" which contended tobacco companies spiked nicotine levels and contained secret additives. The tobacco industry response was swift and intense. Within days Phillip Morris brought a libel suit against *ABC*.[38]

Less than a month before Mike Moore filed the first tobacco litigation, seven tobacco companies testified before Congressional hearings that they believed "nicotine is not addictive." The tobacco industry success at resisting attempts at associating blame or achieving recovery made the actions brought by the Attorneys General a most difficult and perilous endeavor.[39]

At a time when few other Attorneys General had determined to fight the tobacco industry, Darrell formally agreed to join Mississippi AG Mike Moore. Moore, who led the anti-tobacco litigation, described West Virginia's early involvement in the litigation. "We spent a year and a half flying all over America, speaking to AGs, governors…public health groups—whoever would listen. Our strategy always was to amass just as strong and just as large an army as they had...We were basically just assembling an army for the war. One of the first recruits was West Virginia Attorney General Darrell McGraw Jr."[40] Mike went on to explain that "Darrell reviewed the Mississippi suit and then phoned to ask if I would mind if West Virginia basically copied our claim." Mike said, "Darrell you would make me a very happy man if you would do that."[41]

This time it wasn't a personal injury case; it was about equity and recovery of money for an interested party—the state of West Virginia. On September 20, 1994 West Virginia filed suit against the tobacco companies, including RJ Reynolds, Phillip Morris, Lorillard and Liggett and Meyers, in Kanawha County Circuit court. The suit contended that with the highest smokeless tobacco consumption in the nation, West Virginia was spending $500 million a year for tobacco related health care.

There were three major legal components in West Virginia's law suit: 1.) an injunction to prevent future advertisements encouraging children to smoke, which constituted a violation of state consumer protection laws; 2.) a remedy for antitrust violations in which the tobacco companies were conspiring to claim that tobacco didn't harm, and 3.) a recovery of money for state paid health costs for tobacco related diseases. The litigation estimated that recovery for West Virginia was a billion or more. This was not a frivolous law suit.[42]

The pushback to the litigation was immediate and designed to negate the success of the law suit. The Commonwealth Foundation of Virginia attacked West Virginia's law suit as "political." The Foundation charged the suit was meritless and chastised the state for taking on the "Marlboro Man." "West Virginia will gain nothing in its lawsuit. Whatever political benefits befall politicians who promise to 'take the Marlboro Man to court' the economic returns of this type of litigation are not there."[43] The Foundation's reference to the "Marlboro Man" was rather ironic since actor who played the "Marlboro Man" died from lung cancer in 1992.

There is another ironic story, known by few, related to the "Marlboro Man." While at WVU Darrell was the Phillip Morris campus tobacco representative. He was the *Marlboro Man*. In the 1960's tobacco companies often employed student representatives on college campuses. One of Darrell's job responsibilities was to organize raffles. College students wrote their names on empty cigarette wrappers. Darrell collected the wrappers and held drawings for prizes. Phillip Morris gave Darrell cartons of cigarettes to distribute to merchants. The merchants in turn gave free samples to students. Darrell was good at his job. Phillip Morris gave him a certificate for "outstanding performance as Phillip

Morris's college representative." The tobacco companies unabashedly encouraged students to smoke. When Darrell related the Marlboro story he always added the old WV's political axiom, "The question is not whether you are bought but whether you stay bought."

Darrell didn't quit smoking until I was pregnant with our son, Darrell III. Frustrated with all the air quality issues in the house, not to mention the inevitable health issues, I told Darrell if he didn't quit smoking he would never live to see his son become a man. Darrell quit smoking that very evening and never smoked again.

Darrell was chastised for filing the tobacco lawsuit as simply a way to filter money to lawyers: "What is the point in blaming tobacco companies but not smokers? Health is not the reason for this action…Lawyers are…It is doubtful that state taxpayers or smokers will be helped much. There's a chance the state will lose money on the deal. This is not a defense of tobacco companies. This is a call for McGraw to come clean."[44]—*Charleston Daily Mail*

R.J. Reynolds charged West Virginia's lawsuit was political and without merit: "[the lawsuit is] nothing more than a politically motivated attempt on the part of Mr. McGraw to grab headlines and to harass the manufacturers of a legal product. As in other recent lawsuits of this nature, the claims made are without merit and we are confident that these issues ultimately will be resolved in our favor."[45]

Caperton and Tobacco Litigation

Major push back to the litigation came from Governor Caperton whose administration fought the tobacco law suit with much the same fervor as the tobacco companies demonstrated. Six months after the initial filing of the tobacco litigation, Caperton and his legal counsel, Dana Eddy, questioned the viability of the case. The administration demanded an outside lawyer be hired to review the tobacco lawsuit and refused to allow Human Resources and Public Employee Insurance agencies to join the lawsuit. Participation of the agencies was critical in the potential recovery of an estimated $1 billion dollars.

Eddy, who previously worked for Jackson and Kelly, a law firm that represented tobacco, asserted that Darrell "did not have the authority to file suit on behalf of state agencies without being directed to do so by the governor."[46] Darrell countered Eddy's assertion, "[the attorney general] has the power under the law to bring antitrust and consumer protection lawsuits and the state Constitution gives him authority to bring action on behalf of taxpayers. These powers give him standing to recover damages for Medicaid and Public Employees Insurance Agency."[47]

At the conference table, Fran opened the three inch file of documentation on tobacco cost in the state and complained, "Really? The Governor's office resists Public Employee Insurance joining the litigation—what are they thinking?" Darrell responded, "Perhaps they have another agenda." "Are we fighting tobacco and the Governor?" Fran demanded, "They just released a letter to the tobacco companies saying we don't have authority, and now it's part of tobacco's motion to dismiss. It's beyond outrageous." "Fran, Eddy is no match for you," Darrell offered and everyone around the table nodded in agreement.

The actions of the Governor's office in thwarting a case that had potential of recouping millions of dollars in health care cost was disconcerting to the AG staff.[48] There was a heated exchange between Fran with Eddy over hiring outside counsel and the releasing of documents to the tobacco industry:

Fran charged, "All along, Dana Eddy has attempted to obstruct the law suit."[49]

Eddy responded, "Our obligation is to see that the best interests of the state are served, and not the personal political agenda of the attorney general."[50]

Hughes retorted, "Hiring an outside lawyer to review a lawsuit the Attorney General filed against tobacco companies is a waste of time and money."[51]

Eddy countered, "There's a whole host of questions that need to be answered. They need to be answered by someone whose fee is not riding on the outcome."[52]

Fran couldn't resist noting the subterfuge, "Eddy has assisted the tobacco companies by providing them with copies of letters questioning McGraw's authority to file the lawsuit."[53]

Eddy responded, "The letters are public documents, available to anyone who requests them."

Fran quipped, "Exactly who side were they on—big tobacco?"[54]

The Governor's resistance impacted the lawsuit that was pending before Judge Irene Berger in Kanawha County Circuit Court. The disappointment around the AG conference table was palatable when Judge Burger, appointed by Governor Caperton, ruled against the tobacco litigation and refused to allow the Attorney General to add the state Division of Health and Human Resources and Public Employees Insurance Agency to the lawsuit. Berger citing that Governor Caperton objected to the agencies joining the suit said, "McGraw, as attorney general, lacks the authority to try to recover millions of dollars the state has spent treating illnesses of its citizens allegedly related to tobacco use."[55] Judge Berger held the Attorney General's authority was limited to pursuing only the consumer protection and antitrust elements of the case. Judge Berger's ruling meant that without Health and Human Resources and Public Employees Insurance agencies as plaintiffs, the Attorney General would be unable to recover money for the state's tobacco related health costs if the litigation were successful. It also meant WV lost its priority status as an initial litigant.[56] Caperton's objection and Berger's decision negatively impacted the amount of money West Virginia eventually recovered.

In a statement viewed by some as unusual, Judge Berger admonished Darrell's contention that the suit was potentially a billion dollar boon to the state: "I think the public was misled into thinking there could be some sort of huge recovery from this lawsuit. I don't think that's fair to the public, and I don't think that it adds any credibility to the legal profession or the judiciary when it happens."[57]—*Judge Irene Berger*

Legal experts from across the country questioned Caperton's resistance to state agency participation, and Judge Berger's decision. The national law firm of Ness-Motley filed similar suits in other states without the resistance that was taking place in West Virginia.
Darrell, appalled at Berger's ruling, was certainly not ready to quit:

"We're thinking our way through this. Good lawyers are at work, and we do believe we can salvage this lawsuit for the benefit of the state and taxpayers over the long haul."[58]

The tobacco case was all consuming, disrupting the private lives of all those involved in the litigation. Every setback was taken seriously and

311

entailed endless evenings of strategizing and regrouping to determine the appropriate reaction, but they remained determined.

The Governor's refusal to allow the agencies to participate in the litigation was most problematic:

Governor Caperton refused to let his state health officials participate. Oddly, the governor acted as if West Virginia doesn't want any compensation from the tobacco industry...The attorney general repeatedly has clashed with the governor's department heads, especially Environmental Protection Director Dave Callaghan. Was that Caperton's reason for refusing to join the cigarette suit—personal animosity to McGraw?"...Another complicating factor is that the Charleston law firm which handles Caperton's personal affairs also lobbies for R.J. Reynolds Tobacco Company. Surely he wouldn't be influenced by such connections? Whatever the reason, we wish the governor hadn't sabotaged the suit that might have brought millions to West Virginia."[59]—Charleston Gazette

AG team appealed Berger's decision; determined to continue prosecution of the anti-trust and consumer protection elements and resolved to find a way to secure state agencies participation. It was an arduous road. Donovan McClure, of the Kamber Communication said, "Berger's ruling has been getting national attention from various newspapers and reporters outside of West Virginia are asking why Gov. Gaston Caperton wouldn't participate in McGraw's suit, and are astounded why the Judge made such a strong personal attack against the Attorney General when he appeared to be the only one doing his job."[60]

The AG team knew the Governor's refusal to allow agencies to participate damaged the ultimate success of the lawsuit. Privately the legal staff questioned whether the Governor's previous ownership of a major insurance company; his legal counsel, Dana Eddy's association with Jackson and Kelly, a law firm representing the tobacco companies, and his own personal ties to other law firms engaged on the side of "big tobacco" contributed to his resistance. It was reported that lawyers from eight law firms representing tobacco companies were heavy contributors to Caperton's 1992 election.[61]

Dana Eddy responded to any assertion of a conflict of interest by saying, "the campaign contributions and his former employment at

Jackson and Kelly have absolutely no bearing on the legal advice he will give Caperton on whether state agencies should join the lawsuit."[62]

Darrell believed that Berger's decision was perhaps attributable to Caperton's strong personal resistance to the litigation. Cognizant of the negative impact of Berger's decision on ultimate recovery of health care costs, Darrell did not refrain from articulating his observations: "You have a newly appointed judge hearing a case involving the person who appointed her. As she sits there, she looks out over a courtroom of wall-to-wall lawyers in blue-striped suits and pretty little shoes all paid for by the tobacco companies."[63] With tongue in cheek, McGraw continued, "the lawyers will finance the next judicial election in Kanawha County and you guess what the outcome of that case is likely to be?"[64]

Over a year after the tobacco case was filed, the AG's office, unable to secure agency participation as plaintiffs, sent a letter to the state's Medicaid Panel. The letter requested the Panel recommend joining the law suit to the Governor in order to secure reimbursement for state-paid tobacco health care costs. The Medicaid Panel was chaired by Tom Heywood, a future managing partner of Bowles, Rice, McDavid, Graff and Love a law firm that represented R.J. Reynolds in the tobacco litigation.[65] Heywood, Caperton confident and political supporter, also served as Caperton's chief of staff from 1989-1993. Under Heywood's leadership the Medicaid panel demurred from taking action: "McGraw's lawsuit lies outside the panel's charge of proposing immediate steps to respond to Medicaid's budget problems." A curious response with tobacco related costs in West Virginia estimated at $500 million annually.[66]

Emily Spieler, an activist and law professor at West Virginia University, was determined to secure the Public Employees Insurance Agency Board participation in the tobacco litigation. With Spieler leadership the PEIA Board voted in December 1995 to become a plaintiff: "Emily Spieler, a West Virginia University law professor who had served on the board since 1989, pushed for the vote to force Gov. Gaston Caperton to explain his reluctance to let PEIA and the Department of Health and Human Resources join the suit."[67] The PEIA action was important because it showed understanding and support for the litigation from a Board statutorily charged with establishing a plan to discourage tobacco, alcohol and chemical use. In a letter to the Governor, Spieler argued: "Tobacco related illness increase the cost of the PEIA program; tobacco addiction prevents PEIA beneficiaries from quitting the use of cigarettes and snuff; and the tobacco industry directly encourages the behaviors which lead to addition. In essence, the finance board is being forced to decrease benefits or shift costs to employees as a result of the continuing practices of the tobacco industry."[68]

Even with Spieler's request and PEIA's endorsement, Caperton refused to allow PEIA participation in the tobacco litigation. Eddy justified the Governor's continued refusal by saying: "He needs to be convinced that the agencies have at least some chance of winning the case before he would recommend that they become plaintiffs. I can't advise the governor and his agencies to get involved in a lawsuit unless they have a reasonable probability of success."[69] Why was the Governor resisting? States across the nation were now ahead of WV.

Almost two years after the tobacco litigation was filed, Governor Caperton agreed to authorize agencies to participate in the tobacco litigation. The Governor was in a bind. With the notice that WV was set to receive a settlement check from the Liggett tobacco group, the Governor had little choice but to agree to allow the two agencies to become plaintiffs: "[Caperton] became persuaded to allow agencies to join the litigation" when West Virginia received the first $200,000 settlement check. [70] Caperton's agreement came with no public acknowledgement of the importance of the landmark tobacco case.

$200,000 check from Liggett.

The Liggett Group settlement was a turning point in the litigation because it broke the resistance from other large tobacco companies. The settlement established a needed precedent. With the Liggett settlement in hand and PEIA as a plaintiff, the AG returned to Berger's courtroom seeking approval to go forward with the suit. Tobacco lawyers objected to the petition, but Deputy Managing Attorney General Deborah McHenry told Judge Berger: "It is clear in the petition that McGraw's office is pursing the suit on behalf of the insurance agency, referred to as 'the state.' We're simply at a loss here. What more could possibly be required?" This time Judge Berger decided "to allow the state Public Employee Insurance Agency to become the main plaintiff in a lawsuit against the tobacco industry."[71]

Mississippi was the first state to achieve success in the tobacco litigation. In July, 1997, Mississippi settled with the nation's four largest tobacco companies, Phillip Morris, RJ Reynolds, Brown and Williamson and Lorillard. The tobacco companies agreed to pay Mississippi $3.4 billion over the next 25 years. [72] Florida, Texas and Minnesota also settled their cases against the tobacco companies. Florida settled the tobacco litigation for an estimated $11.3-$13 Billion based on their overall domestic tobacco sales.[73] Texas settled their tobacco litigation for 14 billion dollars.[74] Minnesota settled for 6.5 billion over twenty five years.[75]

The administration's resistance to the tobacco litigation cost the state. Governor Caperton's refusal to participate and Judge Berger's negative ruling kept West Virginia from maintaining it priority status in the tobacco litigation. West Virginia lost its status to negotiate a separate settlement like Mississippi, Minnesota, Florida and Texas. Losing its priority status cost the state hundreds of millions. Mississippi, a comparative state in filing status, size and health cost, received $3.4 billion in the settlement as compared to West Virginia's $1.9 billion.[76]

Losing its priority status, West Virginia was limited to participation in the *Master Settlement* that was negotiated by 46 attorneys general with the four largest tobacco companies. In the 1998 *Master Settlement Agreement*, West Virginia did receive a 'strategic status' which provided additional funding for its early, substantive work, but not the amount if WV had retained its priority status. The strategic status

315

allowed WV to receive an additional $196 million for the state's strategic contribution to the overall litigation. This strategic status acknowledged the work of Fran Hughes and Tom Rodd in drafting the original counts against the tobacco industry. WV's consumer protection and anti-trust counts were used as a template/model for other states in their litigation against the tobacco industry.[77]

The *Master Settlement* provided an initial allocation to West Virginia of $1,736,741,427 billion for distribution over the 25 years.[78] The *Agreement* positively impacted the nation's children and adults through the requirements that :

- *Tobacco companies agreed to refrain from engaging in certain advertising practices, particularly ad campaigns that marketed cigarettes towards kids.*
- *Tobacco companies agreed to pay annual sums of money to the states to compensate them for health-care costs related to smoking (a minimum of $206 billion over the first twenty-five years).[79]*

West Virginia tobacco settlement dollars provided funds to state agencies and programs including: Public Employees Agency-$10 million; Workers Compensation Fund-$30 million; Physician Mutual Insurance-$24 million; the first appropriation to the Rainy Day Fund-$234 million; Health and Human Services-$223 million and Teachers Retirement System-$807 million. These were the largest allocations from the tobacco settlement dollars but there were a multitude of other programs and services that benefited from the settlement including senior citizens, mental health, community colleges, colleges, universities, and drug prevention and treatment programs.[80]

The tobacco settlement provided West Virginia with funds based on a 25 year schedule of distributions: 1998-99 - $21,275 Million; 2000-$56,837 Million; 2001-$61,375 Million; 2002-$73,694 Million; 2003-$74,391 Million; 2004-2007-$62,087 Million; 2008-2017 $63,319,864 Million and 2018-2025- $70,952 Million. The settlement terms were formulated to continue in perpetuity based upon the future of tobacco sales.[81]

316

Settlement Fund Initiative to Reduce Tobacco use

Selling Out the Tobacco Settlement

A few years after the tobacco settlement was finalized, states began discussing the possibility of selling bonds against the tobacco settlement in order to secure a large immediate influx of revenue. WV political leaders were also interested in securitizing bonds against the tobacco settlement. Darrell objected to a 40 year bond indebtedness to achieve a onetime pay-out. Darrell referred to it in meetings with two different Governors as nothing more than a "pay-day" lending scheme.[82]

In 2004 Governor Bob Wise proposed the sale of $630 million dollars of revenue bonds in exchange for the tobacco settlement. He was unsuccessful in receiving Legislative approval. Governor Wise wanted to use the money to take care of coal companies' unpaid liability to the state's worker's compensation fund. Darrell was certainly against that one.[83]

In 2007 the sale of the tobacco revenue to the state was again on the table. This time Governor Joe Manchin sponsored legislation to relinquish the $1.4 billion in tobacco settlement money over the next two decades for what was estimated to be $800 million.[84] Darrell opposed the action but knew he was fighting an uphill battle with the Governor and Legislature.

Darrell, Fran and Deputy AG Barbara Allen met with Governor Manchin and his staff to discuss the Governor's desire to take the "money and run":

Manchin started laying out his rationale for taking the tobacco money now. With each point Manchin offered, the "judge" would say "bullshit." The "judge" didn't elaborate. He knew there was no need. One of Manchin's suggestions was to use the tobacco money to forgive the coal companies' indebtedness to the state for the unpaid worker's compensation taxes which they had evaded. The "judge" added "real bullshit" to that one. They were going to do it no matter what the "judge" thought or said. And they did."[85]*—Frances Hughes, Chief Deputy Attorney General*

Darrell wanted the money earned from the tobacco litigation to continue in perpetuity. He believed the tobacco money payments should be applied to the pension systems on an annual basis. He knew a large sell-out simply enriched the bond lawyers and sellers and lacked considered forethought. Not one to easily give up, Darrell sent a letter to the Senate President and Speaker of the House:

By securitizing the $1.4 billion still remaining in the 25-year funding stream—i.e., selling $1.4 billion in future payments for a lump sum of 50 cents on the dollar—we are engaging in a quick fix of today's problems while jeopardizing our ability to deal with what comes up tomorrow.

We are enriching a small group of bond lawyers and Wall Street insiders who don't know and don't care about our ability in upcoming years to facilitate economic development and jobs, build better schools and attract top-quality teachers, and assist our aging and ailing population.

Every lawyer in West Virginia can tell you a cautionary tale about a client who sold his or her structured settlement in order to pay off credit card debt and buy a vehicle. Within a year, the card debt is creeping up again and the vehicle is wrecked—and there's no money coming in. This is securitization, albeit on a smaller scale.[86]

Darrell's longtime friend Michael Moore, the AG from Mississippi who filed the initial tobacco lawsuit, expressed why the securitization of tobacco settlement dollars was inappropriate: "the states that securitized made a "sucker bet" that diverted the winnings of the fight away from their intended purpose. The people making the decisions think that this money fell out of heaven. No. This money was related to a public health battle, probably the biggest public health battle in our

nation's history, trying to combat the No. 1 cause of death and disease."[87]—
Michael Moore

The *Gazette* cautioned against the Manchin's sponsored bill: "A gigantic bond plan seems headed for approval without much discussion, without public debate over whether it's better to grab half the money now or take it all slowly…it seems odd to pass such a big-money plan in the final days of the legislative rush, without really studying it."

Governor Manchin, along with Tom Heywood, Caperton's former chief of staff and partner with Bowles, Rice law firm that represented R.J. Reynolds in the tobacco litigation and a frequent bond counsel for the state, secured passage of the legislation authorizing the sale of tobacco bonds. The sale of tobacco bonds ended up at $911million and was to be repaid with the annual tobacco settlement payments.

The bond funds were used to decrease the unfunded liability in the teachers' retirement pension system which was certainly a worthy cause.[88] In the policy discussions related to the bond sale legislation, it was represented that the infusion of tobacco settlement dollars into the teachers retirement account would inure to the benefit of all systems under the Consolidated Public Retirement Board.

In 2012 articles appeared questioning the action of states that sold the tobacco settlement to bond investors. A *New York Times* report suggested that state governments could default on their bond payments as early as 2024. Ross Taylor, acting secretary of WV Department of Administration said, "Unless there's a dramatic drop, I honestly think we we'll be fine…That's just my personal gut feeling."[89] A most disturbing report in *ProPublica* in 2014 illustrated how unsophisticated or at least non-visionary politicians in leadership positions were in selling out a solid perpetual source of revenue from the tobacco settlement for a huge indebtedness:

*Going forward, nearly every cigarette sold would provide money to states…more than $200 billion in just the first 25 years of a legal settlement that **required payments to be made in perpetuity.** Then Wall Street came knocking with an offer many state and local politicians found irresistible: Cash upfront from those governments willing to trade investors the right to some or all of their tobacco payments.*

State after state struck deals that critics derides as 'payday loans' but proponents deemed only prudent. As designed, private investors—not the taxpayers—would take the hit if people smoked less and the tobacco money fell short. Things haven't exactly worked out as planned.

A ProPublica analysis of more than 100 tobacco deals since the settlement found they are creating new fiscal headaches for states, driving some into bailouts or threatening to increase the cost of borrowing in the future.[90]

The outlook for the state's continued ability to make annual payments to bondholders remains questionable. IHS Global Insight, an economic analysis firm, projects declines in cigarette consumption: "Since 1999, it's not a straight line but cigarettes have declined on average by 3 percent a year."[91] This decline in cigarette sales will eventually impact the state's ability to make its annual payment of $61 million to bondholders. "We would expect that, if the trend continues...there could be missed payments in the future, although I don't think there are any imminent."[92]—*Paul Creedon, Citigroup financial adviser*

More Legal Actions

For the twenty years Darrell was AG the office prosecuted hundreds of legal actions against those who violated the law. The following are examples of the diversity of actions taken by the AG office with the action against pharmaceutical companies presented in more detail.

Housing Market's Equivalent of Junk Bonds
To whose benefit is it to offer mortgages to underqualified borrowers?

In 2008 the unscrupulous practices of financial lending corporations "came home to roost" for many homebuyers. Impacted homebuyers were calling the AG office with anguished accounts of inability to meet their mortgage obligations. Facing foreclosure the homeowners were desperate for a way to salvage their investments.

This is what happened. Homeowners, encouraged by financial institutions, entered into unconventional mortgages. These mortgages provided loans for "high dollar" homes that the borrower's current income did not warrant. The mortgages institutions intentionally encouraged home buyers to move away from the traditional 30-year rate mortgages and to sign up for what is called an Adjustable Rate Mortgages (ARM). ARM's are mortgages with lower initial interest rate but with balloon payments refinanced at higher rates. Encouraged by lending institutions and attracted by the initial lower interest rates, borrowers took the risk of assuming loans that were not warranted based on their current income level. In order to meet the financial obligations of the eventual balloon payments the borrower assumed, and the lending institution reinforced those assumptions, that: 1.) their income would probably continue to grow; 2.) their new house would increase in value, and 3,) the Federal Reserve would keep short term loan rates low indefinitely. For many borrowers it was a catastrophe waiting to happen.[93] Darrell described these mortgages with high default risks as the "housing market's equivalent of junk bonds."

The housing market crashed in 2008 and the ensuing financial crises, viewed by many as the worst since the 1930's Great Depression, negated all of the borrowers' assumptions. Many borrowers lost their jobs or saw reductions in income; the values of their homes plummeted and their Adjustable Rate Mortgages escalated. Many borrowers faced foreclosure on their homes. [94]

After the AG staff researched the intricacies of how these unconventional mortgages were granted, West Virginia became the fifth state to sue Countrywide Financial Corporation. The lawsuit alleged the company repeatedly issued loans to borrowers who simply were not able to afford the mortgage payments. Countrywide Financial settled with West Virginia and agreed to a loan modification program that saved state consumers approximately $8.9 million. The program allowed many West Virginia consumers with Countrywide loans to remain in their homes and assisted in securing home loan interest rates reduced to as low as 2.5 percent for five years.[95]

In a joint state-federal foreclosure settlement against Bank America, JP Morgan, Chase, Wells Fargo, Citi and Ally, West Virginia benefited from \$33.5 million in relief for its homeowners. The settlement money allowed many homeowners to avoid foreclosure.[96]

Microsoft Antitrust Litigation
To whose benefit is it to create a monopoly in a market that results in overcharging the consumer?

In 2001, the AG filed a suit against Microsoft alleging the company's practices violated state anti-trust and consumer protection laws. West Virginia became one of nine states that refused to join the Justice Department in settling a federal case against Microsoft.[97] In a separate litigation, West Virginia alleged that Microsoft unlawfully used anti-competitive means to maintain a monopoly in the market for certain products. Microsoft actions resulted in increased cost to the consumer. West Virginia's case was settled for \$21 million. A major part of the settlement was used to provide vouchers for computers and software in schools with a high percentage of low income students.[98]

Payday Lenders—Treacherous Traps
To whose benefit is it to offer short term loans at exorbitant rates that often place the consumer in unrecoverable debt?

Payday lenders provide short term loans at high interest rates. These short term loans may have interest rates that exceeded 300%. Pay day loans generally stipulate the employee pays back the loan from his next pay check. However if the employee is unable to make the payment by the next paycheck the interest rate increases. The Office of Fair Trade has reported that payday lenders' irresponsible lending often breaches the law.[99]

The unscrupulous tactics of payday lenders, who took advantage of the most vulnerable employees needing cash to make it to the next pay day, were frequently reported to the AG office. The AG team brought action against a multitude of payday companies.

From 2006 to 2010 the Attorney General's Consumer Protection Division reached settlement agreements with 109 Internet payday lenders and their collection agencies. The settlements resulted in nearly \$2.5

million in cash refunds and cancelled debts for 8,044 West Virginia consumers.[100]

In 2012 the AG office won a major litigation against Cash Call, an Internet payday lender. Circuit Judge Louis Bloom found in "favor of the state…and ordered Cash Call to pay $15 million in civil penalties, refunds and canceled debts for the 292 WV consumers who obtained loans and to the state."[101] Darrell reminded consumers that "payday loans are not solutions but treacherous traps that can lead to financial ruin for many West Virginians facing difficult financial circumstances."[102]

Payday loans are now illegal in West Virginia. However, the cyber reach of unscrupulous payday lenders who seek to take advantage remains. These lenders may not operate within the state but in one year there were 333,000 hits on the Internet by West Virginians seeking information on these high interest loans. [103]

Visa and MasterCard
To whose benefit is it to charge excessive debit or credit card fees?

The AG office filed antitrust and consumer protection actions against Visa, Inc. and MasterCard Worldwide alleging the companies forced retailers to accept excessive debit and credit card fees. Visa and MasterCard charged retailers the same fee for debit cards as they did for the more costly credit card transactions. The suit contended the excessive fee charge resulted in higher prices for consumers.

After five years in litigation, the AG office reached a settlement agreement with Visa and MasterCard for $16.2 million dollars. West Virginia was the first state to reach a positive settlement with Visa and Master Card that recovered funds for the consumer rather than the retailer. Settlement funds were placed into a trust account to provide tax relief for West Virginians. "…A settlement with VISA, USA Inc. and Master Card International, Inc. apparently will create three sales tax holidays on appliances that carry the 'Energy Star' label and cost $2,500 or less…"[104]

The Governor's office and the Legislature determined to use the settlement funds to establish "Energy Star" tax free holidays for three years. During this time period consumers purchasing Energy Star

323

appliances were exempt from paying the 6 percent tax on the appliance. This tax avoidance on $2,000 worth of Energy Star appliances meant a savings of $120 dollars for the consumer. The successful settlement provided the opportunity to caution others about violating West Virginia's anti-trust and consumer protection laws: "This has been a long time coming and involved the devotion of a lot of time and resources...I hope that the settlement clips the wings of anyone embarking on a course of illegal conduct in West Virginia."[105]

Big Coal—$56 Million Recovered
To whose benefit is it for coal companies to avoid workers' compensation payments?

It took years but the state finally prevailed in the recovering of "$56 million from 15 coal companies that used independent contractors to duck state worker compensation obligations."[106] These independent contractors routinely went bankrupt and did not pay workers' compensation premiums and numerous other state taxes. The large coal companies who engaged these independent contractors refused any responsibility for payment of taxes. In the 1999 the Affiliated Construction Trades brought suit against Commissioner Vieweg who dismissed more than $200 million in lawsuits against 18 large coal companies. *Affiliated Construction v Vieweg* case was heard by the WV Supreme Court with the majority upholding Vieweg's actions.[107] Justices Starcher and Warren McGraw, in their dissent, described the majority opinion as "Wrong, Wrong, Wrong!"[108]

The state Supreme Court's decision was a major setback in achieving full recovery of debts owed by the coal companies which by 2001 reached $406 million.[109] The large coal companies resisted the notion of any liability but the state's people lawyers persevered and ultimately recovered $56 million. [110]

Wampler Industries
To whose benefit is it for companies to take advantage of farmers?

Hardy County, West Virginia is a place where the South Branch of the Potomac River flows through creating a magnificent valley. A valley with lands so fertile that since the 1730's generation after generation of farmers engaged in stock raising and agricultural farming including apple and peach orchards as well as wheat, corn and much more. The farmers also raised chickens. By the mid-twentieth century poultry farming was transformed to an integrated farm operation that specialized in the production of broilers under contracts to major meat processors. By the last decade of the 20th century the poultry industry in Hardy County and the eastern panhandle was evolving into an industry where 25,000 broilers, no longer housed in tar paper sheds, were raised in six weeks in 40 by 500 foot temperate controlled houses. The appearance of mega poultry processors increased. Perdue Industries acquired Wampler processing operation where 325,000 broilers were processed each day in the Moorefield plant.[111] In this transition to a mega chicken processing area, there was much profit to be made.

Many of the farmers living on these bucolic farms found themselves under pressure from Wampler to produce more chickens. Wampler wanted them to build more chicken houses and promised the farmers greater profits. Many farmers were induced to mortgage their land, land that had been in their family for generations, in order to finance more chicken houses. Wampler provided feed, antibiotics and the baby chickens. Wampler started to cut corners in the quality of baby chickens and the feed and then cut their prices to the farmers. The farmers were facing financial ruination.

The chicken processing business brought currency into local community, and business and community leaders supported Wampler. The farmers, left with little support from local leaders, organized a group to resist Wampler and reached out to the AG for help. The AG office filed legal action against Wampler alleging the chicken processors engaged in unfair and deceptive business practices. The legal action came after attempts by AG office to resolve contractual concerns through meetings with Wampler and a delegation representing the 160 poultry farmers at risk of losing their farms. Wampler refused to negotiate. The AG filed a legal action in Hardy County claiming Wampler violated the state's Consumer Credit and Protection Act. Darrell described the farmers' predicament: "In a time of prosperity for the poultry industry, with low feed prices and high chicken prices, the growers are being squeezed into bankruptcy. These guys are trapped. All these guys built these chicken houses and borrowed money with the idea they were going to make $20,000 to $40,000 per year, per house."[112]

The *Baltimore Sun* commented on the AG's office engagement to assist the farmers: "The complaints of chicken grower Jerry Hahn are nothing particularly new. They're heard these days in more than a dozen states across America's poultry belt from Texas to the Delmarva Peninsula. Expenses are rising, income is hurting and a big impersonal company has a tight grip on his life and his farm…What sets Hahn's grievances apart is that his state has taken up his cause, at a time when government officials elsewhere rarely, if ever, challenge the poultry industry on behalf of farmers."[113]

The litigation sought to have Wampler change its business practices; pay restitution to farmers hurt by the unfair contracts, and pay civil penalties. Hardy County Judge Cookman dismissed the AG's unfair business action lawsuit against Wampler. The AG then appealed to the state Supreme Court in June of 2000.[114] The Court held the state consumer protection laws did not apply to agricultural contracts. [115] There was no remedy provided to the chicken farmers in the eastern panhandle even though the state's Credit and Consumer Protection Act included the protection for agricultural issues: "Agricultural purpose" means a purpose related to the production, harvest, exhibition, marketing, transportation, processing or manufacture of agricultural products by a natural person who cultivates, plants, propagates or nurtures the agricultural products. Agricultural products include agricultural, horticultural, viticultural and dairy products, livestock, wildlife, poultry, bees, forest products, fish and shellfish, and any products thereof, including processed and manufactured products, and any and all products raised or produced on farms and any processed or manufactured products thereof."[116]

The chicken farmers in the eastern panhandle remain subject to the often unfair profit driven policies of the large chicken processors. One Pendleton County farmer, who closed his two caving poultry houses in 2019, said Pilgrim Pride paid him 21 cents a chicken for 15 years without getting a raise. Describing the companies as greedy bastards, the former chicken farmer whose largest profit was $7,000 after paying debts for his chicken houses, said, "They control everything you do without taking responsibility. From the science of LED lighting to the regularity of water droplets, everything is designed to produce the poorest chickens in the shortest amount of time."[117] Many of the 97% of U.S. chicken farmers, under contract with big producers, claim they are being treated unfairly and rules to protect them remain in limbo.[118]

Big Drug Companies
To whose benefit is it for Big Drug Companies to fraudulently market and distribute drugs that hurt people?

March 26, 2001—They were slick; suits expensive and black alligator shoes appropriately shined. Michael Friedman, Chief Operating Officer and three other senior executives of Purdue Pharma had come to Charleston to meet with the Attorney General. Our questions regarding marketing of OxyContin in West Virginia had received no response. Friedman requested the meeting to provide us with answers to our questions. An hour in; not a single question answered and a most professional power point presentation on the company's virtues was completed. The Judge, well versed in diversion tactics used by "wrongdoers," stood and thanked the "suits" for their time. I knew what was going to happen after these guys picked up their brief cases and departed the Capitol. And it did. –Frances Hughes, Chief Deputy Attorney General

Research validates the strong association of "poverty, social exclusion with problematic drug use."[119] In WV where poverty, long term unemployment and a high rate of school dropouts has historically existed, there is a substantial problem with drug abuse.

Substance abuse was not a new problem when Darrell became AG, but it was increasing. The problems surrounding the escalation of drug use were heard at our dinner table. As Kanawha County Superintendent I was most familiar and alarmed at the number of school age children who were born to drug addicted mothers. Teachers, counselors and staff throughout the system were dealing with the problems associated with these children who suffered from neonatal abstinence syndrome (NAS); i.e. health, behavior, emotional and academic maladies. NAS constitutes the array of conditions present when a newborn baby withdraws from drugs (most often opioids) exposed to in the womb. This exposure and withdrawal from drugs results in an array of serious health issues at birth. However, the NAS children often continue to experience long term health problems from hearing and vision to behavior and academic. New specialized school programs and personnel were needed for these in vitro victims of mothers who use drugs. Darrell was inundated nightly with stories of this new kind of epidemic teachers were facing— children with NAS and their often unstable home conditions.

Darrell shared my concerns with his management team. The AG staff began a concentrated effort to learn more and do more about the escalating drug problems including research, data analysis and participation in drug task forces.

In 1996 Purdue Pharmaceutical's marketing of OxyContin set off a wave of drug usage.[120] Purdue Pharmaceutical aggressively promoted OxyContin as a treatment for persons with 'non-malignant' diseases such as arthritis or chronic back pain. Sales of OxyContin grew from $48 million in 1996 to almost $1.1 billion in 2000."[121]

Purdue Pharma marketed OxyContin as a drug that relieved pain for twice as long as other brands. Purdue claimed OxyContin worked for 12 hours. The marketing strategy worked and OxyContin became the bestselling painkiller, with Purdue reaping $31 billion in revenue.[122]

However Purdue's claims for twelve-hour relief weren't correct. Investigative report by the Los Angeles Times, clinical trials, doctor and patient complaints all noted OxyContin weaned off hours early. The company stood by their 12-hour claim of relief to protect their market dominance and hundreds of dollar price per bottle. The 12-hour duration gave Purdue's OxyContin the market advantage over less expensive pain killers. When OxyContin's effectiveness wanes the result can be withdrawal, craving and the need to take another pill. OxyContin, a cousin of heroin, became one of the most abused drugs in U.S. history.[123]

Theodore J. Cicero, researcher on how opioids affect the brain noted, "OxyContin taken at 12-hour intervals could be the perfect recipe for addiction. Patients in whom the drug doesn't last 12 hours can suffer both a return of their underlying pain and the beginning stages of acute withdrawal. That becomes a very powerful motivator for people to take more drugs."[124]

Perdue Pharma wasn't about to admit OxyContin didn't last 12 hours. Perdue Pharma's solution was to develop a campaign in which their representatives recommended to doctors to increase the strength of the dose rather than the frequency. Their training materials told sales representatives to remind doctors there was not a limit on the "amount of OxyContin a patient can be prescribed."[125] "A West Virginia supervisor told one of his highest performing sales reps in a 1999 letter that she could 'blow the lid off' her sales and earn a trip to Hawaii if she persuaded more doctors to write larger doses."[126]

One of the unsung heroes in the fight against opioid use is Dr. William Harris. One day in 2001 Dr. Harris, a tall and imposing family physician in Charleston, picked up the phone and called his patient and friend's work—the office of Attorney General. Dr. Harris, a man known for his lack of tolerance for any form of intimidation was outraged when a Perdue Pharm representative came to his office waiving around a law suit from California where a doctor was sued for not prescribing adequate pain pills for a patient. The representative told Dr. Harris that could happen to him too. Dr. Harris did not take lightly a sales representative telling him how to practice medicine. He was livid.

There is no question that Dr. Harris's phone call led us to look at Purdue Pharma's marketing practices. What we found was most disconcerting. Purdue offered free trips for doctors to seminars in luxury resorts where they touted OxyContin as a safe drug for treating minor pain. We found evidence that Purdue provided seed monies to set up pain clinics. Their representatives intimidated pharmacists claiming they could get in trouble if they didn't fill prescriptions even if they thought someone was an abuser. And the duration of OxyContin's effectiveness was much less than their claim of 12 hours. Patients and family members called and told us their heart-wrenching stories of addiction from the drug. Our investigators interviewed patients, family members, physicians and pharmacists and found the 12 hour claim wasn't true, and Perdue Pharma knew it.

We determined there was a case against Purdue Pharma. But taking on a major pharmaceutical company was akin to taking on Big tobacco—it was fraught with the likelihood of failure and retribution. We didn't fail, but Big drug would retaliate against the Judge."—Frances Hughes, Chief Deputy Attorney General

In June, 2001 West Virginia became the first state to initiate an action against Purdue Pharma alleging Purdue engaged in "coercive and deceptive" marketing of OxyContin. Purdue's sales in West Virginia alone had surpassed $1 billion while the state was left with the cost of treating people addicted due to the misuse of the drug.

Without a doubt patients were seeking relief from their pain. The relief from
OxyContin didn't last as long as the manufacturer claimed. OxyContin was a highly addictive substance. The patients were suffering.

From the time we filed the case, Purdue's legal team made attempt after attempt to get the suit dismissed or moved from state to federal court where the company had succeeded in getting other cases tossed out.

In October, 2004 we were back in Judge Booker T. Stephens' court in McDowell County. Stephens, the first African American elected circuit judge in WV and the son of a coal miner, is a no nonsense judge who to date had rejected Purdue's claims for dismissal. But Purdue was there with their final shot—a request for summary judgement. Purdue brought in a nationally known big gun, Eric Holder, Jr, who was the first African American deputy attorney general, and now in private practice. Holder, who later became Obama's attorney general, argued that 'West Virginia prosecutors didn't have sufficient evidence to warrant a trial.' We had plenty of evidence. Holder and Purdue didn't like the evidence, and they were worried we would prevail.

Thankfully, Judge Stephens didn't buy Holder's argument. In early November, Judge Stephens denied Purdue' request for summary judgement and held there was enough evidence that a jury could find Purdue made deceptive claims, including how long OxyContin lasted.

It was a major victory for us. However we knew that proving damages was one of the major problems with the case. On the other hand Purdue knew a trial meant we would lay out the sealed evidence for

public consumption including class action attorneys, government
investigators, doctors and journalists. The Friday before the trial was to
begin, Purdue offered to settle for $2 million. We rejected the offer.

    On Monday morning the court room was filled with 'suits,'
including Eric Holder. The selection of jury members was to start the
next day. Judge Stephens leaned on us to reach a settlement. We went
into the Judge Stephens' chambers to negotiate. Holder led for Perdue
and offered $10 million but insisted the money must be used for only
three things: Law enforcement, treatment and education. Judge
Stephens accepted the terms of the settlement through his imposed court
order. The $10 million was used in accordance with the settlement
agreement for day reporting centers, law enforcement programs and the
funding of a new pharm program at the University of Charleston. The
Governor and members of the Legislature objected to how the settlement
funds were used, but it was all defined within the Court order.—Frances
Hughes, Chief Deputy Attorney General

    Fran's description of the settlement aligned with others: "The
morning the case was to go to trial, in November 2004, Holder helped
negotiate a settlement. Working in the judge's chambers in West
Virginia, he put together an agreement under which the firm would have
to pay $10 million over four years into drug abuse and education
programs in West Virginia and Purdue Pharma would *not* have to admit
any wrongdoing!"[127]

    Others were watching what was happening in West Virginia's
Purdue Pharm action. Under the leadership of U.S. Attorney John
Brownlee, 600 subpoenas for Purdue's manufacturing, marketing and
distribution records were issued. West Virginia's action was used as a
template for the federal criminal proceeding against Perdue Pharma on
behalf of the entire country. Dr. William Harris provided testimony in
the federal case regarding OxyContin's impact in his community.[128] The
government's investigation revealed that between 1996-2001 oxycodone
related deaths increased fivefold while OxyContin prescriptions increased
twenty fold in the nation.[129] As the result of the investigation, Purdue
was charged with misbranding of a drug with intent to defraud and
mislead by claiming that OxyContin was less addictive than other forms
of oxycodone. In 2007 three Purdue Pharma executives pleaded guilty to

federal charges of fraudulent marketing of OxyContin, and Purdue agreed to pay $634 million in fines.[130] One of the executives was Michael Freeman, the 'suit' that sat in Darrell's office in 2001 with his power point presentation designed to convince the AG team that they were the good guys:

"So it appears that West Virginia AG Darrell McGraw knows what a bad guy looks like after all."[131]—*New York Times*

Big Drug's far reaching influential arms almost derailed the government's case against Purdue Pharma. Alberto Gonzales, attorney general under President George Bush, attempted to fire 9 U.S. Attorneys, including US Attorney John Brownlee who was in the final stages of the Purdue Pharma case:

Brownlee testified before the US Senate Judiciary Committee in July 2007 -- after Purdue Pharma and their three CEO's pleaded guilty in Federal Court to falsely marketing OxyContin as less addictive than other painkiller (by their guilty plea to misdemeanor charges, they avoided jail time). In his testimony, Brownlee recounted that Michael Elston, then chief of staff for Deputy Attorney General Paul McNulty, called him on Oct. 24, 2006, the deadline for Purdue Pharma to accept the government's offer or face other charges. Elston told him that Purdue" had complained it needed more time, Brownlee said. "I sensed that he was inquiring almost on their behalf. ... I simply dismissed him," Brownlee said. Elston had called at McNulty's request "to make sure that Brownlee didn't do anything to jump the gun." Brownlee told Elston that he had authority to settle the case and "he needed to back out of the way." Purdue Pharma accepted the plea that evening. A week later, on November 1, Elston sent an e-mail to Kyle Sampson, then Gonzales' chief of staff, listing U.S. attorneys including Brownlee, to be considered for dismissal. None were fired. Brownlee said he doesn't know why he was targeted. 'I certainly had concerns.'[132]

Like Brownlee, Darrell's intervention into the illegal actions of big drug companies did not set well with government officials and many members of the Legislature. Joe Manchin, WV governor 2005-2010, was not pleased with the AG's continued litigations against pharmaceutical companies. Governor Manchin's daughter was an executive with Mylan Pharmaceutical and later became its president. A top assistant to the

Governor told Darrell that Manchin wasn't happy with all this litigation against drug companies. Darrell, often cryptic in reply said, "Is he against the recovered money too? We will tell just tell the courts to send any settlements to Virginia." Darrell was the only one that laughed.[133]

Big Drug lobbyists were talking with members of the Legislature regarding the Purdue Pharma settlement. They wanted revenge against the AG office, and they had a willing participant in a state senator from the Governor's home county:

I was making a budget presentation to the Senate Finance after the Purdue Pharma case settled. I was questioned regarding the use of the settlement dollars. In the room was John Brown, lobbyist for drug companies and conservative legal reform groups who I'm sure had been meeting with committee members. I explained in detail the use of settlement dollars was framed by Perdue Pharm, signed off by all parties including DHHR and ordered by the court. But the lobbyist had done his work as evident when Sen. Roman Prezioso asked about a Medicaid regulation that required the return of settlement dollars to Medicaid. This was not a question that Preziozo would have known to ask without prodding from the drug company representatives. As a former general counsel to a national consulting firm that specialized in Medicaid financing, I was familiar with the regulation pertaining to Medicaid recovery of money. The regulation was meant for when there was an overpayment to the provider or beneficiary. It was never intended for the recovery of dollars brought about through AG litigation efforts against wrong doers.

But drug companies were orchestrating revenge against the Judge. And it worked. I was told that Sen. Prezioso and John Brown contacted the Center for Medicaid and Medicare Services (CMS) to question whether West Virginia owed them money. I found it amazing that this was an attempt to 'stir the pot by those benefiting from the soup!' When we heard about the call the Judge started to sing, 'Just whose side are you on?'—an old Union song from his youth. After a lot of unnecessary pain, WV ended up losing $2.7 of the $10 million settlement because of the intervention of the state senator and others. It was outrageous.—Frances Hughes, Chief Deputy Attorney General

The state senator's call, along with those from members of the Chamber of Commerce, led the Center for Medicaid and Medicare Services (CMS) to take action. CMS took legal steps to secure not just some but the majority of the settlement dollars. The Appeals Board viewed CMS request as unreasonable. After years of litigation Medicaid recovered approximately $2.7 million of the $10 million settlement.

The money WV recovered in the Purdue settlement was spent in accordance with court approved requirements including the funding of day report centers. The day report centers resulted in counties recouping millions of dollars that would have been spent on regional jail costs for non-violent drug offenders. "For every dollar spent on day report centers, it generated seven dollars in savings in regional jail costs."[134] To whose benefit was it for a state senator to object to the Purdue Pharma settlement with the CMS office? It was not the people.

West Virginia led the way in filing the first litigation against Purdue Pharma for aggressively marketing OxyContin. Addiction to OxyContin is widespread resulting in more than 1,000 lawsuits filed by state and local governments against Purdue Pharma. In March, 2019 Oklahoma settled with Purdue Pharma for $270 million. Oklahoma's claims against Purdue Pharma mirrored "many of the same claims McGraw made 18 years ago."[135]

Perdue Pharma was only one of many cases the AG office filed against drug companies. In 2000 West Virginia was part of a multi-state case against Mylan Industries for price gouging. Mylan settled the case for $100 million after investigations determined that Mylan raised the price of Clorzepate by more than 2200 percent and Lorazepam by more than 2000 percent, drugs used to treat tension, anxiety and insomnia. [136]

In 2006 West Virginia filed a fraud suit against Eli Lily & Company for its marketing practices involving Zyprexa, a drug for the treatment of schizophrenia and bipolar disorder. The suit alleged that "among other things that Eli Lilly & Co. representatives misled and deceived doctors about the safety of the drug, downplayed the risks and side effects and promoted its use for off-label uses including mood swings and ADHD, thus profiting from the drug's prescription for off-label conditions."[137] Evidence included that Eli Lily marketed Zyprexa for medical conditions other than those approved by government regulators. Evidence also showed that Zyprexa increased the risk of diabetes by 50 percent. Eli Lily settled with West Virginia for $15.8 million.[138]

In December, 2012 the AG office filed a suit in Marshall County Circuit Court against Bristol-Myers Squibb, the maker of Plavix, and the U.S. subsidiaries of France's Sanofi SA, which markets the drug, for falsely pushing the drug to doctors.[139] The suit contended Bristol marketed the higher priced Plavix, 100 times the cost of aspirin, with "no additional benefit to the covered patient/beneficiary when compared to aspirin." [140] The suit claimed the drug company touted Plavix's superiority to aspirin so patients would ask their doctors for prescriptions even when evidence showed that wasn't true and that the company had actually manipulated clinical studies. In 2019 West Virginia settled the suit for $3.2 million.[141]

In 2012 the AG also filed suit against Pfizer Industry, manufacturer of Lipitor for antitrust violations including the submission of false patent information and entering into anticompetitive agreements to restrain trade in the market of Lipitor; i.e. measures that increased their profits and hurt consumers.[142] The case remains in litigation.

By 2012 drug usage was increasing in West Virginia at an even more alarming rate. The AG office began an investigation to uncover the reason for the dramatic increase in drug problems. The management team uncovered that drug companies were sending an unending flow of addictive pain pills to retail pharmacies. In a five year period wholesale drug companies had shipped over 2 million pain pills to West Virginia.[143] This influx of addictive pain pills sent to West Virginia was destroying individuals, families and communities.

Dr. Carl Sullivan, drug addiction director at WVU Medical Center, described the "perfect storm" that gave rise to the OxyContin drug problem in WV: "We had a lot of blue collar workers who were in farming and timbering and coal mining and things that were likely to produce injuries. Opioid abuse was further exacerbated by a declining economy and heavy job loss in the state over the last 20 years. With a population primed by prescriptions from work-related injuries, job loss was the gasoline on the fire."[144]

West Virginia remains one of top states in the ingestion of prescription drugs, and "it leads the country in drug-related overdose deaths."[145] As a Justice on the West Virginia Supreme Court, Darrell authored opinions that held for treatment versus incarceration and agency responsibility for the provision of adequate care in such cases as *E.H. et al v. Khan Martin, Mc., Hodge v. Ginsberg and State Ex. Rel Harris v. Calendine*[146] Darrell exhibited the same diligence in instituting actions against drug companies that were harming West Virginians by their indiscriminate and unmonitored shipping of opioid drugs into the state.

In 2012 the AG office filed actions against 14 prescription drug wholesalers including Amerisource Bergen Drug Corp., one of the largest in the United Sates, Miami-Luken, Keysource Medical, Masters Pharmaceutical and others that distributed 60 million oxycodone pills and 140.6 million hydrocodone pills to West Virginia between 2007 and 2012.[147] Litigation was filed against Cardinal Health, the nation's second-largest drug wholesaler, claiming they fueled the drug problem in West Virginia through excessive prescription opioid shipments with over 241 million pills distributed between 2007 and 2012.[148]

The impact of the AG's legal action against drug companies was described by Rusty Webb, who now represents more than two dozen West Virginia cities and counties in pending mass litigation against drug companies. Webb said, "[McGraw's] 2012 lawsuits against three other drug makers, which settled in 2016, paved the way for the current litigation."[149]

As AG, Darrell held drug companies that injured West Virginians through price gouging, inappropriate or false advertising, marketing and shipping excessive number of painkillers to pill mill pharmacies, accountable for their actions. Big Drug knew the AG team was diligent. It was simply too costly for them to have the current AG remain in office. Big Drug determined to elect one their own—a drug lobbyist as attorney general.

During Darrell's twenty year tenure, the Office of Attorney General's work product yielded more than **$2 Billion Dollars** ($2,000,000,000). The funds supported senior citizen services; infused $802 million in a failing teacher retirement system; established domestic violence shelters, day report centers, drug and tobacco prevention

336

programs; enhanced state police programs; funded $24 million for the start up of the Physicians' Mutual Insurance program, and augmented the state's rainy day fund by $234 million and much more.

As attorney general, the state's chief law enforcement officer, Darrell was always in the arena, never on the sidelines and took to heart the words of Etienne de Grellet:

> *I expect to pass this way but once;*
> *And any good therefore that I can do,*
> *Or any kindness that I can show to any fellow creature,*
> *Let me do it now.*
> *Let me not defer or neglect it.*
> *For I shall not pass this way again.*[150]

Chapter XVIII   Attorney General Elections

Elections are foundational procedures of a democracy. And campaigns for elected offices are all about the processes utilized to inform the voters of a particular candidate's stance as it relates to identified issues. In the twenty years that Darrell served in office, campaigns processes changed a great deal including dramatic increases in campaign expenses/expenditures; higher levels of donor contributions; more wealthy candidates with the capacity and willingness to personally incur campaign costs, and expanded use of the Internet and social media to reach voters.

The advent of the Internet and social media substantially transformed campaign processes. Today campaigns rely on Internet and social media and its combined power to secure voters to their way to thinking and ultimately the "correct" candidate. Facebook and twitter, the modern day replacements for hand to hand grassroots campaigns, allow the candidate to personalize outreach. Many people believe these changes alone highlight a need for campaign and election reform. Changes that require the establishment of regulations on how candidates, parties and political action entities participate in campaign processes particularly as it relates to the spending of money. There is no question the amount of campaign money available determines the level outreach; i.e. television, radio, newspaper, mailers, Internet, and social media distribution that impacts voting outcome and ultimate success in an election.

Always the underfunded candidate, Darrell made it successfully through five elections for attorney general. Changes in campaign processes made elections close but two other contributing factors often made success even more problematic. First, Darrell's enforcement of the law was a factor frequently viewed as thwarting those with malign vested interests within the Democratic Party leadership. These status quo leaders reciprocated by lack of observable support and in many cases open opposition to Darrell's campaign efforts. The second factor was the increasing amount of "dark money" contributed by the expanding number of big businesses and corporations, including drug, tobacco, pay day lenders, banks, insurance, coal, and telemarketers, in retaliation for

Darrell's enforcement of environmental and consumer protection laws. This enforcement of the law often interfered with the entities' power and profit base.

Leadership Resistance

Viewed as progressives the McGraw brothers, the late Congressman and Secretary of State Ken Heckler, along with labor leaders for years led the more liberal element of the Democratic Party in West Virginia.[1] Progressives, true believers in the basic concepts inherent in Roosevelt's New Deal and Kennedy's New Frontier, are advocates for working people rights, quality public education, affordable health care, environmental regulations, social and welfare benefits, diversification of the economy, safe working conditions, corporate responsibility and investment in local community growth.

A progressive leader disapproves of tactics that enhance cultural prejudices including sexism, racism, homophobia and regionalism, but rather believes in a leader's responsibility to educate rather than engage in diversionary allusions. The McGraw brothers, as progressives, supported Obama and the Clintons. They understand the phrase "war on coal" is a political allusion reduced to bumper sticker messaging in order to conjure up prejudice of those who live in the region. The reality is that coal jobs in West Virginia decline for many reasons including mechanization of the coal industry; exhaustion of convenient coal seams; worldwide decline in demand for coal, and the rise in competitive energy sources including natural gas production.

Each election found two prominent establishment leaders in West Virginia's Democratic Party avoiding any endorsement or open support of Darrell. Gaston Caperton, insurance executive and governor from1989 to1997and Joe Manchin, coal company special interest politico and governor from 2005 to 2010 and then U.S. senator from 2010 to present are establishment leaders who opposed Darrell's success.[2] As a Justice on the W.Va. Supreme Court and as the state's Attorney General, Darrell's recognition and then enforcement of the law provided ample reasons to engendered their lack of support and disapproval.

Caperton—The Education Governor

It was reported that Governor Gaston Caperton was attending a concert in Wheeling when he learned that Darrell filed for attorney general and acknowledged the news by hitting the wall with his fist. Former principal owner of the tenth largest privately owned insurance brokerage firm in the nation, Caperton's basic philosophy differed with Darrell's progressive views. As a Supreme Court Justice, Darrell's decisions, based on his duty to review the facts and uphold the law regarding workers compensation and other labor issues, were not viewed by some as pro-business. Caperton was a businessman in the insurance industry—an industry that often has a stake in wrongdoers.

In 1992 Caperton was up for reelection. Charlotte Pritt was the labor supported candidate running against Caperton for the Democratic nomination. Darrell supported Charlotte Pritt along with over 100,000 people who signed a petition encouraging Pritt to run against Gaston Caperton. Even with the notoriety gained when she challenged Caperton's opposition to collective bargaining and his grocery and gasoline tax increases, Pritt lost the Democratic nomination for governor. Darrell won the Democratic primary for attorney general against Ed Rebrook who was an attorney for the Lottery Commission in Governor Caperton's administration. Caperton and Darrell were on the same ticket in the general election, but many believed Caperton preferred the Republican nominee for attorney general.

The state's attorney general is duty bound to enforce the law, including against political indiscretions by government leaders and agencies. During Governor Caperton's second term in office it became necessary for the AG to intervene in response to actions or in contradiction to the desires of the Governor's administration; i.e. the lottery scandal, tobacco litigation, IBM computer contract award, bond letting, garbage, sewage sludge and landfill violations, pension fund investments and outside counsel contracts. Governor Caperton's antagonism and those of his associates within the Democratic and Republican parties increased with each intervention.

Caperton liked being called the "education governor." In anticipation of revenue short fall, Governor Caperton authorized a reduction in state aid to local county boards of education. The shortfall did not occur, and the state ended the year with surplus revenue. Governor Caperton, the "education governor," refused to reinstate the school funds. As Kanawha County Superintendent, I recommended the county board file litigation against Caperton and the state in an effort to restore the county's $1.4 million reduction in state aid. The circuit court ruled in favor of Kanawha County, but the county did not prevail on an appeal to the state Supreme Court. The legal action perhaps challenged the notion of Caperton as the "education governor."[3]

As State Superintendent, I refused to authorize a state-wide expansion of a gaming learning system for schools without a contract that adhered to required state purchasing vetting and bidding processes. The gaming system is a product of *Globaloria*, a company founded by Caperton's then wife, Idit. The cost of state wide implementation of *Globaloria* was estimated at $22 million dollars. Governor Caperton was outraged by my lack of support and expressed his disapproval not only to me but to some state Board members. Even with pressure from aligned state Board members to accommodate Caperton, I did not recommend the state-wide expansion of *Globaloria*,

Manchin—Open for Business Governor

Manchin's philosophical stances on corporate tax breaks, strip mining regulation and environmental deregulation are not aligned with Darrell's legal philosophical views. Manchin's long time connection with the Koch brothers' funded American Legislative Exchange Council, (ALEC) is an example of their philosophical differences. ALEC's membership consists of overwhelmingly regressive Republicans with substantial corporate interests. Participating legislators in ALEC bring the bills of interest home to their membership for executive and legislative consideration and action. Manchin, a "habitué" of ALEC's national meetings, served as its state president and national treasurer. ALEC's website lists U.S. Senator Joe Manchin as an alumnus.[4]

In 1984 Manchin, a Delegate in the West Virginia Legislature, filed for a state Senate seat from the 14th district. Manchin claimed he lived in the district, a qualification of residency required by law. His legal residency within the 14th district was contested, and the state Supreme Court was asked to make a determination of Manchin's eligibility. Darrell, as a Justice, speaking for the Court, wrote that Manchin's business and post office box in the 14th district did not qualify as his residence. The opinion resulted in the removal of Manchin's name from the ballot. Manchin lost the opportunity to run for the state Senate until the next election in 1985.[5]

In 1996 Joe Manchin ran for governor. Manchin's opposition in the Democratic primary was Charlotte Pritt, a progressive supported by labor and the McGraw brothers. Pritt defeated Joe Manchin in the primary election. Charlotte Pritt became the first woman to secure the WV gubernatorial nomination of either of the two major political parties. In the general election Pritt, a coal miner's daughter and a public-school teacher, was supported by labor, Senator John D. Rockefeller, IV and the McGraw brothers. Pritt's opponent in the general election was Cecil Underwood, W.Va. governor from 1957-1961. Manchin, in retaliation for his loss in the primary, founded a group called "Democrats for Underwood." Democratic Governor Caperton refused to campaign for Pritt. Pritt narrowly lost the general election to Underwood. Pritt ran a grassroots campaign but lack of support from regressive members of the Democratic Party resulted in her defeat.[6]

Manchin, a carpet store operator, became rich during the time he served in public office. Manchin's net worth of $7.9 million puts him 21st among U.S. Senators.[7] Some think his wealth resonates from his connections to the coal industry. "Sen. Joe Manchin (D-W.Va.) is more than just a supporter of his state's influential coal producers—he's a full-fledged industry insider."[8] Senator Manchin's 2009 and 2010 financial disclosures revealed he earned over $1.7 million from his family owned "coal brokerage company," Enersystems. In 1998 as president of Enersystems, Manchin advocated for pro-growth opportunities for ecologically damaging mountaintop removal projects stating, "Economic development is what's going to make mountaintop removal palatable."[9] Manchin contended his income from Enersystems did not influence his decisions because he previously placed his holdings in a blind trust. Blind trusts are often a paper vehicle established to bring a level of piety between personal interests and a politician's voting record. Mitt Romney

342

described blind trusts as an "age old ruse." Romney noted that politicians can give a blind trust "rules about where and how to invest."[10]

Manchin's long time ties to coal corporations are evident in his campaign financial reports. From 2009-2012 Manchin received almost $1.2 million in coal and oil corporation donations, seventy-five percent of the total coming from the coal industry.[11] "Of the 20 senators who received the most money from coal mining interests in 2018, he [Manchin} ranks 11th and is the sole Democrat."[12] Manchin's voting record continues to reflect those who brought him to the "dance." Senator Manchin voted for a bill to prohibit EPA from taking any action to regulate greenhouse gases and supported a resolution to gut EPA's mercury and toxic standards for coal fired powered plant emissions. Manchin also voted to repeal Big Oil Tax Subsides Act which would result in a loss of $2.4 billion in annual subsidies.[13] "During his first run for the Senate in 2010, Joe Manchin III, the Democrat from West Virginia, took aim—literally—at a climate change bill, shooting a bullet through it in a television ad."[14] Jim Sconyers, chairman of WV Sierra Club described Manchin's long time ties to the coal industry, "Manchin has been nothing but a mouthpiece for the coal industry his whole public life."[15] Manchin votes with President Trump about two-thirds of the time and has opposed virtually any measure that limits U.S. carbon emissions.[16]

In 2014 a *Pulitzer Prize* winning report from the Center for Public Integrity revealed the law firm of Jackson and Kelly "systemically denied coal miners' black lung benefit claims by withholding unfavorable evidence and shaping the opinions of doctors called upon in court…potentially tainted numerous decisions adversely affecting coal miners and their survivors."[17] Only one day after the release of the report, Manchin publically praised the law firm in a speech before the National Western Mining Convention referring to his dear friends at Jackson and Kelly and brushed away questions from reporters of any impropriety by the firm.[18]

As Governor, Manchin sponsored efforts for the passage of bills that reduced corporate taxes from 9 to 6.5 percent. Governor Manchin also led the way for legislation that removed the business franchise tax. It is estimated these two corporate tax breaks for corporations cost the state hundreds of millions of dollars in annual revenue. In recent years with WV facing a $353 million dollar budget shortfall, Manchin admitted, "he's not sure if the business tax cuts he pushed through as governor was a good idea…"[19] Without sufficient revenue West Virginia ranks near the bottom of indicators related to the quality of its infrastructure including roads, bridges and school building capital needs.[20]

As with Caperton, my professional involvement with the Manchin family was not positive. Certainly when I was selected as state superintendent instead of Joe Manchin's first cousin Mark Manchin, the animosity heightened. Joe's wife, Gayle, a member of the State Board, was the leading advocate for her husband's cousin.[21] In addition Gayle and Joe Manchin were supportive of the Caperton's desire to expand *Globaloria* in the state's schools. Governor Manchin provided funds to one of his administration's departments in order to support *Globaloria* without any record of adherence to procurement processes. Both Manchins' advocated for the WV Department of Education to provide funds and technical support for the expansion of *Globaloria*. As state superintendent refused to approve the expansion and funding of *Globaloria* without adherence to proper state bidding requirements.

As state superintendent I criticized the state's Broadband Technology Opportunities Program (BTOP), a $126 million dollar federal grant written, submitted and approved for funding during Governor Manchin's administration. The criticism, based on West Virginia Department of Education staff analysis, included: 1.) awarding the BTOP contract to Verizon, subsequently acquired by Frontier, without letting a new bid; 2.) spending an unnecessary $12.6 million for oversized Cisco routers for schools that an audit report determined " unconscionable," and 3.) allowing Frontier to build the last mile of fiber rather than completing the middle mile solution.[22] A consulting team's audit report confirmed: "Frontier isn't building the correct style of infrastructure for the project, uses products that 'far exceed' what is needed and has problems documenting its work.[23] The criticism did not sit well with either Joe or Gayle Manchin.

In 2016 Citynet, a WV internet provider, brought suit against Frontier alleging that Frontier misused $40.5 million in federal funds to build a high speed proprietary network for their benefit. Citynet's suit alleged there existed a "tight" relationship between Governor Manchin and

Frontier officials.[24] In August, 2016 Frontier moved for the dismissal of the suit. [25] In March, 2018, U.S. District Judge Copenhaver dismissed some elements in the complaint but allowed all counts in Citynet's lawsuit against Frontier Communications to go forward.[26] "The court finds that these allegations, if proven, give rise to the inference that defendants had an implied agreement to violate the FCA, and that Citynet has alleged overt acts committed in furtherance of the conspiracy."[27] The lawsuit remains in litigation. To date the state has been required to send a check for $4.7 million to the federal government for unallowable reimbursements of federal stimulus funds to Frontier in connection with the expansion of broadband.[28]

Manchin, Caperton and their associates' actions often contrasted sharply with progressive actions and law. Their lack of political support for Darrell in elections was a factor that impacted voting outcomes.

Dark Money and Wrong Doers Resistance

A second contributing factor to achieving success in elections was the ever increasing amount of dark money expended for the purpose of defeating Darrell. This dark money, often from "wrong-doers," held accountable for their actions by the Attorney General's office, infiltrated elections to assist the anti-McGraw candidate. By the 2012 election the list of wrong-doers who violated consumer protection, anti-trust, and other statutory or regulatory requirements included tele-marketers, banks, insurance, pharmaceutical, pay-day lenders, tobacco, coal, gas, landfill, sewage dumpers, computer, technology, internet, credit card companies and corporate entities. Often the wrong-doers contributed funds to anti-McGraw efforts either directly or through Political Action Committees associated with such entities as the national and state Chamber of Commerce, the Center for Individual Freedom and other corporate entities.

The Supreme Court decision in *Citizens United,* that held corporations like people have free speech and are eligible to pour millions into political campaigns, dramatically increased the amount of dark money infiltrating elections.[29] The decision gives free reign for corporations to expend money in support of a candidate aligned with their interests versus the interests of the people. Super Political Action Committees (PACs) now can accept unlimited contributions from corporate entities in order to elect supportive candidates. "In the election cycles following *Citizens United,* the balance of power has shifted more and more toward outside spending groups such as a super PACs and 'dark money' political nonprofits, unleashing unprecedented amounts of money toward political advertisements meant to influence voters."[30]

Citizen United also opened up the opportunity for corporations to drive massive amounts of money into the non-profit political world. In this non-profit world corporate disclosure is not required. These non-profit groups fly under the radar by contending they are not required to register with the FEC as a PAC because their primary purpose is not political. One such example of a non-profit heavily engaged in politics is the Center for Individual Freedom (CFIF), a non-profit conservative organization founded by former tobacco industry executives to fight government restrictions on smoking..[31] In 2012 the CFIF, based in metro-Washington, D.C., "made what may be the largest single independent expenditure in state history, at $1.59 million for ads attacking McGraw."[32] Tobacco company executives did not forget Darrell's successful litigation against them.

The changing dynamics of campaigns, including the use of Internet and social media, coupled with lack of support from the status quo Democratic leadership and the influx of dark money made each election increasingly more difficult.

1992 Election

The 1992 election for Attorney General caught most politicos off guard. The late filing of Palumbo for Governor and Darrell's subsequent and equally late filing for Attorney General allowed little time for Republican or Democratic candidates to enter the race. Richard Neely, former Supreme Court Justice when Darrell was on the Court, is a friend of Edward Rebrook III. It was alleged that Justice Neely orchestrated the candidacy of Rebrook for Attorney General. Late on the last night for filing, Richard Neely signed as a witness on Rebrook's candidacy form. Rebrook, the Democratic primary opponent, served as state beer commissioner in the Rockefeller administration and ran unsuccessfully for both Congress and House of Delegates. In a speech before a Rotary Club Rebrook reminded the audience of Darrell's liberal opinions while on the Court and assured the Rotarians that he was endorsed by the WV Bankers Association and other business oriented organizations while "McGraw would be preparing for a rally with his kind of people—the United Mine Workers."[33] Interestingly, Darrell, long time Rotarian, served as President of his award winning Rotary Club.

Rebrook attacked Darrell for opinions he authored while on the state Supreme Court, including one that Rebrook asserted liberalized juvenile laws. Rebrook described Darrell's investigation of the jail cell where a youth hung himself as "his 'notorious' confrontation with deputies at the Kanawha County Jail."[34]

Ethics complaints or requests for an investigation are often used by opponents in an election to establish a negative mind set; i.e. "McGraw is being investigated" or "ethics complaint filed against McGraw." And so it was in this election. Rebrook requested Prosecuting Attorney Bill Forbes investigate the state's purchase of Darrell's law books when he left the state Court. Forbes found the Court historically reimbursed retiring justices for their set of law books. The prosecuting attorney concluded there was no violation.[35]

Establishing a public mind set that a candidate or elected official did something wrong or even worse committed an illegal act is an effective election strategy. The 1992 election found opponents, ads and articles alleging: "McGraw obtained books and other materials at public expense while a Supreme Court Justice," or "McGraw mistreated a secretary while at Supreme Court." Explanations, generally more complicated to communicate than an allegation of misconduct, depend on whether the candidate has sufficient funds to market his/her response. It is strongly believed the public only remembers the negative headline and or sound bite. For Darrell, always without sufficient campaign dollars, his explanations were generally embedded in an article read by a small number of constituents. Darrell stated the obvious, as to why justices should buy and read books: "The judging business is an intellectual business which finds its foundation in the literature of the law and the literature of the people."[36] Unfortunately, voters generally don't spend a lot of time reading and analyzing a response to any given accusation. Darrell's practice was firm on avoiding any conversation privately and most definitely in a public forum regarding an employee. The allegations related to the secretary fell into that category.

Contributions to Rebrook's campaign far exceeded Darrell's and were mainly from banks, insurance, doctors and coal operators.[37] State media did not endorse Darrell, but acknowledgement from Don Marsh, long time Gazette editor, was important to the outcome of the election: "I'm also going to vote for Darrell McGraw who is running for attorney general. McGraw has made mistakes, goodness knows, but the *Daily Mail* has been obsessive in its attacks on him. Ed Rebrook, the other candidate is a second-rater who has raised money from every interest group in the state, including the omnipresent Buck Harless. He also is supported by Hey, Chauncey Browning and Don Robertson and other remnants of the old Statehouse machine."[38]

With the support of the labor base, Darrell won the primary election with 55% of the vote to Rebrook's 45%. In 1993 Rebrook was convicted of wire and securities fraud and sentenced to federal prison.[39]

Robert Gould was the Republican nominee for attorney general in the general election. A New York native, Gould had recently relocated to Monroe County, WV. Gould aligned himself with Rebrook and vowed to keep Rebrook's anti-McGraw coalition intact through the general election. Gould filed complaints with the Federal Election Commission against the UMWA for their ads supporting Darrell in the primary election in an attempt to keep labor involvement out of the general election. The complaint was dismissed by the Federal Election Commission.

Gould's record as a lawyer in West Virginia was sparse. He referred to himself as a Monroe County lawyer and buffalo farmer. Questions arose regarding whether Gould met the five year residency requirement and a complaint was filed, but the Gould remained on the ballot.[40]

Gould's campaign attacked Darrell for his progressive opinions as a Justice, which he alleged ruined the business climate in the state. The anti-business allegations regarding Darrell's service as a Justice were used in this and most future elections. Darrell tried to counter the anti-business claims: "Politics is all about scapegoats…In my case…during the time I served on the Supreme Court, West Virginia went through a very traumatic recession as a consequence of the restructuring of the American economy. A lot of people got hurt as a result and they were looking for scapegoats. One intellectual giant in the business community said I have done more to damage business in West Virginia than any other person ever. That's simply incredible…any reasonable person should realize that the West Virginia Supreme Court didn't manage the American economy."[41] Allegations designed to discredit Darrell impacted the vote. Darrell won the general election. This time the margin was significantly less than the primary election with Darrell receiving 51% of the electorate vote compared to Gould's 48%.

Gould later established a company called Image Development Group, Inc., a public relation firm, that was engaged by Benjamin Suarez to develop a campaign to defeat Darrell in the1996 election.[42] Gould was also actively involved in "Republicans for Manchin in 2004."[43]

1996 Election

Duke Bloom, a Charleston lawyer and member of the Kanawha County Commission, was Darrell's Democratic primary opponent in the 1996 election. Bloom attacked Darrell for hiring outside counsel to prosecute cases and vowed to stop the outside counsel practice if he were elected. Like the anti-business label, the appointing of outside counsel was frequently used against Darrell. Bloom was a locally respected County Commissioner with little state-wide recognition. Darrell's first success in the tobacco litigation occurred just before the primary election with the receipt of a $200,000 settlement check from Liggett. Darrell won the primary election by a large majority. Darrell received 68.5% of the vote compared to Duke Bloom's 31%.[44]

The Republican opponent in the general election for AG was Charlotte Lane, a lawyer and lobbyist for the Charleston Chamber of Commerce, Eastern Associated Coal and the WV Bar Association. Lane's husband was a city councilman whose law firm represented a tobacco company in the ongoing tobacco litigation. In response to her husband-client relationship with tobacco Lane stated, "Those are totally separate issues."[45] Lane served on Public Service Commission. In 1987 Lane resigned from the PSC when Governor Arch Moore appointed her to a brief, but abortive appointment, to serve as U.S. attorney. The appointment viewed as problematic occurred during the time Governor Moore and Republican Mayor Mike Roark were under federal investigation.[46]

Lane was backed by big business and coal executives. In the November pre-election financial reports Lane outraised McGraw by more than three to one. Smoot Fahlgren contributed and sponsored a fund raiser for Lane at his home. As AG, Darrell refused to approve the 1993 Fahlgren's advertising contract with the Lottery Commission.[47]

Suarez and the Better Business Bureau were actively engaged in the 1996 general election for attorney general. Benjamin Suarez, the telemarketer resisted by the AG office for unscrupulous marketing to senior citizens, spent large sums of money in a well-orchestrated and financed anti-McGraw campaign. Suarez filled air waves and mailboxes with ads attacking Darrell's credibility. Suarez vowed to defeat Darrell. Suarez pledged to use the political service division of Suarez Corp, experts in targeting and direct marketing techniques, for that purpose. The Better Business Bureau from Canton, Ohio, an arm of Suarez Industry, funded a separate but coordinated campaign against Darrell. The Better Business Bureau pledged to spend $400,000 and Suarez vowed to spend whatever it took to defeat Darrell.[48] The Suarez and the Canton, Ohio Better Business Bureau attacks were vicious:

- *If Darrell McGraw is re-elected, your taxes could increase;*
- *If Darrell McGraw is re-elected West Virginia jobs could be jeopardized;*
- *Voters need to stop career politician Darrell McGraw who attempted to pocket $937,000 of your tax dollars;*
- *McGraw allegedly tried to storm a state prison and assaulted a guard.*
- *Darrell McGraw was described by a state capital prosecutor as crude and boorish and demonstrates the ethics of a pimp;*

- *By attacking businesses and investors who want to come here [McGraw] sent a message to businesses all across America— West Virginia is hostile to business;*
- *While most West Virginians struggle to pay taxes, he rewarded campaign contributors with huge legal fees, and*
- *McGraw was charged by a former employee of abusive treatment of his secretary, who was suffering from cancer.[49]*

Full page newspaper ads and state-wide mailers contained these and many more false assertions. The ads were in retaliation for Darrell's enforcement of West Virginia's consumer protection laws against Suarez. The ads were designed to intimidate Darrell from any future action; deter any other state attorneys general from enforcement of laws against Suarez Industries and to elect Charlotte Lane attorney general.

Voters often believe negative ads, especially if reinforced with frequency and in a multitude of different mediums. The impact of the negative ads was apparent. The *Charleston Gazette* did not endorse Darrell. The family found a little encouragement when Darrell's resilience was noted, "McGraw's 16 year record in state government could be compared to a worn umbrella: It may not always look the best, but it usually can weather the storm."[50]—*Charleston Daily Mail*

Darrell won the election with 52% of the vote compared to Lane's 48%. The results were in stark contrast to Darrell's primary election victory where he received 68% compared to Bloom's 31%. The dark money used to buy negative ads impacted the election results.[51]

2000 Election

Darrell faced no opponents in the primary or general election in 2000. This miraculous occurrence was the result of two positive events. First, after twelve lawsuits and significant level of harassment, the Suarez attacks ended in December, 1999. Darrell prevailed in the legal challenges. Potential opponents knew that Suarez was no longer a financial source of dark money to fight Darrell. Second, the tobacco litigation reached a successful conclusion with a settlement allocation of $1,736,741,427 billion for WV. The settlement monies were aligned by the Legislature to support teachers' retirement, workers compensation, physician mutual insurance, senior citizen programs and the Rainy Day Fund. Perhaps potential opponents thought the positive impact of the tobacco settlement was too recent in the minds of the voters. It was a most awesome election.

But it didn't last. The dark money from wrong-doers, who had much to benefit from electing a new attorney general, was back in full force in all the future elections.

2004 Election

In the 2004 election Darrell faced Hiram "Bucky" Lewis. Lewis, the Republican nominee, was an Army National Guard Captain. Lewis' advertisements depicted him with a gun in hand projecting his commitment to safe guard the citizenry and protect the gun rights of West Virginians. Lewis, a Morgantown lawyer, had no record of public service or noted legal profile. Hiram held a news conference in front of the Charleston Newspapers headquarters where he called Darrell a chicken for not debating him. Hiram then showed up at the front door of our house with a "person sized chicken," and television cameras. The chicken and Hiram squatted on the doorstep for some time. For some reason I was actually home that day, and was aghast at seeing a large chicken at our front door. Standing on the ledge inside the glassed in sunporch, our dog Malcolm was barking ferociously and begging for me to open the door. As inviting as the thought was for Malcolm to get the chicken, I restrained myself and avoided opening the door. Malcolm loved chicken.

Hiram was hoping to confront Darrell. If Darrell considered debating Hiram, the appearance of a person size chicken made his decision easy. There was no debate scheduled. Hiram though was determined to debate; so he staged a debate with the chicken back at the newspaper headquarters. Some pundits who listened said the chicken won.[52]

Hiram, as others before him, attacked Darrell for his anti-business actions. Hiram promised if elected to accelerate the growth of business in West Virginia and expand criminal work by making the AG office into the West Virginia Department of Justice. It was an interesting platform.

Both of Hiram's promises, growing business and creating a WV Department of Justice, required the Legislature to change the law and the citizenry to change the Constitution.

Hiram attacked Darrell's litigation against Applied Card Systems, a Huntington debt collection agency. Hiram asserted the litigation was as an example of McGraw's anti-business attitude. The AG litigation alleged Applied Card Systems used abusive tactics in collecting debts. In response to the litigation, Applied Card asserted the law suit drove them to close their Huntington business, resulting in 600 West Virginians losing their jobs. Hiram utilized Applied Card assertions in anti-McGraw campaign attacks. However, investigations revealed that Applied Card planned to leave Huntington before the litigation was ever filed. The pattern of unscrupulous debt collecting agencies often includes hiring low paid workers to operate call centers to harass debtors and then moving their phone banks to another location.[53]

Darrell and Warren were both running for re-election in the 2004 primary. Massey CEO Don Blankenship was spending millions against Warren in his reelection bid for the state Supreme Court. Blankenship's negative campaign against Warren was an anti-McGraw effort that reached into the AG election. State Republican Chairman Gary Abernathy commented about the millions of dollars in negative ads dumped against Warren and their impact on Darrell's election: "No doubt about it. Half the people don't know one brother from the other."[54]

The *Gazette* endorsement of Darrell for Attorney General made a difference in what was a very close election: "West Virginia's longtime attorney general, Darrell McGraw, often is at the center of tempests—and its usually because he took bold action in behalf of the public...In contrast, his Republican challenger is a neophyte. We endorse Darrell McGraw for re-election as West Virginia's attorney general."[55] Darrell won the election by a 5,302 votes receiving 50.42% to Hiram's 49.585%.[56]

Hiram was later arrested when he shot a man said to be his roommate in the leg. "Following a preliminary hearing Clay Magistrate Jeffery Boggs found probable cause to bind Hiram C. Lewis IV's case over to the grand jury. [Hiram] was charged with malicious wounding and wanton endangerment."[57] A year after the incident a jury found Hiram not guilty of a crime.

2008 Election

The 2008 general election resonated with dark money expenditures from political action committees focused on defeating Darrell and electing Dan Greear. Greear, a Charleston lawyer who served two years in the House of Delegates, promised to end the activism in the Attorney General's office: "I am not running to be the conservative alternative to Darrell McGraw. I'm running to end the activism in the Attorney General's office." Greear, like others before him, promised that as attorney general he would create a business friendly office, and stop the use of outside counsel.[58]

The AG's appointment of Assistant AGs was the strategy that brought billions into WV at no cost to the taxpayer. Without a state budget that allocates millions for potential enforcement litigation, the appointment of lawyers on a contingency basis under the supervision of the AG was essential in litigation against big corporate "wrong doers."

Citizens for Individual Freedom (CFIF) spent an undisclosed amount of "dark money" in television and radio ads alleging "he [Darrell] misused settlement dollars for his office and giving it away to trial lawyers."[59] The facts were different. Of the nearly $2 billion recovered by the Attorney General's office less than 1% was payment for outside legal services which was actually determined by the judge's approved settlement orders.[60]

Citizens for Individual Freedom contended it was not required to reveal who funded the attack ads, but their web site lists such entities as U.S. Chamber of Commerce, Pfizer Pharmaceutical, Philip Morris, Dow Chemical and the Christian Coalition as clients. CFIF was not registered to do business in West Virginia. Complaints were filed with Republican Secretary of State Betty Ireland. The Secretary did not intervene to enforce the law and stop CFIF infiltration of dark money in the election.[61]

Shortly before the election, the national and state Chamber of Commerce launched $700,000 worth of negative television commercials. West Virginians Against Lawsuit Abuse as well as the American Tort Reform Association expended money in an effort to influence the outcome of the election.[62] The *West Virginia Record*, supported by the national Chamber of Commerce, utilized their newspaper to reinforce whatever negative allegations were generated. The dark money in support of Dan Greear was substantial. A poll close to the race showed Greear winning the election.

The race was complicated by the presidential election. Darrell supported Hilary Clinton in the Democratic primary. Hilary Clinton won WV with a substantial majority 66.7% to Barack Obama's 25.7%, but lost the Democratic nomination. In the general election, Darrell supported Barack Obama. Prior to the November election most national news organizations predicted that the Republican nominee, John McCain, would win in WV. Obama was unpopular with many West Virginians. Many Democratic office holders avoided association with Obama. Darrell did not; he was for Obama. Darrell's support for Obama was used against him in this and future elections. As predicted, McCain won WV by more than 13%. Obama became the first Democratic nominee to win the presidential election but loose WV since Woodrow Wilson in 1916.[63] It was a race issue.

The *Charleston Gazette*, supported Obama and endorsed Darrell. For Darrell the *Gazette* endorsement was instrumental to the outcome of the election. Darrell won the race by only 6,000 votes, a margin of 50.5% to 49.5%.[64]

The dark money was working, and the wrongdoers knew it.

2012 Election

2012 was the year the full impact of the 2010 Supreme Court ruling in *Citizens United* case came into play. *Citizens United* held that corporations like people have free speech and can pour millions into political campaigns. "That is what we get when Chief Justice John Roberts unleased *Citizens United.* It allows anyone with a mega bankroll to become a new type of political boss—elected by no one and beholding to no one, free to share their darkest visions of America with a vast television audience."[65]—*Editorial Sunday Gazette Mail*

And so it was in the 2012 Attorney General election in WV, the dark money from outside corporations, including big drug, flowed into the state. The AG's record of holding corporations and special interests accountable for their actions resulted in an accumulated bevy of "wrong-doers" now ready to spend money against Darrell. The AG office recovered millions against large drug companies that promoted false and mis-leading marketing of drugs. In the fall of 2012, without regard for personal impact, the AG filed action against a dozen of the largest drug companies for their excessive opioid shipments into WV. It was too much; big drug needed a different attorney general.[66]

The drug companies had an answer. They put forth one of their own to run for Attorney General. Patrick Morrisey, a lobbyist for Healthcare Distribution Management Association that represented drug distributors, filed for Attorney General. Morrisey filed just four days after he was admitted to the WV Bar. Morrisey and his wife worked on behalf of Cardinal Health, one of the drug companies the AG sued.[67]

Morrisey, a New Jersey lawyer, bought a cottage in Jefferson County, West Virginia and claimed his residency as Harper's Ferry. Morrisey's wife voted in Virginia and his teenage step daughter attended school in Virginia. Morrisey never practiced law in West Virginia. Prior to his bid for WV AG, Morrisey ran for Congress in New Jersey and lost. Morrisey was a member of a Washington D.C. lobbying firm that represented pharmaceutical corporations. During the election Morrisey articulated his opposition to public health care and federal regulations.[68]

By October, 2012 the Center for Individual Freedom (CFIF), a non profit established by tobacco executives and supported by donors like Karl Rove's political action committee, spent almost $1.6 million in attack ads against Darrell. Determination of the total amount CFIF spent and their funding sources remains difficult because of CFIF success in federal courts in blocking attempts to require full disclosure.[69]

A Des Moines, Iowa group, American Future Fund is another non-profit that claims its "AG Project" is for the purpose is to educate the public on important constitutional issues. In actuality the AG Project's purpose is to elect to office individuals who respond positively to corporate interests. The American Future Fund purchased $600,000 in ads to benefit Morrisey.[70]

In addition to all the corporate and dark money in support of Morrisey, his own campaign expended over $2 million. Morrisey made a $1.4 million personal loan to the campaign and outside contributions

amounted to $531,000.[71] In contrast, Darrell's campaign secured
$236,000 in contributions. The political arm of Democratic Attorney
Generals, Center for Fairness and Justice, funded $345,000 in ads in
support of Darrell.[72]

As a progressive, Darrell openly supported President Obama. The
regressive Democratic leadership in West Virginia did not support
President Barack Obama. In the primary more than 40% of Democrats in
WV voted for Keith Russell Judd, an inmate at a federal correction
institution in Texas. WV Democratic Senator Joe Manchin, who was on
the November ballot, refused to say who he voted for in the presidential
primary. Some suggested a reason for the WV vote for a convicted felon
was racism. Judd was white. [73]

Lack of Democratic leadership support for President Obama was
apparent during the general election. At a large rally at the Teamsters
hall in South Charleston it was said that Senator Manchin and Governor
Tomblin were upset with the remarks delivered by Ed Rabel, a former
national television commentator. An award winning journalist, Ed
Rabel's speech was intended to motivate Democrats and union workers to
get out the vote for President Obama. The speech was more than that for
all who listened. It was a clear and articulate reminder of a greater duty
to what is culturally right—to be like those Democrats who stood up time
and time again in the midst of diversity. Rabel, who had a most
successful national career, came home to bring out the better angels in all
of us when he spoke:

Those who know me see me as the proud son of West Virginia,
born and reared in Appalachia and instructed in the lore of the southern
coalfields. Mine is an all-American story of a lad born in poverty and
enriched in a world-wide experience, one who comes back to rediscover
his roots on Rabel Mountain. For those who do not know me, I introduce
myself simply as a fellow Democrat, a member of the biggest
disorganized political party man has ever known.

John F. Kennedy said this: "The sun does not always shine in
West Virginia, but the people always do." Kennedy said those words
standing in a pouring rain on the statehouse steps in Charleston, West
Virginia, in 1963. I was there, too, on the 100th birthday of our
illustrious state. Kennedy became President in large part because West

Virginia Democrats voted for him in the primary to show the nation that a Catholic could win even among a population in which religious fundamentalism was rampant. That may have been West Virginia's finest hour.

Since then, many Democrats in West Virginia have changed their stripes. No longer are they the honored captains of the party of Franklin Delano Roosevelt and Harry S. Truman and John Fitzgerald Kennedy and Lyndon Baines Johnson and William Jefferson Clinton and, yes, Barack Hussein Obama. No longer do they represent the party of ferocity in war, compassion in peace and hope for the future. In the past, Democrats always led the way on the front lines for civil rights and as the pioneers to reach for the stars by putting a man on the moon. Today we Democrats are losing ground in the ageless struggle to do what is right.

If our history is any guide, we should be trumpeting the rights of the working man, promoting diversity both in human rights and in the economy and jumping on the bandwagon for an environment free of pollution and the cancer it causes. If we would be true to ourselves, we should be forestalling the endless theft of our patrimony by those outside our state who bear us nothing but ill will. If we truly pay homage to our founding as Mountaineers Always Free, we would be about the business of freedom—freedom from a one-dimensional economy, freedom from the tyranny of political corruption in state and local government and freedom to choose progressive leaders to spur us on in the 21st century.

Instead, we are falling victim, once again, to antiquated shibboleths predicated on fear and hopelessness promoted mainly by fossil fuel lobbyists whose only interest is that of their corporate bosses. If they tell you they have your interest at heart, best you head for the hills. If their message is one of hatred and racism, best tell them to get lost. For you and I know that we are better than that.

Our state and our people are known not for intolerance. West Virginia is known not for laziness. Its workers are some of the best and most productive in the world. When called to meet the challenges of the 21st century, we know how to do that. We can produce energy for the world better and faster than anyone else. We can produce talent we can be proud of: Chuck Yeager, Robert Byrd, Pearl Buck, Don Knotts, Jerry West, Walter Reuther and Mary Lou Retton just to name a few. And we

*owe it to them and to ourselves not to dishonor them by allowing
ourselves to become pedestrian, mere followers of the commonplace.*

*I come not today to try to change political minds. For, if I am not
mistaken, many Democrats in the state already have their minds made up
for Mitt Romney in the belief that he would champion their cause by
turning back the tide of environmental protection. In their view, global
warming is a myth to be discredited. Never mind that at least 6,000
scientists avow that the earth is heating up and the oceans are rising up.*

*The truth is, we are living in a season of myths—that the national
budget can be balanced by giving tax breaks to the rich; that the female
body has a way of shutting down conception in what the mythmakers call
a "legitimate rape;" that Israel can avoid global war by attacking Iran.
Why should any rational person believe the mythmakers are telling the
truth about the future of fossil fuels and the jobs that might be produced if
only the so-called war on coal can be ended? In the words of president
Obama, 'That's the biggest whopper of them all.'*

Here are the facts:
*• Employment in West Virginia coal mines is down from 126,000
in 1948 to fewer than 25,000 today.*
*• The biggest private employer in West Virginia is Wal-Mart, not
coal.*
*• Natural gas production in West Virginia is competing with coal
in the production of energy.*
*• Mechanization and modernization in coal mining through
mountaintop removal, in part, means fewer miners are required to
do the job. Hence layoffs occur because coal companies do not
need as many miners as before to dig the coal out of the
mountains.*
*• Since 1950, West Virginia has lost 10 percent of its population.
Instead of five Congressional districts, we're down to three.*
*• The Kanawha Valley lost its chemical company dynamism long
ago.*
*• A modern, international airport to provide thousands of jobs
was nixed by local politicians fearful of losing their fiefdoms.*
*You have the ability to separate fact from fiction. West
Virginians, traditionally, have resisted being buffaloed. We are a proud*

people who do not like to have the wool pulled over our eyes. Too often, in the past, big shots and crooked politicians and religious fanatics have tried. But failed. We sent them to jail for their lies. We did not tolerate them then. And we, as good Democrats, should not tolerate them now.

Now we have work to do. If we, as Democrats, return to our revered foundation forged in the annals of Roosevelt, Truman and Kennedy[74]—as delivered by Ed Rabel

For all those observing, it was apparent that Governor Tomblin and Senator Manchin were upset with Rabel's speech. It was reported by those in charge that they were given a good "tongue lashing" for allowing Rabel to speak. Both the Governor and Senator were running for re-election and wanted no association with Obama in fear that it might negatively impact their success.[75]

Morrisey's campaign ran dark ads connecting the AG and Obama, "Darrell McGraw and Barack Obama: We can't afford another 4 years. Vote against Darrell McGraw." Slick mass mailings sent state-wide pictured President Obama and Darrell together and stated, "McGraw supports Barack Obama and has refused to stand up to his job-killing policies, EPA or the War on Coal." Darrell did not deter from his support for President Barack Obama.

Darrell lost the election by 16,000 votes. Outside corporate interests poured millions of dollars in dark money into the election to silence the voice and work of a progressive, successful Attorney General.[76]

The green light from *Citizens United* gave corporations' permission to spend untold millions for their chosen candidates.[77] Justice Stevens' dissent in *Citizens United* cited what happened in *Caperton v. A.T. Massey Coal Co.* when Don Blankenship spent $3 million to defeat Warren McGraw. Justice Stevens used it as an example of how the majority opinion exacerbated the likelihood that corporate spending would now happen in legislative and executive elections.[78] When *Citizens United* was decided in 2010, Fran Hughes, the Chief Deputy commented to Darrell, "the Justices just put a "for sale sign on the AG office." The dark money twisted, turned and falsified information to sway voters to elect an individual to protect their personal profits:

"When a veteran attorney general whose only 'crime' is his determination to defend the rights of consumers is defeated by a challenger who got his license to practice law in the state four days before launching a campaign that flooded the airwaves with out-of-state money, this is 'Dollarocracy'."[79]

There was no justifiable reason for Morrisey to win the election except for the dark money of those who had much to benefit from defeating an Attorney General who had enforced the law for the benefit of the people he served: "Morrisey's candidacy would have been absurd by traditional measures of credible candidates in West Virginia. But he had an advantage: virtually unlimited—unaccountable—outside money. More money from outside the state poured into Morrisey's race for attorney general than into races for governor or potentially competitive congressional seats."[80]

Big drug was willing to spend the money to secure an Attorney General with favorable ties to the pharmaceutical industry. It was all about protecting their interests. Between 2006 and 2012 the drug companies shipped into West Virginia 67 pills per person annually which paved the way for the state to have the highest per capita death rate from opioids in the country. Unlike Oklahoma, which received 54 opioid pills per person per year, and recently settled lawsuits with Purdue Pharma for $270 million and Teva Pharmaceuticals for $85 million, AG Morrisey settled suits, originally filed by AG McGraw, with Cardinal Health for $20 million and Amerisource Bergen for only $16 million:

"The American Enterprise Institute estimates that the opioid epidemic is costing West Virginia $8.8 billion a year. When former Attorney General Darrell McGraw originally filed the lawsuits, he intended to get justice for the people of West Virginia. So why did Patrick Morrisey settle the cases he inherited with these companies for so little? It might have something to do with his ties to Big Pharma."[81]

The loss of an election impacts not only the officer's life but close associates and staff. A significant number of the Attorneys General's team were part of the entire twenty year journey of enforcing the law against wrongdoers in businesses, corporations or public agencies; educating the public on consumer protection services; resolving hundreds of thousands of consumer complaints; and securing $2 billion in settlement and recovery monies. The AG team secured dollars to fund teacher and public employee retirement systems, the state's rainy day fund, the state physician mutual insurance program, senior citizen services, domestic violence shelters, day report centers, tobacco and drug programs and much more.

The disruption in the lives of those on the AG team was the most difficult part of losing the election. It was an emotional moment when members of the AG team walked out of Capitol together on January 11, 2013 until Darrell commented that the sun was still shining. They all laughed.

Would there be one more next election?

Chapter XIX   One More Time

Do all the good you can. By all the means you can. In all the ways you can. In all the places you can. At all the times you can. To all the people you can. As long as ever you can.—John Wesley,

Darrell and Martha Reese at Marshall University acceptance of Matt Reese' Documents
Martha's husband, Matt Reese, father of *Grassroots Campaigning*

January, 2016, and Darrell, 79 years old, missed his life as a public servant. Darrell, much concerned about the current legal landscape, politics and state government in West Virginia, believed he could help. A regressive Republican majority was in charge of the Legislature and actively engaged in reversing the rights and benefits of laborers and the poor. And in recent years the question of impartiality and recusal of Justices on the state Supreme Court seemed most problematic.[1] There existed a need for a more diverse philosophical representation on the Court in order to stimulate a decision making process that considered various legal perspectives prior to rendering conclusions and opinions of law.

WV Supreme Court Justices

The 2016 West Virginia Supreme Court consisted of Justices Robin Davis, Allen Loughry, Brent Benjamin, Margaret Workman and Menis Ketchum. It was this Court that James Samples of Hofstra Law School described "as a circus masquerading as a Court"—it reputation for impartiality questionable.[2]

Perhaps a factor in this negative impression might have been Don Blankenship's, the convicted ex-Massey Coal CEO, perceived influence with members of the Court. Blankenship's long arm of influence was purported in associations with Justices Ketchum, Benjamin, Davis and Loughry. Blankenship's political outreach perhaps acknowledged when then candidate Menis Ketchum admitted to meeting with Don prior to filing for the state Court.[3] Blankenship's connection with Brent Benjamin was much more apparent for it was Blankenship who spent millions in attack ads with the singular focus to defeat Justice Warren McGraw and elect Benjamin to the Court.[4] As a Justice, Benjamin refused to recuse himself and voted in favor of reversing a $50 million dollar verdict against Massey. Ultimately the case made its way to the U.S. Supreme Court where counsel for the plaintiff argued that "a line needs to be drawn somewhere to prevent a judge from hearing cases involving a person [Don Blankenship] who has made massive campaign contributions to benefit the judge [Justice Benjamin]." Justice Kennedy writing for the Court agreed "there was serious risk of actual bias and Justice Benjamin was wrong in not recusing himself in *Caperton v. Massey.*"[5] The state Court's Judicial Investigation Commission, charged with determining if probable cause exists to formally charge a judge with a violation of the Code of Judicial Conduct, took no action against Benjamin.

Blankenship's connection to Justices Davis and Loughry was less obvious. It perhaps stemmed from Blankenship's longtime friendship with former Justice Spike Maynard who served on the state Court with Justice Davis and who hired Allen Loughry as law clerk. It was alleged that during his term Maynard became close to Justice Davis. "Despite Maynard's lifelong, pro-business voting pattern, he began voting in favor of almost every measure that had Davis's husband's name on it. In twelve of the thirteen cases involving Segal's clients that came before the court between 2005 and 2007, Maynard voted for Segal's side…"[6] When Justice Maynard announced his run for re-election Justice Davis stood next to him, a violation of Canon 5of WV Code of Judicial Conduct that states a judge shall not publically endorse or oppose another candidate for political office. Davis' husband held a fund raiser at her home that garnered over $100,000 for Maynard's reelection campaign.[7] As Chief

Justice, Davis heard *Caperton v Massey* and voted alongside Maynard and Benjamin for Massey.[8]

Allen Loughry who served as law clerk to Justice Maynard authored a book in which he described Justice Maynard as a "kind, intelligent, and an all-around extraordinary person."[9] It was Justice Maynard who vacationed in the south of France with Don Blankenship while Massey's $50 million case was pending in the Court. After public disclosure of the Maynard-Blankenship relationship, Maynard lost his bid for reelection to the state Court. Maynard then switched from Democrat to Republican to run for Congress. Maynard lost. Following in Maynard's footsteps, Loughry changed from Democrat to Republican to run for a seat on the WV Supreme Court.[10]

Negativity about the state Court was exacerbated when Justice Davis became the subject of an *ABC* segment regarding her lack of disclosure and recusal in the *Manor Care, Inc. v. Douglas* case.[11] *Manor Care* was appealed from the Kanawha County Circuit Court where a jury awarded $11.5 million compensatory damages and $80 million in punitive damages for the plaintiff. Justice Davis wrote the majority opinion that held the half million dollar medical malpractice cap didn't apply and awarded $42 million to the plaintiffs.[12] *ABC* revealed connections between Justice Davis and the plaintiff's attorney, Michael Fuller, a lawyer from Plant City, Georgia. *ABC* reported that prior to the decision Scott Segal (Davis's husband) sold his Lear jet to Michael Fuller for an estimated $1.3 million dollars. In addition Mr. Fuller raised from residents of Plant City, Georgia, $37,000 for Davis's last campaign. *ABC* implied that Justice Davis' decision resulted in Fuller and associates receiving an estimated $17 million.[13]

This 2016 Court, described by Hofstra Law "as a circus masquerading as a Court," was in need of reform.[14] With Justice Brent Benjamin's twelve year term expiring, the May primary provided an opportunity to elect a new justice and perhaps begin needed reform.

State Supreme Court Candidates

I did not want Darrell to run for the West Virginia Supreme Court. My journal reflected this trepidation:

It has been four years since Darrell lost the AG election. It has been a most difficult time in so many ways. But the calls keep coming. People respected as lifelong advocates for workers' rights, the environment, and government accountability want Darrell to run for the Court. Darrell is in good health. But the thoughts of another election are so overwhelming. The drug companies, the Chamber of Commerce and all the dark money funding negative commercials against Darrell literally makes me sick. I know so many people believe what they see and hear in ads. I don't want to try and explain again that the family didn't take a state paid for jet to Europe—so ridiculous, so unjust, so outrageous and so hurtful. Or that Darrell didn't rob the state piggy bank from a man who wouldn't even buy a new chair for his office during the 20 years he served as AG.

I know it's not about me. I know it's about helping others. How bad can it be? There is not much time until the primary. Darrell's presence on the Court would make such a difference for this state. But Oh My God, I can hardly breathe at the thought of Darrell running again.

The 2016 process of electing of justices to the state's highest court had been altered by the Legislature. First a new public financing system was established, and second the election was changed from partisan to non-partisan. Both changes were promoted by members of the Legislature, and others who perhaps had much to profit, as necessary to take politics and money out of judicial elections.

In 2012 the Legislature established a new public financing system whereby judicial candidates who meet the Code requirements are eligible to receive $350,000 in public funds. The Legislature mandated the establishment of a pilot program. Allen Loughry, a candidate in 2012 for justice, was the first individual to receive the public funds under the new program.

The pilot program was not without error. In *Loughry v. Tennant*, Loughry, the petitioner contended the pilot program matching fund clause entitled him to receive the amount of money spent by the non-participating candidate during the general election period. In her re-election bid Justice Robin Davis spent $494,472.16. Loughry contended, minus his initial disbursement of $350,000, his campaign was entitled to receive an additional $144,471.46.[15]

At the request of the state Supreme Court, in an Amicus Curia brief submitted by AG McGraw, Managing Deputy Barbara Allen argued the matching fund provisions are unconstitutional and the Election Commission is under no duty to implement an unconstitutional statute. Justice Menis Ketchum, in writing for the majority denied the plaintiff's writ of mandamus and upheld the unconstitutionality of the matching fund provision. However, Justice Ketchum, who sought Blankenship's blessing before filing for the state Court, furthered opined that Loughry, longtime law clerk for Justice Maynard and Blankenship's close friend, was allowed to seek private campaign contributions for his candidacy. Loughry successfully secured a seat on the state Court. The Legislature modified the statute in accordance with the state Court's opinion and increased public financing of justice elections to $500,000.[16]

The second change in the process for electing judges occurred in 2015 when a Republican majority Legislature made the election of judges' non-partisan. The Code change provided for election of all judges and justice to take place in the primary election without designation of party affiliation. Decades earlier when asked his opinion of non-partisan judicial elections, Darrell remarked, "The idea of nonpartisan elections of judges would be a fraud on the public. We have nonpartisan elections for school boards now, and it is the most political election we have."[17]

The Code changes were promoted to take politics and money out of judicial elections.

But would these changes prevent outside interests from expending millions, the wealthy from funding their personal campaign and the established order of Democratic and Republican leadership from supporting their candidates in the 2016 judicial election?

With the midnight hour approaching on the last night to submit candidacy forms, Darrell filed for the West Virginia Supreme Court. Brent Benjamin, William Wooten, Beth Walker, Wayne King and Darrell McGraw were the candidates.

Justice Brent Benjamin was a candidate for re-election who no longer had the monetary assistance of Don Blankenship. And Benjamin's support from the state and national Chamber of Commerce and Citizens Against Lawsuit Abuse (CALA) had evaporated. CALA conjectured that Benjamin's record on the Supreme Court was a "cause for concern…a pattern of judicial activism."[18] But more likely CALA and the Chamber were nervous about Benjamin's connection to Don Blankenship who recently was sentenced to one year in prison for mine safety violations.[19] Benjamin responded that CALA "had abdicated its role as a credible source of information regarding courts, and has instead become just another special interest shilling for partisan candidates."[20] Benjamin defined himself as the most conservative member of state Supreme Court and one who provided the necessary leadership to move the Court in the right direction.

Beth Walker, a Republican and a graduate of Hilldale College who touted her conservatism, worked as counsel for West Virginia University United Health Systems. Walker's strong ties to the coal industry were recognized: "Walker is no stranger to Blankenship and the coal industry…Walker worked for the corporate law firm Bowels Rice, which often represents coal companies. Her husband, Mike Walker, is a former executive of Walker Machinery, which contracts with coal companies and donated $25,000 to And for the Sake of Kids in 2004."[21]

Chris Hamilton, executive director of the West Virginia Coal Association called Walker "a true friend of coal." Hamilton deemed the other candidates as "liberal activist judges, bent on carrying out agendas handed down from likes of Barack Obama and Hillary Clinton, who are harmful to West Virginians."[22] Walker ran for the state Court in 2008 and lost. At that time her campaign manager was Roman Stauffer who in 2016 led Citizens Against Lawsuit Abuse, which was previously led by Greg Thomas, the former Blankenship aide who ran And for the Sake of the Kids.[23]

When Walker announced her candidacy it fractured, and some would say destroyed, Benjamin's base of support with CALA and the Chamber.[24] In addition Walker's campaign had two other distinct advantages: 1.) a $500,000 loan from her husband with connections to a coal mining machinery company, and 2.) the dark money assistance of big business and out of state entities including the Florida based State Republican Leadership Committee and the National Chamber.[25]

William Wooten, a long time Democrat trial lawyer and retired WV National Guard Colonel, had served for 27 years in the Legislature as a Senator and a Delegate. Wooten with little name recognition was dependent upon receiving $500,000 in public financing to build his state-wide base. Wooten was from southern West Virginia and supported by some trial lawyers.

Wayne King, a lawyer from Clay County was a self-described commonsense, country lawyer. King, a former prosecutor and family law master, wanted voters to know that he was a family man and an advocate for children: "There's hundreds and thousands of kids in West Virginia that need stability in their home life,"[26] King was a candidate without an identifiable constituency and any level of financial support. King self-financed his campaign to the tune of $13,860[27]

Darrell McGraw, former Justice and Chief Justice of the state Court and Attorney General, had a long record of service. His service included a lengthy list of state and national awards: Appalachian Hero Award, Defense of Justice Award, Susan B. Anthony Award, Margaret Baldwin Friend of Education Award, Berea College Service Award, Justice on an Outstanding Appellate Court, National Law Review of Landmark Supreme Court Opinions, Nationally Recognized Consumer Protection Office and the Justicia Officium Award, highest award by the WVU Law School. Darrell supported by labor was targeted by big corporations that did not want a "people's judge" returned to the Court.

An early poll showed Darrell with a substantial lead over his opponents: Darrell McGraw 25%, Benjamin 10%, Walker 4%, Wooten 4%, King 2% with 55% undecided. One political pollster noted, "Currently, it seems that name identifications is having impact until the television ads start airing."[28] Analyzing past voting patterns, another political columnist placed Darrell as the winner of the election:

Former Attorney General and Supreme Court Justice Darrell McGraw threw a monkey wrench into the inaugural plans of Beth Walker when he threw his hat in the ring for a term back on the court.

It is my considered, correct and sound opinion that, even though judicial elections are now non-partisan, McGraw is sure to pick up the sound Democrat, liberal left wing vote because he is a Democrat. That leaves his opponents out in the cold. Bill Wooten will either not stay in the race or he will likely vote for McGraw himself. Walker and Brent Benjamin, the sitting justice, will divide the Republican conservative, right wing vote. Voters may be stupid but they know who is liberal and who is conservative, folks.

What all this means is McGraw, who likely would draw 35 percent of the vote in a similar race against any one, two or three is the winner. The other three will divide up the 65 percent. It is likely Wooten will get only 10 percent or so. That leaves 55 percent for Walker and Benjamin. There's not a winning number there, folks. Can you say Justice McGraw again?[29]—Ron Gregory, columnist and political observer

Big Money Impact

After substantial struggle both Benjamin and Wooten campaigns qualified for $500,000 in public financing. Eligibility for public financing requires candidates secure 500 individual contributions of $100 or less; receive $35,000 to $50,000 in total contributions and adhere to strict time lines for submission of required forms.[30] Walker contended that both Wooten and Benjamin missed required deadlines and therefore weren't eligible to receive public finance funds. The Election Commission heard Walker's complaint and ruled in favor of Benjamin's and Wooten's eligibility. On appeal circuit court judges sided with Walker. Finally the state Supreme Court reversed the lower court ruling and granted Wooten and Benjamin eligibility to receive funding.[31]

Darrell opposed public financing of elections. King described public financing of campaigns as "an embarrassment to ask the average citizens of West Virginia in these tough economic times to take on that burden."[32] Darrell questioned the constitutional viability of public financing and noted that without other restrictive measures, "dark money" would continue to infiltrate judicial elections. King and Darrell suggested that public financing dollars be used for other purposes such as schools, roads and health care.

Without public financing and limited campaign dollars Darrell relied on grassroots campaigning and support from labor. From the filing at the end of January to the May election Darrell spent twelve to fourteen hours a day attending meetings and greeting voters in all parts of the state. Forums, Meet the Candidates, spaghetti dinners, ramp dinners, pancake breakfasts, town halls, rallies, receptions, fund raisers, radio and television shows, steak fries, bean dinners and picnics filled the long days and evenings.

For the most part people were positive and encouraged Darrell to ignore the negative ads. But people who attend election events tend to be engaged in the political process and knowledgeable about the issues. These engaged voters are not representative of individuals who are most often influenced by what they see and hear in commercials. Television and the internet ads are now the drivers of how people vote. The frequency of the ads and the appeal of the ad to the voters' own prejudices are game changers. Accuracy and truth are often maligned.

Ten days before the election a poll showed Darrell in the lead. The Republican State Leadership Committee (RSLC), through its Judicial Fairness Initiative, determined to reverse Darrell's lead and unleashed $750,000 in ads for Walker's behalf and $1.9 million on ads against Darrell and Wooten. The primary purpose of the Republican State Leadership Committee, located in Florida and funded by such corporate entities as the Koch brothers, tobacco, drug and insurance companies and the Chamber of Commerce, is the election of individuals who support their interests.[33]

Outraged by the RSLC involvement in the election, Wooten demanded of Walker whether she wanted to be viewed as being a 'purchased justice:' "The RSLC is funded by dark-money from Washington D.C. promoting your candidacy and attacking my reputation. They seem to believe, as Don Blankenship did 12 years ago, that they can purchase a seat on West Virginia's Supreme Court for a candidate who will do their bidding… At this moment, your integrity is called into question, while the integrity of the Court upon which you wish to serve is threatened, as well."[34] Even with Wooten's admonishment, Walker did not object to the involvement of RSLC in the election of a justice for WV's highest court.

The West Virginia Chamber spent almost $220,000 on Walker's behalf. West Virginia for Fair Courts, a PAC established a few weeks before the election by Greg Thomas, former Don Blankenship aide, spent

$228,025 for mailers. West Virginia for Fair Courts received contributions from the American Tort Reform Association ($170,000) and from West Virginia Citizens Against Lawsuit Abuse ($50,000).[35] Moving West Virginia Forward Business and Industry Council PAC spent nearly $55,000 on radio ads. Walker's campaign spent almost $700,000 in the election. Walker's campaign ads depicted Walker as a law and order judge who would lock up criminals, dope dealers even though "locking of the criminals" is not under the purview of a justice. Walker's ads appealed to the voters' prejudice.

Known expenditures in support of Walker's election approached $4 million. The dark money made the odds for success insurmountable.[36] Darrell campaign was financed with only $128,612 which included a personal loan of $18,360.[37] The television, radio and the internet were inundated with ads of Darrell robbing the state piggy bank or the family flying away in a state paid jet for a European vacation or ads linking Darrell and Obama as bad for coal and bad for WV. The ads were false, but the vote confirmed that people believed what they saw and heard. The basic tenant that truth matters did not prevail in this election, rather it was all about appealing to the voters' prejudices and attaching a name to it.

In a recent study a creative research agency conducted experiments on voter emotion related to commercials, or how messages impact ultimate voter support. Using electroencephalograms, galvanic skin responses, micro facial recognition and eye tracking, the research found there was a difference between who someone intellectualizes they support and the subliminal emotional impact of ads on who they might actually vote to elect. The study concluded that negative ads and messaging have a greater emotional interest and level of attentiveness than those messages and ads that provide factual, more 'boring' messages.[38] -Although inconclusive, the study bodes poorly for office holders who have a great record but lack money to produce voluminous commercials that appeal to the voter's prejudices.

The negative messages in the 2016 judicial election were effective in appealing to the voters prejudices: "I (Walker) will lock up all the criminals and throw away the key" (safety); "I (Walker) will bring conservative values back to the office" (security vs unknown); "My opponent (Darrell) is stealing from taxpayers; i.e. the 'state piggy bank for personal use'" (honesty), and "Darrell used a state jet for a family vacation" (morality).

The message framed by the dark money convinced the electorate that Darrell was bad for West Virginia. Walker won a decisive victory with Darrell in second place. The election saw many, many millions from big business and out of state corporate interests coordinated to elect Beth Walker: "Outside groups...dished out more than $3.5 million in a West Virginia Supreme Court race featuring five candidates. Eighty-six percent of that money, over $3 million benefited Beth Walker, who coasted to victory with almost 40 percent of the vote..."

"When the influence of wealthy individuals and corporations enters our courtrooms, West Virginians pay the price with a state government that fails to take into account the needs of all our citizens."[39]— *Natalie Thomas, West Virginia Citizens for Clean Elections*

The New State Supreme Court

Was this new state Supreme Court with Beth Walker, as the newly elected justice, still a circus masquerading as a court? This answer was not long in coming.

Shortly after Walker joined the state Court, a case was brought by mineral owners against EQT, a gas company. The plaintiffs argued that EQT wrongly deducted post-production expenses before paying owners their one-eighth royalty.[40] The gas drillers deducted a variety of expenses including transportation and processing of gas from the payments they owed to the WV resident land owners. Just a few months earlier the state Court, without Justice Walker, held the mineral owners correct and that gas drillers must pay to property owners the agreed upon contract production amounts without the deduction of expenses. Things changed in early 2017 when Justice Walker cast a pivotal vote to reconsider the EQT case. This "new" court then reversed the prior ruling and sided with the industry and against residents. Justice Walker voted for the gas companies at the same time her husband owned stock in a variety of energy companies, "including those participating in WV's growing gas boom."[41]

Plaintiffs argued that "[Justice] Walker should not have taken part in the vote to grant the hearing and that she should have disqualified herself from any consideration of the issue because her husband, Michael Walker, owned stock in natural gas and energy companies." [42] Justice Walker received a $500,000 loan from Michael Walker during her campaign for the Court, but the plaintiffs' argument was ignored. Walker voted for EQT in a case that potentially benefited her husband. [43]

In early 2018 an investigative report and state audit cited concerns related to Justices Davis, Loughry and Ketchum. Lavish expenditures by the Justices Davis and Loughry were uncovered. An office renovation for Justice Davis exceeded $500,000. Davis' office renovation included glass countertops, door and floor cost of $90,000 and rugs priced out at over $28,000. [44] Justice Loughry's office renovation exceeded $363,000 including an oversized blue suede hide couch that cost $32,000. [45] Loughry also authorized the construction of an inlaid wooden map of West Virginia on his office floor. "Each of the counties [55] is made of a different kind of wood. His home county, Tucker, is made of blue granite." [46]

A subsequent Legislative audit uncovered more concerns. [47] The audit revealed that Justice Loughry took a state-owned antique desk, a 1927 Cass Gilbert era desk, valued at $42,000 to his private residence, and that he utilized state vehicles and taxpayer paid rental cars for his personal travel. Legislative Manager Aaron Allred, noting that Justice Loughry was most uncooperative with legislative auditors, recommended an ethics investigation of Justice Loughry's conduct. The "new" Court voted to remove Loughry as Chief Justice in February, 2018 perhaps thinking the removal of Loughry as Chief Justice might put an end to the investigation. [48]

However, talk of impeachment and calls for investigation of Loughry swirled during the 2018 Legislative session. [49] Ultimately, the Legislature passed a resolution for an amendment that "would provide greater legislative oversight for the court systems' budget. Voters would have to approve the proposed amendment to the state Constitution during November's election." [50]

On June 6, 2018 the state Judicial Investigation Committee filed a 32-count complaint with the state Supreme Court finding there is probable cause "to believe Loughry violated judicial codes of conduct," and recommended Loughry's immediate suspension.[51] On June 8, 2018, the West Virginia Supreme Court, comprised of specially appointed justices, suspended Loughry from the bench "over allegations that he repeatedly lied and used his public office for personal gain."[52] Loughry was suspended without pay for the duration of proceedings stemming from the 32 charges that he violated the WV Judicial Code of Conduct.[53]

The Legislative audit also uncovered that Justice Ketchum used a court vehicle to commute to and from his home in Huntington for four and a half years and charged gas purchases totaling $12,250 to the state.[54]

On June 20, 2018 a federal grand jury indicted Justice Loughry on 22 counts of fraud, lying and witness tampering. The indictment stemmed from federal investigations which included Loughry's statements when he met with federal investigators regarding the spending of fellow justices and the court administrator. In announcing the indictment U.S Attorney Mike Stuart responded to questions whether other justices are under investigation: "I'm sure there are a whole lot of people that would like Justice Loughry to be indicted and go down in a great ball of flames and, somehow, the rest of the court escapes uncharged. I don't know whether there will be charges in the future, but I can tell you that we're interested in public corruption....We'll let the facts lead us to where the facts lead us."[55]

On July, 11, 2018, in a state Supreme Court news release, Justice Menis Ketchum announced his retirement from the state Court.

On August 13, 2018 the West Virginia House of Delegates impeached Justices Davis Loughry, Walker and Workman for abuse of their authority stating "they failed to control office expenses, including more than $1 million in renovations to their individual office and not maintaining policies over matters such as working lunches and use of state vehicles and office computers at home." Loughry was impeached on 8 articles. [56]

On August 13, 2018, Justice Robin Davis, facing the possibility of an impeachment trial in the Senate, resigned.[57]

On August 22, 2018 Justice Menis Ketchum pleaded guilty to a felony count of wire fraud related to his personal use of a state vehicle and gas fuel card.

On October 2, 2018 the Republican majority Senate voted to censor Justice Walker for improper spending state funds and poorly managing the Courts administrative affairs, but declined to remove her from office.[58] The Senate's decision did not consider Justice Walker's conflicted vote in the EQT case.

On October 11, 2018, a temporarily panel of 5 circuit court judges, sitting as the WV Supreme Court, issued an injunction blocking the impeachment trial of Justice Workman stating a violation of the separation of powers doctrine. The House of Delegates and Senate leadership appealed to the state Court's decision to the U. S. Supreme Court.

On October 13, 2018 Justice Loughry was found guilty on 11 counts including wire fraud, making false statements to federal investigators, witness tampering and mail fraud.[59]

On November 12, 2018 Justice Loughry resigned from the state Court.

On February 13, 2019 ex-Justice Loughry was sentenced to 24 months in federal prison.[60]

On March 6, 2019 Justice Menis Ketchum was sentenced to a $20,000 fine and ordered to serve 3 years of probation.[61]

On October 7, 2019 the U.S. Supreme Court listed the West Virginia House of Delegates and Senate case under "certiorari denied," which means the Court decided not to hear the case.[62] The U.S. Supreme Court's decision meant the state Supreme Court's injunction preventing the Senate from proceeding with impeachment hearings against Workman remained in place. Justice Workman, who was perhaps swept into the Legislative impeachment fray by the Republican majority, said, "For my whole 30 years serving in the judicial branch, I have always tried to serve with integrity and honesty and fairness."[63]

Chapter XX   Epilogue—Staying in the Arena

Darrell, Jr. and Darrell IV

Warren, Wyoming Circuit Court

"Good work my son, good work"

The McGraw brothers' worked to live by their duty to make life better for others. There were no great monetary riches. They simply acted upon what they were taught was the culturally right thing to do. They never forgot the words they were taught as children, "of one blood are all people." It was the Berea College way.

Resistance to progress often comes from those who have something to benefit, usually power or money. There are always those who have much to gain—those who resist mine safety regulation and enforcement, strip mining regulation, black lung benefits, coal severance taxes, state Supreme Court decisions that protect workers' rights and safety, health, juvenile rights, mental health care, employee pensions and all types of consumer litigation cases including tobacco, drug, insurance, pay day lenders, mortgage firms.

Under the public microscope for over 50 years, the McGraw brothers were never on the sidelines, and their core values based on faith and duty guided their work. By no means, the McGraw brothers were not perfect. But they were, as Teddy Roosevelt saw the role of a citizen, always in the arena striving:

It is not the critic who counts;
not the man who points out how the strong man stumbles, or where
the doer of deeds could have done them better.
The credit belongs to the man who is actually in the arena, whose
face is marred by dust and sweat and blood; who strives valiantly;
who errs, who comes short again and again, because
there is no effort without error and shortcoming, but
who does actually strive to do the deeds;
who knows great enthusiasms, the great devotions;
who spends himself in a worthy cause;
who at the best knows in the end the triumph of high achievement,
and
who at the worst, if he fails, at least fails while daring greatly, so that
his place shall never be with those cold and timid souls who neither
know victory nor defeat.[1]

For the McGraws, life was not easy, but it was pretty wonderful. And in times of great stress, the writings of Joseph Campbell provided encouragement to duty above personal consequence, and ring true for all, including the McGraws, who need to remain in the arena striving to make the world a better place:

The hero emerges from humble beginnings to undertake a journey
fraught with trials and suffering. He or she survives those ordeals and
returns to the community bearing a gift — a "boon," as Campbell called
it — in the form of a message from which people can learn and benefit.
So, properly, the hero is an exceptional person who gives his life over to
a purpose larger than himself and for the benefit of others.[2]

Charleston Gazette Publisher Ned Chilton established and adhered to a philosophy of "sustained outrage" against injustice. *Gazette* Editor Don Marsh shared and applied Chilton's philosophy to fight against social injustice. Chilton and Marsh were heroes by Campbell's definition. Their voices were major factors for progressive reform in West Virginia. The Berea pennant did not hang in the bedroom of Marsh or Chilton, but they lived their lives with the understanding that "of one blood are all people". Their work and the McGraw brothers' stories are inspirational. They stimulate us to rethink our role as a citizen—our duty to others; our duty to be informed; our duty to speak out against wrongdoers, and our duty to stay in the arena.

Don Marsh was Darrell's friend. Marsh's guidance on social issues carried weight with our family, and brought encouragement in some of the darkest hours. Like Ned Chilton, Don Marsh made a positive difference, and perhaps Marsh saw the same in the McGraw brothers when he said:

"So the future is unclear. The past isn't. Things in West Virginia after the McGraws will never be quite the same as they were before them."[3]—*Don Marsh (1922-1999)*

End Notes

Preface
[1] Frank Getlein, "TV Civic Lesson," *Washington Evening Star,* April 23, 1973.

Prologue
[1] Otis Rice and Stephen W. Brown, *West Virginia A History,* 2nd Edition (University of Kentucky Press, 1993), 57-58.
[2] https://www.statista.com/statistics/296501/revenue-coal-mining-in-the-us/, and "Newsmax," http://www.newsmax.com/FastFeatures/industries-in-west-virginia-economy/2015/04/03/id/636341/.
[3] Bryce Gerad, "A Natural Resource Curse: Does It Exist Within the United States?" Claremont McKinley Student Scholarly Thesis, 2011, https://scholarship.claremont.edu/cmc_theses/158/.
[4] Allan Greenblatt, "Different Energy Boom, Same Mistakes," *Governing,* July, 2018, https://www.governing.com/topics/transportation-infrastructure/gov-gas-boom-west-virginia.html.
[5] Richie Bernardo, "2017's Happiest States in America," and "2017's Best & Worst State Economies," http://wallethub.com/edu/states-with-the-best-economies/21697.
[6] "Demographic and Economy Indicators," Henry Kaiser Foundation, http://kff.org/state-category/demographics-and-the-economy/.
[7] "Health Status Indicators," Henry Kaiser Foundation, http://kff.org/state-category/health-status/ and Demographic and Economy Indicators, Henry Kaiser Foundation, http://kff.org/state-category/demographics-and-the-economy/.
[8] "America's Most and Least Educated States," *Huffington Post,* September 9, 2016, http://www.huffingtonpost.com/entry/americas-most-and-least-educated-states_us_57dc22f2e4b053b1ccf2990f.
[9] Phil Kabler, "Lawmakers End Special Session with Budget, PEIA Bills," *Charleston Gazette,* June 14, 2016, http://www.wvgazettemail.com/news-politics/20160614/wv-lawmakers-end-special-session-with-budget-peia-bills.
[10] Otis Rice, *West Virginia A History,* University Press of Kentucky, 1985, 278-288 and Curt Brown, "West Virginia Establishment: The Affluent in Total Control," and Roderick Harless, "The Establishment—Informational and Interpretive Report About West Virginia Establishment," *Sunday Gazette-Mail,* February 7, 1971, 1D.
[11] Rice, *A West Virginia History,* 188.

Chapter I
[1] Mary K. Bowman, *Reference Book of Wyoming County History,* 1965, 475.
[2] "History of West Virginia Mining Industries—Coal," http://www.wvgs.wvnet.edu/www/geology/geoldvco.htm.
[3] Mary K. Bowman, *Reference Book of Wyoming County History.*
[4] McGraw Family Document.
[5] Ibid.
[6] *The West Virginia Capitol: A Commemorative History,* WV Legislature Publication, June 20, 1892, and December, 1995.
[7] Bob Miller, *Broken Bodies and Shattered Dreams: Coal and Corporate Control of West Virginia—A Research Study,* circa 1972, 7.
[8] Lyle Roelofs and Linda Strong-Lee, *The Courier-Journal,* March 8, 2016.
[9] John Prine, *Paradise, http://www.azlyrics.com/lyrics/johnprine/paradise.html.*
[10] Miller, *Broken Bodies and Shattered Dreams,* 28.
[11] Ibid.
[12] Ibid.

[13] Ibid.

[14] Ibid, 29-30.

[15] Ibid.

[16] Henry D. Hatfield, *E-WV,* https://www.wvencyclopedia.org/articles/280.

[17] Rebecca McGraw Thaxton, "Interview with Warren McGraw," Beckley, West Virginia.

[18] Paul F. Lutz, "Governor Marland's Political Suicide: The Severance Tax," *West Virginia History,* Volume 40, No. 1, Fall 1978, 13-27.

[19] Bud Perry and Karl C. Lilly III, *Reopening Glen Rogers*, Pal Productions, circa 1980, Tad WV. 95.

[20] Ibid.

[21] Ibid.

[22] Lutz, "Governor Marland's Political Suicide: The Severance Tax."

[23] Beth Spence, "Whatever Happened to *Pauley v. Bailey:* The Story of Political Corruption,*"* 1998, *http://files.eric.ed.gov/fulltext/ED426839.pdf.*

[24] Perry and Lilly, *Reopening Glen Rogers.*

[25] Tim Murphy, "The Epic Rise and Fall of America's Most Notorious Coal Baron," *Mother Jones,* September 30, 2015.

[26] Robert Lenzner and Matthew Miller, "Buying Justice," *Forbes,* July 21, 2003, 64.

[27] West Virginia Code, Section 49-5-16.

[28] Steve Mullins, "Juveniles' Testimony Confirmed," *Charleston Daily Mail,* October 17, 1979, 1A.

[29] Richard Grimes, "Crisis Brings Results: Attention to Jails,*" Charleston Daily Mail.*

[30] Gene R. Nichol, "Dialectical Federalism: A Tribute to the West Virginia Supreme Court of Appeals," College of William and Mary Law School, William and Mary Law School Scholarly Repository, 907, 1987, and *West Virginia Law Review,* 1987, 91-107.

Chapter II

[1] Larry Leroy Layne, "Affidavit," May 05, 2016, http://www.post-gazette.com/powersource/policy-powersource/2016/09/01/Lawsuit-seeks-to-fix-blame-for-Farmington-mine-disaster-1/stories/201609010159?pgpageversion=pgevoke, and Bonnie Stewart, "No. 9: The 1968 Farmington Mine Disaster," WVU Press, November, 2011.

[2] Len Boselovic, "Almost 50 years Later, Lawsuit Seeks to Fix Blame for Farmington Mine Disaster," *Pittsburg Post-Gazette,* Sept. 1, 2016, http://www.post-gazette.com/powersource/policy-powersource/2016/09/01/Lawsuit-seeks-to-fix-blame-for-Farmington-mine-disaster-1/stories/201609010159?pgpageversion=pgevoke.

[3] Ibid.

[4] Larry Leroy Layne, "Affidavit."

[5] Boselovic, "Almost 50 years Later, Lawsuit Seeks to Fix Blame for Farmington Mine Disaster."

[6] Paul Nyden, "Rank-and-file Rebellions in the Coalfields, 1964-1980," *Monthly Review*, Vol 58, Issue 10, March 2007.

[7] Boselovic, Almost 50 years Later, Lawsuit Seeks to Fix Blame for Farmington Mine disaster."

[8] Paul Nyden, *Miners for Democracy,* PhD Dissertation, Columbia University, 1974 (original) and 1982 (abridged).

[9] Larry Leroy Layne, "Affidavit."

[10] Ibid.

[11] Boselovic, "Almost 50 years Later, Lawsuit Seeks to Fix Blame for Farmington Mine Disaster."

[12] Ibid.

[13] *Michael D. Michael, Administrator of Estate of Jack D. Michael, et. al. v. Consolidation Coal,* June 5, 2019, http://www.courtswv.gov/supreme-court/docs/spring2019/18-0725.pdf.

[14] Joel Ebert, "Assassination of Activist in 1969 Changed Unions," *Charleston Daily Mail,* Dec., 30, 2014.

[15] Richard Fry, "Making Amends: Coal Miners, Black Lung Association and Federal Compensation Reform, 1969-1971," http://www.shfg.org/resources/Documents/FH%205%20(2013)%20Fry.pdf.

[16] Edward Peeks, "Force Legislature, Doctors Tell Miners," *Charleston Gazette,* January 12, 1969, 8C.

381

[17] "Black Lung Strike," *WV State Archives,* 1969.
[18] Fry, "Making Amends: Coal Miners, Black Lung Association and Federal Compensation Reform, 1969-1971."
[19] Edward Peeks, "UMW, Doctors, Operators Hit," *Charleston Gazette,* January 27, 1969, 1A.
[20] Nyden, "Rank-and-file Rebellions in the Coalfields."
[21] Ibid.
[22] Don Marsh, "Former Miners Felt Black Lung Law's Tragedy," *Charleston Gazette,* Feb. 12, 1969, 1A.
[23] Edward Peeks, "West Virginia Acting 40 Years Late," *Charleston Gazette,* February 12, 1969, 15A.
[24] Ibid.
[25] Nyden, "Rank-and-file Rebellions in the Coalfields, 1964-1980."
[26] Ibid.
[27] Ibid.
[28] Ibid.
[29] Ibid.
[30] Associated Press, "State Strike Spread for Black Lung Help," *Charleston Gazette,* Feb. 20, 1969, 1A.
[31] Don Marsh, "House Shows Mixed Coal Strike View," *Charleston Gazette,* February 22, 1969, 1A.
[32] "Best Practices for Dust Control in Mines," *National Institute for Occupational Safety and Health,* https://www.cdc.gov/niosh/mining/UserFiles/works/pdfs/2010-110.pdf.
[33] Don Marsh, "Coal Miners Vow March on Capitol," *Charleston Gazette,* February 24, 1969, 1A.
[34] Fanny Seiler, "Senate Race Features Abolitionist Versus Stripper," *Charleston Gazette,* May 5, 1972, 1B.
[35] "Black Lung Strike," *WV State Archives,* and "Black Lung Strike, 1969," *YouTube, https://www.youtube.com/watch?v=E8TM7AMvhNs.*
[36] Don Marsh, "Black Lung Proposals Sail Through House," *Charleston Gazette,* March 1, 1969, 1A.
[37] Don Marsh, "Both Houses Okay Black Lung Act," *Sunday Gazette-Mail,* March 9, 1969, 1A.
[38] "Federal Coal Mine Health and Safety Act," *Wikipedia,* https://en.wikipedia.org/wiki/Federal_Coal_Mine_Health_and_Safety_Act_of_1969.
[39] Elyssa East, "Black Lung Disease is Still Killing Miners: The Coal Industry Doesn't Want to Hear It," December 13, 2018, https://www.theguardian.com/us-news/2018/dec/13/dr-dust-the-man-who-discovered-a-hidden-black-lung-epidemic.
[40] Chris Hamby, "The New Face of Black Lung," *Sunday Gazette-Mail,* July 8, 2012, E1.
[41] Ken Ward, "Miners Say UBB Mine Cheated on Dust Sampling," *Sunday Gazette-Mail,* 1E, https://publicintegrity.org/workers-rights/miners-say-upper-big-branch-mine-cheated-on-dust-sampling/.
[42] Chris Hamby, "The New Face of Black Lung."
[43] Ibid.
[44] Chris Hamby, "Black Lung Surges Back in Coal Country, *Center for Public Integrity*, July 8, 2012, https://publicintegrity.org/workers-rights/black-lung-surges-back-in-coal-country/.
[45] *Thomas Jefferson to Abbe Arnoux,* 1789. ME 7:423, Papers 15:283, https://famguardian.org/subjects/politics/thomasjefferson/jeff1200.htm.
[46] "Continued Increase in Prevalence of Coal Workers Pneumoconiosis in the US 1970-2017," American Public Health Association, September, 2018, https://ajph.aphapublications.org/doi/10.2105/AJPH.2018.304517.
[47] Howard Berkes, "Black Lung Rule Loopholes Leave Miners Vulnerable," *NPR,* July 10, 2018, https://www.npr.org/2012/07/10/155981916/black-lung-rule-loopholes-leave-miners-vulnerable.
[48] Howard Berkes, "An Epidemic is Killing Thousands of Coal Miners. Regulators Could Have Stopped It," *All Things Considered NPR,* December 18, 2018, https://www.npr.org/2018/12/18/675253856/an-epidemic-is-killing-thousands-of-coal-miners-regulators-could-have-stopped-it.
[49] Nadja Popovich, "Black Lung Comes Storming Back in Coal Country, *New York Times,* February 22, 2018, https://www.nytimes.com/interactive/2018/02/22/climate/black-lung-resurgence.html.
[50] Berkes, "An Epidemic is Killing Thousands of Coal Miners."
[51] Chris Hamby, "Breathless and Burdened: Coal Industries Go To Law Firm Withheld Evidence of Black Lung At Expense of Sick Miners, *Center for Public Integrity,* October 29, 2013,

382

https://publicintegrity.org/environment/coal-industrys-go-to-law-firm-withheld-evidence-of-black-lung-at-expense-of-sick-miners/, and Chris Hamby, "Breathless and Burdened: John Hopkins Medical Unit Rarely Finds Black Lung Helping Coal Industry Defeat Miners' Claims," *Center for Public Integrity,* October 30, 2013, https://publicintegrity.org/environment/johns-hopkins-medical-unit-rarely-finds-black-lung-helping-coal-industry-defeat-miners-claims/, and Chris Hamby, "Breathless and Burdened: As Experts Recognize a New Form of Black Lung Coal Industry Follows Familiar Pattern of Denial, *Center for Public Integrity,* November 1, 2013, https://publicintegrity.org/environment/as-experts-recognize-new-form-of-black-lung-coal-industry-follows-familiar-pattern-of-denial/.

[52] Hamby, "Breathless and Burdened: Coal Industries Go To Law Firm Withheld Evidence of Black Lung At Expense of Sick Miners."

[53] Ibid.

[54] "Rule 3.3: Candor Toward the Tribunal," *American Bar Association*, https://www.americanbar.org/groups/professional_responsibility/publications/model_rules_of_professional_conduct/rule_3_3_candor_toward_the_tribunal/.

[55] Hamby, "Breathless and Burdened: Coal Industries Go To Law Firm Withheld Evidence of Black Lung At Expense of Sick Miners."

[56] Ibid.

[57] Steve Sanders, "Fourth Circuit Fails to Find Fraud on the Court," *Devil in the Dust Black Lung Blog, http://www.blacklungblog.com/2014/01/fourth-circuit-fails-to-find-fraud-on-the-court-fox-ex-rel-fox-v-elk-run-coal-co-inc-f-3d-2014-wl-26556-4th-cir-jan-3-2014/,* and *Fox ex rel. Fox v. Elk Run Coal Co., Inc.,* — F.3d —, 2014 WL 26556 (4th Cir. Jan. 3, 2014).

[58] Hamby, "Breathless and Burdened: Coal Industries Go To Law Firm Withheld Evidence of Black Lung At Expense of Sick Miners."

[59] Hamby, "Breathless and Burdened: John Hopkins Medical Unit Rarely Finds Black Lung Helping Industry Defeat Miners."

[60] Matthew Mosk, "Amid Controversy, Johns Hopkins Quietly Drops Black Lung Program," *ABC News,* September 30, 2015, https://abcnews.go.com/US/amid-controversy-johns-hopkins-quietly-drops-black-lung/story?id=34161753.

[61] Hamby, "Breathless and Burdened: As Experts Recognize a New Form of Black Lung Coal Industry Follows Familiar Pattern of Denial."

[62] Evan B. Smith "Fourth Circuit Affirms Award of benefits to Ted Latusek," Devil in the Dust Black Lung Blog, January 9, 2018, http://www.blacklungblog.com/2018/01/fourth-circuit-affirms-award-of-benefits-to-ted-latusek-after-24-years-of-litigation-and-attention-from-pulitzer-prize-winning-reporting-consolidation-coal-co-v-latusek/, and *Consolidated Coal vs. Latusek,* No. 16, 1768.

[63] Hamby, "Breathless and Burdened: As Experts Recognize a New Form of Black Lung Coal Industry Follows Familiar Pattern of Denial."

[64] *Consolidated Coal vs. Latusek.*

[65] Joseph A. Jock Yablonski Historical Marker, http://explorepahistory.com/hmarker.php?markerId=1-A-2C9.

[66] Nyden, "Rank and File Rebellions in the Coal Field, 1964-1980."

[67] Wolfgang Saxon, "W.A. Boyle Dies, Led Miners Union," *New York Times,* June 1, 1985.

[68] "United Mine Workers Killings," *This Day in History,* January 1, 1970, http://www.history.com/this-day-in-history/the-united-mine-workers-killings.

[69] Joe Dalton, "The Yablonski Legacy," *The Harvard Crimson,* March 20, 1976; Trevor Armbrister, *Act of Vengeance* E.P. Dutton and Co., 340; Wolfgang Saxon, " W.A. Boyle Dies, Led Miners' Union," *New York Times,* June 1, 1985 and Joel Ebert, "Assassination of Activist in 1969 Changed Unions," *Charleston Daily Mail*, Dec. 30, 2014.

[70] Ibid.

[71] Ibid.

[72] Nyden, "Rank-and-File Rebellions in the Coalfields, 1964-1980."

[73] Daryl Worthington, "Cronyism, Mining and Muscle—The Death of Jock Yablonski," *New History,* January 04, 2016, http://www.newhistorian.com/cronyism-mining-and-murder-the-death-of-jock-yablonski/5708/, and

383

"United Mine Workers Killings," *This Day in History,* January 1, 1970, http://www.history.com/this-day-in-history/the-united-mine-workers-killings.

[74] Richard Robbins, "1969 Yablonski Murders Spurred Union Reforms," *Pittsburg Tribune,* Dec. 27, 2009, http://triblive.com/x/pittsburghtrib/news/regional/s_659597.html.

[75] Ibid.

[76] Rebecca McGraw Thaxton, "Interview Warren R. McGraw," Beckley, West Virginia, Nov. 23, 2016.

[77] "United Mine Workers Killings," *This Day in History,* January 1, 1970, http://www.history.com/this-day-in-history/the-united-mine-workers-killings; Richard Robbins, "1969 Yablonski Murders Spurred Union Reforms," *Pittsburg Tribunes,* Dec. 27, 2009, http://triblive.com/x/pittsburghtrib/news/regional/s_659597.html; Dalton, The Yablonski Legacy;" and Armbrister, *Act of Vengeance.*

[78] Ebert, "Assassination of Activist in 1969 Changed Unions."

[79] "W.A. Boyle," *Wikipedia:* https://en.wikipedia.org/wiki/W._A._Boyle, and David J. Krajicek, "United Mine Workers of America Boss Tony Boyle Sends Goons to Kill Rival Jock Yablonski and Family," *New York Daily News,* January 5, 2013, http://www.nydailynews.com/news/justice-story/union-boss-kills-rival-coal-blood-article-1.1234034.

[80] Nyden, "Rank-and-File Rebellions in the Coalfields, 1964-1980."

[81] Laurence Leamer, "The United Mine Workers hold an election," *New York Times,* Nov. 26, 1972, http://www.nytimes.com/1972/11/26/archives/article-9-no-title-the-united-mine-workers-holds-an-election.html?_r=0.

[82] Ibid, and "Arnold Miller," *West Virginia Archives and History,* http://www.wvculture.org/history/labor/millerarnold02.html.

[83] Stuart Ditzen, "Deadly Union Rivalry Capped 60's," *Philly.Com,* December 26, 1999, http://articles.philly.com/1999-12-26/news/25479905_1_jock-yablonski-tony-boyle-killers, and "Jock Yablonski:" *Wikipedia, https://en.wikipedia.org/wiki/Joseph_Yablonski.*

[84] Mary Walton, "Rallying Miners Angrily Confront UMW Officials," *Charleston Gazette,* February 11, 1971, 1A.

[85] Harry Hoffman, "The Rockefeller Bill," *Charleston Gazette,* February 1, 1971, 4A.

[86] Mary Walton, "Strip Hearing Emotions High," *Charleston Gazette,* February 16, 1971, 1A.

[87] "Big Muskie:" *Wikipedia,* https://en.m.wikipedia.org/wiki.

[88] "About Coal Mining Impacts," *Greenpeace,* July 1, 2016, *http://www.greenpeace.org/international/en/campaigns/climate-change/coal/Coal-mining-impacts/.*

[89] Goodell, "The Dark Lord of Coal Country."

[90] Michael Shnayerson, "The Rape of Appalachia," *Vanity Fair,* November 20, 2006.

[91] Goodell, "The Dark Lord of Coal Country."

[92] Tim Murphy, "The Epic Rise and Fall of America's Most Notorious Coal Baron."

[93] Associated Press, "Brotherton Amendment Bruised, But No Dead," *Charleston Gazette,* March 11, 1971, 1A.

[94] Tom Miller, "Who Owns West Virginia," *Herald Dispatch,* 1974, 23.

[95] Ibid.

[96] Garry J. Moes, "New Strip Bill Praised, Chastised," *Charleston Gazette,* March 13, 1971, 2A.

[97] Nelson Sorah, "37 Killed in Logan Flooding, Higher Death Toll is Expected," *Sunday Gazette-Mail,* February 27, 1972, 1A and Nelson Sorah, "Flood Toll 60, Confusion Reigns," *Charleston Gazette,* February 28, 1972 1A.

[98] Ibid.

[99] "Buffalo Creek Disaster," *Coal History, https://www.pophistorydig.com/topics/buffalo-creek-disaster-1972/.*

[100] "Buffalo Creek," West Virginia Division of Culture and History, http://www.wvculture.org/history/buffcreek/frmngtn.html.

[101] "Buffalo Creek Disaster."

[102] Ibid.

[103] "Buffalo Creek," *WV State Archives,* 2015, and "Buffalo Creek Flood and Disaster: Official Report from

384

the Governor's Ad Hoc Commission of Inquiry," West Virginia Archives and History, 1973.
[104] "Buffalo Creek," West Virginia Division of Culture and History, http://www.wvculture.org/history/buffcreek/frmngtn.html.
[105] "40 Years Later: The Buffalo Creek Disaster Its Aftermath," *Daily Kos,* February 7, 2012: http://www.dailykos.com/story/2012/2/7/1062372/-40-Years-Later-The-Buffalo-Creek-Disaster-Its-Aftermath.
[106] Fanny Seiler, "House Bill Asks Check, Action on 'Killer Dams,'" *Charleston Gazette,* Mar. 2 1972, 1A.
[107] "Buffalo Creek:" *Wikipedia:* https://en.wikipedia.org/wiki/Buffalo_Creek_flood.
[108] Paul Nyden, *Miners for Democracy: Struggle in the Coal Fields.* PhD Dissertation: Columbia University, 1974, and *Coal Patrol,* 21, May 1, 1972, 1-3.
[109] "Buffalo Creek Disaster."
[110] Ibid.
[111] "Buffalo Creek," *Wikipedia.*
[112] "Buffalo Creek Disaster."
[113] "Buffalo Creek," WV State Archives, 2015.
[114] "Buffalo Creek Disaster."
[115] "Buffalo Creek," WV State Archives, 2015.
[116] Ibid.
[117] "40 Years Later: The Buffalo Creek Disaster Its Aftermath."
[118] Fanny Seiler, "Death Knell Sounds Loud in House Action," *Charleston Gazette,* March 4, 1972, 1A, *https://www.theatlantic.com/politics/archive/2014/05/trust-your-state-government/362044/ston.*
[119] "If Elected," *Chicago Times: http://articles.chicagotribune.com/keyword/national-coal-association.*
[120] Robert Welling, "Legislature Enters Final Week; Wallace to Speak," *Charleston Gazette,* March 6, 1972, 1A.
[121] "About Coal Mining Impacts," *Greenpeace,* July 1, 2016, *http://www.greenpeace.org/international/en/campaigns/climate-change/coal/Coal-mining-impacts/.*
[122] Brad Plumer, "Why Trump Just Killed a Rule Restricting Coal Companies from Dumping Waste into Streams," *Vox,* February, 16, 2017 https://www.vox.com/2017/2/2/14488448/stream-protection-rule.
[123] Christopher Mele, "What is Coal Ash and Why is it Dangerous," *New York Times,* September 9, 2018, https://www.nytimes.com/2018/09/21/us/coal-ash-spill-dam-breach.html
[124] "Mapping the Coal Ash Containment Sites," *Earth Justice,* November 6, 2019, https://earthjustice.org/features/map-coal-ash-contaminated-sites
[125] 40 Years Later: The Buffalo Creek Disaster Its Aftermath."
[126] Nadja Popovich, Livia Albeck-Ripka and Kendra Pierre-Louis, "85 Environmental Rules Being Rolled Back by Trump," *New York Times,* September 12, 2019, https://www.nytimes.com/interactive/2019/climate/trump-environment-rollbacks.html.
[127] "Trust in Government 1958-2016," *Pew Research Center,* November 23, 2015, http://www.people-press.org/2015/11/23/1-trust-in-government-1958-2015/.
[128] John Tierney, "Do You Trust Your State Government?" *The Atlantic,* May 12, 2014.
[129] "Brazil Dam Catastrophe Sounds Alarm for U.S. Waste Ponds, *Bloomberg Environment,* February 4, 2019, https://news.bloombergenvironment.com/environment-and-energy/brazil-dam-catastrophe-sounds-alarm-for-u-s-waste-ponds.
[130] "MSHA Approves Coal Slurry Impoundment Taller Than Hoover Dam," *Planetsave,* March 27, 2013, https://planetsave.com/2013/03/27/msha-approves-coal-slurry-impoundment-taller-than-hoover-dam/.

Chapter III
[1] Fanny Seiler, "Senate Race Features Abolitionist Versus Stripper," *Charleston Gazette,* May 5, 1972, 1B.
[2] "Matthew A. Reese Collection," Marshall University, Huntington, West Virginia.
[3] www.washingtonmonthly.com/people/Charles-peters/,2001.
[4] *Associated Press,* "Candid Reactions Are Good for the Public, McGraw Believes," *Charleston Gazette,* April 26, 1973, 8A.
[5] Ibid.

[6] Wayne Ewing, *If Elected,* www.ewingfilms.com.

[7] "Mailbag Conflict of Interest Not Hylton's Style, Eh?" *Raleigh Register*, November 6, 1972.

[8] Ibid.

[9] Ibid.

[10] *If Elected.*

[11] Ellis Bailey, "Letter to the Editor," *Raleigh Register,* October 30, 1972.

[12] "Mailbag Conflict of Interest Not Hylton's Style, Eh?" *Raleigh Register*, November 6, 1972.

[13] Wayne Ewing, *If Elected.*

[14] Adam Berstein, "Arch Moore, Jr., Charismatic WV Governor Convicted of Corruption, Dies at 91," *Washington Post,* January 8, 2015, https://www.washingtonpost.com/politics/arch-moore-jr-charismatic-wva-governor-convicted-of-corruption-dies-at-91/2015/01/08/e5857798-974d-11e4-927a-4fa2638cd1b0_story.html.

[15] Wayne Ewing, *If Elected.*

[16] Adam Clymen, "Thomas F. Eagleton, 77, A Running Mate for 18 Days, Dies," *New York Times,* 03/05/07, http://mobile.nytimes.com/2007/03/05/washinton/05eagleton.htm?r=08referer=https://www.google.com.

[17] Ben A. Franklin, "Rockefeller's WV Fund Nears 3 Million in Governor's Race," *New York Times,* October 27, 1976, http://www.nytimes.com/1976/10/27/archives/rockefellers-west-virginia-funds-near-3-million-in-governor-race.html?_r=0.

[18] Ben Franklin, "Rockefeller Outlays Stir West Virginia Concern," *New York Times*, June 2, 1984, www.nytimes.com/1984/06/02rockefeller-outlawys-stir-west-virginia-concern, and Ry Rivard, "Personal Wealth Doesn't Always Result in Wins," *Charleston Daily Mail, http://www.herald-dispatch.com/news/personal-wealth-doesn-t-always-result-in-wins/article_4d23d5da-56af-5b9f-b4b2-ede37a80c57d.html.*

[19] John O'Conner, "TV: One Man's Campaign," *New York Times,* 1973.

[20] Ibid.

[21] Frank Getlein, "TV Civic Lesson," *Washington Evening Star,* April 23, 1973.

[22] Darrell McGraw, "Personal Files Regarding Distribution of *If Elected,* and "Educational Films Don't Have to be Boring," *Washington Monthly, distributor,* 1973.

[23] "Film Boosted State's Image," *Charleston Gazette,* April 26, 1973.

[24] *Associated Press,* "Candid Reactions Are Good for Public, McGraw Believes," *Charleston Gazette,* April 26, 1973, 8A.

[25] Robert Harmel, Matthew Giebert and Kenneth Janda, "American Parties in Context: Comparative and Historical Analysis," Routledge Publishers, 47-48, and "Text to Party Charter Adopted at Democratic Conference Following Compromise," *New York Times,* December 9, https://www.nytimes.com/1974/12/09/archives/text-of-party-charter-adopted-at-democratic-conference-following.html.

[26] Harry M. Caudill, *Watches of the Night,* Jesse Stuart Foundation, Ashland Kentucky, 1976, 203.

[27] John G. Morgan, "$23 Million Coal Severance Tax Bill Causes Senate Stir," *Charleston Gazette,* March 1, 1975, 1A.

[28] Ibid.

[29] John G. Morgan, "Senate Okays Severance Tax on Coal," *Charleston Gazette,* March 4, 1975, 1A.

[30] Rebecca McGraw Thaxton, "Warren McGraw Interview."

[31] Ibid.

[32] John G. Morgan, "Coal Tax Vote Foiled in Senate," *Charleston Gazette,* March 3, 1975, 1A.

[33] The Fairmont Coal Company, http://www.historyinsidepictures.com/Pages/TheFairmontCoalCompanyStory.aspx.

[34] John G. Morgan, "Senate Okays Severance Tax on Coal," *Charleston Gazette,* March 4, 1975, 1A.

[35] Ibid.

[36] Ibid.

[37] Richard Grimes, "Coal Tax Increase Chances Brighter," *Charleston Daily Mail,* March 5, 1975, 1A.

[38] Section 11:13.2L, WV Code, and Stinston, Thomas, *State Taxation of Mineral Deposits and Production,*

Volume I, EPA Office of Energy Mineral and Industrial, U.S. Dept. of Agriculture, Economic Research Service University of Minnesota, January 1977, 43.

[39] Fanny Seiler and John G. Morgan, "Coal Tax Bill Goes to Governor," *Sunday Gazette Mail,* March 9, 1975, 1A.

[40] Phil Kabler, "Justice Signs Mining Tax Cuts," *Charleston Gazette-Mail,* March 28, 2019, 1A.

[41] Ibid.

[42] Rebecca McGraw Thaxton, "Warren McGraw Interview."

[43] Rosalie Earle, "McGraw, See to Lead State Democrats," *Charleston Gazette,* December 8, 1980, 1A.

[44] "Who are the McGraw Boys and Where Do They Come From?" *Charleston Gazette,* December 13, 1980.

[45] Ibid.

[46] Ibid.

[47] Ibid.

[48] Rosalie Earle, "McGraw Pledges Open Debate in Senate," *Charleston Gazette,* January 15, 1981, 1A.

[49] Ibid.

[50] "Senate Journal," *West Virginia Legislature,* Sixty-Fifth Legislature Regular Session, January 14, 1981, 7-8.

[51] Herb Little, "McGraw May Find Winning Job Easier Than Doing It," *Sunday Gazette-Mail,* January 18, 1981, 12B.

[52] John M. Berry, "West Virginia's Almost Heaven Becomes A Nightmare," *Washington Post,* May 16, 1983, *https://www.washingtonpost.com/archive/business/1983/05/16/west-virginias-almost-heaven-becomes-a-nightmare/2f42eb0e-30f1-4932-8023-839072211af4/.*

[53] Ibid.

[54] Paul E. Miller, "Recession Raises Poverty in WV, Especially Among Children," WV Center of Budget and Policy, September 9, 2009, 2, https://d3n8a8pro7vhmx.cloudfront.net/wvcbp/pages/407/attachments/original/1511174855/RI-Poverty090809.pdf?1511174855.

[55] Fanny Seiler, "State Unemployment Benefits Set Record," *Charleston Gazette,* February 2, 1983, 4D.

[56] Beth Spence, "Welfare Lines Frustrating on Both Sides of Counter," *Charleston Gazette,* February 24, 1983, 10B.

[57] "Tax Study Farce," *Charleston Gazette,* February 8, 1983, 4A.

[58] David Lieber, "Senator Downplays Role in Tax Plan," *Charleston Gazette,* February 17, 1983, 2A.

[59] David Lieber, "State Tax Compromise Likely, Chamber Told," *Charleston Gazette,* February 25, 1983, 16A.

[60] David Lieber, "State Has Lowest Business Taxes, Study Says", *Charleston Gazette,* March 10, 1983, 1D.

[61] Fanny Seiler, "FMC Backing Tax Proposal, McGraw Says," *Charleston Gazette,* February 18, 1983, 5B, and Edward Peeks, "McGraw Seeks Tax Package Support, Clarifies Statement," *Charleston Gazette,* February 26, 1983, 3A.

[62] David Lieber, "Legislature to Search," *Charleston Gazette,* February 15, 1983, 1A.

[63] David Lieber, "Jay, McGraw, See Scramble for Spotlight," *Sunday Gazette Mail,* February 20, 1983, 4A, and David Lieber, "$135 Million Tax Bills Passed Senate," *Charleston Gazette,* February 18, 1983, 1A.

[64] David Lieber, "Tax Package Breezes Through Legislature," *Sunday Gazette-Mail,* March 13, 1983, 1A.

[65] Fanny Seiler, "Legislation Lets Jay Borrow $50 Million," *Charleston Gazette,* February 1, 1983, 1A and Fanny Seiler, "Board of Investments Oks $20 Million Loan," *Charleston Gazette,* February 2, 1983, 2D.

[66] David Lieber, "Least Painful Tax Proposal to Be Considered by Senate," *Charleston Gazette,* February 18, 1983, 12A and David Lieber, "Electricity Tax Bill Approved By Committee," *Charleston Gazette,* March 1, 1983, 1B.

[67] Herb Little, "Tax Law Changes May Prove to Be Lawmakers' Biggest move," *Charleston Gazette,* March 20, 1983, 2B.

[68] "Here's List of Bills OK'd in Legislature," *Charleston Gazette,* March 13, 1983, 4A.

[69] "Lottery History," http://www.wvlottery.com/about-us/lottery-history/.

[70] Andrew Gallagher, "Senate Passes State Worker Bargaining Bill," *Charleston Gazette,* February 19, 1983, 2A.

387

[71] Tom Miller, "Mandolidis," *E-WV,* October 8, 2010.

[72] *UPI,* "Jay Signs Mandolidis Bill into Law," *Charleston Gazette,* February 22, 1983, 1A.

[73] David Lieber, "Wheel-Deal-Panic-Run-Worry-Vote; Next Bill, Please," *Charleston Gazette,* March 14, 1983, 1B.

[74] David Liever, "Joe Manchin's First Legislative Deal," *Watchdog Nation,* April 10, 2013, https://watchdognation.com/joe-manchins-first-legislative-deal-30-years-ago/.

[75] David Lieber, "Tax Package Breezes Through Legislature," *Sunday Gazette Mail,* March 13, 1983 and Lieber, "Wheel-Deal-Panic-Run-Worry-Vote; Next Bill, Please."

[76] Lieber, "Joe Manchin's First Legislative Deal."

[77] Ibid.

[78] Ibid.

[79] Mary Catherine Brooks, Judge Warren McGraw Built His Career on Public Service," *Register Herald,* Apr 12, 2015, http://www.register-herald.com/news/sunday_profile/judge-warren-mcgraw-built-his-career-on-public-service/article_cdde542c-004c-5b4c-b821-ceaa65ae8b3b.html.

[80] Lieber, "Wheel-Deal-Panic-Run-Worry-Vote; Next Bill, Please."

[81] David Lieber, "We Need a Raise, She said; 'It Looks Fairly Dim' He said,*" Charleston Gazette,* February 24, 1983, 6A, and David Lieber, "Good Guys, Bad Guys, and Warren McGraw," *Charleston Gazette,* March 7, 1983, 1B.

[82] Thaxton, "Warren McGraw Interview."

[83] Brooks, "Judge Warren McGraw Built His Career on Public Service."

[84] Murphy, "The Epic Rise and Fall of America's Most Notorious Coal Baron."

[85] Ibid.

[86] Ibid.

[87] "Interview with Richard Trumpka," Broadcast on UMWA.org.

[88] "Interview with James Gibbs," Broadcast on UMWA.org.

[89] Rebecca McGraw Thaxton, "Interview with Cecil Roberts," Charleston, West Virginia, December 19, 2016.

[90] Michael Shnayerson, "The Rape of Appalachia," *Vanity Fair,* November 20, 2006, and Goodell, "The Dark Lord of Coal Country."

[91] Thaxton, "Cecil Roberts Interview."

[92] Ibid.

[93] Rebecca McGraw Thaxton, "Joe Carter Interview," Charleston, West Virginia, November 4, 2016.

Chapter IV
[1] Fanny Seiler, "Goodwin Runs," *Charleston Gazette,* February 22, 1983, 2B.

[2] Fanny Seiler, "DEP Director Files Ethics Charge Against Attorney General," *Charleston Gazette* December 10, 1993, 12A.

[3] Associated Press, "Browning Ends Years of Silence on Probe," *Charleston Gazette,* May 27, 1983, 1A.

[4] Richard Brisbin, et. al., *West Virginia Politics and Government,* University of Nebraska, 2nd Edition, 50.

[5] Bill Case, "Jobless Fund Debt Unfair, Candidate Says." *Sunday Gazette Mail,* January 22, 1984, 1B.

[6] Ibid.

[7] Ibid.

[8] Associated Press, "Infighting Part of Daylong Ruckus in Senate," *Charleston Gazette,* February 25, 1984, 1A, and *Saving.org,* https://www.saving.org/inflation/inflation.php?amount=10,000&year=1980.

[9] Thaxton, "Warren McGraw Interview."

[10] Q & A with Editorial Board, "Finding New Coal Uses Top Priority for McGraw," *Charleston Daily Mail,* May 17, 1984, 1D.

[11] Q & A with Editorial Board, "Finding New Coal Uses Top Priority for McGraw."

[12] Ibid.

[13] Ibid.

[14] Ibid.

[15] Ibid.

388

[16] "Warren McGraw," *Sunday Gazette Mail,* May 27, 1984, 10C.
[17] Ibid.
[18] Ibid.
[19] Ibid.
[20] Ibid.
[21] Don Marsh, "Gung Din and Political Interest," *Charleston Gazette,* June 1, 1984, 4A.
[22] Ibid.
[23] "Warren McGraw," *"Sunday Gazette Mail,* May 27, 1984, 10C.
[24] Jorea Marple's Journal.
[25] Chris Knap, "Money-Vote Correlation Shown Within Statewide Primary Races," *Charleston Gazette,* June 13, 1984, 1D.
[26] Patty Vandergrift, "Money Talked Labor Leader say of Election," *Charleston Gazette,* July 7, 1984, 1B.
[27] Ibid.
[28] Murphy, "The Epic Rise and Fall of America's Most Notorious Coal Baron."
[29] Ibid.
[30] Paul Nyden, "Massey Terror Tactics Detailed in NLRB Affidavit," 1A, *Charleston Gazette*, Feb. 3, 1991.
[31] Ibid.
[32] Paul Nyden, "Massey Contracting Made Controversy," *Charleston Gazette,* November 30, 1993.
[33] Tom Kukucka. "Owners Blamed for Latest Battle in Coal Wars," *Charleston Gazette*, June 10, 1985, 1A.
[34] Ibid.
[35] Rebecca McGraw Thaxton, "Interview with Don Barnette,"
[36] Donald Baker and Mark Francis, "Miners Take Strike to the Pulpit," *Washington Post*, February 25, 1985.
[37] *State ex rel. UMWA International Union v. Hon. Elliott R. Maynard,* West Virginia Supreme Court, 342, S.E. 96 (1985).
[38] Rebecca Thaxton McGraw, "Rawles Sales Story."
[39] Paul Nyden, Document Files
[40] Ibid.
[41] Ibid.
[42] Ken Ward, Jr., "Paul Nyden: Coal Reporting Making WV Better," *Charleston Gazette Mail,* 08/21/2015: http://blogs.wvgazettemail.com/coaltattoo/2015/08/21/paul-nyden-coal-reporting-making-w-va-better/.
[43] Paul Nyden, *Miners for Democracy: Struggle in the Coal Fields.* PhD Dissertation: Columbia University, 1974.
[44] Rebecca McGraw Thaxton, "Paul Nyden Interview," November, 2016.

Chapter V
[1] Joseph Albright, *Wikipedia: https://en.wikipedia.org/wiki/Joseph_Albright.*
[2] " Report in the Matter of an Investigation of the WV State Police Crime Laboratory, Serology Division, *West Virginia Supreme Court,* No. 21973, September, 1993, http://truthinjustice.org/zainreport.htm, and William C. Forbes, Forbes Law, http://forbeslawwv.com/attorneys/bill-forbes/.
[3] "Court Invalidates a Decade of Blood Test Results in Criminal Cases," *New York Times,* November 12, 1993, http://www.nytimes.com/1993/11/12/us/court-invalidates-a-decade-of-blood-test-results-in-criminal-cases.html.
[4] Lawrence Messina, "Supreme Court Candidates Differ on Lawyers' Donations," *Charleston Gazette,* October 23, 1998, 2A.
[5] Lawrence Messina, "McCuskey Outspending McGraw in Court Race," *Charleston Gazette,* October 29, 1998, 1C.
[6] Stacey Ruckle, "Jail System Wins Major Court Fights," *Charleston Daily Mail,* July 18, 1998, 1A and *State ex Rel. Regional Jail v. Investment Management,* No 25134 and 25134 Dis, WV Supreme Court, 7/17/98 and 7/22/98.
[7] Lawrence Messina, "GOP Hits Ground Running in High Court Campaign," *Charleston Gazette,* May 14, 1998, 8A.

[8] Editorial, "Justice: Keep Republican John McCuskey on the Bench Helping West Virginians," *Charleston Daily Mail,* October 23, 1998, 4A.

[9] Messina, "McCuskey Outspending McGraw in Court Race."

[10] Lawrence Messina, "Coalfields Spelled Victory: Warren McGraw Could Direct Court in New Direction," *Charleston Gazette,* November 5, 1998, 2C.

[11] "West Virginia Supreme Court," http://www.courtswv.gov/public-resources/press/Publications/2017SupremeCourtBrochure.pdf.

[12] Leamer, 196.

[13] *Affiliated Construction Trades v. Vieweg:* http://www.courtswv.gov/supreme-court/docs/spring1999/26364.htm.

[14] Paul Nyden, "Bill Could Save Coal Millions," *Charleston Gazette,* February 22, 1999, http://www.wvgazettemail.com/News/MiningtheMountains/200807100690.

[15] *Affiliated Construction Trades v. Vieweg.*

[16] Paul Nyden, "Mining Contractors Owe Millions in Fees, Fines, Wages," *Charleston Gazette,* December 26, 1993; Paul Nyden, "Small Mines Shunt Safety Concerns for Large Profits," *Charleston Gazette,* December 19, 1993, and Paul Nyden, "Contractors Fight Bitter Battle Over Deals with AT Massey Coal," *Charleston Gazette,* 12/01/1993.

[17] Nyden, "Mining Contractors Owe Millions in Fees, Fines, Wages."

[18] Ibid.

[19] Ibid.

[20] Nyden, "Small Mines Shunt Safety Concerns for Large Profits."

[21] Rebecca McGraw Thaxton, "Interview with Stuart Caldwell," Charleston, West Virginia, November, 2016.

[22] "Group: Proceed with Coal Lawsuits Petitioner asks Court," *Charleston Gazette,* June 2, 1999, and "Commissioner Vieweg Backs McCuskey for Supreme Court," *Charleston Gazette,* June 22, 1998.

[23] *Affiliated Construction Trades v. Vieweg.*

[24] Paul J. Nyden, "Suits Against Coal Companies Can Be Tossed, Court Rules," *Charleston Gazette,* July 15, 1999, 1A.

[25] *Bower v. Westinghouse Electric,* No. 25338, West Virginia Supreme Court, 1999.

[26] Ibid.

[27] Ibid.

[28] Ken Ward, "Court Allows Medical Monitoring Lawsuit," *Charleston Gazette,* July 25, 1999, 1C.

[29] James R. Thomas, II, "High Court Ruling Makes a Game of It for Potential Victims," *Charleston Gazette,* September 13, 1999, 4A.

[30] Ibid, and "Citizens Against Lawsuit Abuse in Southern West Virginia," *West Virginia Corp-Company Profiles,* http://www.westvirginiacorps.com/corp/11020.html.

[31] www.sourcewatch.org/index.php/Citizens_Against_Lawsuit_Abuse.

[32] "CALA's Greg Thomas Misleading Voters, Perpetuating a Fraud on WV," *West Virginia Association of Justice,* 2014, https://www.wvaj.org/index.cfm?pg=GregThomasMisleadingVoters.

[33] *Bower v. Westinghouse Electric,* No. 25538 Dis, West Virginia Supreme Court, September 20, 1999.

[34] Lawrence Messina, "Maynard Dissents Long After Unanimous Vote Recorded," *Sunday Gazette Mail,* November 7, 1999, 4A.

[35] *Bower v. Westinghouse Electric,* No. 25538 Dis.

[36] Ken Ward, "Maynard's Medical Monitoring Dissent Mirror's Supporters," *Charleston Gazette,* November 12, 1999, 4A.

[37] Lawrence Messina, "Scaife Group Hears Chief Justice Hit 'Medical Monitoring,'" *Charleston Gazette,* March 16, 2000, 6A.

[38] Dan Radmacher, "Kissing Goodbye to a Petty Tyrant," *Charleston Gazette,* September 10, 1999, 4A.

[39] "Kiss Appointment Balances Court, Leaders Say," *Charleston Gazette,* September 10, 1999, 17A.

[40] *SER Rist v.Underwood.* No.26653, WV Supreme Court, 1999.

[41] Ibid.

[42] Ibid.

[43] Ibid.

[44] *SER Rist v. Underwood,* No 26653 Dis., and Paul J. Nyden, "Starcher Backs Decision on Kiss, Court,*"
Charleston Gazette,* December 9, 1999, 1A.

[45] *Carenbauer v. Hechler,* West Virginia Supreme Court, No. 2748, March 31, 2000,
https://caselaw.findlaw.com/wv-supreme-court-of-appeals/1316125.html.

[46] *Carenbauer v. Hechler,* West Virginia Supreme Court, No.27458, Dis., Dec. 14, 2000,
http://www.courtswv.gov/supreme-court/docs/fall2000/27458d.htm.

[47] Ibid.

[48] Lawrence Messina, "McGraw Sues Steptoe and Johnson in Zain Case: Law Firms Considers Allegations
Meritless," *Charleston Gazette,* February 20, 2002, 1A.

[49] Chris Miller, "Board Cautioned Twice in Bond Sale," *Charleston Gazette,* July 16, 1993, 1A, and Chris
Miller, "Caperton to Be Questioned on Memo," *Charleston Gazette,* January 1, 1993, 1A.

[50] Phil Kabler, "Video Lottery to Receive Big Lobbying Effort," *Charleston Gazette,* January 1, 1993, 1C.

[51] *Caperton v. Massey,* 33350, WV Supreme Court, 2008.

[52] Jana Brown, "14 Years Since Devastating WV Flood," *WVVA,*
http://addins.wvva.com/blogs/weather/2015/07/14-years-since-devastating-wv-flood.

[53] "The Floods of 2001," *DEP Report, http://www.wvcoalfield.com/deprecommend.html.*

[54] *Estate of Marjorie I. Verba v. Ghaphery,* 27464 and 27464 Dis, WV Supreme Court, 2001.

[55] Ibid.

[56] Ibid.

[57] Ibid.

[58] Lawrence Messina, "Law on Insurance Reporting Ignored, Lawyers Say," *Charleston Gazette,* Oct. 16,
2000, 4D.

[59] West Virginia Code, Section 29-12B-2.

[60] West Virginia Code, Section 33-20F, West Virginia Physician Mutual Insurance Company.

[61] Lawrence Messina, "Law on Insurance Reporting Ignored, Lawyers Say."

[62] Lawrence Messina, "Medical Assoc. Insurance Firm Makes Secret Deal," *Charleston Gazette,* Feb. 26,
2001, 2A.

[63] Ibid.

[64] Ibid.

[65] Editorial: "Malpractice—Association Distorts Facts," *Charleston Gazette,* March 1, 2001, 4A.

[66] "Medical Misdiagnosis in WV: Challenging the Medical Malpractice Claims of Doctors' Lobby," *Public
Citizen Congress Watch,* January 2003, 1.

[67] Lawrence Messina, "The Price of Malpractice, WV's Medical Malpractice Debate," 2/26/01, 2A,
Charleston Gazette, and "Medical Misdiagnosis: Challenging the Malpractice Claims of the Doctors' Lobby,"
Public Citizen Congress Watch, January 2003, 1.

[68] Ibid.

[69] Ibid.

[70] "Medical Misdiagnosis: Challenging the Malpractice Claims of the Doctors' Lobby."

[71] Messina, "The Price of Malpractice, WV's Medical Malpractice Debate," and "Medical Misdiagnosis:
Challenging the Malpractice Claims of the Doctors' Lobby."

[72] "Medical Misdiagnosis in WV: Challenging the Medical Malpractice Claims of Doctors' Lobby."

[73] Ibid.

Chapter VI

[1] *State v. Arbaugh,* 595 S.E.2d 289, March, 2004.

[2] *State v. Arbaugh,* 595 S.E. 2d 289, Dis., 2004.

[3] Ibid.

[4] Ibid.

[5] Ibid.

[6] Ibid.

[7] *State v. Arbaugh,* 595 S.E.2d 289, Dis., 2004.

[8] Ibid.

[9] Leamer, 207.

[10] *State v. Arbaugh,* 595 S.E.2d 289, Dis., 2004 and Leamer, 207.

[11] *State v. Arbaugh,* 595 S.E.2d 289, Dis and Con, 2004.

[12] *State v. Arbaugh,* 595 S.E.2d 289, March, 2004.

[13] *State v. Arbaugh,* 595 S.E.2d 289, Dis., 2004, and Leamer, 206.

[14] Cody Carliss, "Electing Judges with Cash," *Christian Science Monitor*, January 30, 2008, http://debatepedia.idebate.org/en/index.php/Argument:_Elected_justices_are_corruptly_influenced_by_campaign_funders.

[15] Paul J. Nyden, "Author: W.Va. Supreme Court 'Appalling,' Chief Justice 'Blankenship's Creature,'" *Charleston Gazette,* May 18, 2013, http://www.wvgazettemail.com/News/201305180055.

[16] *Caperton v. Massey,* 33350, WV Supreme Court, 2008.

Chapter VII

[1] Paul Nyden, "Contractors Fight Bitter Battle over Deals with AT Massey Coal," *Charleston Gazette,* December 1, 1993.

[2] *Caperton v. Massey,* 33350, WV Supreme Court, 2008.

[3] Paul Nyden, "Book Details Fall of Harman Mining and Tactics of Massey Energy," *Charleston Gazette-Mail,* May 11, 2013, and Leamer, 39.

[4] Goodall, "The Dark Lord of Coal."

[5] Leamer, 39.

[6] Leamer, 38, 118, 139-144.

[7] *Caperton v. Massey.*

[8] Goodell, "The Dark Lord of Coal Country."

[9] "Miners Seek Payments," *WSAZ:* http://www.wsaz.com/home/headlines/16628666.html.

[10] Lyndsay Steinmetz, "A Perfect Storm: How Speech and Spending are Politicizing State Supreme Courts," Political Science 610, Senior Project, Alleghany College, April 11, 2011, 17.

[11] Murphy, "The Epic Rise and Fall of America's Most Notorious Coal Baron," and Goodell, "The Dark Lord of Coal Country."

[12] Kenneth L. Karst, "Caperton's Amici," *Seattle University Law Review,* Seattle Washington, 2010, 636, http://digi http://digitalcommons.law.seattleu.edu/sulr/vol33/iss3/7/.

[13] Karst, 647.

[14] Karst, 633.

[15] *Caperton v. Massey,* 33350, WV Supreme Court, 2008.

[16] Leamer, 43.

[17] Leamer, 94.

[18] Leamer, 211 and Murphy, "The Epic Rise and Fall of America's Most Notorious Coal Baron."

[19] Ibid.

[20] Karst, 637 and Leamer, 212.

[21] Leamer, 197.

[22] Leamer, 284-285.

[23] Leamer, 248-249.

[24] Leamer, 249-250.

[25] Leamer, 271.

[26] Leamer, 244-245, and Ian Urbina, *New York Times,* October 22, 2006, and David Segal, "The People v. the Coal Baron, *New York Times,* June 20, 2015.

[27] Karst, 638.

[28] Leamer, 269-270.

[29] Ben Fields, "Maynard Trip Raising More Questions," *Herald Dispatch,* January 15: 2008http://www.herald-dispatch.com/news/maynard-trip-raising-more-questions/article_633eb91b-7899-52f9-9922-

392

c6b5bbaae630.html, and *Caperton v. Massey, West Virginia Supreme Court, N0.33350,* *http://www.courtswv.gov/supreme-court/docs/fall2007/33350.htm.*
[30] Leamer, 29.
[31] Paul J. Nyden, "Caperton Wins Massey Trial, but Damages Much Less Than Hoped For," *Charleston Gazette-Mail,* May 25, 2014, http://www.wvgazettemail.com/article/20140525/GZ01/140529536/1419.
[32]Liptak, *"A Justice of the Supreme Court of Appeals,"* and Fields, "Maynard Trip Raising More Questions."
[33] Leamer, 286.
[34] *Deborah K. May v. Mate Creek Security,* WV Supreme Court, No. 3370, June 17, 2008.
[35] Kenneth L. Karst, "Caperton's Amici," *Seattle University Law Review,* Seattle Washington, 2010, 647-649, http://digi http://digitalcommons.law.seattleu.edu/sulr/vol33/iss3/7/.
[36] *Caperton v. Massey* U.S. Supreme Court of Appeals
[37] Leamer, 348.
[38] Leamer, 349.
[39] *Hugh M. Caperton v. A.T. Massey Coal Company, Inc.,* 33350, 2009.
[40] *Hugh m Caperton v. A.T. Massey Coal Company, Inc.,* 33350 and 33350 Dis, West Virginia Supreme Court, 11/12/09.
[41] Leamer, 326-327.
[42] Robert Lenzner and Matthew Miller, "Buying Justice," *Forbes,* July 21, 2003, 64.
[43] Michael Shnayerson, "The Rape of Appalachia," *Vanity Fair,* November 20, 2006.
[44] "Liberal," *Online Etymology Dictionary, http://www.etymonline.com/index.php?term=liberal.*
[45] *WV Constitution,* Article 3, Section 17.
[46] Shnayerson, "The Rape of Appalachia."

Chapter VIII
[1] Don Blankenship, "An American Political Prison," Pamphlet distributed from prison, 2016.
[2] Lenzner and Miller, "Buying Justice."
[3] Cody Carliss, "Electing Judges with Cash," *Christian Science Monitor,* January 30, 2008, http://debatepedia.idebate.org/en/index.php/Argument:_Elected_justices_are_corruptly_influenced_by_campaign_funders.
[4] Don Blankenship, "An American Political Prisoner,"
[5] "Justice Not for Sale," *New York Times,* March 2, 2009, http://www.nytimes.com/2009/03/03/opinion/03tue2.html?_r=0.
[6] "State of the State," *Construction News,* January, 1982, 18.
[7] Joshua Greene, "Karl Rove in the Corner," *Atlantic Monthly,* November, 2004, http://www.theatlantic.com/magazine/archive/2004/11/karl-rove-in-a-corner/303537/.
[8] Ibid.
[9] http://www.thenervousbreakdown.com/wewing/2010/10/21-questions-with-wayne-ewing/
[10] Jesse Rutledge, Editor, "The New Politics of Judicial Elections, 2004," *Brennan Center for Justice and Institute of Money and Politics,* June, 2005, 12, *http://www.justiceatstake.org/media/cms/NewPoliticsReport2004_83BBFBD7C43A3.pdf*
[11] "McGraw Overcomes Negative Ads to Defeat Rowe," *Charleston Gazette,* May 12, 2004.
[12] Leamer, 210-211.
[13] Cody Carliss, "Electing Judges with Cash," *Christian Science Monitor,* January 30, 2008, http://debatepedia.idebate.org/en/index.php/Argument:_Elected_justices_are_corruptly_influenced_by_campaign_funders.
[14] "527 Organization," *Wikipedia, https://en.wikipedia.org/wiki/527_organization.*
[15] Adan Liptak, "Case May Alter Judge Elections Across Country," *New York Times,* February 14, 2009, A29, http://www.nytimes.com/2009/02/15/washington/15scotus.html?_r=0.
[16] Ibid.
[17] Nyden, "Author: W.Va. Supreme Court 'Appalling' Chief Justice 'Blankenship's Creature'."
[18] Leamer, 212-213.

393

[19] Rutledge, "The New Politics of Judicial Elections, 2004," 11.

[20] Liptak, "Case May Alter Judge Elections Across Country."

[21] Wayne Ewing, *Last Campaign,* 2004.

[22] Rutledge, "The New Politics of Judicial Elections, 2004,"4.

[23] Ibid.

[24] Ibid.

[25] Ibid, 25.

[26] "Benjamin Knocks McGraw off the Supreme Court," *Charleston Daily Mail,* November 3, 2004.

[27] Rutledge, "The New Politics of Judicial Elections, 2004."

[28] Morello, "W.Va. Supreme Court Justice Defeated in Rancorous Contest."

[29] Dorothy Samuels, "The Selling of the Judiciary: Campaign Cash in the Courtroom," *New York Times,* April 15, 2008, http://www.nytimes.com/2008/04/15/opinion/15tues4.html.

[30] Richard Brisbin, Jr., "Judicial Elections on the Silver Screen," *Judicature,* Vol. 89 No.1, July-Aug. 2005, 44-47.

[31] Ibid.

[32] Ibid.

[33] *Caperton v. Massey,* 33350, WV Supreme Court, 2008.

[34] Karst, 635, and *Caperton v. A. T. Massey Coal Co.,* 556 U.S. 868 (2009).

[35] Carliss, "Electing Judges with Cash."

[36]Leamer, 347.

Chapter IX

[1] Murphy, "The Epic Rise and Fall of America's Most Notorious Coal Baron."

[2] Ibid.

[3] Ian Urbina, *New York Times,* October 22, 2006, and David Segali, "The People v. the Coal Baron," *New York Times,* June 20, 2015.

[4] Trip Gabriel, "West Virginia Coal Country Sees New Era as Donald Blankenship is Indicted," *New York Times,* November 30, 2014.

[5] *Deborah K. May v. Mate Creek Security,* WV Supreme Court, No. 3370, June 17, 2008.

[6] *Deborah K. May v. Mate Creek Security* and Leamer, 244-245.

[7] *Deborah K. May v. Mate Creek Security.*

[8] "Upper Big Branch," *Governor's Independent Investigation Panel*, May, 2011, 4.

[9] Ibid.

[10] Ibid.

[11] "Upper Big Branch," Governor's *Independent Investigation Panel*, 92.

[12] Ken Ward, Jr. "New Report Details How Disaster Occurred," *Gazette-Mail,* May 22, 2011, 1C.

[13] "Upper Big Branch," *Governor's Independent Investigation Panel*, 106.

[14] Allen Blinder, "Don Blankenship Sentenced to a Year in Prison in Mine Safety Case," *New York Times,* April 7, 2016, http://www.nytimes.com/2016/04/07/us/donald-blankenship-sentenced-to-a-year-in-prison-in-mine-safety-case.html.

[15] Don Blankenship," An American Political Prisoner."

Chapter X

[1] Berea College Service Awards, https://www.berea.edu/psa/.

[2] Chris Wild, "1920s-1950s Living the Havana High Life," http://mashable.com/2014/12/24/havana-before-castro-revolution/.

[3] *"Editorial," Independent Herald,* 1973.

[4] Dylan Matthews, "Everything You Need to Know about the War on Poverty," *Washington Post*, Jan, 4, 2014, https://www.washingtonpost.com/news/wonk/wp/2014/01/08/everything-you-need-to-know-about-the-war-on-poverty/.

[5] Edgar Simpson, "Pressing the Press," *Journalism History 36:4,* Winter, 2011, 196-204.

394

[6] "Lyndon Johnson Biography," *IMDB,* http://www.imdb.com/name/nm0425696/bio.

[7] Capital Comment, "McGraw Was a Rare Breed in Government," *Register Post Herald,* June 22, 1968.

[8] Ibid.

[9] Joe Garofoli, "Obama Bounces Back—Speech Seemed to Help," *The San Francisco Chronicle,* http://www.sfgate.com/politics/article/Obama-bounces-back-speech-seemed-to-help-3289736.php, March 26, 2008.

[10] Jorea Marple, Personal Journal.

[11] John Morgan, "John M. Slack Jr.," *Charleston Gazette,* March 19, 1980, http://www.wvculture.org/history/government/slackjohn03.html.

[12] Ibid.

[13] James Dent "John Slack the Republican," *Charleston Gazette,* 1974.

[14] Associated Press, "McGraw to Run Against Slack," *Charleston Daily Mail,* August 18, 1973, 5A.

[15] Bob Mellace, "No Surprise to Slack," *Charleston Daily Mail,* August 31, 1973, 6A.

[16] Cheryl Caswell, "Bridge to be Dedicated to Late Kaufman Family," *Charleston Gazette-Mail:* June 17, 2011, http://www.wvgazettemail.com/News/201106161058.

[17] Associated Press, "Kaufman, McGraw Kick off Races," *Charleston Gazette,* January 9, 1974.

[18] Stuart Ditzen, "Deadly Union Rivalry Capped 60's," *Philly.Com,* December 26, 1999, http://articles.philly.com/1999-12-26/news/25479905_1_jock-yablonski-tony-boyle-killers, and "Jock Yablonski," *Wikipedia, https://en.wikipedia.org/wiki/Joseph_Yablonski.*

[19] Richard Grimes, "Foe Renews Flood Blame," *Charleston Daily Mail,* 1973.

[20] Associated Press, "Pursuit of Coal Covers Lot of Area," *Charleston Gazette,* October 19, 1973, 10A.

[21] Ibid.

[22] Ibid.

[23] Associated Press, "Coal Firms' Land Taxes Probe Asked," *Charleston Gazette,* September 7, 1973, 3B, and Associated Press, "Testimony Invited At Hearing on Taxes, *Charleston Gazette,* October 10, 1973, 1B.

[24] Darrell McGraw, "Tax Laws Give Rich the Benefit," Charleston Gazette, 1973.

[25] Andrew Gallagher, "McGraw Impresses Miners," Charleston Gazette, May 3, 1974.

[26] Harry Hoffman, "Politics," *Charleston Gazette,* December 7, 1973.

[27] Editorial, *Charleston Gazette,* May 4, 1974, 6A.

[28] Don Marsh, "Editorial" *Charleston Gazette,* May 6, 1974.

[29] Don Marsh, "Slack Runs Away With Nomination," *Charleston Gazette,* May 15, 1974, 1A.

Chapter XI

[1] Justice Darrell McGraw Personal Papers, "The West Virginia Supreme Court of Appeals 1977-1987."

[2] "Candidate Listing," *Charleston Daily Mail,* May 8, 1976, 8A.

[3] Darrell McGraw, Personal Files—Campaign Financial Reports.

[4] Herb Little, AP: "Miller, Camper Ahead in Court Race," *Charleston Gazette,* May 12, 1976, 1C.

[5] Richard Grimes, "Miller, Camper Ahead in Court Race," *Charleston Daily Mail,* May, 12, 1976, 1A, and "Nominees at a Glance," *Charleston Daily Mail,* 1A.

[6] George Steele, "Race for Treasurer, Supreme Court Close," *Charleston Gazette,* May 13, 1976, 1A.

[7] Associated Press, "Winning Vote Totals for State Court Listed," *Charleston Gazette,* June 29, 1976, 2A.

[8] Ibid.

[9] Richard Grimes, "Lawyers Are Sweating It Out," *Charleston Daily Mail,* May 24, 1976, 4A.

[10] Ben A. Franklin, "Rockefeller's West Virginia Funds Near 3 Million in Governor Race," *New York Times,* October 27, 1976, http://www.nytimes.com/1976/10/27/archives/rockefellers-west-virginia-funds-near-3-million-in-governor-race.html?_r=0.

[11] "State Supreme Court Races Called of Major Importance by AFL-CIO," *Talkin Union,* West Virginia Labor Federation, November 1976, 3.

[12] "HDLC Holds Bean Dinner for Candidate Darrell McGraw," *WV AFL-CIO Observer,* October, 1976, and Darrell McGraw for Supreme Court Financial Papers, 1976.

[13] Darrell McGraw, Personal Papers—Campaign Finance Reports.

[14] Associated Press, "Three New Justices People Oriented," *Charleston Gazette,* January 17, 1977, 1B.

[15] "Majestic Splender, 1969-1997," West Virginia Archives and History, http://www.wvculture.org/history/exhibitsonline/inaugural/inaugural7.html.

[16] John Morgan, "New Members Bring New Look To Supreme Court," *Charleston Gazette,* January 1, 1973.

[17] Tom Miller, "Justices Find Court Turning Point," *Herald Dispatch,* January 9, 1977, 1A.

[18] Justice Darrell McGraw Supreme Court Papers, "The West Virginia Supreme Court of Appeals 1977-1987".

[19] Article 3, Section 17, *WV Constitution.*

[20] Don Marsh, "McGraw: Budget Inadequate," *Charleston Gazette,* March 31, 1978, 9A.

[21] Ibid.

[22] John Patrick Hagan, "Policy Activism in the West Virginia Supreme Court of Appeals, 1930-1985," *West Virginia Law Review,* Vol. 89, No.1, Fall 1986.

[23] *Mandolidis v. Elkins Industries, Inc.,* 161 W.Va. 695, 246 W.E.2d 907 (1978), http://law.justia.com/cases/west-virginia/supreme-court/1978/13926-3.html.

[24] "Employer Liability in West Virginia: Compensation Beyond the Law," *Washington and Lee Law Review,* Volume 36, Issue 1, Article 7, http://scholarlycommons.law.wlu.edu/cgi/viewcontent.cgi?article=2747&context=wlulr.

[25] *Mandolidis v. Elkins Industries, Inc.*

[26] "Employer Liability in West Virginia: Compensation Beyond the Law."

[27] Ibid.

[28] *Mandolidis v Elkins Industry, Inc.*

[29] "Employer Liability in West Virginia: Compensation Beyond the Law."

[30] Miller, Tom D "Mandolidis Case." e-WV: *The West Virginia Encyclopedia,* http://www.wvencyclopedia.org/articles/1485.

[31] Jorea Marple Personal Journal, October 16, 1982.

[32] *Mandolidis* Case, http://www.wvencyclopedia.org/articles/1485.

[33] Bowles Rice, "Wrap-Up 2015 Legislative Session," http://www.bowlesrice.com/email/wvacb/2015/wrapup/2015_West_Virginia_Legislative_Wrap_Up.html.

[34] "Legal Reform Bill Draws Emotional Testimony," *Metro News,* January 1, 2015, http://wvmetronews.com/2015/01/21/legal-reform-bill-draws-emotional-testimony-at-capitol/.

[35] Thaxton, "Interview with Stuart Cauldwell," November, 2016.

[36] Darrell McGraw, Personal Papers.

[37] "West Virginia Supreme Court Implied Warranty of Habitability," *Housing Law Bulletin,* Volume IX, Issue 1, February, 1979, http://nhlp.org/files/February%201979.pdf.

[38] *Teller v. McCoy,* West Virginia Supreme Court, *253 SE 2d 114, 1978.*

[39] Ibid.

[40] Tamar Lewin, "West Virginia's Felix and Oscar Show," *National Law Review,* September 3, 1979.

[41] Ibid.

[42] Ibid.

[43] Charles S. Lopeman, *Activism Advocate: Policy Making in State Supreme Courts*, Praeger Publishers, 1999, 50.

[44] Beth Spence, "Whatever Happened to Pauley vs. Bailey? The Story of the Politics of Education in West Virginia!" 1988, 5, http://files.eric.ed.gov/fulltext/ED426839.pdf.

[45] Ibid, 13.

[46] Ibid.

[47] Ibid.

[48] *Pauley v. Kelly,* 162 W.Va. 672, 255 S.E. 2d 859 (1979); later amended to *Pauley v. Bailey* 324 W.Va. S.E. 2d 128 (1984).

[49] Karen DeMoss and Kenneth K. Wong, editors. *The Politics of Education Law: Money, Politics and Law,* Routledge Publishers, New York, 2013, 76.

[50] *Pauley v. Kelly.*

[51] Jorea Marple, Personal Journal.

[52] Ibid.

[53] Ibid.

[54] *Killen v. Logan County Comm.,* 295 SE2d 689, WV 1982.

[55] Justice Oliver Wendell Holmes, Jr., http://www.goodreads.com/quotes/1175738-taxes-are-the-price-we-pay-for-a-civilized-society.

[56] Bob Miller, *Broken Bones and Shattered Dreams,* 20.

[57] Spence, "Whatever Happened to Pauley vs. Bailey? The Story of the Politics of Education in West Virginia," 31.

[58] Robert M. Bastress, Jr., *The West Virginia State Constitution,* Oxford Press, March 30, 2016, Section 1B, https://books.google.com/books?id=4CoRDAAAQBAJ&pg=PT332&lpg=PT332&dq=%E2%80%9CProperty+Tax+Limitation+and+Homestead+Exemption+Amendment+of+1982&source=bl&ots=X6AMebj0KH&sig=0Gj3-ctmuODRfhSkKedg0acLKpk&hl=en&sa=X&ved=0ahUKEwicnrubmqvQAhUKgiYKHRyBCBoQ6AEIOzAG#v=onepage&q=%E2%80%9CProperty%20Tax%20Limitation%20and%20Homestead%20Exemption%20Amendment%20of%201982&f=false.

[59] Ibid.

[60] *Pauley v. Bailey,* 324 W.Va. S.E. 2d 128 (1984).

[61] Spence, "Whatever Happened to Pauley vs. Bailey? The Story of the Politics of Education in West Virginia!" 31.

[62] Ibid, 34.

[63] Ibid, 35.

[64] Bill McGinley, "Recht Decision," *E-WV,* October 10, 2010, http://www.wvencyclopedia.org/articles/19.

[65] Ibid.

Chapter XII

[1] Interview with Francis A. Hughes.

[2] Adam Turl, "The Miners' Strike 1977-1978," *International Socialist Review,* Issue 74, http://isreview.org/issue/74/miners-strike-1977-78, and Bituminous Coal Strike 1977-1978.

[3] Ibid.

[4] No Peace in the Pits," *Time,* June 27, 1977.

[5] "To Work," *Time,* March 20, 1978, and "Carter Invokes Taft-Hartley Act to Force Reopening of Coal Mines." *Facts on File.* March 10, 1978.

[6] "Injunction is a Mistake," *New York Post,* March 8, 1978, 3.

[7] Ibid.

[8] Ibid.

[9] Ibid.

[10] Adam Turl, "The Miners' Strike of 1977-78."

[11] Ben A. Franklin, "Arnold Miller is Dead at 62," *New York Times,* July 12, 1985.

[12] Richard Ballard, "Darrell McGraw," *Penthouse,* September, 1978.

[13] Ibid.

[14] Richard Grimes, "Strong' McGraw Interview Hits Stand," *Charleston Daily Mail,* August 1, 1978, 1A.

[15] Ballard, "Darrell McGraw."

[16] Ibid.

[17] Sen. Sheldon Whitehouse, "Remarks at Gorsuch Confirmation Hearings," March 20, 2017, https://www.whitehouse.senate.gov/news/release/whitehouse-remarks-at-gorsuch-confirmation-hearing.

[18] Ibid.

[19] Ibid.

[20] Sheldon Whitehouse, *Captured,* The New Press, New York, 2017, Book Flap.

[21] Steve Mullins, "Youth 17, Found Dead Hanging in the Kanawha Jail," *Charleston Gazette,* October 1, 1979, 1A, and "Quite Boy Who Had Problems' Hangs Self," *Charleston Daily Mail,* October 1, 1979.

[22] Ibid.

397

[23] UPI, "W.Va. Justice Scuffles with Deputies at Jail," *Journal Star,* October 9, 1979, 1A.

[24] Editorial, "Nobody Won" *Beckley Post Herald,* October 10, 1979.

[25] Paul J. Nyden, "Is Shocked at Beating of McGraw," Letter to Editor, *Beckley Post Herald*, October 12, 1979.

[26] Steve Mullins, "Mike Couldn't Handle All This, Man' Juvenile Inmates Analyze Jeffery's 'Bullpen' Problems," *Charleston Daily Mail*, October 17, 1979, 1A

[27] Steve Mullins, "Juveniles' Testimony Confirmed," *Charleston Daily Mail,* October 17, 1979, 1A.

[28] Ibid.

[29] Bob Minnocci, "Records Falsification Routine at County Jail," *Charleston Gazette,* November 2, 1979.

[30] Ibid.

[31] Ibid.

[32] Justice Darrell McGraw, Personal Files—"Sworn Statement of Deputy J.S. Batman," October 22, 1979.

[33] James Haught, "Juvenile Jungle–Youth Incarceration Laws Being Broken," *Charleston Gazette,* November 12, 1979, 1A.

[34] Justice Darrell McGraw, Personal files—"Letter from Ed Seltzer," Charleston, WV.

[35] "Warrants Against McGraw Dismissed," *Charleston Daily Mail*, July 1, 1980, and "Trial Outcome Draws Varied Perspectives," *Charleston Daily Mail*, July 1, 1980.

[36] Richard Grimes, "Crisis Brings Results: Attention to Jails*,*" *Charleston Daily Mail*, circa 1980.

[37] *State Ex. Rel. MCH v. Kinder,* WV Supreme Court 317 S.E. 2d, 150, 1984, http://law.justia.com/cases/west-virginia/supreme-court/1984/16203-4.html.

[38] Ibid.

[39] Earl Benton, "State High Court Gets Juvenile Award," *Charleston Daily Mail,* 1980.

[40] Sandy Wells, "The Changes Wrought by the Past Ten Years*,*" *Charleston Gazette,* January 1, 1980, 1B.

[41] "Misery Index by Month". *United States Misery Index. Retrieved 9 October 2014,* http://www.miseryindex.us/indexbyyear.aspx.

[42] Drew Von Bergen, "West Virginia had the highest unemployment rate in the nation," *UPI*, May, 1983, http://www.upi.com/Archives/1983/05/17/West-Virginia-had-the-highest-unemployment-rate-in-the/9643421992000/.

[43] *Associated Press,* "Hunger Comes to Family's Table at Month's End," *New York Times,* Nov. 7, 1983, http://www.nytimes.com/1983/11/07/us/hunger-comes-to-family-s-table-at-month-s-end.html.

[44] Richard Grimes, "Chief Justice Pushes Fund to Feed W.V's Jobless," *Charleston Daily Mail,* January 18, 1983, 1A.

[45] "Coalition Unveils Massive Food Drive for Needy," *Charleston Gazette,* February 17, 1983, 16A.

[46] Facing Hunger Food Bank, http://facinghunger.org/.

[47] E.J. Reich, "McGraw Sticking Neck Out For Food Bank," *Charleston Gazette,* January 27, 1983, 2A.

[48] Richard Grimes, "McGraw Says Motivation Comes From Hungry People, Not Politics," *Charleston Daily Mail*, February 3, 1983, 1A.

[49] "Hunger and Ethics," *American Bar Association Journal, May,* 1983, Vol. 69, 573.

[50] Reich, "McGraw Sticking Neck Out For Food Bank."

[51] Herb Little, "Complaint Against Justice McGraw is Dumb," *AP, Sunday Gazette Mail,* May 20, 1979, 13D, and Andrew Gallagher, "McGraw Case Ultimate Silliness," *UPI, Sunday Gazette-Mail,* May 20, 1979.

[52] Ibid.

[53] Gallagher, "McGraw Case Ultimate Silliness."

[54] AP "McGraw Seeks Dismissal Because of Silence," *Charleston Gazette,* July 9, 1980, 12A.

[55] Little, "Complaint Against Justice McGraw is Dumb."

[56] Jorea Marple, Personal Journal.

[57] AP "McGraw Seeks Dismissal Because of Silence."

[58] Ibid.

[59] Tamar Lewin, "West Virginia's Felix and Oscar Show," *National Law Journal,* September 3, 1979.

[60] AP, "McGraw Seeks Dismissal Because of Silence."

[61] Lewin, "West Virginia's Felix and Oscar Show."

398

[62] "Jury's location raises question of Propriety," *Charleston Gazette,* September 24, 1983.
[63] "McGraw Correct," *Charleston Gazette,* October 21, 1983, 4A.
[64] "Charleston, WV, Mayor Admits Cocaine Guilt," *New York Times,* November 18, 1987: http://www.nytimes.com/1987/11/18/us/charleston-wva-mayor-admits-cocaine-guilt.html.

Chapter XIII
[1] Norman Oder, "Supreme Court Ads Project More Image than Issue," *Charleston Gazette,* May 8, 1995, 15A.
[2] Beth Fountain, Internal Memo: "WV Supreme Court: Labor Oriented Opinions of the Court in Recent Years, 1988," Justice McGraw, personal files.
[3] Nichol, Gene R., "Dialectical Federalism: A Tribute to the West Virginia Supreme Court of Appeals," College of William and Mary Law School, William and Mary Law School Scholarly Repository paper 907, 1987, and 90 *West Virginia Law Review* 91-107 (1987).
[4] Deborah Baker, "Fighting the 'New Right' in WV," *UPI,* May 2, 1982.
[5] Ibid.
[6] Ibid.
[7] Lopeman, *The Activist Advocate, 47.*
[8] *State Ex. Rel. Harper v. Zegeer,* WV 296 W.E. 2d 873 (1982).
[9] "County Youth Hangs Himself in S.C. Jail Cell," *Charleston Daily Mail* June 18, 1982.
[10] *West Virginia Code,* Sec. 62-1-5a.
[11] *Dadisman v. Moore,* WV 384 S.E.2d 816 (1989).
[12] Darrell McGraw, Personal Files, "Attorney General's Office, Tobacco Distribution List," *February 2, 2010.*
[13] *Dunlop v. Worker's Compensation Commissioner* (1977).
[14] *Harless v. First National Bank,* 246 S.E. 2d 270 W.Va.(1978).
[15] *Bradley v. Appalachian Power Co.,* 256 S.E.2d 879 W.Va. (1979).
[16] *Hurley v. Allied Chemical Co.,* 262 S.E. 2d 757 W.Va. (1980).
[17] *Peters v. Narick,* 270 S.E. 2d 760 W.Va. (1980).
[18] *Peters v. Narick,* 270 S.E. 2d 760 W.Va. (1980).
[19] *Breeden v. Workmen's Comp.,* 285 S. E. 2d 398 W.Va. (1981).
[20] *Wayne County Board of Education v. Tooley,* 276 S.E. 826 W.Va.(1981)
[21] *E. H., et al v Khan Martin, M.C.* 168, WV 248 (1981).
[22] *Webb v. Fury,* 282 S.E. 2d/28, W.Va. (1981).
[23] *United Mine Workers of America v. Miller,* 291 S.E. 2d 673, W.Va. (1982).
[24] *Hodge v. Ginsberg,* 303 S.E. 2d 245 W.Va. (1983).
[25] *Pittsburg Elevator Co. v. WV Board of Regents,* 310 S.E. 2d 675, W.Va. (1983).
[26] *Adkins v. CSC and PSC,* 324 S.E. 2d 363 (W.Va.1984).
[27] *Javins v. Workers' Compensation Commission,* 320 S.E. 2d 119, W.Va. (1984).
[28] *Hechler v. Casey,* 333 S. E. 2d 799, W.Va. (1985).
[29] *Crain v. Bordenkirchner,* 342 SE2d 422, W.Va. (1986).
[30] *State ex. Rel. Board of Education v. Casey,* 333 S.E. 2d 799, W.Va. (1986).
[31] *Pack v. Van Meter,* 354 S.E. 2d 581, W.Va. (1986).
[32] *Dillon v. Board of Education,* 351 S.E. 2d 58, W.Va. (1986).
[33] *Frank's Shoe Store v. Human Rights Commission,* 366 S.E. 2d 251 No. 16913, W.Va. (1986).
[34] *Wiggins v. Eastern Associated Coal Corp.,* 357 S.E. 2d 745, W.Va., (1987).
[35] Walter C. Massey, Jr., Editorial: "Case for McGraw," *The Register/Herald,* February 21, 1987.
[36] Thomas B. Miller, "Public Service," http://www.ohiocountylibrary.org/history/people/hallfame/Miller.htm.
[37] Nanya Gadd, "Voters Undecided on High Court Race," *Charleston Daily Mail,* Nov. 25, 1987, 1A.
[38] Don Marsh, "The Former Coal Miner's Daughter," *Charleston Gazette,* 1988.
[39] "Gazette Poll," *Charleston Gazette,* January 11, 1988.
[40] Willard & Arnold, "Statewide Poll," *Charleston Gazette,* May 3, 1988, 6A.
[41] Norman Oder, "Workman Loans Campaign $60,000," *Charleston Gazette,* April 12, 1988.
[42] Norman Oder, "McGraw Faces Referendum on Himself in Supreme Court Race," *Charleston Gazette,* May

6, 1988, 10A.

[43] Ibid.

[44] Norman Oder, "Miller Takes Lead in High Court Race," *Charleston Gazette*, May 11, 1988, 1A.

[45] Norman Older, "McGraw's Loss Not Seen Leading to Radical Shift," *Charleston Gazette*, May 12, 1988, 2B.

[46] Justice Darrell McGraw, Personal Files.

Chapter XIV

[1] Jorea Marple, Personal Journal.

[2] Jack Deutsch, "Controversy Way of Life for McGraw, *Charleston Daily Mail*, July 24, 1987, 1A.

[3] Justice McGraw, Personal Files.

[4] Rosalie Earle, "Poor Denied Good Lawyers, Justice Says," *Charleston Gazette*, May 3, 1978, 10B.

[5] Justice McGraw, Personal Files.

[6] Justice McGraw, Personal Files.

[7] Jorea Marple, Personal Journal.

[8] Jorea Marple, Personal Journal.

[9] Joseph Campbell, *Mythology, http://www.goodreads.com/quotes/58966-is-the-system-going-to-flatten-you-out-and-deny*.

[10] Jorea Marple, Personal Files.

[11] John David, "Caperton Stance No Surprise," *Charleston Gazette*, March 13, 1990, 4A.

[12] Ibid.

[13] B. Drummond Ayres, Jr, "Thaw Is Hinted in School Strike in West Virginia," *New York Times*, March 10, 1990, http://www.nytimes.com/1990/03/10/us/thaw-is-hinted-in-school-strike-in-west-virginia.html.

[14] David, "Caperton Stance no Surprise."

[15] Ibid.

[16] Ibid.

[17] West Virginia: "Governor, Striking Teachers Square Off," *Los Angeles Times*, March 12, 1990, http://articles.latimes.com/1990-03-12/news/mn-73_1_west-virginia.

[18] Paul J. Nyden, "Nothing Illegal About Strike Former Justice Says," *Sunday Gazette Mail*, March 11, 1990, 1C.

[19] *E-WV Encyclopedia*, http://www.wvencyclopedia.org/articles/696.

Chapter XV

[1] Peter T. KilBorn, "How a Union Won an Appalachian Struggle, *New York Times*, May 8, 1992, http://www.nytimes.com/1992/05/08/us/how-a-union-won-an-appalachian-struggle.html?pagewanted=all.

[2] Ibid.

[3] Ibid.

[4] Jorea Marple, Personal Journal.

[5] Martha Bryson Hodel, "Attorney General Race Shaping Up As Labor vs. Business," *Charleston Gazette*, April 22, 1992, 5A.

[6] Maryclaire Dale, "McGraw in Control of AG race," *Charleston Gazette*, May 12, 1992, 1A, and "McGraw Wins Bid for State Attorney," *Charleston Gazette*, November 4, 1992.

[7] William Rainey, "Justice McGraw Speaks Out," WVEA School Journal, Vol. 107, No.8, November 22, 1978.

[8] Interview with Frances Hughes, December, 2016.

[9] Ibid.

[10] Ibid.

[11] Emily Gottlieb and Amy Wilman, "State Attorneys' General, The People's Champion," Center for Justice and Democracy at NY Law School, No. 15, March, 2008.

[12] Ibid.

[13] Ibid.

[14] Ibid.

[15] Roderick Harless, "The Establishment – An Informational and Interpretive Report about the West Virginia Establishment," Federal Research Grant Study, 1971, and Curt Brown, "West Virginia Establishment: The Affluent in Total Control, *Sunday Gazette Mail,* 1972.

[16] Ibid.

[17] Bob Weaver, "Remembering Larry Harless: His Sun Did Not Shine Yesterday, *The Hur Herald,* August 7, 2015.

[18] Ibid.

[19] "Social Principles and Social Creed," United Methodist Church, http://www.umc.org/what-we-believe/social-principles-social-creed.

Chapter XVI

[1] *West Virginia Code,* Section 22-1-6: http://www.legis.state.wv.us/wvcode/ChapterEntire.cfm?chap=22, and *Fahlgren Martin v. McGraw,* 438 S.E. 2d 338 (1993).

[2] Jack McCarthy, "Attorney General Rocks Boat on Statehouse Sea," *Charleston Gazette,* September 27, 1993, 1A.

[3] Ibid.

[4] Ibid.

[5] Ibid.

[6] *West Virginia Code,* Section 5-3, Article #, Attorney General, http://www.legis.state.wv.us/wvcode/code.cfm?chap=05&art=3.

[7] Fanny Seiler, "McGraw Blasts Using 'Hand-Holder' Outside Legal Help," *Charleston Gazette,* February 23, 1993, 7A.

[8] Ibid.

[9] Ibid.

[10] Ibid.

[11] "Halt the Contract?" *Charleston Gazette,* February 2, 1993, 4A, and "Saving Millions," *Charleston Gazette,* May 2, 1993, 4A.

[12] Ibid.

[13] Ibid.

[14] *West Virginia Code,* Section 22-1-6, http://www.legis.state.wv.us/wvcode/ChapterEntire.cfm?chap=22

[15] AP, "Judge Upholds Order on Landfill Permit," *Charleston Gazette,* September 1, 1993, 2A.

[16] Fanny Seiler, "DEP Director Files Ethics Charge Against Attorney General," *Charleston Gazette,* December 10, 1993, 12A.

[17] *Lawyers Disciplinary Board v. McGraw,* 461 S.E. 2d 850, WV (1995).

[18] Interview with Frances Hughes, December, 2016.

[19] *Lawyers Disciplinary Board v. McGraw.*

[20] Ibid.

[21] "Legal ethics?" *Charleston Gazette,* February 2, 1994, 4A.

[22] "Political ethics, State Bar's Dubious Actions," *Charleston Gazette,* June 9, 1994, 4A.

[23] Paul Nyden, "Ethics Panel Hives McGraw Welcome News," *Charleston Gazette,* Nov. 14, 1994, 1A.

[24] Ibid.

[25] Fanny Seiler, "Landfill Case Creates Rift Between DEP, Attorney General's Office," *Sunday Gazette Mail,* September 19, 1993, 2B.

[26] *Lawyers Disciplinary Board v. McGraw.*

[27] Richard Grimes, "Suspend McGraw's Law License?" *Charleston Daily Mail,* June 19, 1994.

[28] Paul Nyden, "Caperton Pledges to Review Sludge Disposal Practices," *Charleston Gazette,* February 12, 1993.

[29] Jack McCarthy, "DEP Chief Shuns Stage, but Ready to Wrangle," *Charleston Gazette,* February 7, 1994, 1A.

[30] Ibid.

[31] *Wetzel County Solid Waste Authority v. The Public Service Commission and Lackawanna Transport , No. 33036, http://caselaw.findlaw.com/wv-supreme-court-of-appeals/1011927.html;* Ken Ward, Jr. "Judge Rules Against Mascaro," *Charleston Gazette,* December 8, 2002; Ken Ward Jr., "High Court Will Hear Mascaro Sludge Case," *Charleston Gazette,* December 5, 2003, 10A, and Ken Ward, "DEP's Order to Halt Wetzel Sludge Upheld," *Charleston Gazette,* January 17, 2007, 6A.

[32] Mary Wade Burnside, "Gambling Hurts Poor, Council Says," *Charleston Gazette,* Feb. 20, 1993, 6A.

[33] Ibid.

[34] "Gambling Shadow," Charleston Gazette, January 14, 1993, 4A.

[35] "Dee Caperton, *Wikipedia,* https://en.wikipedia.org/wiki/Dee_Caperton, and "WV First Ladies," WV Culture and History, 2007.

[36] House Resolution 26, West Virginia Legislature, http://wvlegislature.gov/Bill_Text_HTML/2001SESSIONS/RS/Bills?HR26%20intr.htm.

[37] "Rachel Worby, *Wikipedia,* https://en.wikipedia.org/wiki/Rachael_Worby#cite_ref-2, and "WV First Ladies," WV Culture and History.

[38] Jorea Marple, State Superintendent files, 2012.

[39] Idit Harel Caperton, " Be You," *https://redefineschool.com/idit-harel-caperton/*

[40] Stephanie Martz, "Old friends: Bryan's Protégé Reveals Alleged Lottery Deals," *Sunday Gazette-Mail,* September 19, 1993, 1A.

[41] "Lottery Mess," *Charleston Gazette,* May 14, 1993, 6A.

[42] Jack McCarthy, "Ad Agency Takes Case to Circuit," *Charleston Gazette,* May 14, 1993, 1C.

[43] Ibid, and "Lottery contract," *Charleston Gazette,* May 12, 1993, 4A.

[44] *Arnold Agency v. West Virginia Lottery Commission,* 526 S.E. 2d 814 (1999) 206 W.Va. 583, and Stephanie Martz, "Old Friends: Bryan's Protégé Reveals Alleged Lottery Deals," *Sunday Gazette Mail,* September 19, 1993, 1A.

[45] A.V. Gallagher, "Lottery Didn't Evaluate Bid, Ex-official Says," *Charleston Gazette,* May20, 1993, 6A.

[46] Jack McCarthy, *"Ad Firm Asks Court to Overturn Lottery Contract Ruling," Charleston Gazette,* September, 1993, 1A.

[47] Ibid and "Lottery Mess."

[48] McCarthy, "Ad Firm Asks Court to Overturn Lottery Contract Ruling."

[49] "Bryan Guilty of Corruption," *Charleston Gazette,* September 25, 1993, 1A.

[50] McCarthy, "Ad Firm Asks Court to Overturn Lottery Contract Ruling;" *Arnold Agency v. West Virginia Lottery Commission,* and A.V. Gallagher, "Lottery Didn't Evaluate Bid, E-official Says," *Charleston Gazette,* May 20, 1993, 6A.

[51] McCarthy, "Ad Firm Asks Court to Overturn Lottery Contract Ruling."

[52] *Fahlgren Martin v. McGraw,* 438 S.E. 2d 338, (1993).

[53] Ibid.

[54] Phil Kabler, "Attorney Loses Bid to Subpoena Caperton," *Charleston Gazette,* May 23, 1995, 3A.

[55] *Arnold Agency v. West Virginia Lottery Commission.*

[56] Conversation with Linda Arnold, 2017.

[57] Fanny Seiler, "Commission Told to Slow Down Video Lottery Goals," *Charleston Gazette,* January 5, 1993, 1A.

[58] Stephanie Martz, "Old Friends: Bryan's Protégé Reveals Alleged Lottery Deals," *Sunday Gazette-Mail,* September 19, 1993, 1A.

[59] Ibid.

[60] Ibid.

[61] Stephanie Martz, "VLC Given Specs Early, Security Chief Says," *Charleston Gazette,* September 18, 1993, and Martz, "Old friends: Bryan's Protégé Reveals Alleged Lottery Deals."

[62] Martz, "Old friends: Bryan's Protégé Reveals Alleged Lottery Deals."

[63] Ibid.

[64] "Gambling Shadow," Charleston Gazette, January 14, 1993, 4A.

[65] Phil Kabler, "Video Lottery to Receive Big Lobbying Effort," *Charleston Gazette,* January 21, 1993, 1C.

402

[66] Fanny Seiler, "Commission Told to Slow Down Video Lottery Goals."
[67] Fanny Seiler, "Haddad's Lottery Panel Resignation Shocks Caperton," *Charleston Gazette,* January 22, 1993.
[68] *"Caperton Pulls Plug on Video Lottery," Charleston Gazette,* Jan. 26, 1993, 1A.
[69] Ibid.
[70] "Haddad Resigns from Lottery Commission," *Charleston Gazette,* January 22, 1993, 1A, and *"*Caperton pulls Plug on Video Lottery."
[71] "Caperton Pulls Plug on Video Lottery."
[72] Ibid.
[73] Ibid.
[74] *Associated Press,* "Rebrook to Plead Innocent, Attorney Says," *Charleston Gazette,* July 1, 1993, 1B.
[75] Fanny Seiler, "Court Agrees to Hear Video Lottery Case," *Charleston Gazette,* June 3, 1993.
[76] Fanny Seiler, "Bill Takes Aim at AG budget," *Charleston Gazette,* May 19, 1993, 1A, and Seiler, "Court Agrees to Hear Video Lottery Case."
[77] Seiler, "Bill Takes Aim at AG budget."
[78] *State ex rel. Mountaineer Park v. Polan, 438 S.E. 2d 308, WV, (1993).*
[79] Stephanie Martz, "VLC Given Specs Early, Security Chief Says," *Charleston Gazette,* September 18, 1993, 1A.
[80] Martz, "Old friends: Bryan's Protégé Reveals Alleged Lottery Deals."
[81] Ibid, and Phil Kabler, "Caperton Asserts Innocence in Scandal," *Charleston Gazette, "* September 30, 1993, 1A.
[82] Kabler, "Caperton Asserts Innocence in Scandal."
[83] Ibid.
[84] Stephanie Martz, "Bryan Guilty of Corruption," *Charleston Gazette-Mail,* September 25, 1993, 1A.
[85] Stephanie Martz, "Rebrook Convicted," *Charleston Gazette,* November 25, 1993.
[86] Stephanie Martz, "Where's the Line in Office," *Charleston Gazette,* September 26, 1993.
[87] Kabler, "Caperton Asserts Innocence in Scandal."
[88] Fanny Seiler, "Bill Takes Aim at AG budget," *Charleston Gazette,* May 19, 1993, 1A, and Martz, "Bryan Guilty of Corruption."
[89] Stephanie Metz, "Trial May Draw New Conduct Lines," *Sunday Gazette Mail,* September 26, 1993, 4A.
[90] Seiler, "Court Agrees to Hear Video Lottery Case."
[91] "Gambling Opponents Vow Fight," *Charleston Gazette,* January 20, 1995, and "McGraw Defends Paying for Anti-Gambling Seminar," *Charleston Gazette,* January 25, 1995.
[92] "Ad Bid Process Baffles Firms," *Charleston Gazette,* July 20, 2012.
[93] *West Virginia Code,* Sec. 18-2E-7. 1989.
[94] Chris Miller, "IBM Spokesman Says PR Campaign Was State's Idea," *Charleston Gazette,* May 20, 1993, 1C.
[95] Chris Miller, "State Officials Defend Computer Cost," *Charleston Gazette,* May 6, 1993, 1A.
[96] Ibid.
[97] Chris Miller, "IBM Promise of PR Blitz Helped Win Contract," *Sunday Gazette-Mail,* May 16, 1993, 1C.
[98] Miller, "State Officials Defend Computer Cost."
[99] Ibid.
[100] Ibid.
[101] Chris Miller, "School Computer Deal Cost Raises Eyebrows," *Charleston Gazette,* June 3, 1993, 1C.
[102] Ibid.
[103] Chris Miller, "IBM Spokesman Says PR campaign Was State's Idea."
[104] Chris Miller, "Marockie Blasts Midstream Computer Switch," *Charleston Gazette* July 29, 1993, 1A.
[105] Ibid.
[106] Jorea Marple, Activity Report as Kanawha County Superintendent.
[107] Ibid.
[108] *Kanawha County Board of Education v. Caperton,* No. 21907, WV (February 17, 1994).

403

[109] Miller, "Marockie Blasts Midstream Computer Switch."

[110] *McGraw v. Caperton, No. 22011, WV (1994),* and *reHey,* 193 W.Va. 572, 578,457 S.E. 2d 509,515 (1995) and *Lawyer Disciplinary Board, Respondent vs John Hey,* 28239, WV (2003).

[111] Ibid.

[112] *McGraw v. Caperton.*

[113] *Fahlgren Martin v. McGraw* and *McGraw v. Caperton.*

[114] "Obsolete Contracts?" *Charleston Gazette,* July 15, 1993, 6A.

[115] McCarthy, "Attorney General Rocks Boat on Statehouse Sea."

[116] Chris Miller, "Caperton to Be Queried on Memo," *Charleston Gazette,* July 1, 1993, 1A.

[117] *West Virginia State Code,* Section 18-9D, and Ken Ward, "Financing Flap Straining McGraw's Friendly Ties to Labor," *Charleston Gazette,* July 11, 1993, 1B.

[118] Chris Miller, "Board Cautioned Twice on Bond Sale," *Charleston Gazette,* July 16, 1993, 1A.

[119] Ibid.

[120] Miller, "Caperton to Be Queried on Memo."

[121] *State ex rel. Marockie v. Wagoner,* 438 S.E. 2d 810, (1993), *http://www.courtswv.gov/supreme-court/docs/spring1993/21952.htm,* and *State ex rel. Marockie v. Wagoner,* 446 S.E. 2d 680, (1994).

[122] *West Virginia Code* Sec 18-9D-6, http://www.legis.state.wv.us/WVCODe/ChapterEntire.cfm?chap=18&art=9D&section=6.

[123] Associated Press, "Lawmakers Divided on McGraw's Actions," *Sunday Gazette Mail,* July 18, 1993, 3A.

[124] *Dadisman v. Moore,* WV 384 S.E. 2d 816 (December 27, 1988).

[125] Ibid.

[126] Ibid.

[127] Ibid.

[128] Leslie Wayne, "Big Risks, Big Losses, Big Foot," *New York Times,* April 23, 1995, http://www.nytimes.com/1995/04/23/business/big-risks-big-losses-big-fight.html?pagewanted=all&pagewanted=print.

[129] *State v. Morgan V. Stanley Morgan,* No. 22358, (1995), http://www.courtswv.gov/supreme-court/docs/spring1995/22358.htm.

[130] Ibid.

[131] Ibid.

[132] Wayne, "Big Risks, Big Losses, Big Foot."

[133] Ibid.

[134] B. Drumond Ayres, Jr. "West Virginians Out $200 Million," *New York Times*, December 15, 1988, http://www.nytimes.com/1988/12/15/us/west-virginians-are-out-200-million.html.

[135] Wayne, "Big Risks, Big Losses, Big Foot."

[136] Fanny Seiler, "Investing State Pensions in Stocks Called Illegal," *Charleston Gazette,* July 15, 1993, 1A.

[137] *Associated Press*, "Board of Investments to Sue McGraw," *Charleston Gazette,* August 11, 1993, 4C.

[138] *Dadisman v. Moore.*

[139] *West Virginia Trust Fund v. Bailey,* No.23939, March 28, 1997.

[140] Phil Kabler, "Pension: Poster Child," *Charleston Gazette Mail,* February 14, 2017, 1A.

[141] Wayne, "Big Risks, Big Losses, Big Foot."

[142] "Rate of Recidivism," *Pensions and Investments,* August 10, 1998.

[143] Stacey Ruckle, "Jail System Wins Major Court Fights," *Charleston Daily Mail,* July 18, 1988, 1A.

[144] "Rate of Recidivism."

[145] Paul G. Barr, "W.Va. Fund Chained to Law Forcing Prison Loan," *Pensions and Investments,* July 27, 1998, 1, and *State ex rel Regional Jail v. Investment Board,* No., 25134, WV Supreme Court, (1998).

[146] Ibid.

[147] "Rate of Recidivism."

[148] Kabler, "Pensions: Poster Child."

[149] Ibid.

Chapter XVII
[1] Interview with Frances Hughes, October, 2016.
[2] "Telemarketing Fraud," http://www.consumer.ga.gov/consumer-topics/telemarketing-fraud.
[3] *State v. Imperial Marketing,* 506 S.E.2d 799 W.Va., (1998), *http://caselaw.findlaw.com/wv-supreme-court-of-appeals/1388339.html.*
[4] "Firm May be Barred from State," *Charleston Daily Mail,* August, 1994, 2A.
[5] *SCI,* http://www.suarez.com/divisions/lindenwold-fine-jewelers/.
[6] *State v. Imperial Marketing.*
[7] "Firm May be Barred from State."
[8] "Company Loses Bid to Block Release of Customer List," *Charleston Daily Mail,* September 30, 1994, 7A.
[9] Interview with Frances Hughes, December, 2016.
[10] "Firm Says It's Not Behind Veteran Protests," *Charleston Daily Mail,* November 17, 1994, 8A, and "Ohio Company Must Name Its Customers," *Daily Mail,* September 2, 1994, 3C.
[11] "A Piece of WV History," http://www.wvgazettemail.com/article/20150913/GZ05/150919916.
[12] Hoppy Kerchival, "West Virginia's Shining Moment in Civil Rights," *West Virginia Metro News,* November 16, 2018, http://wvmetronews.com/2018/11/16/west-virginias-shining-moment-in-civil-rights/.
[13] Chris Galford, "Attorne.y Shines Light on WV's Unique Civil Rights History with a New Book," *WV Record,* January 22, 2016.
[14] "Climate Change Demands Working Together," *Herald Dispatch,* October 15, 2015, *http://www.herald-dispatch.com/opinion/tom-rodd-climate-change-demands-working-together/article_6e5fc1a1-14cd-530a-9378-d68cc50330ac.html.*
[15] Ron Hutchison, "Judge Won't Grant Restraining Order," *Charleston Daily Mail,* November 30, 1994.
[16] Ibid.
[17] Editorial, *Charleston Gazette,* January 1, 1995, 5A.
[18] "McGraw Opposes Video-Taping Deposition," *Charleston Gazette,* March 29, 1995, 12A.
[19] Kay Michael, "McGraw Victory Not a Runaway: Campaign against Attorney General May Have Helped Opponent," *Charleston Daily Mail*, November 06, 1996, 10A.
[20] Ibid.
[21] Stacey Ruckle, "Lawyer Says Ruling on McGraw Historic," *Charleston* Daily Mail, February 07, 1997, 1C.
[22] Jennifer Bundy, "McGraw to Pay for Use of State Plane," *Charleston Gazette,* June 18, 1997, 5A.
[23] Jorea Marple, Personal Notes.
[24] "Suarez," *Charleston Gazette,* September 08, 1998, 4A.
[25] Lawrence Messina, "Suarez vs. McGraw Most of Suit is Gutted—Haden Throws out Seven of Nine counts," *Charleston Gazette,* November 12, 1998, 1A.
[26] Interview with Frances Hughes, December, 2016.
[27] Lawrence Messina, "McGraw Tirade Prompts Mistrial," *Charleston Gazette,* November 3, 1998, 1A.
[28] Lawrence Messina, "McGraw Suarez Agree to End Battle," *Sunday Gazette Mail,* December 19, 1999.
[29] Ibid.
[30] Ed Meyer, "Stark County Businessman, Ben Suarez Sentenced to 15 months," *Beacon Journal,* November 14, 2014,1.
[31] Ed Meyer, "Who is Ben Suarez? Defense, Prosecution Paint Different Pictures As Trial Enters Second Week," *Beacon Journal,* June 8, 2014.
[32] Interview with Frances Hughes.
[33] *Associated Press, "*Tobacco Toll," *Sunday Gazette Mail,* March 3, 1993, 2B.
[34] Ibid.
[35] "Frontline Settlement Times Lines," *Public Broadcasting Service,* http://www.pbs.org/wgbh/pages/frontline/shows/settlement/timelines/fullindex.html, and Fanny Seiler, "McGraw Files Suit to Recoup the Cost of Smoking in State," *Charleston Gazette,* September 21, 1994, 1A.
[36] "Frontline Settlement Times Lines."
[37] Ibid.
[38] Ibid.

405

[39] Ibid.
[40] Henry Weinstein, "Mississippi Settles Its Tobacco Industry Suit," *New York Times,* July 4, 1997, 1A.
[41] Ibid.
[42] Associated Press, "McGraw Files Lawsuit Against Tobacco Firms," *Charleston Daily Mail,* September 20, 1994, 2A.
[43] Ibid.
[44] "McGraw," *Charleston Daily Mail,* September 22, 1994, 6A.
[45] Seiler, "McGraw Files Suit to Recoup the Cost of Smoking in State."
[46] Paul Owen, "Caperton Lawyer Accused of Holding up Tobacco Suit," *Charleston Daily Mail,* March 23, 1995, 10A.
[47] Ibid.
[48] Editorial, "McGraw Never Expect Consistency from a Political Opportunists," *Charleston Daily Mail* April 1, 1995, 4A.
[49] Owen, "Caperton Lawyer Accused of Holding up Tobacco Suit."
[50] Ibid.
[51] Ibid.
[52] Ibid.
[53] Ibid.
[54] Ibid.
[55] Lawrence Messina, "Judge Guts McGraw's Suit Against Tobacco industry," *Charleston Gazette,* May 4, 1995, 1A.
[56] Associated Press, "Call for Suit Review Draws Fire," *Charleston Daily Mail,* March 22, 1995, *4c,* and Mannis Porterfield, "State Pockets $21.9 million with First Installment from Tobacco Settlement," *Register-Herald,* December 15, 1999, 1A.
[57] Associate Press, "Tobacco Suit Setback Temporary, McGraw Says," *Charleston Daily Mail,* May 4, 1995, 1A.
[58] Fanny Seiler, "McGraw Plans Possible Appeal of Tobacco Lawsuit, If Necessary," *Charleston Gazette,* May 9, 1995, 7A.
[59] "What Happened? Why Governor Opposition?" *Charleston Gazette,* May 8, 1995, 1A.
[60] Seiler, "McGraw Plans Possible Appeal of Tobacco Lawsuit, If Necessary."
[61] Fanny Seiler, "Lawyers in Tobacco Suit Donated to Caperton," *Charleston Gazette,* May 24, 1995, 8A.
[62] Ibid.
[63] Jack McCarthy, "Lawyers Criticize McGraw for Comments," *Charleston Gazette,* August 17, 1995, 1C.
[64] Ibid.
[65] Seiler, "Lawyers in Tobacco Suit Donated to Caperton."
[66] Paul Owens, "Medicaid Panel Won't Support McGraw's Suit," *Charleston Daily Mail,* August 21, 1995, 8A.
[67] Phil Kabler, "PEIA Board Votes to Join McGraw Tobacco Liability Suit," *Charleston Gazette,* December 12, 1995, 1A.
[68] Phil Kabler, "Governor's Office Ready to Discuss Suit," *Charleston Gazette,* December 13, 1995, 1C.
[69] Ibid.
[70] Lawrence Messina, "Caperton Signs on to Tobacco Lawsuit," *Charleston Gazette,* April 10, 1996.
[71] Stacey Ruckle, "PEIA Has Hand in Tobacco Suit," *Charleston Daily Mail,* May 14, 1996, 2A.
[72] Henry Weinstein, "Mississippi Settles Its Tobacco Industry Suit," *New York Times,* July 4, 1997 and *Frontline,* "Full Chronology," http://www.pbs.org/wgbh/pages/frontline/shows/settlement/timelines/fullindex.html.
[73] Mark Howard, "Florida Still Using Tobacco Settlement Money 13 years Later," *Florida Trend,* July 1, 2010, http://www.floridatrend.com/article/3726/florida-still-using-tobacco-money-13-years-later.
[74] *CNN,* "Texas, Tobacco Giants Settle Lawsuit, Avoid Trial," January 16, 1998, http://www.cnn.com/US/9801/16/texas.tobacco/.
[75] Pam Belluck, "Tobacco Companies Settle a Suit with Minnesota for $6.5 Billion," *New York Times,* May

19, 1998, http://www.nytimes.com/1998/05/09/us/tobacco-companies-settle-a-suit-with-minnesota-for-6.5-billion.html.

[76] Mannis Porterfield, "State Pockets $21.9 Million with First Installment from Tobacco Settlement," *Register-Herald,* December 15, 1999, 1A.

[77] Attorney General Personal Files.

[78] "Funds, by State from Settlement Agreement Reached in November, 1998 by 46 State Attorneys General and the Tobacco Industry," *Center for Social Gerontology,* Ann Arbor, Michigan: http://www.tcsg.org/tobacco/settlement/totalfunds.htm.

[79] Kathleen Michon, JD, "Tobacco Litigation and Recent History," *Nolo,* https://www.nolo.com/legal-encyclopedia/tobacco-litigation-history-and-development-32202.html.

[80] "Attorney General Office, Tobacco Distribution List," February 2, 2010.

[81] Ibid.

[82] Editorial, "Bonds Quick Fix," *Charleston Gazette,* March 3, 2007, 2A, and "Float'em If you Got'em Tobacco Bond Market Ripe Now, Analyst Says," *Charleston Gazette, May 6, 2007.*

[83] "WV Governor Wants Tobacco Settlement to Pay for Comp Liability," *WVCompCentral,* January 16, 2004, https://www.workcompcentral.com/news/story/id/j15s04v199514242w43lei/relevant/true

[84] "Manchin Doesn't Want to Wait for Payments," *Charleston Daily Mail,* March 16, 2007.

[85] Interview with Frances Hughes, December, 2016.

[86] Darrell McGraw, Attorney General Personal Files, and "Manchin Doesn't Want to Wait for Payments."

[87] Cezary Podkkul, "How Wall Street Tobacco Deals Left States with Billions in Toxic Debt," *ProPublica,* August 7, 2014, *http://projects.propublica.org/graphics/tbcbonds-statemap.*

[88] "Manchin Doesn't Want to Wait for Payments."

[89] Jared Hunt, "State Avoids Tobacco Bond Default, Officials Say," *Charleston Gazette,* May 31, 2012, http://www.wvgazettemail.com/News/201205300190#sthash.LCj8TMRW.dpuf

[90] Cezary Podkkul, "How Wall Street Tobacco Deals Left States with Billions in Toxic Debt," *ProPublica,* August 7, 2014, *http://projects.propublica.org/graphics/tbcbonds-statemap.*

[91] Phil Kabler, "State's Payment from Cigarette Manufacturers up 2.6 percent," *Charleston Gazette-Mail,* May 12, 2017, 1C.

[92] Ibid.

[93] Lawrence H. White, "Housing Finance and 2008 Financial Crisis," *Down Sizing the Federal Government,* August 1, 2009, http://www.downsizinggovernment.org/hud/housing-finance-2008-financial-crisis.

[94] "Origins of the Financial Crisis-A Crash Course," *The Economist,* September 7, 2013, http://www.economist.com/news/schoolsbrief/21584534-effects-financial-crisis-are-still-being-felt-five-years-article.

[95] John O'Brien, *Legal Newsline,* Huntington, WV, February 3, 2009.

[96] Jessica Borders, "Banks Accountable," *Times West Virginia,* June 3, 2012, www.timeswv.com and AG Publication on Financial Disclosure Settlement.

[97] "West Virginia Sues Microsoft, Again," *Reuters,* November 4, 2001, www.usatoday30.usatoday.com.

[98] Ruth A. Gath, "WV Settles Microsoft Antitrust Suit," *Wall Street Journal,* June 17, 2003, www.wsj.com.

[99] Hilary Osbourne, "What Is a Payday Loan and Why Are They So Controversial," *The Guardian,* July 26, 2013, https://www.theguardian.com/money/2013/jun/27/what-is-a-payday-loan.

[100] Jessica M. Karmasak, "McGraw Settles with 5 Payday Loan Websites," *The West Virginia Record,* July 21, 2010, http://wvrecord.com/stories/510598790-mcgraw-settles-with-five-payday-loan-websites.

[101] "Judge Blooms Finds California Based Internet Lender, Cash Call, Abused WV Consumers," *WVAG Press Release,* September 11, 2012.

[102] Linda Doell, "Payday Loan Company to Refund West Virginia Consumers," *AOL News,* July 22, 2010, http://www.aol.com/article/2010/07/22/payday-loan-company-to-refund-w-va-consumers/19563658/.

[103] "West Virginia Payday Loan," https://www.samedaypayday.com/West-Virginia-Payday-Loan.

[104] John O'Brien, "Everyone on Board with McGraw Settlement," *West Virginia Record,* March 13, 2008, http://wvrecord.com/stories/510593829-everyone-on-board-with-mcgraw-settlement, and Jacqueline Bell, "Credit Card Companies, State Reach $16M Antitrust Accord," *Law 360,* January 16, 2008,

407

http://www.law360.com/articles/44339/credit-card-cos-state-reach-16m-antitrust-accord.
[105] Ibid.
[106] Editorial, "Sabotage Consumer Wipeout," *Sunday Gazette-Mail,"* July 6, 2013, 4A.
[107] "Proceed with Coal Lawsuits Petitioner Asks Court," *Charleston Gazette,* June 2, 1999 and "Suits Against Coal Companies Can Be Tossed, Court Rules," *Charleston Gazette,* July 15, 1999. 1A.
[108] *Affiliated Construction Trades v.Vieweg,* Dis. 1999, *http://www.courtswv.gov/supreme-court/docs/spring1999/26364d.htm.*
[109] "Worker Comp Coal Industry Debt Reaches 406 Million," *Charleston Gazette,* March 4, 2001.
[110] "Sabotage Consumer Wipeout."
[111] "Poultry," *E-WV,* https://www.wvencyclopedia.org/articles/1908.
[112] *Live Stock Weekly,* http://www.livestockweekly.com/papers/99/03/04/whlchickens.asp.
[113] Dan Fesperman, "W.Va. Takes Rare Step of Filing Suit Against a Poultry Company," *Baltimore Sun,* April 16, 1999, http://articles.baltimoresun.com/1999-04-16/news/9904160032_1_poultry-growers-wampler-hahn.
[114] "McGraw Appeals Wampler Decision," *Charleston Gazette,* May 23, 2000.
[115] *Live Stock Weekly.*
[116] Article 1, Section 46A-1-101, West Virginia Consumer Credit and Protection Act, *West Virginia Code,* http://www.wvlegislature.gov/WVCODE/Code.cfm?chap=46a&art=1
[117] Edward Luce, "American's Newest Redneck Rebellion," *Financial Times,* June 26, 2019, https://businessglitz.com/us/americas-new-redneck-rebellion-financial-times/.
[118] Allison Moody, "Fowl Play: The Chicken Farmers Being Bullied by Big Poultry," *The Guardian,* April 22, 2017, https://www.theguardian.com/sustainable-business/2017/apr/22/chicken-farmers-big-poultry-rules.
[119] "Poverty and Substance Abuse": http://alcoholrehab.com/drug-addiction/poverty-and-substance-abuse/.
[120] Richard C. Ausness, "The Role of Litigation in the Fight Against Prescription Drug Abuse, University of Kentucky College of Law, *West Virginia Law Review,* Vol. 116, Spring 2014.
[121] Diane E. Hoffmann, *Treating Pain* v. *Reducing Drug Diversion and Abuse: Recalibrating the Balance in Our Drug Control Laws and Policies,* 1 ST. LOUIS U. J. HEALTH L. & POL'Y 231,273 (2008), 9.
[122] Harriet Ryan, Lisa Girion and Scott Glover, "You Want a Description of Hell? OxyContin's 12-Hour Problem," *Los Angeles Times,* May 5, 2016, http://www.latimes.com/projects/oxycontin-part1/.
[123] Ibid.
[124] Ibid.
[125] Ibid.
[126] Ibid.
[127] Marianne Skolek, "Eric Holder Negotiated an OxyContin settlement in West Virginia-Working for Purdue Pharma!" *Salem News,* June 1, 2011, http://www.salem-news.com/articles/june012011/holder-purdue-ms.php.
[128] Ibid.
[129] Associated Press, "Oxycotin Makers and Execs Fined $634 million," June 20, 2007, http://www.nbcnews.com/id/19877184/ns/health-health_care/t/oxycontin-maker-execs-fined-million/#.WJyNzHkzXVI.
[130] Barry Meir, "Narcotic Makers Guilty of Deceit over Marketing," *New York Times,* May 11: 2007, http://www.nytimes.com/2007/05/11/business/11drug.html.
[131] Skolek, "Eric Holder Negotiated an OxyContin Settlement in West Virginia- Working for Purdue Pharma!"
[132] Ibid.
[133] Jorea Marple, Personal Journal.
[134] Frances A. Hughes and Barbara H. Allen, "Time to Clear Up Misconceptions about Oxycontin Suit," *Charleston Gazette*, October 12, 2012, 4A.
[135] Jeff Jenkins, "Oklahoma Settles with Purdue Pharma Just Like WV But for $260 Million More," *West Virginia Metro News*, http://wvmetronews.com/2019/03/26oklahoma-settles-with-purdue-pharma-just-like-wv-but-for-260-million-more/.
[136] Attorney General William Lochyear's Press Release, July 12, 2000, https://oag.ca.gov/news/press-releases/california-reaches-100-million-multi-state-settlement-drug-giant-mylan-over.

[137] "Time of Legal Actions Against Antipsychotic Manufacturers,"
http://www.woodymatters.com/sept2007Updates/TIMELINE%20OF%20LEGAL%20ACTIONS%20AGAIN
ST%20ANTIPSYCHOTIC%20MANUFACTURERS.pdf.
[138] "McGraw Has Won More than 2Billion for Consumers," *Sunday Gazette-Mail.*
[139] Eric Hornbeck, "Sanofi & BMS Sued by WV AG Over Plavix Marketing," *Law 360,*
https://www.law360.com/articles/412401/sanofi-bms-sued-by-w-va-ag-over-plavix-marketing.
[140] Ibid.
[141] Staff reports, "State Settles Suit for $3.2M," *Charleston Gazette-Mail,* March 22, 2019, 1C.
[142] *West Virginia ex rel. Morrisey v. Pfizer,*
http://www.leagle.com/decision/In%20Adv%20FDCO%20140710-
000124/WEST%20VIRGINIA%20EX%20REL.%20MORRISEY%20v.%20PFIZER,%20INC.
[143] Clay Marsh, M.D., "People and Purpose," *Charleston Gazette,* July 24, 2016, 1D.
[144] Jacobs, Harrison, "Here's Why the Opioid Epidemic Is So Bad in West Virginia—The State with the
Highest Overdose Rate in the US," *Business Insider,* May 1, 2016, http://www.businessinsider.com/why-the-
opioid-epidemic-is-so-bad-in-west-virginia-2016-4.
[145] Ibid.
[146] *E.H., et al v. Khan Martin, M.C.,*168, WV 248, (1981), *Hodge v. Ginsberg,* 303 S.E. 2d 245, (1983) and
State ex rel. Harris v. Calendine, 233 S.E. 2d 318 (1977).
[147] Darrell McGraw, AG Files.
[148] Eric Eyre, "WV High Court Rejects Drug Firms' Request to End Lawsuit," *Charleston Gazette,* January 11,
2016, and Eric Eyre, "Firm Sent 241 Million Pills to W.Va.,"*Sunday Gazette-Mail,* October 9, 2016, 1A.
[149] Jenkins, "Oklahoma Settles with Purdue Pharma Just Like WV But For $260 million".
[150] Etienne de Grellet, http://www.goodreads.com/quotes/131923-i-shall-pass-through-this-world-but-once-
any-good.

Chapter XVIII

[1] Brisbon, et.al, *West Virginia Politics and Government, 50.*
[2] Ibid.
[3] *Kanawha County Board of Education v. Caperton,* No 21907, *WV,* (1994).
[4] ALEC Alumni in Congress, http://www.sourcewatch.org/index.php/ALEC_Alumni_in_Congress.
[5] *White v. Manchin,* 318 S.E. 2d 470, (1984).
[6] Michael Janofsky, "Back in the Statehouse after 4 Decades Away," *New York Times:* December 10, 1996,
http://www.nytimes.com/1996/12/10/us/back-in-the-statehouse-after-4-decades-away.html.
[7] Luce, "America's New Redneck Rebellion."
[8] Manuel Quinones and Elana Schor, "Sen. Manchin Maintains Lucrative Ties to Family-Owned Coal
Company," *New York Times,* July 26, 2011.
[9] Ibid.
[10] Anne Vander May and Nicholas Rapp, "Who Needs a Blind Trust," *Fortune,* October 22, 2012,
http://fortune.com/2012/10/22/who-needs-a-blind-trust/.
[11] "Enersystems," www.dirtyenergymoney.com.
[12] Sheryl Gay Stolberg, "Joe Manchin Faces Liberal Opposition in His Bid to Be Energy Panel's Top
Democrat," *New York Times,* October 6, 2018, *https://www.nytimes.com/2018/12/06/us/politics/joe-manchin-
energy-committee.html*
[13] Quinones and Schor, "Sen. Manchin Maintains Lucrative Ties to Family-Owned Coal Company" and
"Enersystems."
[14] Stolberg, "Joe Manchin Faces Liberal Opposition in His Bid to Be Energy Panel's Top Democrat."
[15] Brad Johnson, "Sen. Joe Manchin Makes Personal Coal Fortune While Acting as a Mouthpiece for Coal,"
Thinkprogress.com, July 27, 2011, https://thinkprogress.org/sen-joe-manchin-makes-personal-coal-fortune-
while-acting-as-mouthpiece-for-coal-e00828d41092#.h8m5un8pk.
[16] Luce, "America's New Redneck Rebellion."
[17] Lee Fang, "Sen. Manchin Defends Law Firm Accused of Concealing Black Lung Medical Evidence," *The*

Nation, April 16, 2014, https://www.thenation.com/article/senator-manchin-defends-law-firm-accused-concealing-black-lung-medical-evidence/.

[18] Ibid.

[19] David Gutman, "With WV $353 Million Budget Deficit, Manchin Unsure If Tax Cuts Were Right Move," *Charleston Gazette,* January, 7, 2016, http://www.wvgazettemail.com/news/20160107/with-wvs-353m-budget-deficit-manchin-unsure-if-tax-cuts-were-right-move#sthash.H8AASOpR.dpuf.

[20] Luce, "America's New Redneck Rebellion."

[21] Zack Harold, "Which Candidate Will Be the Next Superintendent*," Charleston Daily Mail,* February 9, 2011, and "Marple Named Superintendent," *Metro News,* February 10, 2011.

[22] Julie Bort, "West Virginia Accuses Cisco Of Selling It Millions Of Dollars Of Routers It Didn't Need," *Business Insider,* February 25, 2013, http://www.businessinsider.com/west-virginia-slams-cisco-2013-2, and "2010 Purchase of Routers with Broadband Technology Opportunities Program (BTOP) Funding," *West Virginia Legislative Auditor,* PE 12-24-535, February, 2013.

[23] Dave Boucher, "Officials Release Consultants Broadband Report," *Charleston Gazette,* March 21, 2013, 2A, http://www.wvgazettemail.com/News/statenews/201303210165#sthash.lfx2j8bo.dpuf.

[24] Greene, LLP, "FCA Lawsuit Alleges That Frontier Communications Misused Federal funds," http://www.whistleblowerattorneys-blog.com/2016/07/fca-lawsuit-alleges-frontier-communications-misused-federal-funds.html, and Eric Eyre, "Fees Added $4.5 Million to Bills," *Sunday Gazette Mail*, July 24, 2016, 1A.

[25] Eric Eyre, "Frontier: Citynet Seeks Revenge in 6 Year Vendetta," *Gazette Mail,* August 29, 2016, 1A.

[26] *Citynet, LLC ex. rel. United States v. Frontier, W. Va., Inc.,* https://www.casemine.com/judgement/us/5afd11eede4e6135e4a74003

[27] Max Garland, "Most of Citynet's Claim in Frontier Suit Remain After Federal Judge's Order," *Charleston Gazette Mail,* April 18, 2018, https://www.wvgazettemail.com/business/most-of-citynet-s-claims-in-frontier-suit-remain-after/article_6a69ab61-d264-50ee-b253-896a2cba3495.html.

[28] Jeff Jenkins, "State cutting feds check for $4.7 million for broadband expansion missteps," *MetroNews,* May 21, 2019, http://wvmetronews.com/2019/05/21/state-cutting-feds-check-for-4-7-million-for-broadband-expansion-missteps/.

[29] *Citizen United v. Federal Elections Commission* (No. 08-205), https://www.law.cornell.edu/supct/html/08-205.ZS.html.

[30] Karl Evers-Hillstrom, Raymond Arke and Luke Robinson, "A Look at the Impact of *Citizens United* on Its Ninth Anniversary," *Open Secrets.org,* https://www.opensecrets.org/news/2019/01/citizens-united/, January 1, 2019.

[31] "Center for Individual Freedom," *Wikipedia, https://en.wikipedia.org/wiki/Center_for_Individual_Freedom*

[32] Phil Kabler, "Elections after *Citizens United,*" *Charleston Gazette*, October 21, 2012, 1C.

[33] Martha Bryson Hodel, "Attorney General Race Shaping Up As Labor vs. Business," *Charleston Gazette,* April 22, 1992, 5A.

[34] "Running Around," *Charleston Gazette,* March 31, 1992, 8A and "Attorney General's Race Focuses, Costly on One Candidate," *Charleston Gazette,* May 8, 1992, 9A.

[35] David Truman, "Court's Book Purchase Legal, Prosecutor Says," Charleston Gazette," March 19, 1992, 3A.

[36] David Truman, "McGraw, Rebrook Slug It Out," *Charleston Gazette,* April 15, 1992, 1D.

[37] Paul Nyden, "Rebrook Tops McGraw in Fund Raising," *Charleston Gazette,* May 11, 1992, 4A.

[38] Don Marsh, "Reform Voters, Not Elections," *Charleston Gazette,* May 8, 1992, 4A.

[39] "Rebrook Convicted," *Charleston Gazette*, November 25, 1993.1A.

[40] Robert Gould, "Attorney General Candidate Defends His Eligibility," *Charleston Gazette,* October 28, 1992, 5A.

[41] Darrell McGraw, Personal Files circa 1992-2012.

[42] "General Election County by County," *Charleston Gazette,* November 5, 1992.

[43] *Associated Press*, "Veteran GOP Activist Robert Gould Dies," *Denver Post,* August 11, 2007, https://www.denverpost.com/2007/08/11/veteran-gop-activist-robert-gould-dies/.

[44] Lawrence Messina, "Caperton Signs on to Tobacco Lawsuit," *Charleston Gazette,* April 10, 1996 and Maryclaire Dale, "Bloom Would Plan Crime Fighting and McGraw Stays with Fights He Picks," *Charleston Gazette,* April 30, 1996, 1C.

[45] Lawrence Messina, "Lane Target's McGraw's Public Record and McGraw Aids Consumers, Backers say," *Charleston Gazette,* October 3, 1996, 1C.

[46] "Charlotte Lane Endorsed," *Charleston Gazette,* October 16, 1996.

[47] Lawrence Messina, "Lane Backed by Big Business," *Sunday Gazette-Mail*, November 5, 1996, 1A.

[48] Fanny Seiler, "Sweepstakes Firm Vows to Beat Attorney General," *Charleston Gazette*, September 26, 1996, 5A.

[49] "Paid Political Ad by Benjamin D. Suarez and a Publication of the Better Government Bureau of Ohio," *Charleston Gazette,* November 3, 1996.

[50] Carolyn Karr Charnock, "McGraw has Weathered Many Storms in Office," *Daily Mail,* October 29, 1996.

[51] Lawrence Messina, "McGraw Headed to Second Term," *Charleston Gazette,* November 6, 1996.

[52] Jorea Marple, Personal Journal.

[53] Toby Coleman, "AG Candidates McGraw, Lewis Differ on Office," *Charleston Gazette,* October 9, 2008, 1A.

[54] Tom Searle, "One McGraw Wins a Squeaker," *Charleston Gazette,* November 4, 2004, 1C.

[55] Editorial: "Darrell McGraw Attorney General Endorsement," *Charleston Gazette,* October 21, 2004, 4A.

[56] Tom Searle, "One McGraw Wins a Squeaker."

[57] .Lawrence Smith, "Lewis Shooting Case Sent to Clay Grand Jury," *West Virginia Record,* July 21, 2012, http://wvrecord.com/stories/510603009-lewis-shooting-case-sent-to-clay-grand-jury.

[58] P.J. Dickerschied, "Swift Boat Ad Makers Target McGraw," *Sunday Gazette-Mail,* November 2, 2008, 1A.

[59] Paul Nyden, "McGraw Files Election Complaint Concerning Ads," Charleston Gazette," September 5, 2008, 1A, and Paul Nyden, "McGraw to File Complaints Over Group's Attack Ads," *Sunday Gazette-Mail,* September 7, 2008, 1B.

[60] Attorney General Darrell McGraw, Personal Files.

[61] Nyden, "McGraw Files Election Complaint Concerning Ads," and "McGraw to File Complaints Over Group's Attack Ads."

[62] Dickerschied, "Swift Boat Ad Makers Target McGraw," Sunday Gazette-Mail," November 2, 2008, 1A.

[63] "2008 Election Results in WV," https://en.wikipedia.org/wiki/United_States_presidential_election_in_West_Virginia,_2008.

[64] Andrew Clevenger, "McGraw Clings to Small Lead," *Charleston Gazette,* November 5, 2008, 1B.

[65] "Red State," *Saturday Gazette-Mail,* July 21, 2012, 4A.

[66] Eric Eyre, "WV High Court Rejects Drug Firms' Request to End Lawsuit," *Charleston Gazette,* January 11, 2016, and Eric Eyre, "Firm Sent 241 Million Pills to W.Va.,"*Sunday Gazette-Mail,* October 9, 2016, 1A.

[67] Eyre, "WV High Court Rejects Drug Firms' Request to End Lawsuit."

[68] Eric Eyre, "McGraw Attacks Morrisey on Short-Term Ties to W.Va.," *Charleston Gazette,* October 30, 2012, 1A.

[69] Kabler, "Elections After *Citizens United*," and *Dollarocracy,* 52.

[70] Ibid.

[71] Lawrence Messina, "PAC's Spend Over 5.2 million," *Charleston Gazette,* October 23, 2012, 1A and "State Races Featured $6 million From Candidates Personal Wealth," *Charleston Gazette,* December 28, 2012.

[72] Kabler, "Elections after *Citizens' United.*"

[73] Jake Taper, "Prison Inmate wins More Than 40% of Democratic Vote Over President Obama," *Nightline,* May 9, 2012, http://abcnews.go.com/blogs/politics/2012/05/prison-inmate-wins-more-than-40-of-democratic-vote-over-president-obama-in-wv-primary/.

[74] Ed Rabel, Personal Files, 2012.

[75] Jorea Marple, Personal Notes.

[76] Ry Rivard, "New AG Heavily Boosted Own Run," *Charleston Daily Mail,* December 21, 2012, 1A.

[77] *Citizen United v. Federal Elections Commission.*

[78] Ibid.

[79] John Nichols and Robert McChesney, *Dollarocracy,* Nation Books, New York NY, 2013, 66.

[80] *Dollarocracy*, 52.

[81] Ken Hall, "Morrisey Sold Us Out with Drug Settlements," *West Virginia Record,* August 6, 2019, https://wvrecord.com/stories/512875443-morrisey-sold-us-out-with-drug-settlements, and Marla Matzer Rose, "Cardinal Health to Pay 20 Million to Settle WV Suit," *Columbus Dispatch,* January 9, 2017, http://www.dispatch.com/content/stories/business/2017/01/09/cardinal-health-to-pay-20-million-to-settle-west-virginia-suit.html.

Chapter XIX

[1] Cannon 2 of Code of Judicial Conduct, http://www.courtswv.gov/legal-community/court-rules/judicial-conduct/judicial-conduct.html.

[2] Brian Ross and Matthew Mask, "Lear Jet Justice- A Circus Masquerading as a Court," *ABC Nightline Investigates,* December 2, 2014, http://abcnews.go.com/US/lear-jet-justice-west-virginia-circus-masquerading-court/story?id=27291436.

[3] "Walker Explains Ties to Blankenship," *Charleston Daily Mail,* February 15, 2008.

[4]*Caperton v. Massey,* Brennon Center for Justice, June 8, 2009, https://www.brennancenter.org/legal-work/caperton-v-massey and Leamer, page 345.

[5] *Caperton v. A.T. Massey Coal Co.,* 556 U.S. 868 (2009).

[6] Leamer, 197.

[7] Leamer, 249-250, 271

[8] Leamer, 270.

[9] Alan Loughery, *Don't Buy Another Vote, I Won't Pay for a Landslide,* 2006.

[10]"Loughry running as a Republican for WV Supreme Court," *Ballotpedia,* September 15, 2011, https://ballotpedia.org/Loughry_running_as_Republican_for_WV_Supreme_Court.

[11] *Manor Care, Inc. v. Douglas*, No. 13-0470, WV Supreme Court (2014).

[12] Ibid.

[13] Linda Harris, "Nursing Home Trial Raises Concerns Before It Starts," *State Journal,* August 4, 2016, http://www.statejournal.com/story/32684882/nursing-home-trial-raises-concerns-before-it-starts, and Brian Ross and Matthew Mask, "Lear Jet Justice- A Circus Masquerading as a Court," *ABC Nightline Investigates,* December 2, 2014, http://abcnews.go.com/US/lear-jet-justice-west-virginia-circus-masquerading-court/story?id=27291436.

[14] Ross and Mask, "Lear Jet Justice- A Circus Masquerading as a Court."

[15] *State ex. rel Allen H. Loughry v. Natalie Tennant*, 120899, Brief Amicus Curia, 2012, http://www.courtswv.gov/supreme-court/clerk/pdf/cases-of-interest/loughry-funding-2012/brief-amicus-mcgraw.pdf.

[16] Ibid.

[17] Tom Miller, "Justices Find Court Turning Point," *Herald Dispatch,* January 9, 1977, 1A.

[18] Chris Dickerson, "WV CALA says Benjamin's Record is Cause for Concern," *The West Virginia Record,* May 3, 2016, http://wvrecord.com/stories/510722557-wv-cala-says-benjamin-s-record-is-cause-for-concern.

[19] Allen Blinder, "Don Blankenship Sentenced to One Year in Prison in Mine Safety Case," *New York Times,* April 6, 2016, https://www.nytimes.com/2016/04/07/us/donald-blankenship-sentenced-to-a-year-in-prison-in-mine-safety-case.html?_r=0.

[20] Dickerson, "WV CALA Says Benjamin's Record is Cause for Concern."

[21] Alex Kotch, "Outside Money Wins Big in West Virginia Supreme Court Election," *Facing South,* May 13, 2016, https://www.facingsouth.org/2016/05/outside-money-wins-big-in-west-virginia-supreme-co.

[22] "West Virginia Coal Association Endorses Walker," *Connect Clarksburg Local News,* Marc 31, 2016, http://www.connect-clarksburg.com/connect.cfm?func=view&section=News&item=WV-Coal-Association-Endorses-Beth-Walker-for-WV-Supreme-Court-Justice-12104.

[23]Kotch, "Outside Money Wins Big in West Virginia Supreme Court Election."

[24] Hoppy Kerchevl, "Beth Walker Challenging Benjamin for Supreme Court Seat, June 5, 2015, *MetroNews,* http://wvmetronews.com/2015/06/05/beth-walker-challenging-justice-benjamin/.

[25] Beth Walker's Financial Reports, WV Secretary of State, http://www.sos.wv.gov/elections/Pages/default.aspx.

[26] Liz McCormick, "First Time Candidate, King, Runs for Supreme Court," *WV Public Radio*, May 2, 2016, <img src="http://wvpublic.org/sites/wvpn/files/styles/default/public/201605/wayne_king_0.jpg" alt="Wayne King, King, Supreme Court, Candidate">.

[27] Wayne King Financial Election Report, WV Secretary of State, http://www.sos.wv.gov/elections/Pages/default.aspx.

[28] Chris Dickerson, "Poll Shows McGraw Leads in WV Supreme Court Race," *WV Record*, February 26, 2016, http://wvrecord.com/stories/510697699-poll-shows-mcgraw-leads-race-for-state-supreme-court.

[29] Ron Gregory, *Corridor Chronicle*, February 5, 2016.

[30] "2016 Public Campaign Financing, WV Secretary of State, http://www.sos.wv.gov/elections/campaignfinance/Pages/2016%20Supreme%20Court%20Campaign%20Public%20Financing.aspx.

[31] Linda Harris, "Update: WV Supreme Court Rules Two Court Candidates Are Eligible for Public Financing," *The Journal*, March 23, 2016, http://www.statejournal.com/story/31548514/acting-justices-hear-campaign-financing-cases-involving-two-candidates-for-west-virginia-supreme-court-of-appeals.

[32] Liz McCormick, "First Time Candidate, King, Runs for Supreme Court."

[33] Pema Levy, "This Election Inspired a John Grisham Novel. Now It Just Got Even Weirder," *Mother Jones*, May 9, 2016.

[34] William Wooten, "Wooten Asks Walker if She Wants to Be a 'Purchased Justice," *Wooten for Justice*, http://wootonforjustice.com/2016/05/06/wooten-asks-walker-if-she-wants-to-be-a-purchased-justice/.

[35] "Contribution and Expenditure Report for West Virginia for Fair Courts," West Virginia Secretary of State, https://cfrs.wvsos.com/#/committee_filings/30548/en?committeeName=West%20Virginia%20for%20Fair%20Courts.

[36] Alex Kotch, "Outside Money Wins Big in WV Supreme Court Election," *Facing South*, May 13, 2016. https://www.facingsouth.org/2016/05/outside-money-wins-big-in-west-virginia-supreme-co

[37] Darrell McGraw Financial Reports, 2016, WV Secretary of State.

[38] Jacob Bogage , "Study Shows How Candidates Influence Voter's Brain Activity," Reprinted from *The Washington Post* in *Sunday GazetteMail*, June 26, 2016, 3F.

[39] Alex Kotch, "Outside money wins big in WV Supreme Court Election."

[40] Ken Ward, "High Court Reverses Gas Royalties," *Charleston Gazette-Mail*, Saturday, May 27, 2013, 1A.

[41] Ken Ward, "How One WV Supreme Court Justice Gave Natural Gas a Big Victory and Shortchanged Residents," *Charleston Gazette Mail*, August 20, 2018.

[42] Ibid.

[43] Ibid.

[44] Hoppy Kercheval, "Justice Robin Davis's One-Half Million Dollar Office," *West Virginia Metro News*, December 1, 2017, http://wvmetronews.com/2017/12/01/justice-robin-daviss-office-renovation-cost-one-half-million-dollars/.

[45] "Lavish Spending on Justices' Offices shameful," *Huntington Herald Dispatch*, December 3, 2017, http://www.herald-dispatch.com/lavish-spending-on-justices-offices-shameful/article_a7792964-38fa-5a99-a3bd-31f8e70957e4.html.

[46] Editor, "Steve Canterbury Weighs in on Couchgate and the West Virginia Supreme Court," *Corporate Crime Reporter*, January 31, 2018, https://www.corporatecrimereporter.com/news/200/steve-canterbury-weighs-couchgate-west-virginia-supreme-court/.

[47] Phil Kabler, "Legislative Auditors Recommend Ethics Investigation of Justice Loughry," *Charleston Gazette Mail*, April 16, 2018.

[48] Ibid.

[49] Linda Harris, "Turmoil Continues to Swirl Around Loughry in Wake of Spending Controversy," *The State Journal*, February 20, 2018.

[50] Brad McElhiny, "Audit: Justices May Have Violated Lax Laws, Ethics Act for Vehicle Use," *West Virginia*

Metro News, April 16, 2018, http://wvmetronews.com/2018/04/16/audit-justices-may-have-violated-tax-laws-ethics-act-for-vehicle-use/.

[51] John Raby, *Associated Press,* "Suspension Sought of West Virginia Supreme Court Justice," *Los Angeles Times,* June 6, 2018, http://www.latimes.com/sns-bc-wv--supreme-court-loughry-20180606-story.html.

[52] *Associated Press,* "West Virginia Supreme Court Justice Suspended," *Tampa Bay Times,* June 9, 2018, http://www.tampabay.com/west-virginia-supreme-court-justice-suspended-ap_nationalf421c3e67b794a1aa2a7818c507609bc.

[53] Lacie Pierson, "WV Supreme Court Justice Loughry Suspended in Connection to Judicial Conduct Charges," *Charleston Gazette Mail,* June 8, 2018.

[54] Ibid.

[55] Lacie Pierson, "Feds Indict Justice Loughry," *Charleston Gazette Mail,* June 21, 2018, 1A.

[56] Associated Press, "All of WV Justices Impeached Over Spending," *NBC News,* August 14, 2018, https://www.nbcnews.com/news/us-news/all-west-virginia-s-supreme-court-justices-impeached-over-spending-n900461.

[57] Lacie Pierson and Jake Zuckerman, "WV Supreme Court Justice Davis Leaves Court," *Charleston Gazette Mail,* August 14, 2018, https://www.wvgazettemail.com/news/politics/wv-supreme-court-justice-davis-leaves-court-justices-workman-walker/article_91a8f5ae-0030-5c98-b6e2-639827e46929.html.

[58] Lacie Pierson, "U.S. Court Seeks Response from Workman in Impeachment Appeal," *Charleston Gazette Mail, https://www.wvgazettemail.com/news/legal_affairs/us-supreme-court-seeks-response-from-workman-in-impeachment-appeal/article_e1b4f5f4-2fe7-5703-99aa-020aca9b712d.html,* November 13, 2019.

[59] Lacie Pierson, "Justice Loughry Guilty on 11 Counts," *Charleston Gazette Mail,* October 13, 2018, 1A.

[60] Phil Kabler, "Ex-Justice Loughry Gets 2 Years in Jail," *Charleston Gazette-Mail,* February 14, 2019, 1A.

[61] "Former W.Va. SUPCO Justice Will Not Go to Prison," *Metro News,* March 6, 2019.

[62] "U.S. Supreme Court Will Not Intervene in West Virginia Impeachment Case," *Metro News,* October 7, 2019, https://www.wsaz.com/content/news/WVa-Senate-asking-US-SUPCO-to-review-ruling-that-halted-impeachments-507033871.html.

[63] *Associated Press,* "Supreme Court Won't Intervene Over West Virginia Justices," *New York Times,* October 7, 2019, https://www.nytimes.com/aponline/2019/10/07/us/politics/ap-us-supreme-court-west-virginia-justices.html?searchResultPosition=8.

Chapter XX

[1] Teddy Roosevelt, *Citizenship in a Republic.*

[2] Casey Coates Danson, "What Would Joseph Campbell Say About Donald Trump?" *Global Possibilities,* August 23, 2016, http://www.globalpossibilities.org/what-would-joseph-campbell-say-about-donald-trump/.

[3] Don Marsh, *Charleston Gazette,* circa 1986.

Made in the USA
Columbia, SC
10 January 2020